Environmental

Career Directory

Highlights

Gale Research Inc. proudly presents the first edition of the *Environmental Career Directory.* The hallmark of this volume, part of Gale's Career Advisor Series, is the essays by active professionals. Here, industry insiders describe opportunities and challenges in many fields related to the environment, including:

- Soil and water conservation
- Wetland management
- Forestry
- Natural resource and park management
- Ecology
- Fisheries management
- Environmental education
- Geosciences
- Microbiology
- Industrial hygiene
- Solid waste management
- Horticulture
- Botanical gardens

In fully up-to-date articles, they describe:

- What to expect on the job
- Typical career paths
- What they look for in an applicant
- How their specialty is unique

Provides Excellent Job Hunting Resources

Once this "Advice from the Pro's" has given you a feel for environmental careers, the *Directory* offers even more help with your job search strategy:

- **The Job Search Process** includes essays on determining career objectives, resume preparation, networking, writing effective cover letters, and interviewing. With worksheets and sample resumes and letters. **FEATURES:** Resumes are targeted to the realities of environmental fields.

- **Job Opportunities Databank** provides details on hundreds of organizations that hire at entry-level. **FEATURES:** In addition to the entry-level information, entries also include information on all-important internship opportunities.

- **Career Resources** identifies sources of help-wanted ads, professional associations, employment agencies and search firms, career guides, professional and trade periodicals, and basic reference guides and handbooks. **FEATURES:** Resource listings include detailed descriptions to help you select the publications and organizations that will best meet your needs.

Master Index Puts Information at Your Fingertips

The *Directory* is thoroughly indexed, with access to essays and directory sections both by subject and by organization name, publication title, or service name.

ENVIRONMENTAL CAREER DIRECTORY

A Practical, One-Stop Guide to Getting a Job Preserving the Environment

1ST EDITION

Bradley J. Morgan and
Joseph M. Palmisano, Editors
Diane M. Sawinski, Associate Editor

DETROIT • WASHINGTON, D.C. • LONDON

Editors: Bradley J. Morgan and Joseph M. Palmisano
Associate Editors: Joyce Jakubiak and Diane M. Sawinski
Assistant Editor: Wendy H. Mason
Aided by: Mary Alampi, Susan E. Edgar, Susan P. Hutton, Peggy Kneffel Daniels, Katherine H. Nemeh, Lou Ann J. Shelton, and Devra M. Sladics
Senior Editor: Linda S. Hubbard

Research Manager: Victoria B. Cariappa
Research Supervisor: Gary J. Oudersluys
Research Associate: Tracie A. Wade
Research Assistants: Andreia L. Earley, Charles A. Jewell, Colin C. McDonald, Michele L. McRobert, Michele P. Pica, Phyllis Shepherd, and Barbara Thornton

Production Manager: Mary Beth Trimper
Production Assistant: Shanna Philpott Heilveil

Technical Design Services Manager: Art Chartow
Art Director: Cindy Baldwin
Graphic Designer: Mary Krzewinski

Supervisor of Systems and Programming: Theresa Rocklin
Programmer: Timothy Richardson

Data Entry Supervisor: Benita L. Spight
Data Entry Group Leader: Gwendolyn S. Tucker
Data Entry Associates: Beverly Jendrowski and Fredrick L. Penn Jr.

Gale Research Inc.
835 Penobscot Bldg.
Detroit, MI 48226

ISBN 0-8103-9153-8
ISSN

Printed in the United States of America

Published simultaneously in the United Kingdom
by Gale Research International Limited
(An affiliated company of Gale Research Inc.)

Contents

PART ONE

Advice from the Pro's

PART FIVE

Master Index

Acknowledgments

The editors would like to thank all the "pro's" who took the time out of their busy schedules to share their first-hand knowledge and enthusiasm with the next generation of job-seekers. A special thanks to Kathleen M. Daniels, Assistant Director of the Career Planning and Placement Office at the University of Detroit Mercy, who provided much needed help with the job search section.

Thanks are also owed to the human resources personnel at the companies listed in this volume and to the public relations staffs of the associations who provided excellent suggestions for essays. Kevin Doyle of the Environmental Careers Organization deserves special mention.

Introduction

"Corporate America has developed a deep, and perhaps abiding, reluctance to hire."

—*Business Week,* February 22, 1993

As the above quote indicates, getting and keeping a job these days can be a demanding proposition. Despite an economy that is finally recovering from the latest recession, many firms are still downsizing and are reluctant to increase staff levels.

What this means is that the job search is an increasingly competitive process. To beat the competition, job seekers need information. By utilizing the *Environmental Career Directory,* job seekers gain all the information they need to make the best possible decisions about their job search. The *Directory* is a comprehensive, one-stop resource that includes:

- Essays by industry professionals that provide practical advice not found in any other career resource
- Job search guidance designed to help you get in the door in an environmental firm or department
- Job and internship listings from leading companies in the United States
- Information on additional career resources to further the job hunt
- A Master Index to facilitate easy access to the *Directory*

The *Directory* is organized into four parts that correspond to the steps of a typical job search—identifying your area of interest, refining your presentation, targeting companies, and researching your prospects.

Advice from the Pro's: An Invaluable Tool

Instead of offering "one-size-fits-all" advice or government statistics on what the working world is like, the *Environmental Career Directory* goes into the field for first-hand reports from experienced professionals working in all segments of environmentalism. This "Advice from the Pro's" is offered by people who know what it's like to land that first job and turn it into a rich and rewarding career. Learn about:

- how successful environmental internships happen from Kevin Doyle, National Director of Program Development for The Environmental Careers Organization, a group with over 20 years of experience in matching students and recent graduates with paid internships.

- opportunities in ecology available to minorities from Carmen R. Cid, Ph.D., Department of Biology at Eastern Connecticut State University.
- the multi-faceted industry of solid waste management from Anita Blumenthal, Senior Writer, Public Affairs of the National Solid Wastes Management Association.
- and 11 other areas of specialization, including:

Soil and water conservation
Wetland management
Forestry
Natural resource and park management
Fisheries management
Environmental education
Geosciences
Microbiology
Industrial hygiene
Horticulture
Botanical gardens

The essays cover the most important things a job applicant needs to know, including:

- What college courses and other background offer the best preparation
- Specific skills that are needed
- What companies look for in an applicant
- Typical career paths
- Salary information

The Job Search Process: Making Sense of It All

What is the first thing a new job-hunter should do?

What different types of resumes exist and what should they look like?

What questions are off-limits in an interview?

These important questions are among the dozens that go through every person's mind when he or she begins to look for a job. Part Two of the *Environmental Career Directory*, **The Job Search Process**, answers these questions and more. It is divided into five chapters that cover all the basics of how to aggressively pursue a job:

- **Getting Started: Self-Evaluation and Career Objectives**. How to evaluate personal strengths and weaknesses and set goals.
- **Targeting Companies and Networking for Success**. How to identify the companies you would like to work for and how to build a network of contacts.
- **Preparing Your Resume**. What to include, what not to include, and what style to use. Includes samples of the three basic resume types and worksheets to help you organize your information.
- **Writing Better Letters**. What letters should be written throughout the search process and how to make them more effective. Includes samples.
- **Questions for You, Questions for Them**. How to handle an interview and get the job.

Job Opportunities Databank: Finding the Job You Want

Once you're ready to start sending out those first resumes, how do you know where to start? The **Job Opportunities Databank**, Part Three of the *Directory*, includes listings for more than 225 chemical companies, energy companies, paper mills, metal and mining companies, and consumer product manufacturers in the

United States that offer entry-level jobs. These listings provide detailed contact information and data on the companies' business activities, hiring practices, benefits, and application procedures—everything you need to know to approach potential employers. And since internships play an increasingly important role in the career research and employment process, information on the internship opportunities offered by the companies listed is also included.

It should be noted that the companies found in the *Directory* are primarily involved in some segment of the environmental industry. Since almost all companies today are taking a pro-active approach to environmental concerns, students should not limit their job or internship search to the companies listed, but instead, should investigate companies of interest in any field.

For further information on the arrangement and content of the Job Opportunities Databank, consult "How to Use the Job Opportunities Databank" immediately following this introduction.

Career Resources: A Guide to Organizations and Publications in the Field

Need to do more research on the specialty you've chosen or the companies you'll be interviewing with? Part Four of the *Directory*, **Career Resources**, includes information on the following:

- Sources of help-wanted ads
- Professional associations
- Employment agencies and search firms
- Career guides
- Professional and trade periodicals
- Basic reference guides and handbooks

Listings contain contact information and descriptions of each publication's content and each organization's membership, purposes, and activities, helping you to pinpoint the resources you need for your own specific job search.

For additional information on the arrangement and content of Career Resources, consult "How to Locate Career Resources" following this introduction.

Master Index Speeds Access to Resources

A Master Index leads you to the information contained in all four sections of the *Directory* by citing all subjects, organizations, publications, and services listed throughout in a single alphabetic sequence. The index also includes inversions on significant keywords appearing in cited organization, publication, and service names. For example, the "National Association of State Foresters" would also be listed in the index under "Foresters; National Association of State." Citations in the index refer to page numbers.

Information Keeps Pace with the Changing Job Market

This first edition of the *Environmental Career Directory* contains essays in the Advice from the Pro's section that were contributed by leading professionals in the environmental industry on subjects of particular interest to today's job seekers. All employers listed in the **Job Opportunities Databank** were contacted by telephone or facsimile to obtain current information, and **Career Resources** listings were obtained from selected material from other databases compiled by Gale Research Inc.

Comments and Suggestions Welcome

The staff of the *Environmental Career Directory* appreciates learning of any corrections or additions that will make this book as complete and useful as possible. Comments or suggestions for future essay topics or other improvements are also welcome, as are suggestions for careers that could be covered in new volumes of the Career Advisor Series. Please contact:

Career Advisor Series
Gale Research Inc.
835 Penobscot Bldg.
Detroit, MI 48226-4094
Phone: 800-347-GALE
Fax: (313)961-6815

Bradley J. Morgan
Joseph M. Palmisano

How to Use the Job Opportunities Databank

The **Job Opportunities Databank** comprises two sections:

Entry-Level Job and Internship Listings
Additional Companies

Entry-Level Job and Internship Listings

Provides listings for more than 225 chemical companies, energy companies, paper mills, metal and mining companies, and consumer product manufacturers in the United States. Entries in the **Job Opportunities Databank** are arranged alphabetically by company name. When available, entries include:

- **Company name.**
- **Address and telephone number.** A mailing address and telephone number are provided in every entry.
- **Fax and toll-free telephone number.** These are provided when known.
- **Business description.** Outlines the company's business activities. The geographical scope of the company's operations may also be provided.
- **Corporate officers.** Lists the names of executive officers, with titles.
- **Number of employees.** Includes the most recently provided figure for total number of employees. Other employee-specific information may be provided as well.
- **Average entry-level hiring.** Includes the number of entry-level employees the company typically hires in an average year. Many companies have listed "Unknown" or "0" for their average number of entry-level jobs. Because of current economic conditions, many firms could not estimate their projected entry-level hires for the coming years. However, because these firms have offered entry-level positions in the past and because their needs may change, we have listed them in this edition.
- **Opportunities.** Describes the entry-level positions that the company typically offers, as well as the education and other requirements needed for those positions.

- **Benefits**. Lists the insurance, time off, retirement and financial plans, activities, and programs provided by the company, if known.
- **Human resources contacts**. Lists the names of personnel-related staff, with titles.
- **Application procedure**. Describes specific application instructions, when provided by the company.

Many entries also include information on available internship programs. Internship information provided includes:

- **Contact name**. Lists the names of officers or personnel-related contact who are responsible for the internship program.
- **Type**. Indicates the type of internship, including time period and whether it is paid, unpaid, or for college credit. Also indicates if a company does not offer internships.
- **Number available.** Number of internships that the company typically offers.
- **Number of applications received**. Total number of applications received in a typical year.
- **Application procedures and deadline**. Describes specific application instructions and the deadline for submitting applications.
- **Decision date**. Final date when internship placement decisions are made.
- **Duties**. Lists the typical duties that an intern can expect to perform at the company.
- **Qualifications**. Lists the criteria a prospective applicant must meet to be considered for an internship with the company.

Additional Companies

Covers those companies that elected to provide only their name, address, and telephone number for inclusion in the *Directory*. Entries are arranged alphabetically by company name.

How to Locate Career Resources

The **Career Resources** chapter contains six categories of information sources, each of which is arranged alphabetically by resource or organization name. The categories include:

▼ Sources of Help-Wanted Ads

- **Covers:** Professional journals, industry periodicals, association newsletters, placement bulletins, and online services that include employment ads or business opportunities. Includes sources that focus specifically on environmental concerns, as well as general periodical sources such as the *National Business Employment Weekly.*
- **Entries include:** The resource's title; name, address, and telephone number of its publisher; frequency; subscription rate; description of contents; toll-free and additional telephone numbers; and facsimile numbers.
- **Sources:** *Job Hunter's Sourcebook* (published by Gale Research Inc.) and original research.

▼ Professional Associations

- **Covers:** Trade and professional associations that offer career-related information and services.
- **Entries include:** Association name, address, and telephone number; membership; purpose and objectives; publications; toll-free or additional telephone numbers; and facsimile numbers. In some cases, the publications mentioned in these entries are described in greater detail as separate entries cited in the Sources of Help Wanted Ads, Career Guides, Professional and Trade Periodicals, and Basic Reference Guides and Handbooks categories.
- **Sources:** *Encyclopedia of Associations* (published by Gale Research Inc.) and original research.

▼ Employment Agencies and Search Firms

- **Covers:** Firms used by companies to recruit candidates for positions and, at times, by individuals to pursue openings. Employment agencies are generally geared towards filling openings at entry- to mid-level in the local job market, while executive search firms are paid by the hiring organization to recruit professional and managerial candidates, usually for higher-level openings. Also covers temporary employment agencies because they can be a method of identifying and obtaining regular employment. Includes firms that focus specifically on environmentalism, as well as some larger general firms.

- **Entries include:** The firm's name, address, and telephone number; whether it's an employment agency, executive search firm, or temporary agency; descriptive information, as appropriate; toll-free and additional telephone numbers; and facsimile number.
- **Sources:** *Job Hunter's Sourcebook.*

▼ Career Guides

- **Covers:** Books, kits, pamphlets, brochures, videocassettes, films, online services, and other materials that describe the job-hunting process in general or that provide guidance and insight into the job-hunting process in environmental careers.
- **Entries include:** The resource's title; name, address, and telephone number of its publisher or distributor; name of the editor or author; publication date or frequency; description of contents; arrangement; indexes; toll-free or additional telephone numbers; and facsimile numbers.
- **Sources:** *Professional Careers Sourcebook* and *Vocational Careers Sourcebook* (published by Gale Research Inc.) and original research.

▼ Professional and Trade Periodicals

- **Covers:** Newsletters, magazines, newspapers, trade journals, and other serials that offer information to environmental professionals.
- **Entries include:** The resource's title; the name, address, and telephone number of the publisher; the editor's name; frequency; description of contents; toll-free and additional telephone numbers; and facsimile numbers. Publication titles appear in italics.
- **Sources:** *Gale Directory of Publications and Broadcast Media* and *Newsletters in Print* (published by Gale Research Inc.) and original research.

▼ Basic Reference Guides and Handbooks

- **Covers:** Manuals, directories, dictionaries, encyclopedias, films and videocassettes, and other published reference material used by professionals working in environmental careers.
- **Entries include:** The resource's title; name, address, and telephone number of the publisher or distributor; the editor's or author's name; publication date or frequency; description of contents; toll-free and additional telephone numbers; and facsimile numbers. Publication titles are rendered in italics.
- **Sources:** *Professional Careers Sourcebook, Vocational Careers Sourcebook*, and original research.

Advice from the Pro's

CHAPTER ONE

Make the Earth Your Office: Careers in the Geosciences

Nick Claudy, Manager, Human Resources, American Geological Institute

The geosciences offer an unparalleled diversity of career path opportunities that reflect a unique integration of many scientific subdisciplines and the objective of exploring, understanding, and protecting Earth's environment. Whether it is conducting scientific research, applying research and development to problem solving, assessing and developing natural resources, or creating and disseminating geologic knowledge, the geosciences offer a rewarding sphere of professional endeavors.

Geoscientists gather and interpret data about the Earth for the purpose of increasing our understanding and improving the quality of society. Geoscientists investigate the materials, processes, products and history of the Earth. They usually specialize in one the following areas:

- **Geophysicists** study the Earth's interior and magnetic, electric, and gravitational fields.
- **Geochemists** investigate the nature and distribution of chemical elements in rocks and minerals.
- **Petroleum geologists** are involved with the exploration for and production of oil and natural gas.
- **Economic geologists** explore for and develop geologic materials that have profitable uses.
- **Hydrologists** investigate the movement and quality of surface water.
- **Engineering geologists** study the geologic factors that affect engineering structures such as bridges, buildings, airports, and dams.
- **Environmental geoscientists** work to solve problems with pollution, waste disposal, and urban development, and hazards such as flooding and erosion.
- **Seismologists** study the location and force of earthquakes and trace the behavior of earthquake waves to interpret the structure of the Earth.

- **Planetologists** study the moon and other planets to understand the evolution of the solar system.
- **Geochronologists** determine the age of certain rocks by calculating the rates of decay of certain radioactive elements and thus help reconstruct the geologic history of the Earth.
- **Geomorphologists** study the effects of Earth processes and investigate the nature, origin, and development of present landforms and their relationship to underlying structures.
- **Glaciologists** study the physical properties and movement of glaciers and ice sheets.
- **Marine geologists** investigate the oceans and continental shelves.
- **Mineralogists** study the formation, composition, and properties of minerals.
- **Paleontologists** study fossils to understand past life forms and their changes through time and to reconstruct past environments.
- **Petrologists** determine the origin and genesis of rocks by analyzing mineral or grain relationships.
- **Sedimentologists** study sedimentary rocks and the processes of sediment formation, transportation, and deposition.
- **Stratigraphers** investigate the time and space relationships of layered rocks and their fossil and mineral content.
- **Structural geologists** study deformation, fracturing, and folding that has occurred in the Earth's crust.
- **Volcanologists** investigate volcanoes and volcanic phenomena.

One obvious advantage of being a geoscientist is the variety of locales where one works; one may divide time among work in an office, a laboratory, and in the field. Generally, anyone who enjoys the outdoors, travel, discovery, and analysis will find the geosciences a rewarding career choice. In addition, the geosciences offer a unique opportunity to apply interdisciplinary science concepts to problem solving—a feature of the profession that accommodates a wide variety of background training.

What Does It Take to Get Hired?

Each category of employer has its own list of preferred credentials for new hires. However, all employers seek a few basic requisites. A master's degree is usually required today to work as a professional geoscientist. In 1991 there were far more BA/BS geoscience graduates than geoscience jobs available, but the situation was quite the opposite for those with a master's degree. Basic undergraduate and graduate courses should include physical and historical geology, mineralogy, petrology, sedimentation and stratigraphy, paleontology, structural geology, geomorphology, and field training. Diversity of course work is highly valued since it allows greater adaptability to employer needs. Independent study may also be a useful factor for employment. Any work experience (full-time, part-time, or summer) is also a valuable asset; such experience can often enhance the employability of those with a BA/BS degree. Skills in oral and written communication are also frequently cited as a necessity for new hires. The increased emphasis on environmental issues in geoscience programs is probably a response to predicted employment opportunities, and some course work in these environmental topics will be beneficial for every professional path.

Career Opportunities

Factors that generally support career opportunities in science and technology are also valid for the geosciences: a far lower unemployment rate than that of the total civilian labor force and a potential shortages of workers due to a decline in the 18-24 year age group, depressed enrollments, too few new graduates, and the aging of the current work force. In addition, the creation of a national energy plan is likely to stimulate employment opportunities in the geosciences.

Available career options are best defined by those who employ geoscientists. What follow are a few current and emerging trends for the major geoscience employer categories; the figures in parentheses are the employment percentage (as of 1991) of the total domestic professional geoscience work force.

Oil/gas exploration and production companies (50%): For decades, the oil and gas industry has been the major employer of geoscientists. Recent downturns in the industry, however, have caused this employment sector to trim its workforce. Moreover, in a recent survey of undergraduate students' employment plans following graduation, only 12 percent were considering petroleum geology as a career. Nevertheless, the oil and gas industry will continue to be a major employer of geoscientists. There is a remarkable variety of employment specializations within this field, such as basin evaluations, regional structural or stratigraphic studies, oil-field studies that analyze the nature of hydrocarbon trapping, problems of reservoir distribution, and predicting oil and gas charge. The techniques used in modern exploration and development are varied as well: seismic reflection, well logs, computer modeling, 3-D work stations. The business aspects of assessing the economic risk of investment and the excitement of making deals are additional employment incentives.

Mining/minerals companies (9%): For the past few years, employment in the mining and minerals industry has been flat; most hiring has been to replace those who resign or retire. As with oil and gas, however, the country's continued dependence on coal and strategic minerals will guarantee the need for specialists in this field. Once prices have stabilized, employment should improve in mining and minerals.

Federal/state agencies (12%): In the past few years, the federal government has been exercising a freeze on most new hires. As a consequence, federal employment for the near-term does not seem promising, although fresh incentives—especially in the environmental fields—could open up new jobs. At the state government level, most employment is associated with state geological surveys. Employment opportunities in this sector are usually controlled by state budgets, the tightening of which causes a similar tightening in employment.

Research institutions/DOE national laboratories (4%): Research institutions are generally associated with colleges and universities, and geoscience departments usually share their staff with such research facilities. National laboratories, funded by the U.S. Department of Energy, may also employ college/university faculty as adjunct researchers. However, the most pressing needs at these national labs concern environmental clean-up and remedial waste disposal, especially of nuclear and toxic waste materials. It is predicted that this activity will generate significant employment opportunities for the foreseeable future. A Ph.D. is generally required for senior research staff in this sector, but employment opportunities are available and will increase for those with a master's degree.

Environmental/hydrogeology/geotechnical firms (11%): This category comprises the broad field of consulting, and it has been the fastest growing geoscience employment sector for the past few years. Because there are so many different types of geoscience consulting, and because such a diverse population (from farmers to bankers) requires geologic expertise, the employment possibilities are tremendous. In addition, new environmental laws and redoubled efforts to implement existing laws and regulations will generate employment growth across a broad range of job sectors. And because the federal government has selective freezes in hiring, it relies heavily on consulting firm contracts. Employment growth will continue throughout the 1990s.

Academia (14%): College and university geoscience departments are the primary employer in this category, although earth science teachers are needed at every educational level, from kindergarten through high school. Academic employment almost always requires a Ph.D., although community colleges may relax that standard. Teaching and research are the primary activities, and nearly all faculty regularly write articles for publication and for textbooks.

Employment as a **geotechnician** is another area that has been experiencing significant growth. A geological technician is one who is skilled in the application of tools and techniques that facilitate geoscience investigations in a variety of settings. Opportunities for BA/BS graduates are also numerous in this category, and such employment can provide a practical means to gain experience for advancement.

NICK CLAUDY has been employed at the American Geological Institute since 1979 and involved in human resources activities since 1983. He is the editor of the *AGI Directory of Geoscience Departments* and is responsible for annual surveys of student enrollments in the geosciences, geoscience employment and hiring, and faculty salaries. Claudy earned his B.A. from Brown University in 1965 and his M.A. from the University of North Carolina in 1970.

CHAPTER TWO

Your Career in Microbiology: Unlocking the Secrets of Life

American Society for Microbiology

Microorganisms. Tiny infectious agents. They invade your body and can make you sick. They also cure and prevent diseases. They are everywhere—in the air you breathe, the food you eat, and the water you drink. They help clean up oil spills and toxic waste sites. Their genetic material can be broken down and moved to other organisms. Sometimes simple, often complex, these *microbes* have had an impact on our planet—the environment, your body, food, and health.

Few fields offer the excitement, challenges, and rewards of microbiology. It is a broad field that enables you to discover a vast living world of organisms. As a **microbiologist**, you are at the frontier of modern biology. You will change the way we live and improve our quality of life. Look at today's microbiologists. They are working on cures to life-threatening diseases such as Lyme's disease, cancer, and AIDS. They are finding ways to clean up toxic wastes and oil spills without using dangerous chemicals. They are investigating ways to provide better tasting fruits and vegetables, healthier, more productive livestock, and natural pest controls. The list is endless.

Why do individuals become microbiologists? For some, it is a strong curiosity. For others, the yearning to find out how things work. In all cases, it is a desire to make a difference in our world. For you, a biology course may spark an interest in finding out the secrets of life. A special teacher may stimulate your curiosity about the unseen world. Or, perhaps, it will be the fascination of organisms interacting with the environment.

A career in microbiology is not just a job, but ongoing adventures that open doors to discovering new phenomenon. As a microbiologist, you will have numerous opportunities to make significant contributions to mankind.

What Is a Microbiologist?

Although known by many different titles, a microbiologist is a scientist who studies living organisms and infectious agents, many of whom can only be seen with a microscope. They also study the interaction of microorganisms with people. Every day, microbiologists around the world explore, investigate, and discover how these organisms, called microbes, exist and affect our lives. Microbes range from submicroscopic infectious agents, such as viruses to tapeworms, which can grow to several feet in length and have a large number of genes.

Microbiologists' findings are critical to research in health, agricultural, and environmental sciences. They contribute significantly to the quality of life. To conduct their studies, microbiologists combine the techniques of genetics, chemistry, biochemistry, physiology, physics, ecology, and pathology. Some of the many accomplishments of microbiologists have significantly affected our lives:

- Developing vaccines for infectious diseases such as whooping cough and polio;
- Testing for infections at early stages when they are more treatable;
- Finding out how microorganisms cause diseases, such as toxic shock syndrome, Legionnaires' disease, and AIDS;
- Preventing tooth decay and gum disease;
- Harnessing microbes to recycle waste and clean oil spills;
- Improving crop and livestock production to help feed the world's hungry;
- Making food taste better and preventing spoilage; and
- Understanding the nature of all living things.

A Multitude of Options

As a microbiologist, you will work with many other scientists and have a vast range of opportunities. Microbiologists work in almost every industry and have many different responsibilities. The following is a partial list of overlapping roles you may have. You will collaborate with many other scientists, many of whom are identified here. Depending on your specific situation, you may perform more than one function or role.

Bacteriologist—studies how bacteria infect humans, animals and plants, reproduce, and cause disease.

Biochemist—studies how organisms derive energy, use nutrients, and reproduce.

Cell Biologist—studies how cells grow and differentiate.

Epidemiologist—studies the pattern of disease outbreaks.

Geneticist—studies the processes by which organisms inherit and transmit genetic information to other microorganisms and investigates how genetic information is stored and processed.

Immunologist—studies the body's ability to resist infectious diseases and cancer.

Microbial Physiologist and Biochemist—studies life processes of microbes and how organisms use nutrients and divide.

Molecular Biologist—studies the structure and function of genetic material, as well as how cells translate this material into life's products.

Mycologist—studies fungi, molds, and yeast to discover how they infect living matter, reproduce, and cause disease.

Parasitologist—studies parasitic organisms to find out how they infect living hosts, reproduce, and cause disease.

Virologist—studies viruses or pieces of genetic material that are only active inside living cells.

In addition, microbiologists are writers, artists, and illustrators. They may also work in public relations, sales, and technical support positions.

Career Avenues for Microbiologists

Depending on your experience and education, there are a number of options and opportunities to choose from in your career as a microbiologist. Microbiology is a rapidly expanding field with extensive opportunities in many areas. These include human health, the environment, genetic engineering, and microbial ecology. Listed below are examples of the opportunities available to you as you complete your education.

Two-Year Technical Training Degree

One option is obtaining an associate of arts or an associate of applied science degree from a community college or technical institution. There are increasing opportunities for laboratory assistants and this training will give you the necessary qualifications. The curriculum covers a two-year program and includes courses in biology, life sciences, chemistry, physics, mathematics, and computer science.

Baccalaureate Degree

Upon graduation, your baccalaureate degree in biology or microbiology will help you qualify for many technical, research, environmental, and clinical positions. These include:

- **Research Assistant**—A key player to research teams, providing technical support to conduct research. A research assistant participates in a team with a director and other technical specialists (e.g., biochemists, geneticists, cell biologists), as well as marketing, administrative, and sales professionals.
- **Food, Industrial, or Environmental Microbiologists, Quality Assurance Technologists**—Identifies disease or harmful microorganisms in water, food, dairy, pharmaceutical, and environmental products. In addition, they check for the quality and safety of vitamins, vaccines, antibiotics, antiseptics, and disinfectants.
- **Clinical and Veterinary Microbiologists, Medical Technologists**—Identifies harmful or disease-causing microorganisms in humans and animals.

Another option available to students with a bachelor's degree is to complete laboratory training that qualifies you for higher-level positions in a laboratory environment. These are usually one-year training programs resulting in certification.

Master's Degree

A master's degree will broaden your career choices in marketing, sales, administrative, teaching, and technical support positions. Your master's degree will typically offer you better positions with a higher salary, greater prospects for advancement, more responsibility, and increased independence. Opportunities include:

- **Supervisor or Laboratory Manager**—Supervises day-to-day activities in a variety of laboratories.
- **Research Manager or Associate**—Performs experiments and provides technical support to research teams.
- **Instructor**—Teaches courses at the community and junior college levels.

Doctoral Degree (or equivalent)

A Ph.D. or M.D. is almost always required for higher-level positions in microbiology and other sciences. Achieving your doctoral degree will greatly enhance your opportunities as there is a tremendous need for microbiologists with a Ph.D. You will be able to perform independent research, teach undergraduate and graduate students, and assume executive-level responsibilities in government and industry. Specific jobs include:

- Scientist—Formulates hypotheses for experimental investigation, conducts research, and trains students and laboratory personnel.
- University or College Professor—Teaches in the classroom or laboratory, trains students, conducts research, and performs community service.
- Academic Science Administrator—Serves as college or university dean or in other administrative positions such as vice president or president.
- Research Director—Leads research team that explores and tries to understand unanswered questions and unproven theories.
- Corporate Executive—Oversees part or all of a company such as a biotechnology, pharmaceutical, agricultural, or environmental firm.
- Consultant—Advises and reports information to organizations such as businesses or government agencies.
- Science Advisor/Administrator—Leads programs concerned with safety of new devices, food, drugs, and chemicals and helps influence laws, regulations, and research for government agencies.

Combining a Science Education with Another Discipline

You may choose to combine your undergraduate degree in a science-related field with a graduate degree in another area, such as business, marketing, or journalism. This will enable you to pursue opportunities in scientific sales, technical support, writing, public relations, communications, regulatory affairs, or management. Completing a bachelor's degree in microbiology also gives you the necessary foundation to continue an education in the medical, veterinary, dental, or legal fields.

How Much Does a Microbiologist Make?

Salaries among microbiologists vary a great deal depending on education, experience, type of job, and location. The following chart provides a general guide to what you could expect to earn, given the indicated educational level of achievement and type of company or institution. The lower end of the salary scales represents salaries for people starting a career in microbiology, and the higher end represents a microbiologist with many years of experience.

A Diversity of Settings

Microbiologists work in many different organizations studying a broad range of issues. The potential places to be a microbiologist are numerous. They include:

Education—undergraduate and graduate institutions; research institutions; community and junior colleges; and medical, dental, and veterinary schools.

Industry—pharmaceutical, food, geological, and agricultural companies; biotechnology companies, environmental, and pollution control companies; and hospitals, health maintenance organizations, clinics, and physicians' offices.

Government—research and regulatory laboratories of the U.S. Department of Health and Human Services, Department of Agriculture, Department of Energy, Department of Education, Department of Defense, Central Intelligence Agency, Federal Bureau of Investigation, Environmental Protection Agency, and Patent Office; state and municipal laboratories such as water and waste management companies; and public health institutions such as hospitals, clinics, and public health laboratories.

Within these specific areas, the options are far reaching. For example, if you enjoy helping others and would like to teach, there is a tremendous demand for professors at all educational levels. An academic career offers fulfillment in the classroom, laboratory, and community. For Joan W. Bennett, a professor of cell and molecular biology, no two days are the same. Her work combines teaching, administration, and research. She nurtures future microbiologists by teaching and helping students with research projects. She writes proposals, serves on editorial review boards, and authors articles. In her research, she studies fungi, both for their helpful and harmful effects. While she studies a poisonous toxin released by fungi that can spoil food, she also searches for positive ways to use fungi, such as for destroying munitions like TNT.

Working for an independent research firm, Jim Harvey helps coordinate scientific workshops that focus on protecting our environment. One of his programs will bring together scientists from around the country to discuss how microorganisms can destroy insects and reduce our dependency on harmful pesticides.

Reginald Bennett, a research microbiologist at the Food and Drug Administration, helps develop methods for detecting microbial toxins in food. Because of the efforts of Dr. Bennett and his colleagues, we can feel secure that the food we eat is safe and free of contamination.

A Life of Intrigue

Microbiologists the world over find their work interesting, fulfilling, and highly rewarding. Discovering a cure for fatal diseases or isolating genetic materials that can prevent these diseases are only two facets of microbiology that provide life long gratification. Knowing your research saves lives, improves the quality of life, or protects the environment is a reward unattainable in other careers. Microbiology boasts some of the most illustrious names in science such as Leeuwenhoek, Pasteur, and Salk. A third of all Nobel prizes in physiology and medicine have been awarded to microbiologists.

As a microbiologist, you can expect to:

- Explore the unknown microscopic world;
- Collect and analyze data;
- Collaborate and share information; and
- Transform research findings into beneficial products.

You will ask questions and test theories that lead to new discoveries. You will explore how the body responds to infectious agents. You will isolate and modify microorganisms that are valuable and beneficial in the natural world. And you will work with other scientists in teams, sharing and exchanging information. The microbiologist's world is exciting and ever-changing. You will be on the cutting edge of technology and can make a significant contribution to our world.

The Chance to Make a Difference

Why do individuals become microbiologists? For some, it is a strong curiosity. For others, the yearning to find out how things work. In all cases, it is a desire to make a difference in our world. For you, a biology course may spark an interest in finding out the secrets of life. A special teacher may stimulate your curiosity about the unseen world. Or, perhaps, it will be the fascination of organisms interacting with the environment.

The Frontier of Science

Exciting studies are performed in microbiology every day. Many of them incorporate biotechnology which encompasses the latest diagnostic, genetic engineering, cellular, and tissue techniques. Advances are being made in all areas of the environment, agriculture, and health.

Environment

Environmental microbiologists play an increasingly important role in studying and improving the world around us. For example, George Skladany, a microbiologist working for a biotechnology company collaborates with scientists and government researchers to solve problems caused by contaminated waste sites and ground water. He provides information and research that helps to improve the quality of our water supply and to reduce the dangers of hazardous waste. As an environmental microbiologist you can:

- Identify organisms to accelerate the cleaning up of oil spills and hazardous waste sites;
- Develop genetic probes to detect microbial contaminants in the water supply, in seafood, estuaries, and other natural settings; or

- Evaluate new water treatment and filtering processes ensuring the safety of our water supply.

Agriculture

Agricultural research is helping to produce safer and better food products with greater efficiency. If you choose to become an agricultural microbiologist, you will have numerous options ranging from developing genetically-engineered crops that are resistant to frost, drought, spoilage, disease, and pests to producing vaccines that protect domestic animals from rabies. Joe Robinson is an agricultural microbiologist at the Upjohn Company. He researches ways cattle break down food. His studies may lead to the discovery of a diet for cattle to gain weight quickly with fewer pounds of feed.

Working for an agricultural company may provide you with an opportunity to:

- Develop organisms to help produce healthier, tastier, and cheaper foods;
- Identify organisms that can reduce the use of chemical pesticides;
- Develop sensitive, rapid methods to detect signs of food spoilage or microbial contaminants to ensure the safety of our food supply.

Health

In the area of human health, clinical and medical microbiologists improve our lives by managing and preventing diseases. Some, like Janet Hindler at the University of California at Los Angeles, study patients with poor immune systems (such as people with AIDS, organ transplants, and cancer) to find out which antibiotics are effective. Others, like Marie Pezzlo at the University of California at Irvine, perform tests to detect disease-producing microorganisms. Research you may conduct as a clinical or medical microbiologist includes:

- Identifying culprit microorganisms and infectious agents that cause Legionnaires' disease, toxic shock syndrome, AIDS, and Lyme's disease;
- Developing new vaccines or antibiotics for preventing diseases or delivering protection against several diseases at once;
- Developing new methods that help diagnose diseases rapidly and more accurately.

Preparing to Become a Microbiologist

In your quest to become a microbiologist, you must build a solid foundation with emphasis in reading, writing, mathematics, computer science, and communication. As a microbiologist, you will probably specialize in one area. In order to do that, however, you will need to be familiar with many scientific disciplines. Your coursework in high school provides a basic foundation. Four years of college gives breadth to that knowledge and post-graduate studies enable you to probe into your selected area. Here are specific actions you can take as you continue your education.

High School

Your coursework should include biology, chemistry, physics, computer science, and mathematics. English courses are also important because microbiologists spend much of their time communicating results through speeches, articles, and manuscripts. In addition, foreign languages are critical for exchanging information with scientists around the world.

You should participate in extracurricular activities such as science fairs and clubs. If possible, work in a research laboratory of a university or science related company part-time or during the summers. These activities provide valuable insight and actual experience in a scientific environment.

Undergraduate

As an undergraduate, if there is no microbiological sciences degree available, you should major in biological or life sciences, or chemistry and take all offered courses in microbiology. These could include general microbiology, microbial genetics, cell biology, immunology, virology, pathogenic microbiology, and environmental microbiology. Your other coursework should include qualitative and quantitative chemistry, organic and biochemistry, calculus, physics, computer science, statistics, and English. It is extremely important to have a multidisciplinary foundation in order to increase your options and obtain the qualifications for many microbiology careers.

To receive the greatest benefit of your undergraduate program, work in a laboratory and participate in extracurricular programs such as microbiology or biology clubs and honor societies. Join local and national scientific professional societies and take advantage of student-oriented events. If these kinds of opportunities are unavailable, ask your departmental chairperson to charter these organizations on your campus. To develop necessary hand-eye coordination and group interaction skills, participate in activities that develop manipulative, precision, and team building skills.

Additional Preparations

In addition to your formal education, you should maintain an awareness of microbiological developments by watching the news and reading science-related articles appearing in newspapers, magazines, information pamphlets, and journals. You should meet with an advisor early in your college career and develop a relationship with a professor who can share his or her research experiences and advise you throughout your education. Visiting microbiologists who perform research at biotechnology firms, pharmaceutical companies, universities, and medical centers will also provide you with valuable knowledge, as well as important contacts. In general, these individuals are eager to assist aspiring microbiologists. Finally, you can volunteer to work with microbiologists in hospitals, universities, government agencies, or companies. These endeavors will add to your educational foundation by providing practical, hands-on experiences and helping you understand the available options.

Financial Assistance

To help finance your education, there are numerous scholarships, fellowships, and student loan programs available. For more information, contact your school's financial aid office.

Your Future in Microbiology

Opportunities for scientific achievement are limitless. As Dr. Ronald Cape, chairman and founder of a large biotechnology company says, "There are lots of Nobel prizes waiting to be earned!" Your choices are not only exciting, but vast. Projections for the next 20 years indicate thousands of scientific positions will go unfilled with a huge demand for microbiologists. A variety of special programs will make opportunities for women, members of under-represented groups, and people with disabilities especially favorable.

The image of a microbiologist spending the entire day sequestered in a laboratory peering down a microscope is no longer valid. In addition to working in the laboratory, microbiologists work with many different people—in hospitals, clinics, universities, research institutions, industries, and government agencies.

Where you end up is your choice. Your future is bright and promising. With a solid foundation in science and the desire to discover the unknown world of microbiology, your possibilities and opportunities are numerous.

THE AMERICAN SOCIETY FOR MICROBIOLOGY promotes the advancement of scientific knowledge in order to improve education in microbiology. The society encourages high professional and ethical standards, and the adoption of sound legislative and regulatory policies affecting the discipline of microbiology at all levels.

CHAPTER THREE

Career Opportunities in Ecology

Frederic H. Wagner, Director,
Ecology Center, Utah State University

As a Texas college student in the late `40s and early `50s, I already knew that I wanted to make my career in ecology. My best friend, a New England urbanite, who was studying business administration and bent on making his first million, had no idea what ecology was. But like a true friend, he was tolerant and supportive, if disinterested. When I saw him after we had gone separate ways for 20 years at the height of the environmental movement in the `70s, he was wide-eyed and exuberant. "My gosh," he said, "now I know what you were into. I see the word *ecology* more often in the press than I see the word *sex*."

Still, Charlie really had no more sense of the field than most people today. It is relatively new. It is extremely diverse. It is surrounded by emotion, contention, and misinformation. Most people have a hazy idea at best of what it is and many misconceptions about what it is not.

What is Ecology?

Ecology, like chemistry and physics, is a science. This means that, like the other sciences, it strives through research to develop systematic, disciplined, factual descriptions and explanations of some aspect of reality. Its aspect of reality is the interrelationship between living organisms and their environments.

What makes ecology so diverse is the breadth of its subject matter. Physics deals with less than two dozen particles and less than 10 each of forces and kinds of energy. Chemistry studies the interactions of about 100 elements. The living world, on the other hand, consists of several hundred thousand species of plants, several million species of animals, and uncounted species of microorganisms. They live in most environments on the earth's surface: in salt water on the lightless ocean bottom two miles deep, near the surface in mid-ocean, in estuaries and mangroves around continental margins; in fresh water streams, lakes, and marshes; and on land in polar tundra, deserts, grasslands, tropical forests, and even bare rock.

At its lowest level of integration, ecology studies how individual organisms relate to their environments. How do individual plants or animals take up and give off heat, water, oxygen, and carbon dioxide from the atmosphere; and in the case of plants, how do they take up sunlight and convert it to their own tissues which then become energy-bearing food for animals?

Top 10 Job Markets

Ranked by: Total new jobs by 1995.

1. Washington, DC, with 118,200 new jobs
2. Anaheim, CA, 108,800
3. Atlanta, GA, 104,600
4. Phoenix, AZ, 92,000
5. San Diego, CA, 77,100
6. Tampa-St. Petersburg, 76,300
7. Orlando, FL, 70,300
8. Dallas, TX, 69,300
9. Riverside, CA, 67,700
10. Minneapolis-St. Paul, 64,700

Source: *Money*

The science also studies organisms in groups called populations. How fast do they reproduce, die, fluctuate in number, achieve high or low densities? Why do some populations go extinct, others increase to the point of becoming pests? How do still others, like salmon and tuna, maintain substantial numbers in the face of human harvest?

At its most complex level, ecology studies the functioning of whole ecosystems by looking at the processes of energy and chemical exchange among the plants and animals collectively and their physical environment. How much energy-bearing plant material does the vegetation convert through photosynthesis, how much of it is eaten by plant-eating animals, and in turn, how many of them are eaten by predators? The answer bears on the cost of the tuna, a large predator in the ocean, on your dinner table. How well do the different kinds of organisms in a forest conserve essential elements needed by all living creatures and originally taken from the soil by the vegetation? Does plant decomposition by microorganisms, which return the elements to the soil for reuse by new plants, create a tight enough cycle to maintain fertility and keep the elements from eroding downhill into streams and out into the ocean?

Ultimately, the condition of all the earth's ecosystems affects human welfare in someway. But some effects are more obvious and immediate to our concerns than others. Most people know from the media that ecologists are predicting global warming in the years ahead. This is expected to result from an imbalance in the earth's carbon cycle. Burning fossil fuel, breathing by people and domestic and wild animals, and bacterial breakdown of organic matter all add carbon dioxide to the atmosphere faster than the world's vegetation can take it up in photosynthesis. Carbon dioxide acts like glass, letting sunlight through to the earth, but then trapping it as heat. This is expected to change world climates and affect agricultural production.

Releasing certain chemicals into the atmosphere destroys the ozone layer that blocks some of the sun's ultraviolet radiation. Our immediate concern is that the increase in ultraviolet radiation will increase our skin cancer rate, but most people are less aware that some plants are sensitive to increased levels of it. This is true of the microscopic phytoplankton in the ocean which capture carbon dioxide and, thereby, help with the carbon-balance problem, but are also the base of the food chain that may top off with the tuna on your dinner table.

So What Are the Opportunities?

There are a lot. And like the question, *what is ecology?*, there are no one-line answers. First of all, it depends on whether a person wants to stay in the science itself. That pretty much means research and teaching. Most ecological research is done by people in universities, state and federal government agencies (e.g., U.S. Environmental Protection Agency, U.S. Fish and Wildlife Service, USDA Forest Service, state departments of natural resources, etc.), and in some private organizations and laboratories. So there are a good many positions in ecological research.

Obviously, most teaching is done in educational institutions. Not many high schools offer separate courses in ecology. It is usually included as a part of courses in biology, of which it is a subdiscipline. Typically, ecology is first taught as a full-fledged course in university undergraduate curricula along with other biology courses like physiology, botany, genetics, entomology, etc. It is at the university graduate level where courses proliferate into specialized ecology offerings. At my own university, we offer more than 50 specialized ecology courses not counting those in related sciences like meteorology, climatology, soils, geology, hydrology, and related areas of biology; and not including those in applied areas of ecology to be discussed below. So there are teaching opportunities at the high school level for biology teachers who can provide competent instruction in ecology and for college professors who have specialized in ecology in their graduate education.

But just as engineering is the application of physics, and medicine is the application of such sciences as physiology, epidemiology, and pathology, there are numerous professions that apply to ecology. To name a few, forestry, fisheries and wildlife management, range management, conservation, various aspects of environmental protection, economic entomology, and some aspects of agriculture are all applied ecology. These fields provide extensive employment opportunities for persons educated in the science. Foresters, park rangers, wildlife managers, insect pest control experts, and oceanographers are all applied ecologists.

There are many of these kinds of positions in state and federal government agencies. Additionally, there are numerous jobs in private environmental advocacy organizations like the Audubon Society and Nature Conservancy and in a large number of environmental consulting firms. Some people trained in ecology enter law school, get law degrees, and are either employed in the above government and private organizations or are hired by law firms. Some legal firms have sections in environmental law, while others specialize entirely in environmental issues.

Ecology, in its many manifestations, is a huge field that relates to human welfare in ways that the average person is only dimly aware of. Its importance will increase over the years as the world's human population rises, makes increasing demands on the globe's ecosystems for its necessities and luxuries, and increasingly impacts the global environment in the process.

What Kinds of Training Make an Ecologist?

We are talking about a science, and so the necessary training is intensive, just like in any other science. There are some labor or maintenance positions open to people without college educations, but realistically these people are not ecologists.

An undergraduate degree is the required minimum degree to enter this field. However, people with no more than a bachelor's degree are at a disadvantage in progressing beyond technician-level jobs or entry-level positions as conservation officers or park rangers. The bachelor's degree had been sufficient in the past, but for some years, a master's degree has virtually become the required minimum for professional positions in the government agencies and many private organizations.

For anyone aspiring to a research career and certainly for academia, the Ph.D. is the necessary credential. Many individuals going into upper management and administrative posts are well served by having a doctorate. The field is simply too complex to gain significant competence with anything less.

People planning to go into the field should be prepared for, *more importantly,* should enjoy, studying math and the sciences. A casual approach, based on an emotional attachment to the beauties of nature, doesn't get the job done. All of us who go into the field have that attachment, and it serves as a motivation for the hard work ahead. But we all have put our shoulders to the wheel and applied ourselves to the demanding disciplines. It is rewarding in the end, for our emotional appreciation of nature is vastly enriched by an intellectual understanding of those things that we were aesthetically drawn to in the first place.

In general, both income potential and the number and stature of employment opportunities rise with increasing education. In no way is the earning power comparable to such professions as law and medicine. No one gets rich in ecology. But neither do most of the people who have gone into the field regret having done so. Job satisfaction is high when one can work on things that s/he finds attractive and interesting and, at the same time, have a sense of the social worth of one's efforts. There is a need for people who are willing to make a commitment to the field.

FREDERIC H. WAGNER became interested in nature at an early age. As a teenager, he served as a refuge patrolman on a large, federal wildlife refuge. With his interest in ecology solidified, Dr. Wagner enrolled at Southern Methodist University, where he received a B.S. in biology. Afterwards, he attended graduate school at the University of Wisconsin, where he earned a M.S. in wildlife management and later his Ph.D. in zoology and wildlife management.

Since completing his doctorate, Dr. Wagner has been a professor at the College of Natural Resources, Utah State University. During his academic career, he has taught courses in ecology and wildlife management and has conducted research or consulted in such diverse subjects as desert ecology, predation, herbivory, wild horses, national park management, natural resources, environmental policy, and other topics in North America, Africa, and Australia.

Among his many professional commitments, Dr. Wagner acts as secretary-treasurer of the American Institute of Biological Sciences and chair of the National Academy of Sciences Committee on Wild and Free-Roaming Horses and Burros. He is also past president of the Association of Ecosystem Research Centers.

CHAPTER FOUR

Minority Opportunities in Ecology: The Importance of Diversity

Carmen R. Cid, Ph.D., Department of Biology, Eastern Connecticut State University

Ecology is the branch of biology that is concerned with the preservation and restoration of the local and global diversity of living organisms. **Ecologists** study how those various species interact with each other and their surroundings, through competition, predator-prey, parasite-host, or mutualistic interactions. The results of their study are used to manage needed resources in a way that allows for maximum species diversity. To accomplish this multifaceted mission requires a variety of perspectives from all cultural and educational backgrounds.

Biodiversity Preservation

To preserve biodiversity, we need to coordinate the expertise of researchers in various areas of ecology with that of other scientists such as chemists, engineers, planners, hydrologists, and geologists. Species diversity management plans generated by the scientists must be coordinated with the local, state, and federal government policies and policymaking bodies. At times, there may even be a need for managed disturbance of sections of the environment. We need to acquire funding from private and public agencies and support from the general public.

Restoration and preservation of diversity requires communication with and cooperation from many communities of people, be they directly involved in the environmental management plans or be they groups of concerned citizens. Recently, the Ecological Society of America (ESA) published a report that outlines the research priorities for ecologists in the coming decades. This report, entitled the *Sustainable Biosphere Initiative*, clearly exposes that in order for global ecological problems to be solved, we must communicate the results of our ecological research to all citizens and help incorporate that knowledge into public policy and management decisions. Ecologists are often asked to devise a compromise among human economic and spiritual needs and the survival requirements of other species. Fortunately, there is a growing realization that the preservation of *all* other species and natural resources is *essential* for human survival.

Preservation and restoration of biodiversity, even at the local scale, may involve interactions among communities from all over the world. In general, people are often more willing to interact and cooperate with people with whom they feel a common bond (e.g., third world countries and U.S. ethnic minority groups). In spite of that need, the 1992 ESA membership survey indicated that African-Americans, Hispanic-Americans, Asian-Americans, and Native Americans are greatly underrepresented among ecologists, relative to their numbers in the national population.

Environmental Problems Need a Global Solution

The perspectives of these underrepresented ethnic groups are needed to solve today's ecological problems. For example, the improvement of air and water quality, land field use, and other waste management issues are of primary concern in urban areas. These environmental problems involve much coordination among the local and state governments, the people affected, and a variety of ecology experts. Unfortunately, the ethnic groups that are underrepresented in ecology make up the largest proportion of people in these urban areas. There are very few minority ecologists with the personal experience of growing up in these urban environments to provide a solid understanding of all the nonenvironmental aspects of those problems, and to provide the most equitable solutions for all parties involved. The restoration of urban habitats requires that all people (especially those who have grown up in inner-city neighborhoods) work together, not just to clean up the water, land, and air, but to increase and maintain species diversity in urban parks, for the sake of those species and for people to preserve the privilege to appreciate the beauty of nature.

Expected Earnings

Educators, advisors, and ecologists need to convey to students that the salaries in ecology careers are comparable to those in other fields currently being favored by minorities. For example, the starting salary with a bachelor's degree in a variety of fields that an ecologist may major in (e.g., biology, wildlife management, chemistry, geology, or environmental earth science) ranges from $17,000 to $23,000 per year. With a master's degree, an ecologist can expect a starting annual salary ranging from $23,000 to $30,000. A recent Ph.D. graduate interested in an ecology position can expect to earn between $30,000 and $45,000 per year. The ESA 1992 membership survey indicated that the median annual salary for ecologists ranges from $40,000 to $50,000, and the maximum annual salary of respondents was $175,000.

Additionally, many global environmental problems are concentrated in third world countries where ecologists of color would be welcomed to interact with the local people to coordinate solutions. Also, bilingual Hispanic-Americans would be very helpful throughout South America in coordinating with local environmental groups.

Now is the time to unite with the emerging majority groups of the U.S population to solve the environmental problems of the 21st century. The ethnic groups currently underrepresented among ecologists have a cultural tradition of caring for the land and managing biodiversity, including the development of innovative, environmentally safe agricultural techniques, and plant and animal breeding programs. African-Americans, Hispanic-Americans, Native Americans, and Asian-Americans, particularly in geographical areas of the U.S. where these ethnic groups abound, should be encouraged to take pride and continue with their cultural heritage of stewardship.

Career Options in Ecology

Several academic and sociological factors are emerging as possible reasons for the currently low ethnic diversity among ecologists. Among those factors is the lack of adequate preparation that students from underrepresented groups are receiving toward science careers, which may be due to unavailable science resources, or tracking in high school into course schedules devoid of math and science courses. Due to low expectations from educators, family and/or peer, minority students are often discouraged or receive no positive reinforcement in choosing science—and especially—ecology careers. Additionally, cultural barriers, lack of exposure to ecology as a career choice, lack of field trip experience, or simply misinformation about career opportunities in ecology may prevent minorities from pursuing a career in ecology.

Because of the general public's growing concern for environmental issues, there is an endless number of career opportunities in ecology for *all* students, (e.g., interdisciplinary career tracks, lab and field work, and greenhouse and computer work). For example, students with interests in business and the environment, have good writing skills, and care about environmental issues; or who are good at debating public policy issues and are interested in environmental causes, currently have many opportunities in the newly emerging environmental careers with an interdisciplinary focus. Students interested in combining inside work with field work can explore the wonders of new computer programs and new laboratory techniques in improving plant species and develop computer models to assess the impact of environmental changes made to various plant and animal species.

To understand the potential changes in the world's biodiversity as a result of global warming, we need people to coordinate information from a variety of fields, which involves a great deal of computer expertise. The study of how a variety of organisms adapt physiologically to changes in temperature and water availability can be done at the molecular or organismal level in laboratories and greenhouses and is crucial to understanding the ecological changes occurring in today's biosphere.

However, information on the variety of career options in ecology is not clearly disseminated to target the interests of underrepresented students in ecology, nor to answer their questions. For example, ecology is sometimes perceived erroneously as an esoteric science, with few types of jobs to offer and in which promotions are infrequent. The environment in which most minorities grow up is not conducive to taking jobs in fields perceived as difficult for advancement or as having mostly low-paying jobs. The difficulties that most minority groups face in graduating from high school—and even more so—in obtaining a college degree require that upon college graduation, there be more security and greater promise of improvement of their socioeconomic scale.

Salaries

Educators, advisors, and ecologists need to convey to students that the salaries in ecology careers are comparable to those in other fields currently being favored by minorities. For example, the starting salary with a bachelor's degree in a variety of fields that an ecologist may major in (e.g., biology, wildlife management, chemistry, geology, or environmental earth science) ranges from $17,000 to $23,000 per year. With a master's degree, an ecologist can expect a starting annual salary ranging from $23,000 to $30,000. A recent Ph.D. graduate interested in an ecology position can expect to earn between $30,000 and $45,000 per year. The ESA 1992 membership survey indicated that the median annual salary for ecologists ranges from $40,000 to $50,000, and the maximum annual salary of respondents was $175,000.

Strategies for Diversity

Getting Them Informed/Interested

Although graduate degrees are needed for advancement in most ecological careers, many industries are willing to help defray the cost of graduate school for minority employees. Because ecological research integrates various branches of science, and because environmental problems often require solutions that affect the quality of life of all species, including humans, ecology work is exceedingly diverse, exciting, and rewarding. Ecology research brings a high level of personal satisfaction in helping preserve nature and in attempting to divine the answer to its complex puzzles of species interactions.

The low ethnic diversity among current ecology students is based largely on lack of information, misinformation, and a greater need for money to embark into such a career. First, professional organizations need to develop brochures and other advertising materials and provide the information to minorities in an efficient, systematic way. They need to make it feasible for minorities to opt for ecology careers. Ultimately, all of these changes require setting short-term and long-term goals.

For a rapid increase in the recruitment pool, advisors, educators, and professional organizations must target ecology career information to high school seniors and undergraduates who already have good preparation for college science courses and good support systems. We need to expound on the future importance of environmental science to other fields, such as business, economics, and law, emphasizing the aspects of ecology that can enhance the lifestyle of the inner-city student. We need to inform university co-op education programs and career planning and placement offices of jobs and internships in ecology. We need to show students in our local schools what type of research ecologists do, and develop advertising materials showing minorities in a variety of ecological settings doing exciting, interesting work. Lastly, to have a more lasting impact on recruitment of minority ecologists, ecology career options need to be presented to pre-high school students. The ESA membership survey showed that 41 percent of today's ecologists became interested in the subject in their elementary and early middle school years.

Getting Them to Stay

In order to retain minority students in ecology programs in college, we need to continue developing support networks from high school through undergraduate and graduate school levels. Various scientific professional organizations, such as the Society for the Advancement of Chicanos and Native Americans in Science (SACNAS), the Minorities in Agriculture, Natural Resources, and Related Sciences Association (MANRSS), the Ecological Society of America (ESA), and the Association for Women in Science (AWIS) are sponsoring career fairs, developing mentor programs, and holding strategy-planning workshops to help increase retention of minorities in ecology. Additionally, minority graduate students need easier access to mentoring programs (as is being done by large corporations for business students and staff), updated guides to graduate ecology programs, and greater variety of and easier access to financial assistance throughout their graduate school studies.

Large-Scale Efforts

Fortunately, a wide range of educational associations, environmental organizations, and professional groups are joining forces in the mission of increasing representation of minorities in ecology. *All* students need greater access to ecology educational brochures, videos, mentoring programs, summer work and research experiences in ecology, trips to nature preserves, and participation in environmental preservation projects. Professional and private organizations are setting up scholarships for minorities interested in ecological careers. Marine and terrestrial biological stations throughout the country (e.g., Woods Hole Oceanographic Institute, MA; W.K. Kellogg Biological Station, MI; Archbold Biological Station, FL; and the Institute of Ecosystem Studies, NY) and private environmental organizations (e.g., the Environmental Career Organization, MA; the Nature Conservancy) have organized summer internship and research experience programs for minorities in environmental fields. Publishers are developing educational aids (videos and high school biology texts) that show minorities doing ecological research. Science museums throughout the country are connecting an increasing number of minority scientists with elementary and middle school children through correspondence networks, such as *Science by Mail* chapters. National environmental organizations, such as the Sierra Club, and local environmental mentoring groups, such as the Natural Guard (in New Haven, CT) are taking elementary school students from urban neighborhoods to nearby nature preserves to expose them to the joys of field studies. Private environmental organizations, such as the Nature Conservancy and the International Wildlife Coalition, are encouraging the public to participate in environmental preservation projects in Latin America and along U.S. coasts through *Adopt an Acre* and *Adopt a Whale* programs respectively, which target students of all ages.

Promote...Recruit...Succeed

As one of few Hispanic ecologists in the United States, I see a great need for minority scientists to serve as role models to encourage minority students to consider careers in *all* areas of science. I find great satisfaction in sharing my curiosity and delight in learning about nature's mysteries with other minorities. I want to bring to all the joy I experience in learning how species interact with one another and how to restore species diversity to disturbed forests and wetlands. I also see that the solution to many environmental problems depends on all people becoming involved in the restoration and preservation of these ecosystems. It is crucial for the education and career development of groups currently underrepresented in ecology (i.e., African-Americans, Hispanic-Americans, Asian-Americans, and Native Americans) and for the preservation of global and local biodiversity, that students at *all* educational levels be encouraged to pursue a career in ecology.

DR. CARMEN R. CID came from Havana, Cuba to the United States in 1968 and became enchanted by nature when she took a plant ecology course in her junior year at New York University. The course entailed busing students out of the Greenwich Village campus every Saturday for an all-day adventure into New York and New Jersey forests and wetlands. She received her master's degree in botany from Ohio State University where she studied the regulation of population growth of flood plain plants. She obtained her Ph.D. in plant ecology from Michigan State University, where she enjoyed living at the Kellogg Bird Sanctuary, while studying factors that regulate the distribution of annual plants of forests and abandoned agricultural fields. She presently teaches at Eastern Connecticut State University and continues her studies of forests and wetlands in the New England area, while working to recruit and retain women and minorities in ecology.

CHAPTER FIVE

Diversifying the Environmental Movement

Mariella C. Puerto, National Director, Minority Opportunities Program, The Environmental Careers Organization

Biodiversity is one of the most frequently used battle cries of the mainstream environmental community. Diversity is touted as vital to nature's well-being. Upon closer examination, one soon realizes that the diversity that is being referred to is that of plants, animals, and insects, not humans. Since its beginnings in the 19th century, the traditional conservation movement was led by men of European heritage. Their interest has been in preserving America's pristine wilderness, of perpetuating ecological diversity so that future generations will be guaranteed their scenic playgrounds. For many decades, they seemed to ignore the undeniable fact that their own leadership, staffs, boards agenda, and image were homogeneous. Even though the environmental movement has undergone some changes and growth, expanding its focus to include the amelioration of the negative effects of industrial and agricultural pollution through technical and legal means has been a slow process. Furthermore, it still remains, to a large extent, white, middle class, and male-dominated. Any review of the history of mainstream environmental organizations fails to show any significant involvement of people of color and women, and almost no attention to environmental concerns specific to communities of color.

The implications of the exclusion of people of color and women from the environmental field are clear. It is apparent in the way communities of color have borne the brunt of environmental hazards. The following is a summary of some of the evidence that exists to support the claim that communities of color are disproportionately impacted by environmental hazards.

According to the Commission for Racial Justice of the United Church of Christ's *Toxic Wastes and Race: A National Report on the Racial and Socio-economic Characteristics of Communities with Hazardous Waste Sites,* there is statistically significant evidence that race, not income, is the primary determinant in siting commercial hazardous waste facilities and toxic waste sites. Among the findings were: three out of the five largest commercial hazardous waste landfills in the United States are located in predominantly Black or Hispanic communities; approximately half of all

Asian/Pacific Islanders and American Indians lived in communities with uncontrolled waste sites.

A study entitled *Breathing Polluted Air: Minorities are Disproportionately Exposed* by D.R. Wernette and L.A. Nieves found that out of the whole population 57 percent of whites, 65 percent of African-Americans and 80 percent of Hispanic-Americans live in 437 counties with substandard air quality.

In 1988, the Agency for Toxic Substances and Disease Registry reported that 44 percent of urban black children are at risk from lead poisoning, which is four times the rate of white children.

According to the U.S. Department of Labor, the nation's three to four million farm workers have the highest rate of exposure to pesticide poisoning of any occupational group in the U.S. of this workforce, 80 to 90 percent is Chicano; African-Americans comprise the next largest group, with a smaller number of Haitians, Filipinos, Vietnamese, and others.

However, since the 1980s, large numbers of people of color have organized themselves into community-based organizations to demand environmental justice after realizing that they had been forced to take on a disproportionate amount of the waste and pollution burden of the United States. The movement from being victims to activists was a response to the failure by government agencies to adequately enforce laws in their communities, as well as to being largely ignored by the mainstream environmental organizations. The environmental justice issues became linked with the civil rights issues that emerged out of the 1960s and was redefined to include the notion that a safe and clean environment is a basic right for all regardless of race or color.

Women, too, are present in large numbers at the grassroots level; many of whom are mothers who became active in environmental justice when their children fell ill or they themselves suffered health problems from pollutants in their communities. Lois Gibbs is a notable example of a woman who woke her community up to the environmental health crisis at "Love Canal", after she discovered that her son and other children were being poisoned from a leaking dump site on which their school was built. Jesse DeerInWater, founder of the grassroots group Native Americans for a Clean Environment, organized her community in Vian, OK, when she discovered that Sequoyah Fuels was planning an injection well that would place radioactive waste into the earth between two fault lines.

While thousands of women are involved in raging struggles at the grassroots level, they are, unfortunately, incongruously absent at the top of most mainstream organizations, government agencies, and corporations, where we find a predominantly male leadership. Former Congresswoman Bella Abzug, of the Women's Environmental and Development Center charges that "Women have been almost invisible in policy-making on environment and development issues."

Fortune magazine's examination of the highest paid officers and directors of 1,000 of the largest U.S. industrial and service companies, found that less than one half of one percent were women. In the area of science and engineering, the MS. Foundation asserts that science and math skills of girls plummets along with their self-esteem as they get older due to cultural, attitudinal and structural biases in society. A recent publication by the Commission on Professionals in Science and Technology entitled *What is Holding up the Glass Ceiling? Barriers to Women in the Science and Engineering Workforce* states that women in science and engineering continue to have higher rates of unemployment and make lower salaries than male counterparts. Women in these professions are less likely to be promoted and more likely to be laid off first, especially when seniority is a factor. In academia, women are more likely to be outside the tenure track or not yet tenured.

Changes in the Cultural Landscape

Superimposed over this backdrop of homogeneity in the environmental field is the reality that the there are dramatic changes occurring in the nation's population and workforce. The Hudson Institute's *Workforce 2000* predicts that by the 21st century, 75 percent of new employees in the labor pool will be women, minorities, and immigrants. White males, thought of only a few years ago as the mainstays of the economy, will comprise only 15 percent of the net additions to the labor force between 1985 and 2000. The Department of Labor forecasts that the workforce is also becoming older, with fewer young people entering the workforce.

Facing the Challenge

The environmental movement is changing gradually, and the notion of young women and minorities not only entering the environmental movement, but also leading is no longer inconceivable. My advice to you is to seek out those opportunities, face the challenges with integrity and, once you are in the profession, try as much as possible to advance the cause of diversity within your organizations.

Likewise, the employment statistics of women in the environmental arena bear out the same results. In 1985, four and a half percent of all those in the forestry profession were women. In wildlife agencies, 38 percent of the workforce is women. However, only eight percent are in higher-level positions.

Forecast for the Environmental Field

The environmental profession is one of the fastest-growing career fields. Since the formation of the EPA in the early 1970s, there has been an explosion of professions to conserve, protect, monitor, test, litigate, and research the environment. The passage of the Clean Air Act of 1990 alone is estimated to generate 60,000 new jobs by 1995. Corporations who in the past relied on a handful of environmental consultants have formed large internal divisions that handle regulatory compliance and other environmental concerns. In 1990, the EPA estimated that the nation spends more than $200 billion every year on environmental protection. That number is expected to rise throughout the rest of the decade.

As with many other career fields, the environmental profession will experience a labor shortage. With the profound demographic changes and the expansion of the environmental field, there must be changes in the human resource approach of employers, particularly in attracting and retaining people of color and women. It is critical that the environmental field redefine its priorities and plan for the future now.

Efforts to Change Recruiting Methods

Attempts to improve the cultural diversity of the environmental community vary from one organization to another. Several government agencies have begun to address some of the concerns affecting communities of color by stepping up recruitment efforts, initiating internship and training programs, establishing task forces, sponsoring conferences, and setting up pilot programs aimed at promoting environmental clean-up in communities of color. The U.S. EPA recently established an Environmental Equity Office to assist its various departments and regions in addressing environmental equity issues, as well to provide technical assistance to communities needing environmental remediation and protection. The recent appointments of Carol Browner, Hazel O'Leary, Mike Espy, and Federico Pena as heads of the U.S. EPA, the Department of Energy, Department of Agriculture and Department of Transportation, respectively, reflect a consciousness in government to promote the leadership of women and people of color in the environmental field.

Some mainstream environmental organizations have taken on the challenge seriously by devoting resources to programs aimed at fostering collaboration with communities of color, as well as increasing staff, board, and membership diversity. Notable among them is the Natural Resources Defence Council (NRDC), which has achieved 23 percent people of color representation overall on its staff, with 14 percent being at the professional level. NRDC's success is apparent not only by looking at the numbers, but also its agenda and programming. Some examples of its activities include working with the Greening of Harlem and West Harlem Environmental Action. Another organization, Friends of the Earth, works with Native Americans concerned about nuclear waste transportation.

The Sierra Club in the past year funded 12 grassroots organizing projects ranging from a lead poisoning prevention effort in San Francisco's Chinatown to a campaign against toxic waste dumping on the Rosebud Reservation in South Dakota. According to Vivien Li, Chair of the Sierra Club's Ethnic Diversity Taskforce, the club is "trying to connect traditional Sierra Club work with community- based efforts." She also cautions that "it should never be a question of a token minority on the board of directors...one of the things that we are trying to do is to ensure that diversity is an issue throughout the Sierra Club, for both staff and volunteers." It is also important to note that the move to embracing diversity must include the ability to manage and celebrate all the unique perspectives that diverse people bring with them. In an interview with EarthWork, a publication by the Student Conservation Association, Forest Service Chief Dale Robertson voiced his views: "We are not talking about hiring people and trying to mold them to Euro-American values. They should bring their own cultures and values with them and integrate them into our work."

Efforts to Offer Greater Educational Opportunities

One of the major obstacles in developing young environmental professionals of color has been the lack of encouragement and opportunities for students of color at an early age to pursue courses and fields of study that lead to environmental careers. People of color are underrepresented in environmental fields of study. For instance, African-Americans, Asian/Pacific Islanders, Native Americans and Latinos together comprise only 6.6 percent of students graduating with bachelor's degrees in forestry, natural resources, and environmental sciences; women make up just 37 percent. People of color are also less likely than their white counterparts to be on campus in the first place and experience high attrition rates.

This situation has often compelled some environmental employers to use the argument that there isn't a sufficient number of women and people of color applying for their jobs. They have always had the luxury of having a steady supply of candidates, "the old boys network", that precluded a need to dedicate significant resources to recruiting. They also have narrow definitions of what "qualified" is. According to a study released by the Environmental Careers Organization (ECO) entitled *Beyond the Green: Redefining and Diversifying the Environmental Movement,* the unwritten expectations for "qualified candidates" has whittled away the number of people of color who may be hired. They often hire people "with a discerning eye toward the college the candidate attended, socially correct etiquette, and previous volunteer or intern experience...candidates are being turned away who may just as well get the job done."

This makes only all too clear that not only is it imperative that colleges and universities across the country be more aggressive in recruiting people of color, it is also important that partnerships be forged between government, industry, academia, and local communities to enhance environmental education, training, and internship opportunities for people of color and women in order to prepare them for the environmental fields such as forestry, engineering, planning, solid waste management, environmental health, and others.

The U.S. Forest Service, along with other land management agencies, has been known as being conspicuously white and male in its makeup. To ensure that its programs reflect a multicultural constituency, the U.S. Forest Service in the Pacific Southwest Region has developed a strategy called Commencement 2000, a 10-year statewide initiative in California which targets children and youth of underrepresented populations and enhances their education with an environmental studies curriculum that remains consistent through graduation from a four-year college or university.

The Student Conservation Association established the Career Conservation Development Program (CCDP) to provide fellowships and conservation leadership training primarily for women and people of color who are in high school and college. The Environmental Careers Organization, in collaboration with government agencies, corporations, nonprofits, and consulting firms, offers paid and challenging apprenticeship positions to college students of color across the country.

Although there are several success stories are out there, the environmental community still faces formidable challenges in moving towards serving the needs and concerns of a multicultural nation and including the valuable perspectives of different cultures. There is good some news, however. Women and people of color who have decided to dedicate their lives to the protection of the environment and the development of their communities will find that there are more opportunities now than there have ever been before in this country's history. They have trailblazed the way and have not been disappointed.

Stories of Successful Environmental Pioneers

The following are some profiles of young people who launched their environmental career paths by pursuing apprenticeship opportunities.

Mustafa Ali (MS, Public Administration, West Virginia University, 1992) is an alum of the Environmental Careers Organization's Minority Environmental Summer Associate (MESA) Program who was offered a permanent position in the U.S. Environmental Protection Agency's Office of Environmental Equity immediately after he completed his apprenticeship in that office during the summer of 1992. He says: "The MESA program gave me the necessary experience to move my career forward. Right now, I'm working on my doctoral thesis, but the MESA program helped me work while I finished my master's. It was also a great opportunity to work with people such as Administrator William Reilly, Dr. Clarice Gaylord, and Dr. Warren Banks, all from the EPA."

Mary Andes (BS, Biology and Women's Studies, Oberlin College, 1992), another alum of the MESA program, encourages young people to "seize the day...you will see very quickly that there is a world of opportunities out there." Mary worked for BP America in Cleveland, OH on environmental grants during the summer of 1991. The next fall, she worked on hazardous waste issues with a local nonprofit, Ironbound Community Corporation, in Newark, NJ. Mary says that both apprenticeships had a significant impact on her career: "They gave me a firsthand understanding of the issues and ideas of what was possible in the field...they also made me feel more strongly about incorporating environmentalism in everything that I do." Mary now works for a consulting firm in Manhattan, NY.

Take an Aggressive Approach

The environmental movement is changing gradually, and the notion of young women and minorities not only entering the environmental movement, but also leading is no longer inconceivable. My advice to you is to seek out those opportunities, face the challenges with integrity and, once you are in the profession, try as much as possible to advance the cause of diversity within your organizations.

Mariella C. Puerto is currently the national director of the Minority Opportunities Program of the Environmental Careers Organization in Boston, MA. Among her voluntary activities, she is vice chair of the Asian Task Force Against Domestic Violence, a steering committee member for the Asian Shelter and Advocacy Project, and coordinator of recruitment and referral committee for the Environmental Diversity Forum, all of which are based in Boston.

Mariella received a Malaysian Certificate of Education in 1982 from Sekolah Menengah Bukit Nanas in Kuala Lumpur, Malaysia, her bachelor's degree in political science from Brandon University in Brandon, Manitoba, Canada in 1986, and her master's degree in political science from Ohio University in Athens, OH, the following year.

CHAPTER SIX

Environmental Internships: Beginning Your Career

Kevin Doyle, National Director of Program Development, The Environmental Careers Organization

To get a job, get some experience. To get experience, get a job. Who hasn't heard that old, creaky line? Well, it may be old and stale, but it's also true, as many talented college seniors have found out when they start to look for that elusive first job. Experience, they learn, is what can separate the job seeker from the job finder.

So, how do you get the job that gets you experience that gets you a job? In a word: intern! Internship opportunities are ubiquitous in the environmental field. In fact, in some environmental disciplines and organizations, internships are almost a required rite of passage, proof that you have *paid your dues* and are truly committed to the field. Not surprisingly, internships are also a way for organizations to check you out; a low-risk way to discover how they feel about having you around everyday.

If a successful internship can provide you a big advantage in your environmental career search, an unsuccessful one can potentially set you back. More often, a poorly designed and executed intern experience will simply be a big waste of time for you and the sponsoring organization.

What makes an internship successful? How can you find (or create!) an internship that will be educational, fun, challenging, and help develop your career? For over 20 years, The Environmental Careers Organization has been organizing paid, professional-level, internships at environmental agencies, businesses, and nonprofit groups. We've learned some things from our own experience and from talking to the nearly 5,000 intern alumni and supervisors who have participated in the ECO program.

By following a few simple rules and using some creativity and a lot of common sense, you'll have the internship you want, and get started on the road to a great environmental career.

Finding Your Internship

It is estimated that there are some 60,000 for-profit *environmental* companies in the United States, 2,000 to 8,000 environmental nonprofits, and thousands of local, state, and federal government agencies concerned with environmental issues. Add to this some 3,000 universities and community colleges and several times that many elementary and secondary schools with environmental education needs. Then figure in thousands of banks, real estate developers, insurance companies, television stations, newspapers, magazines, law offices and...well, you get the picture.

There are a lot of places to do an environmental internship.

Two Rules for the Internship Search

Obviously, you will only be able to focus effectively on a tiny fraction of all available intern opportunities. This means that Rule Number One in the internship search is: Know what you want.

What are you trying to accomplish by doing an internship? You would be surprised how many people enter the internship search without thinking about this basic question. To avoid being one of them, take some time to think about questions like:

- What do you hope to learn?
- What kind of people do you want to work with?
- What skills would you like to develop?
- Where would you like to work?
- What results would you like to achieve?

Answering these questions can be a huge help in finding the right internship. For instance, if you know that you want to develop new field biology skills, work closely with professional scientists, gain an understanding of a particular geographic area, and have your name on a report which can boost your resume, you can successfully narrow your search and present yourself as the kind of confident, self-directed person employers like to see.

That self-knowledge, however, won't count for much if you can't match it with the right opportunity. That's why Rule Number Two is: Know what intern employers want.

Why would an environmental business, advocacy group, or agency take on an intern? We have found that there are four basic reasons. It's important for you to find out what is motivating your employer to avoid mixed messages, false expectations, and bruised feelings. The basic internship *types* are:

1. Educational

Educational internships are designed primarily to further a student's academic learning. They are often linked to college degree requirements and may include non-work requirements such a thesis or paper to verify the learning content of the experience. Such internships are especially common when the content of a master's or doctoral thesis is of interest to an environmental employer.

2. Project

Project internships are focused on completing a specific piece of work. They are usually measured by the quality and timeliness of the *deliverables* expected from the intern. For example, an intern may be taken on to complete a literature review or prepare a newsletter.

3. Recruitment

Recruitment internships are used as entry-level training for future permanent employees. When an employer is recruiting for such internships, they are already interviewing you with an eye toward your suitability as a future colleague.

4. Temporary Help

These internships provide a steady stream of interns who are essentially low-cost labor. Such interns are expected to help out on whatever needs to be done. You may be doing a professional-level task one week and camping out by the copy machine the next.

Obviously, many internships involve a mix of these types. Most opportunities, however, will be built around one of these four ideals. Ask a lot of questions to determine what is motivating your employer and what they expect to receive from your intern experience. By combining your own desires with the expectations of prospective intern sponsors, you will come closer to the right *match*—and finding that *match* is what the intern search is all about for you and for the sponsor.

Largest Environmental Groups

Ranked by: U.S. membership, as reported by individual groups on March 1, 1992.

1. Greenpeace, with 1,800,000 members
2. World Wildlife Fund, 1,000,000
3. National Wildlife Federation, 975,000
4. Nature Conservancy, 644,000
5. The Sierra Club, 625,000
6. National Audubon Society, 600,000
7. Ducks Unlimited, 520,000
8. The Wilderness Society, 350,000
9. Environmental Defense Fund, 200,000
10. Natural Resources Defense Council, 180,000

Source: *Public Relations Journal*

Five Rules for Successful Internships

A few years ago, we managed a research venture called the National Environmental Intern Action Project. We were trying to discover why some internships were successful, while others fizzled. The *secrets* we discovered were not secrets at all, just common sense taken to uncommon levels. In the end, we discovered five deceptively simple rules for good internships. Following these guidelines can help you make the most of a valuable opportunity.

Rule Number One: Be Sure You Are the Right Person for the Job

Huh? An environmental manager with extensive intern experience told us, "Getting the right person is 90 percent of good management." It's true. Although you may believe you can handle anything, you know that's just not possible. For example: if you are not a gregarious person who thinks quickly on her feet and loves to *mix it up* verbally, it's probably not a good idea to take a position that requires these qualities, even if it is offered to you. You can bet that the intern sponsor is checking to see if you are a good match for the job. You should be just as rigorous in asking whether the job is right for you.

Rule Number Two: Know Your Supervisory Needs and Try to Get Them Met

In our internship research, we found out that the biggest success factor by far is the quality of supervision. What makes a good supervisor *good*? It often depends on your supervisory needs. Will you need a lot of help? Do you like a supervisor who provides a lot of structure and guidance, or do you prefer a more open approach? Talking through these issues with prospective supervisors can help both you and him/her to come to an agreement and avoid confusion in the future.

Rule Number Three: Develop a Plan and Schedule for Your Work

Though it may appear to be obvious, this important first step is the one that is regularly ignored by even good intern supervisors. Your active involvement can help get it done. Preparing such a plan doesn't have to be a hard task. Simply work backwards for the final product or goal of the internship. Then, brainstorm a list of everything, no matter how small, which must be done to get there. Finally, attach deadlines to each of the tasks and review these with the supervisor. Don't be surprised if she is shocked by your incredible organization. You'll learn that it is extremely rare in the workplace!

Rule Number Four: Get Adequate Resources to Complete Your Internship

Easier said than done. Here are some simple things which almost any intern will need. A quiet, well-lit place to work. Access to phones and computers. Basic materials and supplies. Some training in the use of office equipment, especially computer programs used. A reasonable call on the time of others in the organization. Some background reading in the internship issue area. These sound pretty minimal, right? Don't bet on it. Think things through with someone to assure that your internship won't grind to a halt for lack of a phone or desk.

Rule Number Five: Check Your Attitude

Are you prepared to work hard, to be actively responsible for the success of your internship? Is your sense of humor and your patience intact? Do you really care about what you are doing, not only for yourself but for the organization and, ultimately, the future environmental quality of our world? Is your curiosity high and your mind engaged? Are you truly open to learning and to accepting constructive criticism from colleagues?

The spirit behind these five "rules" is honored in words more often than it is in practice. By being one of the rare interns who actually embodies them in the real world, you will be remembered, respected, and (very possibly) offered a permanent job. Go to it!

Places to Look for an Environmental Internship

There are three basic ways to secure an internship in our field. First, you could work through a established, national or regional environmental intern program. Second, you could identify internships at specific organizations through a good internship or environmental directory (like this one!). Third, you could identify organizations of interest to you and approach them directly, whether or not they have a formal internship program. Taking the third approach gives you the most latitude and control, but also involves some serious skill in job-hunting. A book like *What Color is Your Parachute?* by Richard Bolles (Ten Speed Press) provides a great outline for your search.

Good luck!

Kevin Doyle is the national director of program development for The Environmental Careers Organization, a private, national, nonprofit organization with over 20 years of experience in matching students and recent graduates with paid internships. He is also the co-author (with Bill Sharp) of The New Complete Guide to Environmental Careers (Island Press, 1993) and the co-author (with Lori Colombo) of Beyond the Green: Redefining and Diversifying the Environmental Movement (ECO, 1992).

CHAPTER SEVEN

Environmental Careers: Let Your Imagination Soar!

Ginger Wandless, Special Assistant, Office of Environmental Education, Environmental Protection Agency

The most wonderful thing about working with professionals dedicated to protecting our environment is their great enthusiasm for what they do and their seemingly endless supply of energy. Protecting our environment is a cause that any individual, any age, in any academic discipline can embrace and pursue. One way to explore an environmental career is to do an internship with the Environmental Protection Agency (EPA) during your academic career.

Entering the Environmental Protection Agency

The Environmental Protection Agency is a regulatory agency responsible for implementing the federal laws designed to protect our environment. Currently, the EPA is not a Cabinet-level agency and is therefore headed by an **Administrator** and not a Secretary. The Administrator is supported by three **Associate Administrators** (Congressional and Legislative Affairs; Regional Operations; and Communication, Education, and Public Affairs) and nine **Assistant Administrators** (International Activities; Administration and Resource Management; Enforcement and Compliance Monitoring; Policy, Planning, and Evaluation; Solid Waste and Emergency Response; Water; Air and Radiation; Prevention, Pesticides, and Toxic Substances; Research and Development.) The Agency also has an Office of General Counsel and an Office of Inspector General. Each of these offices, as well as our 10 regional offices and our laboratory facilities, provides internship opportunities to qualified graduate and undergraduate students.

Internship Opportunities with the EPA

Internships at the EPA are designed to provide undergraduate and graduate students pursuing a degree in any academic discipline with an opportunity to work with environmental professionals; to observe and participate in the daily activities of these professionals; and to have a real world experience that will supplement course work. An internship experience can bring professional and personal rewards and will help to strengthen your resume in the current, highly competitive job market.

EPA has three types of internships available. The first is an educational internship. These are comprised of a course work component as well as on-site work experience. Students complete courses for credit while working 30 to 40 hours a week. The stay- in-school and co-op programs are examples of this type of internship. These programs can either be for a semester, quarter, or year-round. In many cases, internships are becoming a requirement for graduation, and many universities have developed their own programs to help students develop internship opportunities in the public and private sectors.

The second type of internship at the EPA is a recruitment internship. These are designed to recruit individuals for future employment, while allowing both employer and perspective employee the opportunity to see if there is mutual interest. The Presidential Management Internship (PMI) Program and the Environmental Management Internship (EMI) Program are examples of recruiting internship programs. Both are highly competitive and are designed to attract individuals from a variety of academic disciplines who have a clear interest and commitment to a career in public service. These interns are given temporary assignments to different program and field offices as well as a variety of project assignments. Individuals who have completed either an undergraduate degree (the EMI Program) or a graduate degree in any academic discipline (the PMI Program) are eligible.

EPA Internships Open Doors

An internship with the EPA is very appealing because a student pursuing a degree in any academic discipline could turn an interest in the environment into a profession. The nearly 18,000 employees of the EPA represent academic disciplines ranging from law to journalism, from science and engineering to business, from medicine to communication, and everything in between. Their actual job titles range from lawyer to international affairs specialist, from research chemist to budget analyst, from toxicologist to communication specialist, and many, many more. Only your imagination can limit the choices you have in pursuing an environmental protection career.

The third and most popular type of internship at EPA is the project specific internship. Work experience is designed around a specific set of duties or tasks that the student is to perform, based on their unique set of skills, abilities, and knowledge. Through this internship program, the Agency encourages students from a variety of academic disciplines to apply their education to the vast array of environmental protection problems. A law student might be asked to follow the progress of a piece of environmental legislation on the Hill; a communications major could help write a brochure to be used by homeowners on the dangers of radon in homes; a chemist could help refine techniques for detecting pesticides in soils; and a computer major could help design an interactive computer game to help grade school children understand drinking water and groundwater protection issues in their communities. The variety of projects is endless and will vary in number and activities from year to year. In general, this type of internship is available to matriculating students only.

All in a Day's Work

In general, an intern is expected to do the same type of work that the professionals are doing, as it relates to his/her particular internship. You would be expected to do your own library research, write issue papers and analyze action options, manage your time and respond to deadlines, communicate with your supervisor, and with others who are involved with your work, and do your own clerical work. For a typical environmental professional at the EPA, each day is different; there is no typical work day. Organization priorities can supersede any daily activity. This can make your day interesting and create a challenge to accomplish the duties for which you are responsible. An internship with the EPA will make you feel like you are making a difference; that you are helping in some way to preserve our clean air and water and protecting our natural resources for future generations—and that is an incredible feeling!

Applying for an EPA Internship

The best way to begin exploring your internship options is to contact the Office of Recruitment at the EPA headquarter office in Washington, DC, or the regional office nearest you. The time to start thinking about a summer internship—the majority of the project internships are in the summer between semesters—is not when it starts to get warm out, but in the fall or winter *before* you want to start. Most EPA internship programs have deadlines of at least six months before the actual internship begins.

You should also have a clear idea of the type of work you want to do and what type of work setting appeals to you. If you know that you are most comfortable in an office setting, a field work or laboratory experience is probably not going to be as appealing. If, however, you are not sure what type of work you would like to do, an internship as an undergraduate student would be a good way to explore your career options, in order to try different work settings and to experience the difference between the public and private sectors.

An Opportunity that Awaits Everyone

An internship with the EPA is very appealing because a student pursuing a degree in any academic discipline could turn an interest in the environment into a profession. The nearly 18,000 employees of the EPA represent academic disciplines ranging from law to journalism, from science and engineering to business, from medicine to communication, and everything in between. Their actual job titles range from lawyer to international affairs specialist, from research chemist to budget analyst, from toxicologist to communication specialist, and many, many more. Only your imagination can limit the choices you have in pursuing an environmental protection career.

GINGER WANDLESS received her bachelor of arts degree at George Mason University in Virginia, where she majored in chemistry. She has also done undergraduate and graduate work in business management. She started her career as a research chemist with the U.S. Geological Survey, after doing a year-long internship with that agency. She is currently a special assistant in the Office of Environmental Education in EPA.

CHAPTER EIGHT

Consider a Career in Soil and Water Conservation

Timothy J. Kautza, Director of Education and Professional Development, Soil and Water Conservation Society

Soil and Water Conservationists: Not Specialists, but General Practitioners

Do you have a genuine interest and enthusiasm to help others conserve soil and water resources? Are you looking for a career that requires some expertise in most aspects of natural resource management and interpersonal communications? Then consider a career as a soil and water conservationist, the general practitioner among natural resource conservationists!

Soil and water conservation is a broad field of work that involves many individuals with different specialties working together with generalists to carry out a mission of conserving soil and water resources. These specialist positions include sociologists, economists, wildlife biologists, foresters, journalists, agronomists, and agricultural and civil engineers, to name only a few.

Four positions that are most prominently involved in soil and water conservation and that are less specialized than those mentioned are soil conservation technician, soil conservationist, range conservationist, and soil scientist.

What Will I Do as a Soil and Water Conservationist?

The responsibilities of soil and water conservationists vary greatly by employer and geographic region. Most are employed by government agencies at national, state, and local levels. However, an increasing number are being employed in the private sectors by consulting firms. Employment opportunities in all sectors may increase if the federal government changes the way in which it performs its soil and water conservation mission. But in all cases, opportunities for promotion beyond the following common entry-level positions arise as you gain experience in the profession and in management of projects and people.

Soil conservationists work with land users—farmers and ranchers, homeowners, developers, and government officials—that need help in wisely managing soil and water resources. Soil conservationists create conservation plans that will help the land users meet their land use goals within government regulations. They suggest ways to conserve soil, preserve or restore wetlands, increase wildlife populations, rotate crops for better yields and soil conservation, reduce water pollution, and other ways to help land users make good land management choices. They may give talks to clubs and organizations and write articles for local newspapers to inform land users and the public about how to conserve soil and water resources. Soil conservationists make their recommendations to land users based in part upon information provided to them by soil scientists.

Soil scientists determine limitations for the use of land, based upon the properties of soils. They examine soil on the land to gather information which they use to identify problems such as wetness, dryness, stoniness, steepness, and high erosion potential that can limit the ways a soil can be used. They also suggest precautions that land users can take to overcome soil limitations. Although they spend a lot of time examining soils on the land, they also spend some time at the office writing reports of their findings. Some soil scientists spend most of their time doing research on experiment farms and in laboratories.

Range conservationists are the soil conservationists of range country. They help ranchers plan livestock grazing systems that increase livestock production, while preventing overgrazing and damage to rangeland. They suggest ways to control brush, improve water management, and produce more and better forage. Whether land users want their rangeland to support livestock, wildlife, recreation, or a combinations of these, range conservationists, like soil conservationists, tailor conservation plans to meet land users' goals within government regulations.

The **soil conservation technician** is the generalist that works most directly with land users on their lands in putting conservation plans into practice. They make engineering surveys and design and stake conservation practices like terraces, contour strips, and grassed waterways. Technicians work closely with contractors that construct conservation structures and practices to ensure that they are built according to approved standards.

What Will I Be Paid?

If you have a college degree with the appropriate coursework, a typical entry-level position as a soil conservationist will pay a starting annual salary of about $18,000. If you have a cumulative grade point average of at least 3.0 or have a master's degree and two years work experience, your starting annual salary will be about $22,000.

It is not uncommon for soil conservationists to be promoted three to four times during the first ten years of employment, the first coming within the first two years, which could boost your salary to about $40,000 to $50,000. Increased management responsibilities can boost salaries to $65,000 over another five to ten years, with many top management officials in the soil and water conservation field making more than

$70,000 per year. Generally, promotions also mean relocation to different states or areas within a state.

If you do not have a college degree and want to work as a soil conservation technician, the entry-level annual salary is about $12,000. Top pay in this position will be about $18,000 per year.

What's the Best Way to Enter the Field?

I recommend that you do everything you can to gain experience in soil and water conservation while you're going to school. The experience will give you a head start over others entering the field, may help you get a higher starting salary, and will speed your progress toward your career goal.

The federal government, most states, and some private employers offer some outstanding programs to help you gain that experience. All of the programs help you to explore career options, develop your personal and professional skills, and enhance your knowledge about the missions and responsibilities of soil and water conservation agencies. Many federal programs offer competitive pay based on the education and work experience you already possess that can help you meet your educational expenses. Some programs even offer the same health and life insurance benefits that professional employees are eligible for, training and tuition assistance, and payment for transportation between school and your work place, too.

Volunteer service programs offer unpaid training opportunities to students in high school and college that related to their academic program. Work may be performed during the school year and/or during summer or school vacation periods, and, in some cases, for college credit.

For more details about such programs, contact your school guidance office or any governmental agency personnel office.

Largest Authorized Water Resources Development Projects

Ranked by: Total cost, in millions of dollars.

1. American River (CA), watershed flood control, with $662.0 million
2. Monongahela River (PA), move locks and dams 2 and 4, remove lock and dam 3, $556.4
3. Tennessee River (KY), new lock, $468.0
4. Kissimmee River (FL), restoration, $426.9
5. Delaware River (DE, NJ, PA), deepening $278.3
6. Las Vegas Wash (NV), watershed flood control, $196.0
7. Rio Grande de Loiza (PR), flood control, $118.8
8. Saugus River Basin (MA), flood control, $95.7
9. Intracoastal Waterway (TX), bank protection, $75.4
10. Amite River Basin (LA), flood control, $65.9

Source: *ENR*

What Are the Educational Requirements?

Courses necessary to qualify for soil and water conservation positions are available at all land grant universities and many other colleges.

At least 30 college credit hours and solid work experience are needed to be considered for a soil conservationist or range conservationist position with the federal government. A bachelor's degree in a natural resource field such as agronomy, forestry, wildlife biology, agricultural education, range management, or agricultural engineering is helpful; at least three credit hours in soil science are required. Many recently hired soil conservationists have master's degrees in a natural resource field.

To work as a soil scientist in the federal government, you need a college degree with a minimum of 15 college credit hours in soil science and related work experience.

College education is not required for soil conservation technician positions. However, an aptitude for mathematics, problem solving, interpersonal communications, and detail is helpful.

What Benefits Can I Expect?

Benefits vary a great deal from one employer to another. Federal employees are entitled to 10 paid holidays per year. You earn 13 days of vacation leave each year during the first three years; 20 days after three years; and 26 days after 15 years. You earn 13 days of sick leave each year, which can be accrued to cover serious illness, injury, or maternity leave.

The government pays for part of your health and life insurance costs, too. Life insurance is also offered with the amount dependent upon your salary. Career government employees are covered under a good retirement system and are eligible to participate in a tax-deferred investment plan in government securities, stocks, or bonds.

The government provides on-the-job and formal training opportunities to help you meet your career goals. Because the federal government has many different agencies throughout the nation involved in soil and water conservation, there are many opportunities to transfer to other states.

The personal satisfaction received and the knowledge that one is protecting our environment and the productivity of natural resources are additional benefits.

▼

Timothy J. Kautza received his bachelor of science degree at St. Norbert College, WI, where he majored in biology and education. He received his master of science degree in education at Drake University, IA, after studying soil science at the University of Wisconsin, Stevens Point. He taught science upon receipt of his bachelor degree.

Timothy has worked at all levels of government since starting his career in soil and water conservation as a part-time soil conservation technician's aide. He has worked as a soil scientist, a conservation program consultant, and is currently director of education and professional development for the Soil and Water Conservation Society, a private, nonprofit association headquartered in Ankeny, IA.

CHAPTER NINE

Natural Resource and Park Management

National Recreation and Park Association

Conservation work has expanded rapidly and accomplished much in recent years, and the need for qualified individuals to fill natural resource and park management related positions has never been greater. Natural resource management is the art of making land and water produce adequate yields of products and services for social and economic use. Thus, the manager in this field, educated in the sciences and techniques involved, controls both plant and animal species and their environment for optimum protection. Or, the manager might apply knowledge of natural laws in the maintenance of soil and water resources upon which other renewable resources depend. Accordingly, there are numerous specialized lines of work to address this field. Wildlife management, park management, soil conservation, watershed management, and forestry are just a few examples of the diverse range of professions within the scope of natural resource and park management.

Job Titles and Descriptions

Natural resource and park management staff are usually employees of national, state, county, or municipal park systems, with conservation efforts being the primary focus of work. Duties may include wildlife management, fire control, and gathering information on the environment. Individuals employed in this field may also be responsible for law enforcement, violation investigation, accidents, and search and rescue operations. Campground operators, tour guides, and information center staff may also work in natural resource and park areas.

Most professionals in natural resource and park management specialize in one area of conservation. For example, park rangers generally focus on enforcing laws and regulations in national, state, county, or municipal parks; wildlife managers concentrate on protecting animals or plants; foresters work to protect and maintain trees; watershed managers direct and regulate the use of an area's water resources; and soil conservationists concentrate on maintaining soil health. Some specific examples of jobs within the natural resource and park management industry include:

Park Rangers—park rangers enforce laws and regulations in national, state, county, or municipal parks. They help care for and maintain parks, as well as inform, guide, and assure that visitors are able to fully experience the natural and cultural heritage of the country in which they live. However, the first responsibility of the park ranger is to ensure the safety of park visitors. Rangers in parks with treacherous terrain, dangerous wildlife, or severe weather conditions must make sure hikers, campers, backpackers, and others follow outdoor safety codes. Rangers also protect parks from inappropriate use and threats from visitors.

The duties of park rangers also extend to conservation efforts not connected to visitor use. They may study wildlife behavior, plants, water quality, pollution, and visitor use of park lands. Additionally, rangers may be involved with such projects as park planning, record keeping, facility construction and maintenance, trail building, and landscaping. In some parks, rangers may serve as specialists in certain areas of park protection, safety, or management. For example, in areas where there are many snow avalanches, experts in avalanche control and snow safety may be designated snow rangers.

Park Police—park police staff are employed by the National Park Service. They are generally stationed in large urban areas, such as around the Mall in Washington, D.C. Most staff members begin their employment in Washington, D.C. and then, after training, may be assigned to any of the locations within the park system. Staff includes the mounted police; the motorcycle, helicopter, canine, and special equipment and tactics teams; and the investigations units.

All in a Day's Work

Most natural resource and park management employees are hired to work 40 hour weeks. However, their hours can be long and irregular, with much overtime. They may receive extra pay or time off for working overtime. Some rangers and foresters are on call all the time for emergencies, with the longest hours occurring during busy tourist seasons.

Ranger Aids or Park Technicians—aids and technicians help park rangers and superintendents manage national, state, and local parks, historic sites, and recreation areas. Their chief responsibilities include facility maintenance, greeting park guests and visitors, checking camp sites, enforcing park policy, and giving tours.

Foresters—foresters maintain forests and natural areas as well as supervise the planting of new trees. They choose and prepare sites using controlled burning, bulldozers, or herbicides to clear weeds, brush, and logging debris. They also advise on the type, number, and placement of trees to be planted. Foresters monitor trees to ensure healthy growth and to determine the best time for harvesting timber. If foresters detect signs of disease or harmful insects, they decide on the best course of treatment to prevent contamination or infestation of healthy trees. Foresters must be knowledgeable about insects, diseases, soil erosion, and forest fire fighting occupations.

Foresters who work for government agencies usually manage public parks and forests. They may also design campgrounds and other outdoor recreation areas. Those working in private industry may be responsible for procuring timber from private landowners and negotiating timber sales and distribution.

Wildlife Managers—wildlife managers work to protect animals in various environments. They work to monitor animal populations to determine guidelines and regulations for hunting particular species and maintaining the species' ability to reproduce. The wildlife manager may also be responsible for providing treatment to injured animals in certain situations. They also plan and supervise the construction of shelters, water resources, and the planting of vegetation to feed and protect animals.

Fish and Game Wardens—Wardens are responsible for enforcing laws that protect wildlife. They must have a thorough knowledge of federal, state, and/or local game laws to protect wildlife and arrest violators if necessary. In many cases, the warden may have to prepare and present evidence at court trials of alleged game law violators. Governing bodies count on wardens to enforce hunting and fishing laws. Without these laws, improper hunting and fishing could destroy entire species populations within the parks and other protected natural resource areas.

Soil Conservationists—soil conservationists provide technical assistance to farmers, ranchers, and others concerned with the conservation of soil, water, and other related natural resources. They develop programs that are designed to attain the most productive use of land without damaging it. Conservationists visit areas with erosion problems, find the source of the problem, and help landowners and managers develop management practices to combat it.

Watershed Managers—watershed managers observe the use and maintenance of reservoirs, aqueducts, and other water storage facilities. These resources provide water for large areas, including homes, schools, businesses, and other institutions. The watershed manager must have an understanding of chemistry and water purification. Mechanical aptitude is also desirable because duties sometimes involve regulating engines and other equipment in water plants and making minor repairs on the equipment.

Range Managers—range managers improve, protect, and manage rangelands to maximize their use without damaging the environment. Rangelands cover about one billion acres in the United States, mostly in the western states and Alaska. They contain many natural resources, including grass and shrubs for animal grazing, wildlife habitats, water from vast watersheds, recreation facilities, and valuable mineral and energy resources. Range managers help ranchers attain optimum livestock production by determining the number and kind of animals to graze and the best season for grazing. At the same time, they maintain soil stability and vegetation for uses such as wildlife habitats and outdoor recreation.

Related job titles in the natural resource and park management industry include:

- Adventure Travel Coordinator
- Campground Director
- Environmental Interpreter
- Interpretive Specialist
- Museum Director
- Natural Resource Planner
- Outdoor Recreation Manager
- Park Maintenance Director
- Park Manager
- Recreation Manager

Education and Training

Employment as a federal, state, county, or municipal employee in natural resource and park management will usually require a bachelor's degree in parks and recreation management or forestry. Course work in natural sciences such as biology, botany, chemistry, ecology, geology, and other applicable subject areas is also desirable.

There are over 300 baccalaureate programs and more than 280 associate degree programs in parks and recreation offered by colleges and universities in the United States. The National Recreation and Park Association, in cooperation with the American Association for Leisure and Recreation, has developed standards of accreditation for four-year programs. NRPA accredits over 90 of these programs. Additionally, there are more than 100 graduate degree programs in the field of parks and recreation.

Without at least a bachelor's degree, applicants should have a minimum of three years experience in parks or conservation, must show they understand natural resource and park work, and have good communications skills. Those individuals who desire to move into management positions may need to obtain a graduate degree.

Professional Certification

As a means of attesting to the education and experience qualifications of persons employed in the parks, recreation, and leisure service field, the National Recreation and Park Association certifies those individuals who meet the eligibility requirements for professional, provisional, and technical levels.

Hours and Earnings

Natural resource and park management employees work in federal parks and forests all over the country. They work in the mountains and forests of Hawaii, Alaska, and California, in urban and suburban parks throughout the United States, and in many historic sites east of the Mississippi River. Rangers in the National Park Service are employed by the U.S. Department of the Interior. Entry-level rangers are usually hired at the GS-5 grade level. More experienced or educated rangers may enter the Park Service at the GS-9 level, which paid approximately $24,000 to start in the early 1990's. Rangers who work in state, county, or municipal parks are generally employed by that particular governing body, such as a state government. They receive comparable salaries and benefits, including paid vacations, sick leave, paid holidays, health and life insurance, and pension plans, to those individuals employed by the federal government. Most graduates entering the federal government as foresters, range managers, or soil conservationists with a bachelor's degree started at $17,000-$21,000 a year in 1991. Those with more education or experience could start at $21,000-$25,000. In 1991, the average salary for all foresters was $38,600; for range managers, $34,000; and for soil conservationists, $35,800.

Most natural resource and park management employees are hired to work 40 hour weeks. However, their hours can be long and irregular, with much overtime.

They may receive extra pay or time off for working overtime. Some rangers and foresters are on call all the time for emergencies, with the longest hours occurring during busy tourist seasons.

Although many employees work in offices, many work outside in all types of climates and weather, and the work can be physically demanding. Many rangers, foresters, and conservationists work in extreme weather conditions, sometimes in isolated areas. To get to these areas, the use of airplanes, helicopters, four-wheel drive vehicles, and horses may be required. It may be necessary for some employees to walk long distances through densely wooded land in order to carry out their work. They may also work long hours fighting fires or in other emergencies. Additionally, most employees spend considerable time working with people. They deal regularly with tourists, landowners, loggers, forestry technicians, farmers, ranchers, government officials, and special interest groups.

Employment Outlook

Employment in certain natural resource and park management positions is expected to grow slowly through the year 2000 primarily due to budgetary constraints in federal, state, and local governments, where employment is concentrated. However, an expected wave of retirements throughout the federal government in the 1990s should create many openings for foresters. Jobs for soil conservationists should continue to be competitive in the federal government. In the private sector, more foresters and range managers should be needed to improve forest, logging, and range management practices and increase output and profitability. State governments and private owners of timberland may employ more natural resource managers due to increased interest in environmental protection and land management.

Park ranger jobs are scarce and competition for them fierce. The National Park Service reports that the ratio of applicants to available positions is as high as 100 to 1. Individuals who intend to compete for these positions must attain the widest variety of applicable skills and may wish to study subjects they can use in other fields such as forestry, conservation, wildlife management, history, and natural sciences. The scarcity of available federal positions is expected to continue indefinitely. Job seekers should apply for outdoor work with agencies other than the National Park Service, including other federal land and resource management agencies and similar state and local agencies, where position openings are far more frequent.

Entry Methods

Many individuals obtain full-time natural resource and park management positions after working part-time or seasonally at different parks, forests, or other natural resource areas. These individuals often work at information desks, fire control and law enforcement positions, while others help to maintain trails, collect trash, or perform forestry activities. Persons interested in applying for positions with federal agencies should write their local Federal Job Information Center of the Federal Office of Personnel Management in Washington, D.C. Job seekers should write to state parks departments for information on applying for jobs in state parks.

Another effective way to secure an initial quality experience in natural resource and park management is through fieldwork or an internship with an established public or private agency. Such an experience is an opportunity to have intensive, work-based exposure to a broad range of operations within the field. During an internship the student should expect to perform regular, productive duties within one or more areas of the agency. Additionally, the student should strive for opportunities offered through a quality field experience even if it requires volunteer work beyond the standard work week.

Professional Associations

The natural resource and park industry is extremely diverse and fragmented. There is no single professional association that bridges the spectrum of industries and provides career guidance, contacts, and job placement services. There are separate professional associations for park management, forestry, soil conservation, water conservation, and wildlife management that address federal, state, and local levels. The student would be well advised to investigate membership in two or three associations and strive to attend national, state, or regional conferences whenever possible. The National Society for Park Resources, a professional branch of the National Recreation and Park Association, serves professionals and citizens who are currently involved or concerned with protection and conservation of national open space and park resources.

This essay was contributed by the **NATIONAL RECREATION AND PARK ASSOCIATION (NRPA)**, a public interest organization dedicated to improving the human environment through improved park, recreation, and leisure opportunities.

CHAPTER TEN

Forestry: The Chance to Make a Difference

Dr. Klaus Steinbeck, Professor, School of Forest Resources, University of Georgia

Foresters are responsible for the management and conservation of trees and associated forest resources. Most of them have chosen their profession because of their love for the outdoors and for the chance to contribute toward the well-being of society and the environment. Traditionally, they have been responsible for establishing, nurturing, and harvesting forests, improving habitat for wildlife, protecting water quality, and providing recreational opportunities. Today, forestry graduates also are working as environmental engineers, private consultants, urban foresters, educators, hydrologists, researchers, and business leaders.

The days when foresters dealt only with trees are long past. Today, they must deal with often conflicting concerns about the proper use of forests. It can happen that one interest group argues that a particular area in a national forest be set aside for recreation, whereas another group might want it preserved as a wilderness area, and a third group may want that area to be a working forest where the timber being grown is utilized economically. Oral and written communication skills are very important. In order to participate meaningfully in these kinds of discussions, foresters must be articulate, diplomatic, and informed.

Forestry schools emphasize the natural sciences as well as familiarity with statistical procedures and computer science in their courses of study. Such an educational background is useful in many other disciplines as well, such as engineering, education, geology, and computer science. Forestry graduates are also well prepared for graduate studies in a variety of science and math related disciplines.

Career Opportunities: Trees and Forests Grow in Most Regions

Employment opportunities vary somewhat with the region of the country. Public lands managed by the U.S. Forest Service, the National Park Service, the Bureau of

Land Management, and the Fish and Wildlife Service predominate in the Western United States. Therefore, many Western foresters are employed by these federal agencies or by state forestry commissions, and environmental protection agencies. In the Midwest and East, however, forest land is mostly owned by private individuals or by forest industries. Consequently, foresters there also serve as consultants to individual landowners or manage forests for timber companies. The U.S. Army Corps of Engineers and the Environmental Protection Agency also offer opportunities. I don't mean to say that in the West only government agencies hire foresters and in the East only private employment is available. A variety of jobs exists in all regions, and the balance shifts in different parts of the country.

The increase in environmental legislation as well as renewed public interest in the environment have led to a variety of new job opportunities for forestry graduates. Environmental consulting companies and conservation organizations are hiring foresters. International opportunities exist in the Peace Corps, with forest products companies, and organizations such as the World Bank and the U.S. Agency for International Development.

Biggest U.S. Corporations in the Pollution Control Industry

Ranked by: Market value as of March 6, 1992, in millions of dollars. (Also notes rank in top 1,000, percentage change in 1991-92 market value, sales, profits, assets, return on invested capital, and return on equity.)

1. Waste Management, with $20,916 million
2. Chemical Waste Management, $4,169
3. Browning-Ferris Industries, $3,547
4. Chambers Development Co., $2,155
5. Calgon Carbon, $866
6. Rollins Environmental Services, $805
7. Mid-American Waste Systems, $491
8. International Technology Corp., $353

Source: *Business Week*

Entry-Level Forestry Jobs

If you want to get rich, chances are that you won't do so as a forester. Entry-level salaries for graduates with a bachelor's degree range roughly between $20,000 and $30,000, with an average of about $24,000 per year in the Southeast. I suspect that beginning salaries in other areas of the country are comparable.

There is no such thing as a *typical* day for a forester on her or his first job. The absence of repetitious tasks is one of the attractions of the field. Duties change with the seasons—supervising tree planting operations during winter and spring, planning for thinning and harvesting of trees during dry weather conditions, measuring trees and assessing their growth, evaluating wildlife habitat, locating boundary lines of the land, laying out roads and locations for bridges, buying and selling of timber, planning of budgets, searching for endangered plant or animal species, measuring streamflow of a creek, assessing the quality of groundwater, managing a recreation area—any of these activities and many more may be included in an ordinary day in the field.

Office work generally involves use of computers for keeping track of inventory and predicting future growth of various forest stands. Computers are also used for storing geographic information relating to soils, wetlands, scenic values, and recreation area use. A forest resource manager may also evaluate aerial photographs or satellite imagery to spot insect or disease problems, inventory resources, and map terrain. Global positioning systems are frequently used to locate stand boundaries, roads, or wildfire fronts. Also, budget and report writing are just as important in forestry as in any other profession and business.

Foresters are frequently called upon to explain the effects of various forest management alternatives to civic clubs, business groups, or conservation associations.

People are becoming more aware of the limits of our planet and the importance of diverse forested systems to the continued well-being of mankind and earth. A growing population places apparently insatiable demands for wood, recreation, wildlife, and water resources on the land. At the same time, more and more forested areas are set aside as wilderness areas, wetlands, or habitat for endangered species. The practicing forester also meets many individual people face-to-face in his or her daily rounds. An open, friendly person who can communicate with all kinds of people is at an obvious advantage in such situations. A sense of stewardship—that is, a desire to leave the land and associated forest resources in better shape than we found them—is essential for a good forester.

Career Ladders

After an initial three to five years in the woods, most foresters will be promoted. This usually means more administrative and planning responsibilities in the office and less field work. It may also mean a move from a rural location to a more urban setting, although many forest district offices are located in relatively small towns.

Beyond these generalities, it is difficult to identify typical progress in a career. Individual advancement depends on three things: the type of employer (e.g., government agency, forest industry, or consulting firm); the kind of position (e.g., whether it deals more with the resource management or the business side of the profession); and the goals of the individual.

As we become more aware of the limits of our planet, we also become more concerned about improving its life support systems. Forested ecosystems and landscapes around the world are of critical importance for the long-term ecological welfare of earth. At the same time, they provide basic raw materials for human physical and mental well-being. Foresters have been and will continue to be involved in the forefront of these endeavors.

DR. KLAUS STEINBECK received his B.S. and M.S. at the University of Georgia and his Ph.D. at Michigan State University. He worked as a research forester for the U.S. Forest Service for several years. He then joined the faculty of the School of Forest Resources at the University of Georgia, where he teaches Silviculture—literally the cultivation of forests. As undergraduate coordinator for the school, Dr. Steinbeck also enjoys counseling undergraduate students about career choices in the forestry profession.

CHAPTER ELEVEN

Wetland Management: Career Opportunities in a Rapidly Changing Field

Mark M. Brinson, Ph.D., East Carolina University

These are exciting times to be involved in wetland management. As wetlands become scarcer and the controversies surrounding them more publicized, the public at large becomes more attuned to the values that wetlands provide. There are many facets to wetland management. They include protection, regulation, restoration, and legal and political aspects. Each of these is undergoing continuous change as we learn how to translate natural resource science and law into practical results. Being a part of this process can be frustrating at time, but it is never boring.

The reason for so much attention on wetlands is their importance in meeting the goals of the Clean Water Act passed by Congress in 1972. Without protecting wetlands, it would be virtually impossible to meet the Act's goal "...to protect and maintain the physical, chemical, and biological integrity of the Nation's waters." The challenge for society is to maintain what all of us consider the essentials of civilized life (i.e., adequate housing, food, and work) at the same time that we maintain clean water and an otherwise healthy environment.

Because wetlands are almost everywhere in the landscape, it is virtually impossible to completely avoid negatively impacting wetlands. They are so prevalent that the straightforward task of building or widening a road one mile long cannot be carried out without damaging or eliminating some or all of a wetland.

Issues Wetland Managers Face

One way to illustrate the career opportunities for **wetland managers** is to discuss ongoing issues of national importance, such as the contentious situation in the Florida Everglades where wetland managers have been involved from many perspectives.

The Everglades

Although the problems with the Florida Everglades are too far- ranging and complex to do justice to in a couple of short paragraphs, some of the issues illustrate how wetland managers and those in collateral fields become involved. As most people know The Everglades is a 40 mile-wide "river of grass" when it undergoes shallow flooding with flow extending from Lake Okeechobee, some 100 miles to the tip of the Florida where mangrove swamps are located. The southernmost part of this extensive wetland is Everglades National Park. North of the park and roughly southeast of the lake are several land holdings. One is a large sugarcane growing area which is privately held; Another consists of water conservation areas that store water for the thirsty populations of the Miami metropolitan area. The juxtaposition of Everglades National Park, a growing metropolitan area, and intensive agriculture is the crux of the problem: Both water quality (nutrient levels) and water quantity (rates of supply) are at stake.

Water is pumped from sugarcane fields to canals which enriches the normally nutrient-poor Everglades vegetation. Excessive nutrients change the natural sawgrass and algae-based food chains to areas often dominated by cattail, a plant that is considered to be a weed species by comparison. The water conservation areas store water that would otherwise be available to flood the Everglades National Park. Instead, the water is slowly diverted through canals away from the Everglades National Park to the Miami area. One doesn't need a degree in wetland management to figure out that The Everglades, one of the Nation's largest and most valuable wetlands, is in big trouble.

It does, however, require an understanding of wetlands to be part of the effort to find solutions to the problem. For example, wetland managers work for the State of Florida, which is responsible for maintaining water quality. They employ environmental scientists who sample water to make sure that nutrient rich waters are not being discharged into the Park. The sugarcane producers hire consulting firms who employ wetland scientists. In order to cut down on the phosphorus-rich water that is flowing from the fields, wetland scientists help design wetlands to act as filters for removing phosphorus. Wetland managers working for these firms also make recommendations on flow rates, wetland size, etc., for these artificial wetlands designed for removing nutrients. **Wetland scientists** working for the National Park Service monitor the rate at which cattails, an undesirable wetland plant in that region, are invading the natural stands of sawgrass.

How to Prepare for a Career

Because wetland management is a relatively new field, few people have been specifically trained in the area or have even had a course called *wetland ecology* or *wetland management.* Consequently, many have had to learn on the job and apply their background in limnology (study of lakes and streams), soil science, geology, hydrology, etc., to the problems that affect wetlands.

However, wetland managers are expected to have a college degree. Your chances for promotion and advancement will improve by having advanced or graduate degrees. In the basic sciences, it is very common for college students with adequate grade point averages to continue in school until they have earned a master's degree. This makes them more competitive in the job market.

Types of Training Available

The types of training to prepare for a career in wetland management closely follows the disciplines discussed above. None of these are dependent on having a course in wetland ecology or wetland management. This is quickly changing, however, as more and more of students and faculty recognize the demand for trained wetland managers. For the college bound, there are two tracks, either of which provide opportunities. For those not interested in graduate degrees, a focused technical approach might be appropriate. These could include associate or bachelor degrees in:

- Wildlife management
- Silviculture (forestry)
- Agriculture (horticulture, crop science, eta.)
- Hydraulic or environmental engineering
- Soil science and other environmental sciences

For those contemplating graduate work or who want a broader, less technical, background, the best advice is to get a degree in one of the traditional scientific disciplines. These include:

- Biology, botany, or zoology with emphasis in ecology, taxonomy, or some field courses, especially plant identification.
- Geology including ground water hydrology, sedimentary petrology, geomorphology, and surface water hydrology.
- Chemistry with emphasis in organic chemistry, biochemistry, or environmental chemistry.

Wetland science is a highly interdisciplinary or multidisciplinary field. Therefore, it is advisable to take some courses in related areas such as statistics, economics, public speaking, and writing. Many of those working in the management fields give oral presentations to their coworkers, the public, and to private environmental groups. Written presentations in the form of reports or study plans are a constant part of life when working in the wetland management field. If you don't place enough importance on these skills, your opportunities for advancement are limited.

What You Can Expect to Earn

By entering the job market with a bachelor's degree and no experience, you can expect to start with a salary of less than $25,000 in government and roughly $5,000 more in the private sector. Many companies and agencies would like a candidate to have at least one to two years of experience. This is how a short-term course or workshop might give you the edge over others.

Because wetland science is moving so rapidly, the wetland management professional must continue his or her education. Short-term courses are often available to both governmental and private employees. While you are taking course work, it might be advisable to get a head start with an internship, which would allow a break in your college work to gain some experience. Both federal and state cooperative arrangements are available.

What Are the Major Career Opportunities?

In the Everglades example given above, it became apparent that two major groups were involved: government employees and those working in the private sector. Government positions are offered at the federal, state, county, and even municipal levels. In the private sector, the career options range from being on the environmental staff of a large engineering consulting firm to working for a regional conservation group. For a broader overview of the career opportunities offered in the government and private sectors, see the following chart.

CAREER CATEGORIES
(by employer and discipline)

Government Employer	Private Employer
Federal Regulatory • Army Corps of Engineers • Environmental Protection Agency • Fish and Wildlife Service • National Marine Fisheries Service • Federal Dept. of Transportation Research and Management—technician positions in agencies above, including some additional ones that manage large areas of public land such as: • Forest Service (Nat. Parks and Monuments) • Fish and Wildlife Refuge (Refuges) • National Park Service (Nat. Parks and Monuments) • Bureau of Land Management (mostly west of the Mississippi **State** Regulatory (names may vary by state) • Department of Natural Resources • Division of Coastal Management • State Department of Transportation • Department of Health and Environment Research • Technician positions in agencies and universities	**Consulting Firms** Delineation • Contracts with developers for delineation and planning Restoration • Nurseries to planting **Non-Governmental Organizations** Mostly conservation groups, such as: • Sierra Club • Audubon • The Nature Conservancy • Environmental Defense Fund And also some lobbying groups, such as: • Farm Bureau • Association of Realtors

The fact that most of the research is conducted at universities and by government agencies doesn't mean that work in the private sector can't be creative and innovative. In fact, some of the most exciting and creative work is being done by private firms in the design of new wetlands and the restoration of damaged wetlands.

Many individuals in these firms and government keep abreast of the latest information through their membership in professional societies of wetland managers and scientists.

Careers by Discipline

Most wetland managers have a technical background in a field that is biologically based, such as ecology, forestry, botany, and wildlife management. However, those trained in alternate areas have opportunities to bring their special talent to the management forum. The disciplines of soil science, hydrology, and geology also produce people that have much to contribute to the field.

A number of lawyers are involved in wetland management because they find that environmental organizations, such as the World Wildlife Fund and The Nature Conservancy, are most effective when conflicts are brought to court. The Everglades case involved a disproportionate number of lawyers, since the resource controversies were so strong that science and technology played a minor role. The situation is improving, however, because ultimately management, not litigation or scientific knowledge, is needed *to get the job done.*

Career Advancement

Currently, the field appears to be stabilizing after a period of rapid growth. This does not mean that jobs are lacking, but that more time is needed to get that first interview. A position advertised below your level of training, but in the general area of environmental management, may be worthwhile to accept, especially in the government sectors. Lateral movement within most government organizations is much easier than trying to *get that perfect job.*

By entering the job market with a bachelor's degree and no experience, you can expect to start with a salary of less than $25,000 in government and roughly $5,000 more in the private sector. Many companies and agencies would like a candidate to have at least one to two years of experience. This is how a short-term course or workshop might give you the edge over others. Once you have some experience, through, job entry and greater pay are more accessible.

Opportunities for promotion and advancement vary greatly from region to region. However, a professional in an average-sized city with 15 years experience might expect to earn the equivalent of $50,000. In the private sector, entrepreneurial approaches make it difficult to provide reliable estimates. However, Ph.Ds. who do full-time consulting may make as much as $830.00 to $1,000.00 per day. Such rates are usually not sustainable over long periods; they usually only apply if the individual is providing services for his area of specialty.

As with many careers, the further you advance, the greater the management opportunities and responsibilities. This includes managing personnel projects and negotiating contracts both in government and private enterprise.

One final note: wetland management appears to be attractive to many women—a disproportionate number of them are actively involved in the field and are making significant career advances.

Professional Support and Continuing Education

Wetland managers must keep up with advances in their field, whether they work for state government as a regulator or serve as president of a prestigious consulting firm. There are several national and international societies that have newsletters and research journals to keep their members abreast of the latest findings. The Society of Wetland Scientists includes members from all over the world, but the center of activity is in the U.S., where nearly 2,500 members reside. The State Association for Wetland Managers has multiple meetings annually and supports a broad range of professionals.

In addition to activities in these societies, there are short- term courses, training sessions, workshops, and other forms of continuing education to provide members and other professionals with transfer of science to management. This gives a chance for professionals to get together to compare notes, share problems, and seek solutions. Through professional membership and workshops, you will find that wetland management is not isolated to one type of profession.

Dr. Mark M. Brinson is professor of biology at East Carolina University. He received his B.S. at Heidelberg College in Ohio and an M.S. in botany from the University of Michigan. Before pursuing his Ph.D. at the University of Florida, Mark served with the Peace Corps in Costa Rica, assisting small scale farmers in the development of fish culture in ponds. His Ph.D. work was done on a lowland tropical lake in Guatemala.

Since his move to North Carolina in 1973, he has been involved in research in many wetland types, including brackish marshes and river swamps. He has taught undergraduate courses in general ecology and environmental biology and graduate courses in physiological plant ecology and wetland ecology. In 1980, he took a one-year leave of absence to work on riparian ecosystems with the U.S. Fish and Wildlife Service. He has continued to interact extensively with federal and state government agencies in providing research and advice on wetland issues and participating in training courses. Dr. Brinson is past president of the Society of Wetland Sciences, which encourages the sustainable management of wetland resources.

CHAPTER TWELVE

Careers in Fisheries

American Fisheries Society

Fisheries: Professionals Needed Today and Tomorrow

With your imagination, put on your scuba diving gear and let's go down to explore the inviting world of career opportunities in fisheries. You're reading this chapter, no doubt, because water and fish attract you so strongly that recreation involving them may not be enough—you'd like to *work* with fish and water, or *write* about them, or *conduct research* relating to them.

Perhaps you're concerned about solving the world's food problems. A **career in fisheries** relates directly to supplying the world with very possibly the healthiest protein of all—fish. Maybe you want to manage the fish populations in cold mountain streams or warm ponds or even in parts of the ocean. Whatever the reason for your interest in fisheries, the following information will help you discover how to convert your fascination with aquatic life into a lifelong career.

In 1988, in the United States alone, commercial fishermen harvested five million metric tons of finfish and shellfish products worth four billion dollars. Aquaculture (fish farming) of fishes and invertebrates in ponds and other closed systems has grown rapidly in North America in the last 20 years. Aquacultural production in North America is roughly 360,000 metric tons—mostly catfish, crawfish, trout, and salmon—valued at $600 million. Given the increasing demand for fisheries products, future expansion of the aquaculture industry is certain. Perhaps you'd like to investigate further a career in aquaculture or management of commercial fisheries.

> **Where the Jobs Are**
>
> State, federal, or provincial fish and wildlife agencies in the United States and Canada are the largest employers of fisheries biologists in North America. International agencies, such as the Peace Corps and the Food and Agriculture Organization of the United Nations, hire fisheries biologists and provide opportunities to work abroad, particularly in developing nations. Nongovernmental employers include power companies, universities, the aquaculture industry, environmental consulting firms, and nonprofit organizations, such as the Sport Fishing Institute.

Another fascinating career is **management of recreational fisheries**. Next to swimming, sport fishing is the most popular outdoor activity in North America: in 1985, U.S. anglers numbered 59 million, or nearly 27 percent of all Americans! Anglers fished a total of 988 million days and spent over $28 billion on licenses, tackle, food, lodging, boats, motors, transportation, and fuel.

Our fisheries resources need help. The demands and stresses that have been placed on many fisheries continue to threaten their productivity. Dredging, dam building, and shoreline erosion physically alter aquatic habitats and can kill fish and invertebrates or interfere with reproduction. Withdrawal of water from lakes and streams for domestic, industrial, and agricultural purposes also reduces available habitat. Release of pollutants into the water threatens survival of all aquatic organisms. *Over*fishing also threatens many fisheries, and competition for various species of fish by sport, commercial, and subsistence fishermen often leads to conflicts and complicates management.

Finding solutions to these problems is one task confronting fisheries scientists of today and tomorrow. Fisheries professionals at all levels are concerned with effective management of living resources in ponds, lakes, streams, estuaries, rivers, and oceans. Fisheries scientists, managers, and administrators work to understand how aquatic systems function, and to determine how to keep our aquatic resources healthy and productive for public use and enjoyment as we approach the 21st century.

Employment Opportunities

The number of available fisheries positions has expanded in recent years as a result of increased funding under the Federal Aid in Sport Fish Restoration Act, which distributes funds collected from a federal tax on fishing tackle and other items to the states for fisheries management programs. The increasing demand for fish in our diets has improved the employment picture for students trained in aquaculture. Graduates with strong educational backgrounds and experience in aquaculture and fisheries research and management are always in demand.

State, federal, or provincial fish and wildlife agencies in the United States and Canada are the largest employers of fisheries biologists in North America. International agencies, such as the Peace Corps and the Food and Agriculture Organization of the United Nations, hire fisheries biologists and provide opportunities to work abroad, particularly in developing nations. Nongovernmental employers include power companies, universities, the aquaculture industry, environmental consulting firms, and nonprofit organizations, such as the Sport Fishing Institute. As a minimum background, the fisheries professional needs a bachelor's degree in fisheries science, aquatic ecology, or another closely related field. In recent years, the master's degree has become a prerequisite for many entry-level research and management positions with state, federal, and private organizations. The doctorate degree may be required for some federal positions and is usually required for faculty positions at most colleges and universities.

Educational Background

A broad education is essential for finding employment in fisheries. Such high school courses as biology, chemistry, physics, mathematics, computer science, English, and communications will help provide the base on which you can build a fisheries education. Consult your guidance counselor for help. Visit a nearby college or university that offers courses in fisheries, aquatic biology, or marine ecology. Volunteer to work with state, federal, and private fisheries and aquaculture organizations. Talk with professors, fisheries biologists, and students studying fisheries to get different views on educational needs and what college or university programs might suit you best.

Beyond the high school level, you will find that, although some colleges and universities offer undergraduate programs in fisheries science, students often obtain degrees in other disciplines, such as biology, zoology, engineering, marine science, economics, or animal science. A good undergraduate curriculum includes courses in biological sciences, physical sciences, mathematics, statistics, and computer science. Courses in writing and public speaking, social studies, and the humanities are also important because fisheries professionals must understand not only the scientific basis of a fishery, but also how to communicate their understanding to the public. Undergraduate programs usually provide a general education stressing all aspects of fisheries science or aquatic ecology. In contrast, a graduate education typically involves specialized study on selected aspects of fishery science.

A summer job, internship, or cooperative education program, although not generally a *requirement* for a fisheries position, is an excellent way for a college student to gain valuable experience and increase chances for employment. Volunteer work in fisheries-related activities can also contribute to a strong resume.

Basic Qualifications for Fisheries Jobs

All high-quality universities should provide you with a broad education in the humanities and basic sciences, enhance your abilities to be an independent and creative individual, and leave you with a continuing desire for additional education. In addition, you should select a university program that provides instruction or experience with the following topics which are desired by employers of entry-level fisheries professionals. All topics listed are not equal; some may be acquired in one lecture or hour of experience, others are acquired over an entire college career. Although the list appears formidable, most high-quality university fisheries programs cover these topics:

- Physical, chemical, and biological processes (including population, community, and ecosystem processes) in aquatic environments (limnology or marine science, stream ecology).
- Concepts of natural resources management and related social and economic issues.
- The scientific method, experimental design, and sampling procedures.

- Fish ecology and biology, especially to understand fish growth, environmental requirements, food resources, reproduction, mortality, life history, movement, and distribution.
- Estimation of fish population characteristics and assessment of the impact of fishing on fish populations.
- Fish anatomy/morphology, in order to identify species, sexes, and stomach contents; mark fish; and use anatomical structures for determining age.
- Fish sampling methods such as netting, electrofishing, marking/tagging.
- Routine analysis of fish samples for length, weight, age, and sex.
- Routine water quality analysis and interpretation.
- Identification of common aquatic invertebrates, algae, and vascular plants.
- Library research and information retrieval.
- Oral and written communication, public speaking, and public relations.
- Basic statistics, word processing and computer analysis, management, and summarization of data.
- Fundamentals of budget preparation and management and employee supervision.

Students who satisfy these requirements will qualify for entry-level fisheries positions requiring a bachelor's degree. Some of this education and training may be obtained in course work, laboratory exercises, university-sponsored intern programs with employers, and part-time employment. You should select a university that provides field courses in the curriculum and promotes the opportunity for students to work with faculty and graduate students on research projects and with agencies on internships.

Other Qualifications

Many employers also look for other important skills not typically obtained as part of the university education. They are:

- Operation, routine maintenance, and simple repairs of vehicles, boats, and boat motors.
- Construction skills (electrical, mechanical, carpentry, plumbing).
- Fishing and outdoor living skills.
- First aid skills.

Master's Degree

You should be aware that individuals with master's degrees frequently apply for entry-level positions and tend to be more competitive than those with bachelor's degrees. University graduate programs in fisheries do not typically require undergraduate degrees in fisheries. Students with any liberal arts or science-based undergraduate degrees may pursue a fisheries career by obtaining a master's degree in fisheries. A master's degree program should provide greater depth of understanding of the items listed for the bachelor's degree and the following:

- Design, implementation, and evaluation of fishery management and research programs.
- Design and implementation of fish population and community surveys.
- Technical writing for scientific reports and publications

Specialization

Many fisheries professionals choose to specialize in certain areas related to fisheries. Two areas in which bachelor's degree graduates may find entry-level positions are water quality and aquaculture (fish culture/hatchery management).

Water Quality

If you want to specialize in water quality, you should make sure the university program can offer you education in the following topics *in addition* to many of those above:

- Environmental toxicology.
- Environmental and assessment principles and procedures.
- Environmental laws and regulations.
- Pollution abatement methods.
- Analytical chemistry principles and procedures.
- Watershed management.
- Basic hydrology and hydraulic engineering.

Fish Culture

If you wish to specialize in fish culture, you should be sure the university program can provide you with classroom or laboratory training in:

- Principles and operation of aquaculture systems including water quality management.
- Reproduction, selective breeding, genetic principles, and artificial spawning techniques.
- Common fish diseases and treatment techniques.
- Fish behavioral responses in aquaculture systems.
- Basic nutrition.
- Harvest techniques.
- Microeconomics and marketing.
- Laws and regulations pertaining to aquaculture.
- Hatchery and business management techniques.

Examples of other fisheries specializations include fish health, genetics, and physiology; fisheries statistics, bioengineering, and socioeconomics. These specializations are typically achieved by obtaining an advanced degree after acquiring the basic fisheries background. In some cases, individuals who have obtained their primary education in the specialization apply that expertise to fisheries problems.

Questions You Should Ask

There are a number of questions that students should ask to determine if a university program is likely to provide them with the required knowledge and abilities for the general or specialized fisheries positions.

- Does the university teach the courses required for professional certification?
- Does the content of the fisheries/aquatics courses cover the topics needed to qualify for entry-level positions?
- Are internship programs, field courses, and relationships with natural resource management agencies sufficient for students to gain practical experiences?
- Is there a fisheries student organization to provide opportunities outside of the classroom for interaction among students with common interests?
- What is the program's record in placing students in fisheries/aquatics jobs?

Availability of these opportunities in a university program does not ensure a high-quality fisheries education, but their absence is likely to result in a less-than-satisfactory education.

Career Choices

Five examples of rewarding and challenging careers in fisheries are:

Fisheries research biologists study aquatic organisms, their interactions with their environment, the effects of recreational and commercial activities on fish populations, and the relationships between aquatic resources and man. Research provides the basis for sound management of fisheries resources. Typical areas of research include ecology, physiology, behavior, genetics, aquaculture, economics, pathology, limnology, marine biology, population dynamics, and computer modeling. Broad training in biology, ecology, statistics, mathematics, and communication skills is important for research scientists.

Fisheries managers use research results to manipulate the various components of a fishery to achieve specific objectives, such as increasing the number or size of fish being harvested, or improving lake access. Managers routinely design and evaluate fish stocking programs, harvest regulations (fishing laws), and fishermen access programs in marine and fresh waters. They also interview anglers to gather important social and economic information for use in development of management programs. Enforcement of harvest regulations is also part of a fisheries management agency's mission. An effective manager knows that public relations is essential to successful management. Therefore, in addition to biology requirements, communications, public policy and administration, and sociology are important subjects in a fisheries manager's education.

Administrators plan and coordinate the work of researchers, managers, aquaculturists, and enforcement officers. Fisheries administrators develop and put into effect regulations and policies. They also establish priorities among the many activities conducted by research and management biologists by coordinating program objectives, preparing budgets and monitoring spending, and supervising staff. Understanding relationships between a fishery, the management agency, and the public is important for sound management programs. Administrative positions in state, federal, and private organizations are usually held by senior professionals with considerable experience in fisheries research and management.

Aquaculturists produce catfish, crawfish, trout, salmon, oysters, shrimp, and other fish for markets and restaurants, stocking programs, and the live-bait industry. They need to understand the physiological, nutritional, and environmental requirements of the organisms being raised. Because most fish and shellfish are cultured at very high densities and are quite susceptible to disease, culturists must also be familiar with disease or health problems that may affect survival of an organism or its value to potential customers. A background in fish health and nutrition, water chemistry, and genetics, and an understanding of business operations and market economics are important for those interested in aquaculture.

Educators teach in approximately 200 colleges and universities in North America where there is a fisheries degree program or where fisheries courses are part of a program in natural resources, zoology, or ecology. Teaching careers typically involve the development of fisheries courses and research programs that contribute to the training of students at both the undergraduate and graduate levels. A doctorate degree is usually required for faculty positions at most colleges and universities, but the educational paths leading to the Ph.D. are as diverse as the field of fisheries science and depend on individual interests.

Within each of the career options summarized above, there are many areas of specialization, such as marine or freshwater fisheries, recreational or commercial fisheries, and laboratory or field work. Expertise in such diverse areas as vertebrate and invertebrate biology, physiology, pathology, oceanography, conservation, enforcement, nutrition, genetics, or limnology can be applied to several different career options.

Food technologists are important in commercial fishing and aquaculture industries. Knowledge of economics, law engineering, statistics, and oral and written communication is always useful to a fisheries professional and may be essential in some job specialties. Land and resource management planning, habitat enhancement, recreation management, public relations, and political science are also becoming increasingly important as we learn more about the relationships between fisheries resources, their habitats, and people.

The **AMERICAN FISHERIES SOCIETY (AFS)** is an international organization of 8,000 aquatic science professionals, students, and nonprofessionals with an interest in fisheries science. Though members are primarily from the United States and Canada, more than 75 other countries are represented. Chartered in 1870, AFS is dedicated to the advancement of fisheries science and the conservation of renewable aquatic resources. The AFS produces a variety of books and other special publications covering the full range of fisheries science.

CHAPTER THIRTEEN

Careers in Waste Management

Anita Blumenthal, Senior Writer, Public Affairs, National Solid Wastes Management Association

Careers in the waste services industry are so varied that a short essay can describe only a few options. Here are a few snapshots from different angles of this multi-faceted field that is in the forefront of environmental protection.

Running a Small Garbage Hauling Business: Collecting Garbage and Recyclables

Robert Haspel is president of Environmental Control Inc., a small waste hauling and recycling business in Sante Fe, NM. Here's how he describes his and his managers' jobs, where flexibility and willingness to learn are key to success:

"As president, I have day-to-day responsibility for all functions as well as strategic planning. I supervise the office and operations managers and also negotiate contracts, market our services and our recyclables, and participate in task forces on solid waste issues. I also answer phones and supervise other employees. ECI's work force of 45 includes an office staff of five, with the rest working in the maintenance, refuse, and recycling departments.

"Both of my managers started at entry-level positions. My **office manager** started as a part-time receptionist nine years ago and, as the company grew, her duties and responsibilities grew as well. My **operations manager**, who has two foremen and supervises 40 people, started as a truck driver nine years ago and worked his way up to foreman, and eventually, to his current post. Both of my managers have high school educations and, as equally important, continue to take work-related training. They attend seminars and workshops on hiring/firing employees and other relevant subjects. My office manager is taking accounting classes at the local community college."

Nothing Is Typical

"There's no such thing as a *typical* day in this business. The best laid plans can be interrupted by an emergency connected with a vehicle or route, or by the potential for a big contract, or by the need to testify before the legislature or at a hearing. Any of these situations can arise at a moment's notice. However, my mornings generally start by making sure that all of our routes are covered (and employees have shown up for work) and by checking on the equipment due to be worked on in the shop. Also, I work on bids, proposals, and reports for contracts. Working out these ideas, I generally brainstorm with my managers, then I go off by myself to crunch the numbers and write it all up. I probably spend four hours a day on the phone."

Going the Extra Mile...

"The ideal candidate to work at ECI should have a sense of responsibility and be ready and willing to go the extra mile to do what needs to be done. Candidates should communicate well with people in English and (this is New Mexico) Spanish. A clean driving record is a must for anyone who will be driving the trucks. All of our drivers must have a commercial drivers license. Also, I look for a stable work history (not changing jobs every year or two)."

...And Rolling up Your Sleeves

"A small business like this has no place for some one who says, 'It's not my job.' Unfortunately, some MBA courses seam geared only toward jobs in Fortune 5OO companies. Some of my *former* employees with college degrees figured they would start at the top, but that's not the way it is in a small, start-up company. You have to be able to roll up your sleeves and get dirty, work on the back of a truck, drive a truck, bale paper, and staff the phones during lunch."

Managing a Recycling Facility

To learn about the multi-sided and challenging job of managing a recycling facility, we spoke to several people in the business (with special thanks to Mark Finney, Recycling Coordinator, Mid-American Waste Systems, Inc., Canal Winchester, OH). Here is the picture that emerged:

Collecting, separating, and marketing recyclables on the scale that's happening in this country is a new business, so we're all learning as we go.

The Manager Wears Many Hats

At a recycling facility, a complex series of mechanical separators and hand pickers produces clean, consistent, recyclable material (old newspaper, cardboard, steel cans, aluminum, glass, and certain plastics). The **recycling manager** has overall responsibility for the facility's day-to-day operation as well as for finding new markets and ensuring profitability.

The day begins at about 6 am, when the assistant manager opens the shop and the first shipments of recyclables begin to arrive. The first order of business is to be sure that the staff has shown up and are at their jobs. If someone is absent, the assistant manager is likely to *work the line*, until that slot is filled.

Paperwork starts early and continues throughout the day. The weights of incoming loads and the percentages of different recyclable materials must be recorded and reported to each customer (such as municipal governments).

Safety is a constant concern. Managers, assistant managers, and supervisors must always be vigilant and constantly be educating their staffs in safety matters, making sure that gloves, goggles, back supports, and hard helmets are worn when required. They must also deal with any injuries that occur.

Of course, the facility deals with outgoing as well as incoming shipments. The manager (with middle managers' help) must know which customers are arriving that day to pick up the collected and separated recyclables, and s/he must ensure that those shipments are ready. Quality control is vital if entire shipments are not to be rejected (customers can do that). Tiny bits of foreign material can contaminate entire loads, so managers must inspect the shipments again while they are being loaded.

Also, the manager needs human resources experience. Recycling at this point is labor-intensive, with many low-skilled minimum-wage level jobs. Turnover in those positions can be a problem.

To Market, to Market...

The manager's other essential tasks include negotiating with brokers and other buyers and prospecting for more marketable materials. S/he must keep up on pricing and supply conditions and always, always look for new customers. Remember, other recycling companies are trying hard to find markets, too!

People skills are very important. For example, in the continual search for markets, a manager deals with many types of people. From one phone call to the next, you could go from seat-of-the-pants to state-of-the-art: from a local scrap merchant who's been in the business forever to a marketing professional at a high-tech paper mill.

Crucial to success is the manager's ability to justify costs for each particular commodity and customer. This is where business and financial training come in. After all, our recycling operation is a business. The big question is, how can this business turn a reasonable profit—or any profit at all?

Sometimes, unfortunately, profit is not possible. That's when other considerations come into play. For example, if the market is so bad that you are not being paid for the old newspaper you've collected and baled, you still want the loads to be picked up in clean, good-looking trucks because the image of the facility is very important.

You Gotta Believe...

This is certainly not a position for someone just looking for any old job. You need to be really enthusiastic about recycling and concerned about the environment. Also, you need a business and production background so that you understand *how* the job is done. Couple all this with the interest and ability to keep up with new laws and regulations and to understand environmental issues. A college education, with emphasis on business/marketing, is desirable.

Clearly, this is *not* a nine-to-five job. Recycling managers are expected to attend meetings outside of work hours. If the facility is part of a larger hauling company, the recycling manager could be called upon to present part of the firm's contract proposal to a city council or a prospective corporate customer. S/he could be called upon to help set up recycling programs, to speak before schools and civic groups, and generally to educate and motivate the community. Public speaking skills are a big plus.

...And Keep on Believing

Along with conviction and enthusiasm, a manager needs another major personal quality: the ability to cope with frustration. You know you want to do the right thing, but with volatile markets and low-value commodities, try as you might, your efforts can sometimes be thankless. You must be resilient and be able to pick yourself up and keep going. Your rewards are those that dedicated recyclers can understand: The genuine satisfaction of knowing you are actually doing the right thing, while other people are just talking about it.

Of course, material rewards are nice, too. Because recycling on this scale nationwide is such a new industry, it's hard to say where you can be in five or ten years' time. In a family of companies, it's possible to move into another segment of the organization, given the talent and interest. It is also possible to build yourself a higher position within recycling. This is a growing field with a web of opportunities.

Be Willing to Keep Learning

Advice to the new graduate entering this field: look, listen, and learn. Don't stop learning just because you've finished school. Also, don't think you have to talk a lot—open your mouth to ask questions.

Designing and Building Waste Facilities

Michael McLaughlin is an office director at SCS Engineers, an engineering consulting firm specializing in designing and building solid and hazardous waste facilities. Here's what he has to say about starting out and moving up in this field:

Junior staff at our firm have the opportunity to learn about complex and expensive projects from the ground up. Entry-level jobs include **technicians** and **assistant staff engineers/scientists/analysts**. Let's follow, for example, the career path of a **landfill engineer**.

Starting Out

A typical day for a young, entry-level landfill engineer might include travel to a job site to collect survey or other background information, slope stability calculations, stormwater system design and supporting calculations, and/or preparation of portions of permit applications, feasibility studies, or cost estimates.

Many people are attracted to consulting by the variety of the work. No two projects are alike, and junior engineers who do not like the project they are working on one day need only wait a few days or weeks to be working on another one: But do not expect a nine-to-five job. Especially in the early part of one's career, it is important to put in extra effort and time to learn about the industry and our work. Because clients should not have to pay to educate our less experienced engineers, a beginner needs to show individual initiative to supplement formal training budgets.

A junior landfill engineer should work towards having a reputation for making project managers look good, by completing assignments quickly and well within budget. This generally entails more work than fits into an eight-hour day.

Moving Up

Successful junior staff can expect promotion within two years to the position of **staff engineer**, which carries responsibility to manage smaller tasks and to perform more complicated ones. After two or three years (during which time, the engineer is expected to gain his/her professional license), a staff engineer can expect promotion to **project engineer**. Project engineers have considerable independence of activity and begin to take on management responsibility for some project tasks.

Project-level staff members (including scientists and analysts as well as engineers) assist in business development, which is an essential function in a consulting engineering firm. Projects are won on the basis of the strong technical skills of the proposed project team, as demonstrated in the written proposal and face-to-face interviews. Project-level staff help write proposals and often participate in interviews. Typical salaries for project- level staff range from the mid-$30's to the mid-40's.

In 10 years, a successful technical professional could well achieve the title of **senior project engineer/scientist/analyst, project manager**, or **senior technical advisor**. A successful professional at this level will have a lead role in attracting new work to the firm and in assuring it is performed well, on time, and within budget. Typical salaries after ten years of experience range from the mid-$5O's to the mid-$70's (sometimes higher).

What It Takes

The ideal entry-level candidate will have strong technical and communication (especially writing) skills. Also important is an interest in working as a member of a multi-disciplinary team. Few engineering consulting firms have "managers" because good management requires a thorough understanding of the technical aspects of the work. Very valuable to a firm, however, is a young engineer or scientist with an understanding of and interest in regulatory matters, because modern solid waste projects are governed by an intricate maze of regulations.

Entry-level positions on a professional track (engineers, scientists, and analysts) normally require a college degree in a technical discipline (civil, geotechnical, mechanical, electrical, and environmental engineering; environmental sciences and/or management). Higher degrees—technical, M.B.A., or law—are desirable.

In addition, the firm offers some positions for candidates without college degrees, such as **technicians, senior technicians**, and **construction personnel**.

Senior engineering technicians are among the more important of our staff in assuring that field work is performed properly.

A Word of Caution....

Some ambitious, entry-level staff try to avoid field work and move up quickly into *management*. This is a mistake. Consulting engineering firms don't have true management positions. Field experience is invaluable for a candidate who wants to move up in this industry.

...And a Word of Advice

Spend your first few months on the job establishing a reputation as a *can do* individual. Ask questions, but take care not to ask the same question more than once. Demonstrate your initiative and your integrity as well as your thoroughness and attention to detail, all in the context of working smartly and efficiently, and you will have no problem whatever in this or most other industries.

Careers in Hazardous Waste

Douglas MacMillan, director of hazardous waste issues at the National Solid Wastes Management Association, gives a brief overview of this specialization:

> Careers in hazardous waste centers mainly on: clean-up of contaminated hazardous waste sites and response to oil and chemical spills; or management of commercial hazardous waste laboratories and treatment, disposal, or recycling facilities. Entry-level jobs in both areas include **chemical** and **civil engineers, geohydrologists, environmental science specialists, laboratory analysis specialists**, and **data managers**.

Biggest U.S. Corporations in the Pollution Control Industry

Ranked by: Market value as of March 6, 1992, in millions of dollars. (Also notes rank in top 1,000, percentage change in 1991-92 market value, sales, profits, assets, return on invested capital, and return on equity.)

1. Waste Management, with $20,916 million
2. Chemical Waste Management, $4,169
3. Browning-Ferris Industries, $3,547
4. Chambers Development Co., $2,155
5. Calgon Carbon, $866
6. Rollins Environmental Services, $805
7. Mid-American Waste Systems, $491
8. International Technology Corp., $353

Source: *Business Week*

Cleaning Up

The clean-up jobs are tackled by remedial response contracting firms, whose engineers assess contaminated sites and design and execute plans to eliminate or minimize the contamination. Specific tasks include setting up groundwater sampling programs, conducting laboratory analyses of soils, reviewing available technologies to determine clean-up options, and managing the actual clean-up activities on site.

There is no *typical* day at a clean-up site because activity is based on the particular needs of the operation and the urgency of the situation. During emergencies, hours can be long and weekends ignored. By its very nature, remedial contracting requires travel. Of course, laboratory work and headquarters jobs have more regular hours.

Geohydrologists and chemical engineers are the most sought-after specialists in hazardous waste clean-up.

Treating and Disposing

The second major career opportunity involving hazardous waste is in the management of treatment, disposal, and recycling facilities. Here, chemical engineers design and oversee processes to destroy or detoxify the wastes. Hours for these jobs are more predictable than for site clean-up jobs, but special projects or contingencies periodically require overtime. Facilities are generally located in either heavily industrialized or sparsely populated areas.

To give an example of a non-engineering position, let's look at the data entry function at a *facility*. This job involves tracking samples that prospective customers send to the facility. These samples must be sent to the lab, where analysts determine whether the material can be treated by the plant's technologies. If so, the data manager indicates tentative acceptance of the material. When that shipment arrives, a quick confirmatory sample must be taken, and the material must be stored and scheduled for treatment. The data manager must then return completed shipping forms to the customers. Careful and extensive documentation is a basic requirement in this highly regulated industry.

Salaries depend on many factors, including location, but again, chemical engineers and geohydrologists are finding a buyer's market.

Robert Haspel, president of Environmental Control, Inc., Sante Fe, NM, holds a B.A. in geography from the University of Colorado and an M.B.A. from the University of New Mexico. **Mark Finney**, recycling coordinator, Mid- American Waste Systems, Inc., Canal Winchester, OH, entered recycling through an internship during his senior year at Xavier University, in Cincinnati. He holds a B.S. in business administration (marketing). **Michael McLaughlin** directs the Reston, VA, Office of SCS Engineers. He received his bachelor's degree in civil engineering from Virginia Tech and a law degree from Washington and Lee University. **Douglas MacMillan**, currently director of Hazardous Waste Programs at the National Solid Wastes Management Association (NSWMA), previously worked for the U.S. Environmental Protection Agency and in private industry and holds graduate degrees in law from Georgetown University and Public Administration from Harvard.

Anita Blumenthal, senior writer in public affairs at NSMWA, holds two degrees in English from Brandeis University and from the New University of Ulster in Northern Ireland.

CHAPTER FOURTEEN

Career Opportunities in Public Gardens

A. Jefferson Lewis III, Ph.D., Director,
The State Botanical Garden of Georgia

Careers in public gardening are as diverse as public gardening itself. Botanical gardens, horticultural gardens, arboreta, parks, campuses, and other institutions offer numerous career opportunities for students in horticulture, botany, landscape architecture, biology, forestry, and related fields of study.

What Do Public Gardens Do?

Public gardens teach people about plants, gardening, landscaping, nature, and related topics. They provide a setting in which children can develop an early appreciation for nature and the environment. They introduce new plants to the nursery and home gardening trade through breeding, collection, and selection programs. Public gardens provide a forum for global issues regarding the environment and provide a refuge for rare and endangered plants. They provide a place of beauty and tranquility away from crowded cities and busy lifestyles and offer recreational opportunities from walking to bird watching. Public gardens serve as centers of community pride and community involvement in city beautification programs, historic preservation, arts and educational programs, lectures, flower shows, and a wide assortment of other social, recreational, cultural, and educational activities.

What Are Some Career Options?

Career opportunities are many and varied, requiring a wide range of talents and skills. Because botanical gardens, arboreta, municipal parks, etc., vary so in size and mission, career opportunities also vary. The size of the unit will often determine how general or specialized the job title and responsibilities will be. In addition to jobs that require training in the plant sciences, many other jobs exist in public information, volunteer management, journalism, financial and office management, development, education, and visitor services.

The **director** is responsible for implementing policy, funding, planning, organizing, staffing, directing, and/or supervising all activities, usually answering to a board of directors or board of advisors. In large and more complex organizations, an **assistant director** may handle the more routine administrative matters.

The **horticultural manager** or **supervisor** is responsible for greenhouse, nursery, conservatory, and/or grounds management. Larger gardens may employ **assistant horticulturists** or **curators** for special gardens or collections with specific management, accessioning, and record keeping responsibilities. The horticultural manager or supervisor generally has responsibility for day-to-day management of the grounds section including personnel, supplies, pest control, and equipment and vehicle maintenance.

Horticulturists/curators are responsible for the maintenance and upkeep of the garden, specific areas or collections within the garden or specific tasks, e.g., turf management or pest management. The number of such positions will generally depend on the size of the garden, number of accessions, and intensity of cultivation.

Larger organizations often employ an **accessions manager** whose principal responsibility is to keep accurate records on the plants comprising the collection(s). Such records are generally computerized for rapid sorting/retrieval and may be *online* for query from other locations. Integrated mapping systems allow the precise location of specific accessions to be quickly determined.

The **propagator** produces plants from seeds, cuttings, tissue culture, and other propagation techniques for use in the garden, display beds, conservatory, and education and/or research programs. In smaller gardens, horticulturists or curators may assume this responsibility.

Gardens with a strong research mission will generally have a **research director**. Areas of research may include plant breeding, plant evaluation, conservation of rare and endangered species, and a variety of other topics congruent with the mission of the garden. Research may vary from applied studies to basic research, both on and off-site. Botanical gardens are at the forefront of issues such as biodiversity, loss of habitat destruction, and the consequences of tropical deforestation. Gardens with extensive library holdings, an herbarium, and university-affiliated botanical gardens often conduct literature research and taxonomic studies.

The **development officer** works with the director, board of advisors, membership organization, and other support groups to develop funding strategies that ensure the operation and long range growth and development of the garden. While training in plant sciences is not essential, it is important nonetheless that the development officer have a good working knowledge of the garden, future plans, etc.

The **educational coordinator** develops, implements, schedules and supervises educational activities including lectures, workshops, classes, teacher training, and other special events. Audiences vary from school children to senior citizens and amateurs to professionals. A variety of printed and audio/visual media may be used in communicating and interpreting various components within the garden.

The **public relations/information specialist** works with the director, development officer, educational coordinator, and other staff and support groups in promoting and publicizing the garden and its activities through leaflets, brochures, booklets, guides, news releases, newsletters, advertising, displays, public service announcements, videos, and radio and television.

The **Visitor Services Manager** is responsible for the maintenance and management of public buildings to include scheduling, visitor services, safety, and operation of auxiliary enterprises, e.g., gift shops and food service. Many gardens, parks, and arboreta rent their facilities to outside groups as a source of operating income.

The **volunteer coordinator** recruits, trains and manages volunteers who supplement the work of the permanent staff. Volunteers are an integral part of the operation of most botanical gardens and arboreta. The volunteer coordinator serves as a *clearinghouse* to match the needs of the garden with the desires of the volunteers.

Other titles and positions include accountants, business managers, groundskeepers, librarians, gift shop managers, urban horticulturists, naturalists, ecologists, plant information specialists, botanists, and editors.

Advice From The Pro's

The Working Environment

Public gardens offer a pleasant working environment, particularly for people who like to be outdoors. Not all the work is glamorous; some positions require physical exertion sometimes in adverse weather conditions. On the other hand, office workers may be inside most of the day. In some departments, work schedules must be arranged to provide for seven-days-a-week coverage and 24-hours-a-day emergency response. Regardless of the job, most positions require the ability to interact and relate to people effectively.

Salaries and fringe benefits vary with the institution, its size, governance, and method of funding. Median salaries for selected positions are director, $48,000; assistant director, $40,000; head horticulturist, $31,104; curator (of horticulture), $28,184; plant records keeper, $23,184; and gardener, $21,254.

What Training Do I Need?

Educational requirements vary depending on the position and job title. A bachelor's degree in the plant sciences or related disciplines is generally required to pursue a career in the horticultural aspects of public gardens. A master's degree is usually required for leadership or research positions. Some gardens and arboreta, particularly those associated with colleges and universities, require the director and director of research to have a Ph.D.

Many jobs at public gardens do not require professional training in the plant sciences. Public gardens require staff with a broad range of expertise who can prepare reports, grants, brochures, educational materials, agreements, policies, and who are skilled in personnel and financial management. Most such jobs require a B.A. or equivalent degree.

Want to Learn More?

Visit public gardens in your area; talk with the staff to learn about their jobs and responsibilities. Call your local library or contact the American Association of Botanical Gardens and Arboreta (AABGA) for a listing of public gardens in your state and area. Consider gaining practical experience through an internship or summer job. Most botanical gardens and arboreta offer one or more internships annually. An internship directory is published annually by the AABGA; it also maintains a jobs hotline.

Internships may be general, exposing the student to the many facets of a botanical garden or they may be specific, e.g., horticulture, education, etc. The garden or arboreta pays a modest salary and often subsidizes the intern by providing housing assistance. Many colleges and universities offer credit for supervised internship and work/study experiences.

Get to know more about local, state, regional, and national plant societies and organizations. Join the AABGA and attend a regional or annual meeting if possible. Competitive student travel awards are available through AABGA to attend regional meetings.

DR. JEFF LEWIS received his B.S. and M.S. degrees in horticulture and his Ph.D. in plant physiology from Clemson University. He has held teaching, research, extension, and administrative positions at Clemson University, Virginia Polytechnic Institute and State University, and the University of Georgia. He currently lives in Athens, GA, where he is professor of horticulture and director of The State Botanical Garden of Georgia.

CHAPTER FIFTEEN

Opportunities in Horticulture

Lois Berg Stack, Ph.D., Associate Professor, Department of Plant, Soil, and Environmental Sciences, University of Maine

What is Horticulture?

Horticulture is the study, production, and management of fruits and nuts, vegetables and herbs, and ornamental plants such as trees, shrubs, and flowers. It is such a diverse field with so many career options, that no matter what your interests are, there is a career for you in horticulture.

Find Your Niche Based on Your Interests

If you enjoy growing plants, you might consider producing apples or oranges in an orchard, trees or shrubs in a nursery, or potted plants or cut flowers in a greenhouse. Our growing population means that the future is bright for **crop producers**—more people will eat more fruits and vegetables, plant more landscapes, enjoy more city parks, and play on more golf courses.

You can find out more about growing plants by getting a summer job with a local producer than by preparing for a career as a grower by studying horticulture, soil management, and production technology at a university or technical college. With specialized training, you might grow tomatoes in a hydroponic greenhouse or young plants in a tissue culture lab. You might even manage the first vegetable farm at a space station!

Did you ever think about where new plants come from? **Plant breeders** select plants from the wild and improve them. They develop earlier tomatoes, bigger melons, tastier sweet corn, prettier roses, and longer-lasting poinsettias. Exciting new things are happening in the world of plant breeding. Breeders are learning to take a trait from one plant and incorporate it into another plant. The possibilities for these **biotechnologists** are limited only by their imaginations: beans with more protein, flowers of colors not found in nature, trees that resist damage from insects, and plants that survive in droughty locations.

If you are interested in plant breeding, you could train for an exciting career by completing a four-year university degree, then continuing in graduate school to study horticulture, genetics, and plant breeding. Most plant breeders work for private companies, such as seed or plant suppliers, or for government agencies and universities.

If you enjoy design and art, you might become a landscape professional. **Landscape architects, landscape designers**, and **landscapers** turn artistic visions into beautiful and functional parks, botanic gardens, and other outdoor areas. They help reduce air pollution in cities by creating tree-lined streets, reduce soil erosion by terracing hillsides and planting dense groundcovers, solve wind problems with windbreaks, and reduce our dependence on air conditioning by designing landscapes with shade trees. Find out if you are interested in designing outdoor areas by getting a job with a landscaper in the summer. Pursue a career by studying horticulture and design at a university or technical college and by completing internships with landscape professionals. To become a licensed landscape architect, you should pursue graduate studies and also gain on-the-job training with a licensed landscape architect.

If you are interested in art and design but would prefer to work indoors, you might consider a career in floral design or interiorscaping. **Floral designers** create flower arrangements for use in people's homes and businesses. They study horticulture and artistic design at a floral design school, technical college, or university. Most floral designers own their own businesses and find that courses in business and personnel management are also useful. An **interiorscaper** designs and installs plantings in large business complexes, shopping malls, and similar public buildings. The tropical plants they use in their designs create an exotic setting that brings the outdoors in. Interiorscapers study horticulture at a technical college or a university.

With all these designs, there are almost endless opportunities for people who enjoy managing plants. Both indoor and outdoor landscapes are kept in top condition by **landscape maintenance professionals.** These people work in botanic gardens and conservatories, home and business landscapes, public parks, and on golf courses. Some are employed by cities to keep urban forests healthy.

To prepare for a career in landscape maintenance, you should learn about a great variety of plants and how to manage them by taking courses at a technical college or university in the areas of horticulture, plant care, and pest management. To advance in this career, you may want to add courses in business and personnel management.

If you like using computers and figuring out how things work, you can find a great career as a **horticultural engineer**. Horticulture is becoming more and more specialized, and engineers help solve problems like how to harvest fruits and vegetables by machine, how to store crops and transport them to market, how to manage the environment in a greenhouse by computer; how to turn apples, oranges, and blueberries into jams, jellies, and juices; and how to create landscape designs on computerized CAD systems. Some engineers specialize in highly technical equipment, such as the instruments used in laboratories for research. Horticultural engineers take some horticulture courses, but concentrate on how to solve horticultural problems by getting a strong background in engineering. Appropriate courses are found at universities.

By now, you can see that horticulture is big business! To grow plants, producers need tools and equipment. The plants they produce must be marketed. With over half the households in the U.S. participating in some form of gardening, there are endless tools, seeds, and related products for home gardeners, too. There are tremendous opportunities for **horticultural business managers**. To get the best job and develop it into a career, take business courses at a university. Gain an appreciation for the unique nature of horticultural businesses by working summers in crop production, plant maintenance, or some other aspect of the industry. Then concentrate on the part of business that interests you the most—marketing, personnel management, or business management, for example.

A Job vs. a Career

You can get a job in horticulture right out of high school. But to advance and make a career of it, you need technical training. The experience you gain will immediately help you determine what direction you want to pursue. From there, you can take courses at a technical college or university. Your next summer job may be a little closer to what you want to do as a career and so on. By the time you complete your training, you will also have gained the summer experience to help you land that first professional job. From there, the sky is the limit. Horticulture is such a broad field with so many opportunities, you can create your own goals and work toward them.

Many people who study horticulture find it so fascinating that they want to share their knowledge with others. **Teachers** at public schools, technical colleges, and universities provide training in the classroom and lab. **Cooperative extension professionals** work with members of the horticulture industry to assess problems and identify solutions. **Consultants** teach members of the industry how to be more productive by providing professional advice directly for their businesses. Some people share their knowledge of horticulture by becoming **writers**, providing technical information, crop knowledge, and gardening advice through books, technical journals, and gardening magazines. And someone has to write all those seed catalogs!

Some people who study horticulture want to go beyond what is known. They pursue graduate degrees at universities and make a career of investigating new aspects of horticulture. These **researchers** find out how plants function, and how we can better use them. Many researchers work at universities, but many also work in private industry. Some work primarily in laboratories, while others work in the field with crops. Researchers often start their studies with basic courses about plants and become more and more focused in later course work, as they define the specific areas they want to investigate.

If you are concerned about the environment, horticulture may help you to make a difference. Some **environmental horticulturists** work to identify and preserve natural ecosystems. Others grow native plants to replant habitats such as woodlands and wetlands. Still others work with the public at botanic gardens and nature preserves to teach people the importance of nature.

What Does an Employer Look For?

It is important to study and do well in school, but employers look for other things, too. Here are some things most horticultural employers look for:

- A progression of summer jobs or internships in horticulture, with each one more responsible than the last.
- A good work ethic.

- An ability to get along with co-workers.
- Goals—your goals can change over time, but you should at least be thinking about what you want to do after a few years of experience.
- A desire to learn.

What Are the Benefits?

Horticulturists specialize in one area or another because of their strengths and interests, but they all have one thing in common: They love plants. This provides a strong motivation to succeed. People who love what they do generally earn a good living. Salaries are commensurate with training: more technical positions pay higher salaries. But horticulture is more than a career. For many people it is a way of life, and it provides tremendous satisfaction that money cannot buy. Even professional horticulturists garden when they get home!

Dr. Lois Berg Stack is a faculty member at the University of Maine. As an associate professor of landscape horticulture, she teaches three undergraduate courses. As a cooperative extension specialist in ornamental horticulture, she works closely with Maine's nursery, greenhouse, and garden center industry. She holds an M.S. in floriculture and a Ph.D. in horticulture education from the University of Wisconsin-Madison. Before completing her graduate work, she taught courses and managed the educational greenhouses at the Brooklyn Botanic Garden and worked as a landscaper.

CHAPTER SIXTEEN

Balancing Work, Health, Technology, and Environment: Careers in Industrial Hygiene

American Industrial Hygiene Association

Definition and Background of the Profession

Basic Definition and Job Description

Industrial hygiene is the recognition, evaluation, and control of workplace environmental factors that may affect the health, comfort, or productivity of the worker. Industrial hygiene is considered a *science*; however, it is also an art that involves judgement, creativity, and human interaction.

Although some occupations may appear more dangerous than others, potential short-term and long-term health hazards occur in every profession, whether a person is employed as a banker or a construction worker. Industrial hygienists play an important role in ensuring that the workplace is as free from hazards as possible and that the workers and the community at large are protected from potential health threats. As our world moves through the *information age*, where new, possibly hazardous technologies are emerging every day, the industrial hygienist's job function becomes more valuable to the health and well-being of workers, the community, and the environment.

Some areas that industrial hygienists may get involved in include:

- **Asbestos**—testing for and possibly removing asbestos. This mineral fiber, which has fire-resistant capabilities and was used for insulation in buildings, is now thought to cause cancer and other illnesses.
- **Biological Monitoring**—determining if toxic materials have reached a person by searching for them in the person's body and by evaluating the body's *by-products*, such as blood.
- **Biosafety**—ensuring that materials, such as bacteria, viruses, used syringes and needles, etc., are handled safely so as not to infect workers.

- **Confined Spaces**—establishing procedures to safely enter closed spaces not designed for human occupancy, such as storage tanks.
- **Ergonomics**—helping to limit cases of disabilities due to repetitive and/or prolonged movement, such as typing at a keyboard, sitting at a desk all day. One disability industrial hygienists frequently encounter is carpal tunnel syndrome, a common stress injury; another is lower back trauma.
- **Environmental Lead**—finding solutions to problems occurring from unsafe levels of lead found in old paint, contaminated water, and other materials.
- **Exposure Assessment Strategies**—measuring human exposures to toxins (i.e., solvents, asbestos).
- **Hazard Evaluation**—determining the real potential for ill health effects by performing such functions as testing for potentially hazardous gases and vapors, measuring noise levels, and evaluating results from such measurements and tests.
- **Indoor Environmental Quality**—ensuring that inside air is safe and free from irritants and toxins, including problems such as sick building syndrome and second-hand tobacco smoke.
- **Radiation**—testing and controlling radiation emitted from power lines, electromagnetic fields, radioactive materials, etc.
- **Laboratory Health and Safety**—protecting workers involved in research and development.
- **Toxicology**—studying the nature and action of poisons and exactly how they cause ill health effects.
- **Workplace Environmental Exposure Levels**—sets limits on exposure levels and provides guidelines for control of chemicals, noise, and radiation in the workplace.

The Development of Industrial Hygiene as a Profession

Industrial hygiene is a relatively new profession, gaining prominence in the last half of this century, mainly due to the advent of the Occupational Safety and Health Act of 1970. Although evidence suggests the field of industrial hygiene began as early as the fourth century B.C. with Hippocrates' recognition of lead poisoning as an occupational disease, our time line begins with Ramazzini, the *father of industrial hygiene*, in the year 1700.

Today, the industrial hygienist's role is proactive; instead of correcting problems *after* they occur, industrial hygienists work with management to anticipate problems that *could* occur and take action to prevent them *before* they happen. Management now recognizes that industrial hygienists are not just scientists who tell employers they are doing things wrong and cost them money. Managers realize that industrial hygienists can and should play an important role in the organization to help increase worker productivity and reduce insurance and medical costs, thus lowering overall costs while keeping workers safe and healthy.

The Federal Government's Role

Industrial hygienists have played an important role in shaping and implementing government policy concerning worker health and safety. In 1970, Congress passed the Occupational Safety and Health Act, which formed the Occupational Safety and Health Administration (OSHA). OSHA, which is part of the U.S. Department of Labor, is responsible for setting and enforcing health and safety standards across the country. In addition, some special OSHA-approved offices that are administered by individual states also conduct health and safety inspections.

The National Institute for Occupational Safety and Health (NIOSH), a branch of the U.S. Department of Health and Human Services, was created to learn more about occupational illnesses and how to prevent them. Some of the most exciting research in the field of industrial hygiene is performed at NIOSH. NIOSH also aids in the training of industrial hygienists. A large number of industrial hygienists who received master's degrees since 1970 received graduate scholarships paid for by NIOSH.

Job Diversity Within the Industrial Hygiene Profession

Job diversity is a major benefit to consider when choosing a career in the health/environmental sciences. A wealth of unique employment opportunities exists for industrial hygienists. Unlike many other professions, industrial hygienists are not limited to one particular type of industry; they are employed in a variety of organizations such as:

- Public Utilities
- Government
- Academia
- Labor Unions
- Research Laboratories
- Hospitals
- Hazardous Waste Companies
- Insurance Companies
- Consulting Firms
- Chemical Companies
- Manufacturing Companies

Many industrial hygienists work for private corporations or federal and state government agencies as salaried employees. However, the fastest growing segment of industrial hygiene is self-employment/consulting. The need for competent industrial hygiene professionals is growing rapidly, and the demand is sure to increase even more in the coming years. In fact, a 1992 *U.S. News & World Report* survey ranks industrial hygiene as one of the top professions of the future. As the world changes, the industrial hygiene profession is constantly faced with new challenges. The industrial hygienist will find that an even greater number of job opportunities will evolve as more government and corporate leaders realize the importance of health and safety in all phases of planning and daily operations.

Many of these opportunities will lead to upper management positions, as employers realize the industrial hygienist's job is a multifaceted one that touches every aspect of an organization. The industrial hygienist acts as an advisor, making recommendations and setting standards to keep the workplace safe. This calls for working with employees at all job levels and requires a genuine commitment to caring about people and the environment.

Preparing for a Career in Industrial Hygiene

Educational Requirements

Although more schools are beginning to offer undergraduate programs in industrial hygiene, currently few schools have an industrial hygiene *major.* Industrial hygienists generally prepare for their careers by pursuing an undergraduate degree in one of the sciences, such as engineering, chemistry, biology, etc. Many then continue on to attain a master's or doctoral degree in industrial hygiene.

Some colleges offer a one- to three-year associate degree and a certificate program that qualifies students as industrial hygiene technicians. A technician assists an industrial hygienist and other occupational health and safety professionals in gathering and analyzing data and in ensuring that programs and regulations are enforced.

After you have worked in the industrial hygiene field for five years, you are eligible for certification. To become certified, you must take a comprehensive two-day certification exam, similar in form and intensity to the CPA exam that accounting professionals take. When the exam is passed and all requirements are met, an industrial hygienist becomes a Certified Industrial Hygienist (CIH). To maintain certification, the industrial hygienist participates in a continuing education program. The certification process distinguishes an industrial hygienist and also advances the profession in general. Regulatory agencies, such as the EPA, have recognized the special competency of CIHs in their environmental regulations and many employers see the CIH designation as one of their selection and promotion criteria.

Educational Norms

According to a 1991 member survey by the American Industrial Hygiene Association (AIHA), which is composed of more than 11,000 health and safety workers, 98 percent of AIHA members are college graduates, 54 percent have master's degrees, and 13 percent have doctoral degrees.

Salary and Other Benefits

If you are a self-starter who takes pride in his or her work and cares about people and the environment, industrial hygiene may be the career for you. Besides having the ability to choose among many types of employment opportunities, industrial hygienists frequently have the luxury of scheduling their own hours. Plus, there is always the opportunity of working for yourself by becoming a consultant, or starting your own business if *total* employment freedom is your goal.

The salary you earn, of course, depends on the type of business you choose to work for and your own ability, but entry-level industrial hygienists are generally paid between $28,000 and $33,000. Mid-level industrial hygienists make about $40,000 to $60,000. Top-level industrial hygienists can earn anywhere between $60,000 and $130,000, or higher.

▼

THE AMERICAN INDUSTRIAL HYGIENE ASSOCIATION, founded in 1939, is an organization of professionals dedicated to the prevention of workplace-related illness or injury that may affect the health and well-being of workers or the community. With more than 11,000 members, AIHA is the largest international association serving the needs of occupational and environmental scientists and engineers practicing industrial hygiene in industry, government, labor, academic institutions, and independent organizations. The purposes of AIHA are to promote the field of industrial hygiene, to provide education and training, to provide a forum for the exchange of ideas and information, and to represent the interests of industrial hygienists and those they serve.

AIHA offers its members and other interested professionals a wide range of products and services on a variety of topics within the occupational health and safety field. AIHA publishes an extensive library of books and guides.

CHAPTER SEVENTEEN

Working to Improve the Environment: A Career in Environmental Education

Deborah Simmons, Ph.D.

They often dream of living in a cabin deep in the woods, spending their days teaching visiting school children about a delicate ecosystem, and observing the crystal clear heavens at night. It is a love of nature and a deep seated desire to protect the environment that draws dedicated people into the field of environmental education. The task, as seen by environmental educators, is to help citizens become aware of and knowledgeable about the environment. Environmental education hopes to promote the development of the necessary skills and motivation that enables environmentally responsible behavior.

Environmental educators can be found in a wide variety of jobs and settings. As teachers, naturalists, rangers, writers, and education curators they work in parks, zoos, museums, nature centers, schools, government agencies, and resident camps. To better describe the functions of environmental education, it is typically divided into three interrelated and somewhat overlapping subfields or settings: formal, nonformal, and informal environmental education. Activities that take place within the kindergarten through twelfth grade school system come under the umbrella of formal environmental education. The nonformal setting involves work at zoos, museums, nature centers, and the like, as well as with youth organizations, government agencies, and extension services. Finally, informal environmental education includes use of various forms of media (e.g., film, newspapers, magazines) to reach the public. Although few environmental educators may get that cabin deep in the woods, environmental education jobs can be found in every state, from the biggest cities to the most remote mountain tops. With thousands of programs nationwide and hundreds of jobs advertised every month in employment bulletins, the career opportunities in environmental education seem to be good. But what does it *really* take to be an environmental educator?

The Economic Realities of Environmental Education

For many, being an environmental educator means stringing together part-time jobs to make ends meet, moving from one seasonal job to another, or competing with unpaid volunteers for an interesting assignment. It means earning a master's degree and making less than a typical first-year teacher. Because the vast majority of environmental education programs are housed in nonprofit organizations and public agencies, with the typical environmental education program boasting a total annual budget of less than $250,000, personnel funds are often limited. Consequently, organizations use a variety of strategies to staff their programs. Some rely on full-time paid personnel, while others fill in the gaps with part-time staff, college interns, or volunteers. Nearly two-thirds of the environmental education programs in the United States utilize volunteers and part-time employees to staff their activities according to a recent survey. Astonishingly, nearly 10 percent rely entirely on volunteers or part-time employees, hiring no full-time paid staff at all. These alternative staffing patterns allow programs to meet their needs economically. Volunteers, in particular, play an important role. It was not unusual for programs to report using as many as one hundred volunteers on a regular basis. However, the reliance on volunteers presents a dilemma to professionals within the environmental education field. Without volunteers, programs would not be staffed, and without programs, the centers would be in an even worse position of being able to hire professionals.

It should be remembered, however, that society does not value, in economic terms, education as a profession. Until these values change, anyone contemplating a career in environmental education must recognize that pay will fall below most other professions. Although it is difficult to generalize in a field that is as diverse as environmental education, starting salaries typically range from $150 per week, plus room and board, to $22,000 per year. Administrators and others at the top of their field may realize annual salaries of $40,000 to $60,000. As a rule of thumb, those who work for school districts or other public agencies will probably make more than those employed by small, nonprofit organizations.

On Becoming an Environmental Educator

For most, becoming an environmental educator was not a conscious decision, but the natural result of a particularly unplanned progression within their lives. Time after time, I meet professionals who recount stories of significant childhood experiences in nature, finding within themselves a growing passion for the environment. These childhood adventures, from camping and fishing with their families to exploring a nearby stream or vacant lot with neighborhood chums, all seem to engender a love of nature and a strong motivation to help protect it. Having been bitten by the bug, they sought out opportunities to spend even more time out in nature. Many spent summer vacations at camp and when they were old enough became camp counselors, experiencing for the first time the satisfaction of sharing one's passion for the outdoors with others. Often through mere happenstance, they found themselves drawn to college courses in natural resources or education. Some were lucky enough to stumble upon an undergraduate major in environmental education or natural history interpretation. But for most, they pieced together the knowledge, experience, and love to become environmental educators.

The job requirements for environmental educators are not standardized. There are no licenses, review boards, or exams as with law, engineering, or even teaching. Because there are few undergraduate degree programs available in environmental education, job announcements typically ask for a bachelor's in environmental education, while also listing a number of other related fields, such as education, natural science, resource management, or environmental studies. Although most entry-level positions require only the bachelor's degree, a master's is becoming indispensable for those wishing to advance in the field and particularly important for those wishing to move into administration. Master's degree programs in environmental education and outdoor/environmental education are a bit more abundant than those at the bachelor's level. But where a specific degree program is not available, colleges and universities often allow students to specialize in environmental education within the context of a master's in science education, natural resources, or environmental studies.

The Future Looks Bright

The statistics may make the prospects of a career in environmental education look bleak—perhaps unreasonably so. The vast majority of environmental education programs do have full-time paid staff, and nearly 80 percent of those surveyed experienced an increase in staff in the last five years. As the field matures, more and more programs offer their employees health benefits, vacation leave, and retirement plans. The limitations of the field that necessitate the use of volunteers, part-time workers, and interns also mean that staff must be hired to recruit, train, and supervise them.

Environmental education is defined in very broad, interdisciplinary terms. Consequently, preparation for environmental education requires some knowledge and expertise drawn from a number of fields. It would not be unusual to include courses in ecology, teaching methods, curriculum development, natural history, environmental issues, environmental policy, and environmental psychology in a course of study. For those interested in particular specializations, additional coursework or training will be necessary. Those wishing to work directly in the classroom will need to follow a program leading to teacher certification. An interest in informal environmental education may direct the student toward courses in journalism or film, while coursework in animal husbandry may be beneficial for those wishing to work in wildlife rehabilitation.

Getting that First Job

Experience is probably as important as education. I recognize that this statement sets up the common *catch 22*: one cannot find a job without experience, but cannot get experience without a job. Fortunately, environmental education as a field provides numerous opportunities for internships (paid and unpaid); summer employment in camps, day care programs, and recreation programs; and volunteer activities. Most environmental educators got their start through one of these vehicles. The pay will be minimal, if you get paid at all, but you will receive some of the best training available. Although employers obviously want to see a strong employment history, internships, volunteer assignments, and summer camp employment are all considered legitimate forms of experience. When it comes down to it, the intangibles are probably the most important: enthusiasm, professionalism, and a dedication to the field.

Typical Days and Nights

There are, of course, no typical jobs within environmental education. As an environmental educator you could find yourself working in a zoo, museum, aquarium, national park, film studio, urban center, school, wildlife preserve, resident camp, university, newspaper office, or any number of other settings. You could spend your time designing exhibits, teaching school children, developing curricula, writing news articles, running teacher training programs, leading family-oriented interpretive walks, or administering a nature center. What is typical is that most environmental educators are generalists. You might teach a group of ten-year-olds about recycling in the morning, put the finishing touches on an article about endangered species for your center's newsletter before lunch, work with a group of teachers developing a curriculum concerning water quality in the afternoon, and lead a night hike and astronomy walk that evening. Most environmental educators wear a number of hats. The variety of responsibilities is exciting and requires a person who enjoys challenges. The work schedule is also varied, often requiring evening and weekend assignments.

The Future of Environmental Education

The field is constantly changing as it reflects the challenges within society. Traditional environmental education programs have expanded over the last several years to meet the needs of senior citizens, latchkey children, and at-risk youth. The simple walk in the woods is now joined by multimedia presentations and various computer applications. The particular slice of environmental education is up to the individual. Careers in administration, program development, and teaching exist in a wide range of settings. And while few expect to become wealthy on their salaries, the riches of working in environmental education are immeasurable. The statistics can't capture the magic of watching a child's face light up at the sight of gleaming dew drops on a spider's web.

The Job Search Process

CHAPTER EIGHTEEN

Getting Started: Self-Evaluation and Career Objectives

Getting a job may be a relatively simple one-step or couple of weeks process or a complex, months-long operation.

Starting, nurturing and developing a career (or even a series of careers) is a lifelong process.

What we'll be talking about in the five chapters that together form our Job Search Process are those basic steps to take, assumptions to make, things to think about if you want a job—especially a first job in some area of the environment. But when these steps—this process—are applied and expanded over a lifetime, most if not all of them are the same procedures, carried out over and over again, that are necessary to develop a successful, lifelong, professional career.

What does all this have to do with putting together a resume, writing a cover letter, heading off for interviews and the other "traditional" steps necessary to get a job? Whether your college graduation is just around the corner or a far distant memory, you will continuously need to focus, evaluate and re-evaluate your response to the ever-changing challenge of your future: Just what do you want to do with the rest of your life? Whether you like it or not, you're all looking for that "entry-level opportunity."

You're already one or two steps ahead of the competition—you're sure you want to pursue a career that helps the environment. By heeding the advice of the many professionals who have written chapters for this *Career Directory*—and utilizing the extensive entry-level job, organization, and career resource listings we've included—you're well on your way to fulfilling that dream. But there are some key decisions and time-consuming preparations to make if you want to transform that hopeful dream into a real, live job.

The actual process of finding the right company, right career path and, most importantly, the right first job, begins long before you start mailing out resumes to potential employers. The choices and decisions you make now are not irrevocable, but this first job will have a definite impact on the career options you leave yourself. To help you make some of the right decisions and choices along the way (and avoid some of the most notable traps and pitfalls), the following chapters will lead you through a series of organized steps. If the entire job search process we are recommending here is properly executed, it will undoubtedly help you land exactly the job you want.

If you're currently in high school and hope, after college, to land an environmental career, then attending the right college, choosing the right major, and getting the summer work experience many companies look for are all important steps. Read the section of this *Career Directory* that covers the particular field and/or job specialty in which you're interested—many of the contributors have recommended colleges or graduate programs they favor.

If you're hoping to jump right into any of these fields without a college degree or other professional training, our best and only advice is—don't do it. As you'll soon see in the detailed information included in the **Job Opportunities Databank,** there are not that many job openings for students without a college degree or training. Those that do exist are generally clerical and will only rarely lead to promising careers.

The Concept of a Job Search Process

As we've explained, a job search is not a series of random events. Rather, it is a series of connected events that together form the job search process. It is important to know the eight steps that go into that process:

1. Evaluating yourself

Know thyself. What skills and abilities can you offer a prospective employer? What do you enjoy doing? What are your strengths and weaknesses? What do you want to do?

2. Establishing your career objectives

Where do you want to be next year, three years, five years from now? What do you ultimately want to accomplish in your career and your life?

3. Creating a company target list

How to prepare a "Hit List" of potential employers—researching them, matching their needs with your skills and starting your job search assault. Preparing company information sheets and evaluating your chances.

4. Networking for success

Learning how to utilize every contact, every friend, every relative, and anyone else you can think of to break down the barriers facing any would-be environmental professional. How to organize your home office to keep track of your communications and stay on top of your job campaign.

5. Preparing your resume

How to encapsulate years of school and little actual work experience into a professional, selling resume. Learning when and how to use it.

6. Preparing cover letters

The many ordinary and the all-too-few extraordinary cover letters, the kind that land interviews and jobs.

7. Interviewing

How to make the interview process work for you—from the first "hello" to the first day on the job.

8. Following up

Often overlooked, it's perhaps the most important part of the job search process.

We won't try to kid you—it is a lot of work. To do it right, you have to get started early, probably quite a bit earlier than you'd planned. Frankly, we recommend beginning this process one full year prior to the day you plan to start work.

So if you're in college, the end of your junior year is the right time to begin your research and preparations. That should give you enough time during summer vacation to set up your files and begin your library research.

Whether you're in college or graduate school, one item may need to be planned even earlier—allowing enough free time in your schedule of classes for interview preparations and appointments. Waiting until your senior year to "make some time" is already too late. Searching for a full-time job is itself a full-time job! Though you're naturally restricted by your schedule, it's not difficult to plan ahead and prepare for your upcoming job search. Try to leave at least a couple of free mornings or afternoons a week. A day or even two without classes is even better.

Otherwise, you'll find yourself, crazed and distracted, trying to prepare for an interview in the ten-minute period between classes. Not the best way to make a first impression and certainly not the way you want to approach an important meeting.

The Self-Evaluation Process

Learning about who you are, what you want to be, what you can be, are critical first steps in the job search process and, unfortunately, the ones most often ignored by job seekers everywhere, especially students eager to leave the ivy behind and plunge into the "real world." But avoiding this crucial self-evaluation can hinder your progress and even damage some decent prospects.

Why? Because in order to land a job with a company at which you'll actually be happy, you need to be able to identify those firms and/or job descriptions that best match your own skills, likes, and strengths. The more you know about yourself, the more you'll bring to this process and the more accurate the "match-ups." You'll be able to structure your presentation (resume, cover letter, interviews, follow up) to stress your most marketable skills and talents (and, dare we say it, conveniently avoid your weaknesses?). Later, you'll be able to evaluate potential employers and job offers on the basis of your own needs and desires. This spells the difference between waking up in the morning ready to enthusiastically tackle a new day of challenges and shutting off the alarm in the hopes the day (and your job) will just disappear.

Creating Your Self-Evaluation Form

If your self-evaluation is to have any meaning, you must first be honest with yourself. This self-evaluation form should help you achieve that goal by providing a structured environment to answer these tough questions.

Take a sheet of lined notebook paper. Set up eight columns across the top—Strengths, Weaknesses, Skills, Hobbies, Courses, Experience, Likes, Dislikes.

Now, fill in each of these columns according to these guidelines:

Strengths: Describe personality traits you consider your strengths (and try to look at them as an employer would)—e.g., persistence, organization, ambition, intelligence, logic, assertiveness, aggression, leadership, etc.

Weaknesses: The traits you consider glaring weaknesses—e.g., impatience, conceit, etc. Remember: Look at these as a potential employer would. Don't assume that the personal traits you consider weaknesses will necessarily be considered negatives in the business world. You may be "easily bored," a trait that led to lousy grades early on because teachers couldn't keep you interested in the subjects they were teaching. Well, many entrepreneurs need ever-changing challenges. Strength or weakness?

Skills: Any skill you have, whether you think it's marketable or not. Everything from basic business skills—like typing and word processing—to computer or teaching experience and foreign language literacy. Don't forget possibly obscure but marketable skills like "good telephone voice."

Hobbies: The things you enjoy doing that, more than likely, have no overt connection to career objectives. These should be distinct from the skills listed above, and may include activities such as reading, games, travel, sports, and the like. While these may not be marketable in any general sense, they may well be useful in specific circumstances.

Courses: All the general subject areas (history, literature, etc.) and/or specific courses you've taken which may be marketable, you really enjoyed, or both.

Experience: Just the specific functions you performed at any part-time (school year) or full-time (summer) jobs. Entries may include "General Office" (typing, filing, answering phones, etc.), "Office Assistant," "Retail Clerk" etc.

Likes: List all your "likes," those important considerations that you haven't listed anywhere else yet. These might include the types of people you like to be with, the kind of environment you prefer (city, country, large places, small places, quiet, loud, fast-paced, slow-paced) and anything else which hasn't shown up somewhere on this form. Try to think of "likes" that you have that are related to the job you are applying for. For example, if you're applying for a job at a major corporation, mention that you enjoy reading the Wall St. Journal. However, try not to include entries which refer to specific jobs or companies. We'll list those on another form.

Dislikes: All the people, places and things you can easily live without.

Now assess the "marketability" of each item you've listed. (In other words, are some of your likes, skills or courses easier to match to an environmental job description, or do they have little to do with a specific job or company?) Mark highly marketable skills with an "H." Use "M" to characterize those skills which may be marketable in a particular set of circumstances, "L" for those with minimal potential application to any job.

Referring back to the same list, decide if you'd enjoy using your marketable skills or talents as part of your everyday job—"Y" for yes, "N" for no. You may type 80 words a minute but truly despise typing or worry that stressing it too much will land you on the permanent clerical staff. If so, mark typing with an "N." (Keep one thing in mind—just because you dislike typing shouldn't mean you absolutely won't accept a job that requires it. Almost every professional job today requires computer-based work that make typing a plus.)

Now, go over the entire form carefully and look for inconsistencies.

To help you with your own form, there's a sample one on the following page that a job-hunter might have completed.

The Value of a Second Opinion

There is a familiar misconception about the self-evaluation process that gets in the way of many new job applicants—the belief that it is a process which must be accomplished in isolation. Nothing could be further from the truth. Just because the family doctor tells you you need an operation doesn't mean you run right off to the hospital. Prudence dictates that you check out the opinion with another physician. Getting such a "second opinion"—someone else's, not just your own—is a valuable practice throughout the job search process, as well.

So after you've completed the various exercises in this chapter, review them with a friend, relative, or parent—just be sure it's someone who knows you well and cares about you. These second opinions may reveal some aspects of your self-description on which you and the rest of the world differ. If so, discuss them, learn from them and, if necessary, change some conclusions. Should everyone concur with your self-evaluation, you will be reassured that your choices are on target.

Establishing Your Career Objective(s)

For better or worse, you now know something more of who and what you are. But we've yet to establish and evaluate another important area—your overall needs, desires and goals. Where are you going? What do you want to accomplish?

If you're getting ready to graduate from college or graduate school, the next five years are the most critical period of your whole career. You need to make the initial transition from college to the workplace, establish yourself in a new and completely unfamiliar company environment, and begin to build the professional credentials necessary to achieve your career goals.

If that strikes you as a pretty tall order, well, it is. Unless you've narrowly prepared yourself for a specific profession, you're probably most ill-prepared for any

	Strength	Weakness	Skill	Hobby	Course	Experience	Like	Dislike
Marketable?								
Enjoy?								
Marketable?								
Enjoy?								
Marketable?								
Enjoy?								

real job. Instead, you've (hopefully) learned some basic principles—research and analytical skills that are necessary for success at almost any level—and, more or less, how to think.

It's tough to face, but face it you must: No matter what your college, major, or degree, all you represent right now is potential. How you package that potential and what you eventually make of it is completely up to you. It's an unfortunate fact that many companies will take a professional with barely a year or two experience over any newcomer, no matter how promising. Smaller firms, especially, can rarely afford to hire someone who can't begin contributing immediately.

So you have to be prepared to take your comparatively modest skills and experience and package them in a way that will get you interviewed and hired. Quite a challenge.

There are a number of different ways to approach such a task. If you find yourself confused or unable to list such goals, you might want to check a few books in your local library that have more time to spend on the topic of "goal-oriented planning."

But Is the Environmental Industry Right for You?

Presuming you now have a much better idea of yourself and where you'd like to be, let's make sure some of your basic assumptions are right. We presume you purchased this *Career Directory* because you're considering a career in some area of the environment. Are you sure? Do you know enough about the industry as a whole and the particular part you're heading for to decide whether it's right for you? Probably not. So start your research now—learn as much about your potential career field as you now know about yourself.

Start with the essays in the Advice from the Pro's section—these will give you an excellent overview of the environmental industry, some very specialized (and growing) areas, and some things to keep in mind as you start on your career search. They will also give you a relatively simplified, though very necessary, understanding of just what people who work in all these areas of environment actually do.

Other sources you should consider consulting to learn more about this business are listed in the Career Resources section of this book.

In that section, we've listed trade associations and publications associated with environmental professions (together with many other resources that will help your job search. (Consult the front of this directory for a complete description of the Career Resource section.) Where possible in the association entries, we've included details on educational information they make available, but you should certainly consider writing each of the pertinent associations, letting them know you're interested in a career in their area of specialization and would appreciate whatever help and advice they're willing to impart. You'll find many sponsor seminars and conferences throughout the country, some of which you may be able to attend.

The trade publications are dedicated to the highly specific interests of environmental professionals. These magazines are generally not available at newsstands, but you may be able to obtain back issues at your local library (most major libraries have extensive collections of such journals) or by writing to the magazines' circulation/subscription departments. We've also included regional and local magazines.

You may also try writing to the publishers and/or editors of these publications. State in your cover letter what area of the environment you're considering and ask them for whatever help and advice they can offer. But be specific. These are busy professionals and they do not have the time or the inclination to simply "tell me everything you can about working with nature."

If you can afford it now, we strongly suggest subscribing to whichever trade magazines are applicable to the specialty you're considering. If you can't subscribe to all of them, make it a point to regularly read the copies that arrive at your local public or college library.

These publications may well provide the most imaginative and far-reaching information for your job search. Even a quick perusal of an issue or two will give you an excellent feel for the industry. After reading only a few articles, you'll already get a handle on what's happening in the field and some of the industry's peculiar and particular jargon. Later, more detailed study will aid you in your search for a specific job.

Authors of the articles themselves may well turn out to be important resources. If an article is directly related to your chosen specialty, why not call the author and ask some questions? You'd be amazed how willing many of these professionals will be to talk to you and answer your questions, and the worst they can do is say no. (But *do* use common sense—authors will not *always* respond graciously to your invitation to "chat about the business." And don't be *too* aggressive here.)

You'll find such research to be a double-edged sword. In addition to helping you get a handle on whether the area you've chosen is really right for you, you'll slowly learn enough about particular specialties, companies, the industry, etc., to actually sound like you know what you're talking about when you hit the pavement looking for your first job. And nothing is better than sounding like a pro—except being one.

The Environment Is It. Now What?

After all this research, we're going to assume you've reached that final decision—you really do want a career working to benefit the environment. It is with this vague certainty that all too many of you will race off, hunting for any firm willing to give you a job. You'll manage to get interviews at a couple and, smiling brightly, tell everyone you meet, "I want a career in the environment." The interviewers, unfortunately, will all ask the same awkward question—"What *exactly* do you want to do at our company?"—and that will be the end of that.

It is simply not enough to narrow your job search to a specific industry. And so far, that's all you've done. You must now establish a specific career objective—the job you want to start, the career you want to pursue. Just knowing that you "want to get into the environment" doesn't mean anything to anybody. If that's all you can tell an interviewer, it demonstrates a lack of research into the industry itself and your failure to think ahead.

Interviewers will *not* welcome you with open arms if you're still vague about your career goals. If you've managed to get an "informational interview" with an executive whose company currently has no job openings, what is he or she supposed to do with your resume after you leave? Who should he or she send it to for future consideration? Since *you* don't seem to know exactly what you want to do, how's he or she going to figure it out? Worse, that person will probably resent your asking him or her to function as your personal career counselor.

Remember, the more specific your career objective, the better your chances of finding a job. It's that simple and that important. Naturally, before you declare your objective to the world, check once again to make sure your specific job target matches the skills and interests you defined in your self-evaluation. Eventually, you may want to state such an objective on your resume, and "To obtain an entry-level position as a microbiologist at a major chemical company," is quite a bit better than "I want a career in the environment." Do not consider this step final until you can summarize your job/career objective in a single, short, accurate sentence.

CHAPTER NINETEEN

Targeting Prospective Employers and Networking For Success

As you move along the job search path, one fact will quickly become crystal clear—it is primarily a process of **elimination**: your task is to consider and research as many options as possible, then—for good reasons—**eliminate** as many as possible, attempting to continually narrow your focus.

Your Ideal Company Profile

Let's establish some criteria to evaluate potential employers. This will enable you to identify your target companies, the places you'd really like to work. (This process, as we've pointed out, is not specific to any industry or field; the same steps, with perhaps some research resource variations, are applicable to any job, any company, any industry.)

Take a sheet of blank paper and divide it into three vertical columns. Title it "Target Company—Ideal Profile." Call the lefthand column "Musts," the middle column "Preferences," and the righthand column "Nevers."

We've listed a series of questions below. After considering each question, decide whether a particular criteria *must* be met, whether you would simply *prefer* it or *never* would consider it at all. If there are other criteria you consider important, feel free to add them to the list below and mark them accordingly on your Profile.

1. What are your geographical preferences? (Possible answers: U.S., Canada, International, Anywhere). If you only want to work in the U.S., then "Work in United States" would be the entry in the "Must" column. "Work in Canada or Foreign Country" might be the first entry in your "Never" column. There would be no applicable entry for this question in the "Preference" column. If, however, you will consider working in two of the three, then your "Must" column entry might read "Work in U.S. or Canada," your "Preference"

entry—if you preferred one over the other—could read "Work in U.S.," and the "Never" column, "Work Overseas."

2. If you prefer to work in the U.S. or Canada, what area, state(s) or province(s)? If overseas, what area or countries?
3. Do you prefer a large city, small city, town, or somewhere as far away from civilization as possible?
4. In regard to question three, any specific preferences?
5. Do you prefer a warm or cold climate?
6. Do you prefer a large or small company? Define your terms (by sales, income, employees, offices, etc.).
7. Do you mind relocating right now? Do you want to work for a firm with a reputation for *frequently* relocating top people?
8. Do you mind travelling frequently? What percent do you consider reasonable? (Make sure this matches the normal requirements of the job specialization you're considering.)
9. What salary would you *like* to receive (put in the "Preference" column)? What's the *lowest* salary you'll accept (in the "Must" column)?
10. Are there any benefits (such as an expense account, medical and/or dental insurance, company car, etc.) you must or would like to have?
11. Are you planning to attend graduate school at some point in the future and, if so, is a tuition reimbursement plan important to you?
12. Do you feel that a formal training program is necessary?
13. If applicable, what kinds of specific accounts would you prefer to work with? What specific products?

It's important to keep revising this new form, just as you should continue to update your Self-Evaluation Form. After all, it contains the criteria by which you will judge every potential employer. Armed with a complete list of such criteria, you're now ready to find all the companies that match them.

Targeting Individual Companies

To begin creating your initial list of targeted companies, start with the **Job Opportunities Databank** in this directory. We've listed many major chemical, paper, metal and mining, and home care product companies that offer the most potential for those seeking an environmental career; most of these companies were contacted by telephone for this edition. These listings provide a plethora of data concerning the companies' overall operations, hiring practices, and other important information on entry-level job opportunities. This latter information includes key contacts (names), the average number of entry-level people they hire each year, along with complete job descriptions and requirements.

One word of advice. You'll notice that some of the companies list "0" under average entry-level hiring. This is more a reflection of the current economic times than a long-range projection. These companies have hired in the past, and they will again in the future. We have listed these companies for three reasons: 1) to present you with the overall view of prospective employers; 2) because even companies that don't plan to do any hiring will experience unexpected job openings; and 3) things change, so as soon as the economy begins to pick up, expect entry-level hiring to increase again.

We have attempted to include information on those major firms that represent many of the entry-level jobs out there. But there are, of course, many other companies of all sizes and shapes that you may also wish to research. In the Career Resources section, we have listed other reference tools you can use to obtain more information on the companies we've listed, as well as those we haven't.

The Other Side of the Iceberg

You are now better prepared to choose those companies that meet your own list of criteria. But a word of caution about these now-"obvious" requirements—they are not the only ones you need to take into consideration. And you probably won't be able to find all or many of the answers to this second set of questions in any reference book—they are known, however, by those persons already at work in the industry. Here is the list you will want to follow:

Promotion

If you are aggressive about your career plans, you'll want to know if you have a shot at the top. Look for companies that traditionally promote from within.

Ask the Person Who Owns One

Some years ago, this advice was used as the theme for a highly successful automobile advertising campaign. The prospective car buyer was encouraged to find out about the product by asking the (supposedly) most trustworthy judge of all—someone who was already an owner.

You can use the same approach in your job search. You all have relatives or friends already out in the workplace—these are your best sources of information about those industries. Cast your net in as wide a circle as possible. Contact these valuable resources. You'll be amazed at how readily they will answer your questions. I suggest you check the criteria list at the beginning of this chapter to formulate your own list of pertinent questions. Ideally and minimally you will want to learn: how the industry is doing, what its long-term prospects are, the kinds of personalities they favor (aggressive, low key), rate of employee turnover, and the availability of training.

Training

Look for companies in which your early tenure will actually be a period of on-the-job training, hopefully ones in which training remains part of the long-term process. As new techniques and technologies enter the workplace, you must make sure you are updated on these skills. Most importantly, look for training that is craft- or function-oriented—these are the so-called **transferable skills**, ones you can easily bring along with you from job-to-job, company-to-company, sometimes industry-to-industry.

Salary

Some industries are generally high paying, some not. But even an industry with a tradition of paying abnormally low salaries may have particular companies or job functions (like sales) within companies that command high remuneration. But it's important you know what the industry standard is.

Benefits

Look for companies in which health insurance, vacation pay, retirement plans, 401K accounts, stock purchase opportunities, and other important employee benefits are extensive—and company paid. If you have to pay for basic benefits like medical coverage yourself, you'll be surprised at how expensive they are. An exceptional benefit package may even lead you to accept a lower-than-usual salary.

Unions

Make sure you know about the union situation in each industry you research. Periodic, union-mandated salary increases are one benefit nonunion workers may find hard to match.

Making Friends and Influencing People

Networking is a term you have probably heard; it is definitely a key aspect of any successful job search and a process you must master.

Informational interviews and **job interviews** are the two primary outgrowths of successful networking.

Referrals, an aspect of the networking process, entail using someone else's name, credentials and recommendation to set up a receptive environment when seeking a job interview.

All of these terms have one thing in common: Each depends on the actions of other people to put them in motion. Don't let this idea of "dependency" slow you down, however. A job search *must* be a very pro-active process—*you* have to initiate the action. When networking, this means contacting as many people as you can. The more you contact, the better the chances of getting one of those people you are "depending" on to take action and help you out.

So what *is* networking? How do you build your own network? And why do you need one in the first place? The balance of this chapter answers all of those questions and more.

Get your telephone ready. It's time to make some friends.

Not the World's Oldest Profession, But...

Networking is the process of creating your own group of relatives, friends, and acquaintances who can feed you the information you need to find a job—identifying where the jobs are and giving you the personal introductions and background data necessary to pursue them.

If the job market were so well-organized that details on all employment opportunities were immediately available to all applicants, there would be no need for such a process. Rest assured the job market is *not* such a smooth-running machine—most applicants are left very much to their own devices. Build and use your own network wisely and you'll be amazed at the amount of useful job intelligence you will turn up.

While the term networking didn't gain prominence until the 1970s, it is by no means a new phenomenon. A selection process that connects people of similar skills, backgrounds, and/or attitudes—in other words, networking—has been in existence in a variety of forms for centuries. Attend any Ivy League school and you're automatically part of its very special centuries-old network.

And it works. Remember your own reaction when you were asked to recommend someone for a job, club or school office? You certainly didn't want to look foolish, so you gave it some thought and tried to recommend the best-qualified person that you thought would "fit in" with the rest of the group. It's a built-in screening process.

Creating the Ideal Network

As in most endeavors, there's a wrong way and a right way to network. The following tips will help you construct your own wide- ranging, information-gathering, interview-generating group—*your* network.

Diversify

Unlike the Harvard or Princeton network—confined to former graduates of each school—your network should be as diversified and wide-ranging as possible. You never know who might be in a position to help, so don't limit your group of friends. The more diverse they are, the greater the variety of information they may supply you with.

Don't Forget...

...to include everyone you know in your initial networking list: friends, relatives, social acquaintances, classmates, college alumni, professors, teachers, your dentist, doctor, family lawyer, insurance agent, banker, travel agent, elected officials in your community, ministers, fellow church members, local tradesmen, and local business or social club officers. And everybody they know!

Be Specific

Make a list of the kinds of assistance you will require from those in your network, then make specific requests of each. Do they know of jobs at their company? Can they introduce you to the proper executives? Have they heard something about or know someone at the company you're planning to interview with next week?

The more organized you are, the easier it will be to target the information you need and figure out who might have it. Begin to keep a business card file or case so you can keep track of all your contacts. A small plastic case for file cards that is available at any discount store will do nicely. One system you can use is to staple the card to a 3 x 5 index card. On the card, write down any information about that contact that you might need later—when you talked to them, job leads they provided, specific job search advice, etc. You will then have all the information you need about each company or contact in one easily accessible location.

Learn the Difference...

...between an **informational** interview and a **job** interview. The former requires you to cast yourself in the role of information gatherer; *you* are the interviewer and knowledge is your goal—about an industry, company, job function, key executive, etc. Such a meeting with someone already doing what you soon hope to be doing is by far the best way to find out everything you need to know—before you walk through the door and sit down for a formal job interview, at which time your purpose is more sharply defined: to get the job you're interviewing for.

If you learn of a specific job opening during an informational interview, you are in a position to find out details about the job, identify the interviewer and, possibly, even learn some things about him or her. In addition, presuming you get your contact's permission, you may be able to use his or her name as a referral. Calling up the interviewer and saying, "Joan Smith in your human resources department suggested I contact you regarding openings for assistant editors," is far superior to "Hello. Do you have any job openings at your magazine?"

(In such a case, be careful about referring to a specific job opening, even if your contact told you about it. It may not be something you're supposed to know about. By presenting your query as an open-ended question, you give your prospective employer the option of exploring your background without further commitment. If there is a job there and you're qualified for it, you'll find out soon enough.)

Don't Waste a Contact

Not everyone you call on your highly-diversified networking list will know about a job opening. It would be surprising if each one did. But what about *their* friends and colleagues? It's amazing how everyone knows someone who knows someone. Ask—you'll find that someone.

Value Your Contacts

If someone has provided you with helpful information or an introduction to a friend or colleague, keep him or her informed about how it all turns out. A referral that's panned out should be reported to the person who opened the door for you in the first place. Such courtesy will be appreciated—and may lead to more contacts. If someone has nothing to offer today, a call back in the future is still appropriate and may pay off.

The lesson is clear: Keep your options open, your contact list alive. Detailed records of your network—whom you spoke with, when, what transpired, etc.—will help you keep track of your overall progress and organize what can be a complicated and involved process.

Informational Interviews

So now you've done your homework, built your network, and begun using your contacts. It's time to go on your first informational interview.

A Typical Interview

You were, of course, smart enough to include John Fredericks, the bank officer who handled your dad's mortgage, on your original contact list. He knew you as a bright and conscientious college senior; in fact, your perfect three-year repayment record on the loan you took out to buy that '67 Plymouth impressed him. When you called him, he was happy to refer you to his friend, Carol Jones, a human resources manager at XYZ Pollution Control, Inc. Armed with permission to use Fredericks' name and recommendation, you wrote a letter to Carol Jones, the gist of which went something like this:

> *I am writing at the suggestion of Mr. John Fredericks at Fidelity National Bank. He knows of my interest in a microbiology career and, given your position at XYZ Pollution Control, Inc., thought you might be able to help me gain a better understanding of this specialized field and the career opportunities it presents.*
>
> *While I am majoring in microbiology, I know I need to speak with professionals such as yourself to learn how to apply my studies to a work environment.*
>
> *If you could spare a half hour to meet with me, I'm certain I would be able to get enough information about this specialty to give me the direction I need.*
>
> *I'll call your office next week in the hope that we can schedule a meeting.*

Send a copy of this letter to Mr. Fredericks at the bank—it will refresh his memory should Ms. Jones call to inquire about you. Next step: the follow-up phone call. After you get Ms. Jones' secretary on the line, it will, with luck, go something like this:

> *"Hello, I'm Paul Smith. I'm calling in reference to a letter I wrote to Ms. Jones requesting an appointment."*
>
> *"Oh, yes. You're the young man interested in microbiology. Ms. Jones can see you on June 23rd. Will 10 A.M. be satisfactory?"*
>
> *"That's fine. I'll be there."*

Well, the appointed day arrives. Well-scrubbed and dressed in your best (and most conservative) suit, you are ushered into Ms. Jones' office. She offers you coffee (you decline) and says that it is okay to light up if you wish to smoke (you decline). The conversation might go something like this:

You: "Thank you for seeing me, Ms. Jones. I know you are busy and appreciate your taking the time to talk with me."

Jones: "Well it's my pleasure since you come so highly recommended. I'm always pleased to meet someone interested in my field."

You: "As I stated in my letter, my interest in microbiology is very real, but I'm having trouble seeing how all of my studies will adapt to the work environment. I think I'll be much better prepared to evaluate future job offers if I can learn more about your experiences. May I ask you a few questions about XYZ?"

Jones: "Fire away, Paul".

Ms. Jones relaxes. She realizes this is a knowledge hunt you are on, not a thinly-veiled job interview. Your approach has kept her off the spot—she doesn't have to be concerned with making a hiring decision. You've already gotten high marks for not putting her on the defensive.

You: "I have a few specific questions I'd like to ask. First, at a company such as yours, where does an entry-level person start?"

Jones: "In this company, you would be assigned to an experienced therapist to work as that person's assistant for the first month of your employment. This gives you a chance to see the way we work and to become comfortable with our facilities. After that, if you had progressed well, you would receive your own projects to work on."

You: "Where and how fast does someone progress after that?"

Jones: "Obviously, that depends on the person, but given the proper aptitude and ability, that person would simply get more responsibilities to handle. How well you do all along the way will determine how far and how fast you progress."

You: "What is the work environment like—is it pretty hectic?"

Jones: "We try to keep the work load at an even keel. The comfort of our workers is of prime importance to us. Excessive turnover is costly, you know. But this is an exciting business, and things change sometimes minute-to-minute. It's not a profession for the faint-hearted!"

You: "If I may shift to another area, I'd be interested in your opinion about environmental careers in general and what you see as the most likely areas of opportunity in the foreseeable future. Do you think this is a growth career area?"

Jones: "Well, judging by the hiring record of our company, I think you'll find it's an area worth making a commitment to. At the entry level, we've hired a number of new people in the past three or four years. There always seems to be opportunities, though it's gotten far more competitive."

You: "Do you think someone with my qualifications and background could get started in occupational therapy? Perhaps a look at my resume would be helpful to you." *(Give it to Ms. Jones.)*

Jones: "Your course work looks appropriate. I especially like the internships you've held every summer. I think you have a real chance to break into this field. I don't think we're hiring right now, but I know a couple of firms that are looking for bright young people with qualifications like yours. Let me give you a couple of phone numbers." *(Write down names and phone numbers.)*

You: "You have been very generous with your time, but I can see from those flashing buttons on your phone that you have other things to do. Thank you again for taking the time to talk with me."

Jones: "You're welcome."

After the Interview

The next step should be obvious: **Two** thank-you letters are required, one to Ms. Jones, the second to Mr. Fredericks. Get them both out immediately. (And see the chapter on writing letters if you need help writing them.)

Keeping Track of the Interview Trail

Let's talk about record keeping again. If your networking works the way it's supposed to, this was only the first of many such interviews. Experts have estimated that the average person could develop a contact list of 250 people. Even if we limit your initial list to only 100, if each of them gave you one referral, your list would suddenly have 200 names. Presuming that it will not be necessary or helpful to see all of them, it's certainly possible that such a list could lead to 100 informational and/or job interviews! Unless you keep accurate records, by the time you're on No. 50, you won't even remember the first dozen!

So get the results of each interview down on paper. Use whatever format with which you're comfortable. You should create some kind of file, folder, or note card that is an "Interview Recap Record." If you have access to a personal computer, take advantage of it. It will be much easier to keep your information stored in one place and well-organized. Your record should be set up and contain something like the following:

Name: XYZ Pollution Control, Inc.

Address: 333 E. 54th St., Rochester, NY 10000

Phone: (212) 555-4000

Contact: Carol Jones

Type of Business: Pollution control

Referral Contact: Mr. Fredericks, Fidelity National Bank

Date: June 23, 1993

At this point, you should add a one- or two-paragraph summary of what you found out at the meeting. Since these comments are for your eyes only, you should be both objective and subjective. State the facts—what you found out in response to your specific questions—but include your impressions—your estimate of the opportunities for further discussions, your chances for future consideration for employment.

"I Was Just Calling To..."

Find any logical opportunity to stay in touch with Ms. Jones. You may, for example, let her know when you graduate and tell her your grade point average, carbon her in on any letters you write to Mr. Fredericks, even send a congratulatory note if her company's year-end financial results are positive or if you read something in the local paper about her department. This type of follow up has the all-important effect of keeping you and your name in the forefront of others' minds. Out of sight *is* out of mind. No matter how talented you may be or how good an impression you made, you'll have to work hard to "stay visible."

There Are Rules, Just Like Any Game

It should already be obvious that the networking process is not only effective, but also quite deliberate in its objectives. There are two specific groups of people you must attempt to target: those who can give you information about an industry or career area and those who are potential employers. The line between these groups may often blur. Don't be concerned—you'll soon learn when (and how) to shift the focus from interviewer to interviewee.

To simplify this process, follow a single rule: Show interest in the field or job area under discussion, but wait to be asked about actually working for that company. During your informational interviews, you will be surprised at the number of times the person you're interviewing turns to you and asks, "Would you be interested in...?" Consider carefully what's being asked and, if you *would* be interested in the position under discussion, make your feelings known.

Why Should You Network?

- To unearth current information about the industry, company and pertinent job functions. Remember: Your knowledge and understanding of broad industry trends, financial health, hiring opportunities, and the competitive picture are key.
- To investigate each company's hiring policies—who makes the decisions, who the key players are (personnel, staff managers), whether there's a hiring season, whether they prefer applicants going direct or through recruiters, etc.
- To sell yourself—discuss your interests and research activities—and leave your calling card, your resume.
- To seek out advice on refining your job search process.
- To obtain the names of other persons (referrals) who can give you additional information on where the jobs are and what the market conditions are like.
- To develop a list of follow-up activities that will keep you visible to key contacts.

If the Process Scares You

Some of you will undoubtedly be hesitant about, even fear, the networking process. It is not an unusual response—it is very human to want to accomplish things "on your own," without anyone's help. Understandable and commendable as such independence might seem, it is, in reality, an impediment if it limits your involvement in this important process. Networking has such universal application because **there is no other effective way to bridge the gap between job applicant and job.** Employers are grateful for its existence. You should be, too.

Whether you are a first-time applicant or reentering the work force now that the children are grown, the networking process will more than likely be your point of entry. Sending out mass mailings of your resume and answering the help-wanted ads may well be less personal (and, therefore, "easier") approaches, but they will also be far less effective. The natural selection process of the networking phenomenon is your assurance that water does indeed seek its own level—you will be matched up with companies and job opportunities in which there is a mutual fit.

Six Good Reasons to Network

Many people fear the networking process because they think they are "bothering" others with their own selfish demands. Nonsense! There are good reasons—six of them, at least—why the people on your networking list will be happy to help you:

1. **Some day you will get to return the favor.** An ace insurance salesman built a successful business by offering low-cost coverage to first-year medical students. Ten years later, these now-successful practitioners remembered the

company (and person) that helped them when they were just getting started. He gets new referrals every day.

2. **They, too, are seeking information.** An employer who has been out of school for several years might be interested in what the latest developments in the classroom are. He or she may be hoping to learn as much from you as you are from them, so be forthcoming in offering information. This desire for new information may be the reason he or she agreed to see you in the first place.
3. **Internal politics.** Some people will see you simply to make themselves appear powerful, implying to others in their organization that they have the authority to hire (they may or may not), an envied prerogative.
4. **They're "saving for a rainy day".** Executives know that it never hurts to look and that maintaining a backlog of qualified candidates is a big asset when the floodgates open and supervisors are forced to hire quickly.
5. **They're just plain nice.** Some people will see you simply because they feel it's the decent thing to do or because they just can't say "no."
6. **They are looking themselves.** Some people will see you because they are anxious to do a friend (whoever referred you) a favor. Or because they have another friend seeking new talent, in which case you represent a referral they can make (part of their own continuing network process). You see, networking never does stop—it helps them and it helps you.

Before you proceed to the next chapter, begin making your contact list. You may wish to keep a separate sheet of paper or note card on each person (especially the dozen or so you think are most important), even a separate telephone list to make your communications easier and more efficient. However you set up your list, be sure to keep it up to date—it won't be long before you'll be calling each and every name on the list.

C H A P T E R   T W E N T Y

Preparing Your Resume

Your resume is a one-page summary of you—your education, skills, employment experience and career objective(s). It is not a biography, but a "quick and dirty" way to identify and describe you to potential employers. Most importantly, its real purpose is to sell you to the company you want to work for. It must set you apart from all the other applicants (those competitors) out there.

So, as you sit down to formulate your resume, remember you're trying to present the pertinent information in a format and manner that will convince an executive to grant you an interview, the prelude to any job offer. All resumes must follow two basic rules—excellent visual presentation and honesty—but it's important to realize that different career markets require different resumes. The resume you are compiling for your career in environmental work is different than one you would prepare for a finance career. As more and more resume "training" services become available, employers are becoming increasingly choosy about the resumes they receive. They expect to view a professional presentation, one that sets a candidate apart from the crowd. Your resume has to be perfect and it has to be specialized—clearly demonstrating the relationship between your qualifications and the job you are applying for.

An Overview of Resume Preparation

- **Know what you're doing**—your resume is a personal billboard of accomplishments. It must communicate your worth to a prospective employer in specific terms.
- **Your language should be action-oriented,** full of "doing"-type words. And less is better than more—be concise and direct. Don't worry about using complete sentences.

- **Be persuasive.** In those sections that allow you the freedom to do so, don't hesitate to communicate your worth in the strongest language. This does not mean a numbing list of self-congratulatory superlatives; it does mean truthful claims about your abilities and the evidence (educational, experiential) that supports them.
- **Don't be cheap or gaudy.** Don't hesitate to spend the few extra dollars necessary to present a professional- looking resume. Do avoid outlandish (and generally ineffective) gimmicks like oversized or brightly-colored paper.
- **Find an editor.** Every good writer needs one, and you are writing your resume. At the very least, it will offer you a second set of eyes proofreading for embarrassing typos. But if you are fortunate enough to have a professional in the field—a recruiter or personnel executive—critique a draft, grab the opportunity and be immensely grateful.
- **If you're the next Michelangelo,** so multitalented that you can easily qualify for jobs in different career areas, don't hesitate to prepare two or more completely different resumes. This will enable you to change the emphasis on your education and skills according to the specific career objective on each resume, a necessary alteration that will correctly target each one.
- **Choose the proper format.** There are only three we recommend—chronological, functional, and targeted format—and it's important you use the one that's right for you.

Considerations in the Electronic Age

Like most other areas of everyday life, computers have left their mark in the resume business. There are the obvious changes—the increased number of personal computers has made it easier to produce a professional-looking resume at home—and the not so obvious changes, such as the development of resume databases.

There are two kinds of resume databases: 1) An internal file maintained by a large corporation to keep track of the flood of resumes it gets each day (*U.S. News and World Report* stated that Fortune 50 companies receive more than 1,000 unsolicited resumes a day and that four out of every five are thrown away after a quick review). 2) Commercial databases that solicit resumes from job-seekers around the United States and make them available to corporations, who pay a fee to search the database.

Internal Databases Mean Some of the Old Rules Don't Apply

The internal databases maintained by large companies are changing some of the time-honored traditions of resume preparation. In the past, it was acceptable, even desirable, to use italic type and other eye-catching formats to make a resume more visually appealing. Not so today. Most of the companies that have a database enter resumes into it by using an optical scanner that reads the resume character by character and automatically enters it into the database. While these scanners are becoming more and more sophisticated, there are still significant limits as to what they can recognize and interpret.

What does this mean to you? It means that in addition to the normal screening process that all resumes go through, there is now one more screening step that determines if the scanner will be able to read your resume. If it can't, chances are your resume is going to be one of the four that is thrown away, instead of the one that is kept. To enhance the chances of your resume making it past this scanner test, here are some simple guidelines you can follow:

- Use larger typefaces (nothing smaller than 12 point), and avoid all but the most basic typefaces. Among the most common are Times Roman and Helvetica.
- No italics or underlining, and definitely no graphic images or boxes.
- Do not send copies. Either print a fresh copy out on your own printer, or take the resume to a print shop and have it professionally copied onto high-quality paper. Avoid dot matrix printers.
- Use 8 1/2 x 11 paper, unfolded. Any words that end up in a crease will not be scannable.
- Use only white or beige paper. Any other color will lessen the contrast between the paper and the letters and make it harder for the scanner to read.
- Use only a single column format. Scanners read from right to left on a page, so two- or three-columns formats lead to nonsensical information when the document is scanned.
- While it is still appropriate to use action words to detail your accomplishments (initiated, planned, implemented, etc.), it is also important to include precise technical terms whenever possible as well. That's because databases are searched by key words, and only resumes that match those key words will be looked at. For example, if a publishing company was seeking someone who was experienced in a desktop publishing, they might search the database for all occurrences of "PageMaker" or "Ventura," two common desktop publishing software packages. If your resume only said "Successfully implemented and oversaw in-house desktop publishing program," it would be overlooked, and you wouldn't get the job!

National Databases: Spreading Your Good Name Around

Commercial resume databases are also having an impact on the job search process in the 1990s, so much so that anyone about to enter the job market should seriously consider utilizing one of these services.

Most of these new services work this way: Job-seekers send the database company a copy of their resume, or they fill out a lengthy application provided by the company. The information is then loaded into the company's computer, along with hundreds of other resumes from other job-seekers. The cost of this listing is usually nominal—$20 to $50 for a six- to 12-month listing. Some colleges operate systems for their graduates that are free of charge, so check with your placement office before utilizing a commercial service.

Once in the system, the resumes are available for viewing by corporate clients who have openings to fill. This is where the database companies really make their money—depending on the skill-level of the listees and the professions covered, companies can pay thousands of dollars for annual subscriptions to the service or for custom searches of the database.

Worried that your current employer might just pull up *your* resume when it goes searching for new employees? No need to be—most services allow listees to designate companies that their resume should not be released to, thus allowing you to conduct a job search with the peace of mind that your boss won't find out!

One warning about these services—most of them are new, so do as much research as you can before paying to have your resume listed. If you hear about a database you think you might want to be listed in, call the company and ask some questions:

- How long have they been in business?
- What has their placement rate been?
- What fields do they specialize in? (In other words, will the right people even *see* your resume?)
- Can you block certain companies from seeing your resume?
- How many other resumes are listed in the database? How many in your specialty?
- Is your experience level similar to that of other listees in the database?

The right answers to these questions should let you know if you have found the right database for you.

To help you locate these resume databases, we have listed many of them in the **Career Resources** chapter of this book.

The Records You Need

Well, now that you've heard all the dos and don'ts and rules about preparing a resume, it's time to put those rules to work. The resume-writing process begins with the assembly and organization of all the personal, educational, and employment data from which you will choose the pieces that actually end up on paper. If this information is properly organized, writing your resume will be a relatively easy task, essentially a simple process of just shifting data from a set of the worksheets to another, to your actual resume. At the end of this chapter, you'll find all the forms you need to prepare your resume, including worksheets, fill-in-the-blanks resume forms, and sample resumes.

As you will soon see, there is a great deal of information you'll need to keep track of. In order to avoid a fevered search for important information, take the time right now to designate a single location in which to store all your records. My recommendation is either a filing cabinet or an expandable pocket portfolio. The latter is less expensive, yet it will still enable you to sort your records into an unlimited number of more-manageable categories.

Losing important report cards, citations, letters, etc., is easy to do if your life's history is scattered throughout your room or, even worse, your house! While copies of many of these items may be obtainable, why put yourself through all that extra work?

Making good organization a habit will ensure that all the records you need to prepare your resume will be right where you need them when you need them.

For each of the categories summarized below, designate a separate file folder in which pertinent records can be kept. Your own notes are important, but keeping actual report cards, award citations, letters, etc. is even more so. Here's what your record-keeping system should include:

Transcripts (Including GPA and Class Rank Information)

Transcripts are your school's official record of your academic history, usually available, on request, from your high school's guidance office or college registrar's office. Your college may charge you for copies and "on request" doesn't mean "whenever you want"—you may have to wait some time for your request to be processed (so **don't** wait until the last minute!).

Your school-calculated GPA (Grade Point Average) is on the transcript. Most schools calculate this by multiplying the credit hours assigned to each course times a numerical grade equivalent (e.g., "A" = 4.0, "B" = 3.0, etc.), then dividing by total credits/courses taken. Class rank is simply a listing of GPAs, from highest to lowest.

Employment Records

Details on every part-time or full-time job you've held, including:

- Each employer's name, address and telephone number
- Name of supervisor
- Exact dates worked
- Approximate numbers of hours per week
- Specific duties and responsibilities
- Specific skills utilized and developed
- Accomplishments, honors
- Copies of awards, letters of recommendation

Volunteer Activities

Just because you weren't paid for a specific job—stuffing envelopes for the local Democratic candidate, running a car wash to raise money for the homeless, manning a drug hotline—doesn't mean that it wasn't significant or that you shouldn't include it on your resume.

So keep the same detailed notes on these volunteer activities as you have on the jobs you've held:

- Each organization's name, address and telephone number
- Name of supervisor
- Exact dates worked
- Approximate numbers of hours per week
- Specific duties and responsibilities
- Specific skills utilized

- Accomplishments, honors
- Copies of awards, letters of recommendation

Extracurricular Activities

List all sports, clubs, or other activities in which you've participated, either inside or outside school. For each, you should include:

- Name of activity/club/group
- Office(s) held
- Purpose of club/activity
- Specific duties/responsibilities
- Achievements, accomplishments, awards

If you were a long-standing member of a group or club, also include the dates that you were a member. This could demonstrate a high-level of commitment that could be used as a selling point.

Honors and Awards

Even if some of these honors are previously listed, specific data on every honor or award you receive should be kept, including, of course, the award itself! Keep the following information in your awards folder:

- Award name
- Date and from whom received
- What it was for
- Any pertinent details

Military Records

Complete military history, if pertinent, including:

- Dates of service
- Final rank awarded
- Duties and responsibilities
- All citations and awards
- Details on specific training and/or special schooling
- Skills developed
- Specific accomplishments

At the end of this chapter are seven **Data Input Sheets**. The first five cover employment, volunteer work, education, activities, and awards and are essential to any resume. The last two—covering military service and language skills—are important if, of course, they apply to you. I've only included one copy of each but, if you need to, you can copy the forms you need or simply write up your own using these as models.

Here are some pointers on how to fill out these all- important Data Sheets:

Employment Data Input Sheet: You will need to record the basic information—employer's name, address, and phone number; dates of employment;

and supervisor's name—for your own files anyway. It may be an important addition to your networking list and will be necessary should you be asked to supply a reference list.

Duties should be a series of brief action statements describing what you did on this job. For example, if you worked as a hostess in a restaurant, this section might read: "Responsible for the delivery of 250 meals at dinner time and the supervision of 20 waiters and busboys. Coordinated reservations. Responsible for check and payment verification."

Skills should enumerate specific capabilities either necessary for the job or developed through it.

If you achieved *specific results*—e.g., "developed new filing system," "collected over $5,000 in previously-assumed bad debt," "instituted award-winning art program," etc.—or *received any award, citation or other honor*—"named Employee of the Month three times," "received Mayor's Citation for Innovation," etc.—make sure you list these.

Prepare one employment data sheet for each of the last three positions you have held; this is a basic guideline, but you can include more if relevant. Do not include sheets for short-term jobs (i.e., those that lasted one month or less).

Volunteer Work Data Input Sheet: Treat any volunteer work, no matter how basic or short (one day counts!), as if it were a job and record the same information. In both cases, it is especially important to note specific duties and responsibilities, skills required or developed and any accomplishments or achievements you can point to as evidence of your success.

Educational Data Input Sheet: If you're in college, omit details on high school. If you're a graduate student, list details on both graduate and undergraduate coursework. If you have not yet graduated, list your anticipated date of graduation. If more than a year away, indicate the numbers of credits earned through the most recent semester to be completed.

Activities Data Input Sheet: List your participation in the Student Government, Winter Carnival Committee, Math Club, Ski Patrol, etc., plus sports teams and/or any participation in community or church groups. Make sure you indicate if you were elected to any positions in clubs, groups, or on teams.

Awards And Honors Data Input Sheet: List awards and honors from your school (prestigious high school awards can still be included here, even if you're in graduate school), community groups, church groups, clubs, etc.

Military Service Data Input Sheet: Many useful skills are learned in the armed forces. A military stint often hastens the maturation process, making you a more attractive candidate. So if you have served in the military, make sure you include details in your resume. Again, include any computer skills you gained while in the service.

Language Data Input Sheet: An extremely important section for those of you with a real proficiency in a second language. And do make sure you have at least conversational fluency in the language(s) you list. One year of college French doesn't count, but if you've studied abroad, you probably are fluent or proficient. Such a talent could be invaluable, especially in today's increasingly international business climate.

While you should use the Data Input Sheets to summarize all of the data you have collected, do not throw away any of the specific information—report cards, transcripts, citations, etc.—just because it is recorded on these sheets. Keep all records in your files; you'll never know when you'll need them again!

Creating Your First Resume

There are many options that you can include or leave out. In general, we suggest you always include the following data:

1. Your name, address and telephone number
2. Pertinent educational history (grades, class rank, activities, etc.) Follow the grade point "rule of thumb"—mention it only if it is above 3.0.
3. Pertinent work history
4. Academic honors
5. Memberships in organizations
6. Military service history (if applicable)

You have the option of including the following:

1. Your career objective
2. Personal data
3. Hobbies
4. Summary of qualifications
5. Feelings about travel and relocation (Include this if you know in advance that the job you are applying for requires it. Often times, for future promotion, job seekers **must** be willing to relocate.

And you should never include the following:

1. Photographs or illustrations (of yourself or anything else) unless they are required by your profession—e.g., actors' composites
2. Why you left past jobs
3. References
4. Salary history or present salary objectives/requirements (if salary history is specifically requested in an ad, it may be included in your cover letter)

Special note: There is definitely a school of thought that discourages any mention of personal data—marital status, health, etc.—on a resume. While I am not vehemently opposed to including such information, I am not convinced it is particularly necessary, either.

As far as hobbies go, I would only include such information if it were in some way pertinent to the job/career you're targeting, or if it shows how well-rounded you are. Your love of reading is pertinent if, for example, you are applying for a part-time job at a library. But including details on the joys of "hiking, long walks with my dog and Isaac Asimov short stories" is nothing but filler and should be left out.

Maximizing Form and Substance

Your resume should be limited to a single page if possible. A two-page resume should be used **only** if you have an extensive work background related to a future goal. When you're laying out the resume, try to leave a reasonable amount of "white space"—generous margins all around and spacing between entries. It should be typed or printed (not Xeroxed) on 8 1/2" x 11" white, cream, or ivory stock. The ink should be black. Don't scrimp on the paper quality—use the best bond you can afford. And since printing 100 or even 200 copies will cost only a little more than 50, if you do decide to print your resume, *over*estimate your needs and opt for the highest quantity you think you may need. Prices at various "quick print" shops are not exorbitant and the quality look printing affords will leave the impression you want.

Use Power Words for Impact

Be brief. Use phrases rather than complete sentences. Your resume is a summary of your talents, not a term paper. Choose your words carefully and use "power words" whenever possible. "Organized" is more powerful than "put together;" "supervised" better than "oversaw;" "formulated" better than "thought up." Strong words like these can make the most mundane clerical work sound like a series of responsible, professional positions. And, of course, they will tend to make your resume stand out. Here's a starter list of words that you may want to use in your resume:

accomplished
achieved
acted
adapted
addressed
administered
advised
allocated
analyzed
applied
approved
arranged
assembled
assessed
assigned
assisted
attained
budgeted
built
calculated
chaired
changed
classified
collected
communicated
compiled
completed
composed
computed
conceptualized
conducted
consolidated
contributed
coordinated
critiqued
defined
delegated
delivered
demonstrated
designed
determined
developed
devised
directed
discovered
drafted
edited
established
estimated
evaluated
executed
expanded
fixed
forecast
formulated
gathered
gave
generated
guided
implemented
improved
initiated
installed
instituted
instructed
introduced
invented
issued
launched
learned
lectured
led
litigated
lobbied
made
managed
marketed
mediated
negotiated
obtained
operated
organized
overhauled
oversaw
participated
planned
prepared
presented
presided
produced
programmed
promoted
proposed
publicized
ran
recommended
recruited
regulated
remodeled
renovated

researched	selected	suggested	upgraded
restored	served	supervised	utilized
reviewed	sold	systematized	won
revised	solved	taught	wrote
rewrote	started	tested	
saved	streamlined	trained	
scheduled	studied	updated	

Choose the Right Format

There is not much mystery here—your background will generally lead you to the right format. For an entry-level job applicant with limited work experience, the chronological format, which organizes your educational and employment history by date (most recent first) is the obvious choice. For older or more experienced applicants, the functional—which emphasizes the duties and responsibilities of all your jobs over the course of your career, may be more suitable. If you are applying for a specific position in one field, the targeted format is for you. While I have tended to emphasize the chronological format in this chapter, one of the other two may well be the right one for you.

A List of Do's and Don't's

In case we didn't stress them enough, here are some rules to follow:

- **Do** be brief and to the point—Two pages if absolutely necessary, one page if at all possible. Never longer!
- **Don't** be fancy. Multicolored paper and all-italic type won't impress employers, just make your resume harder to read (and easier to discard). Use plain white or ivory paper, black ink and an easy-to-read standard typeface.
- **Do** forget rules about sentences. Say what you need to say in the fewest words possible; use phrases, not drawn-out sentences.
- **Do** stick to the facts. Don't talk about your dog, vacation, etc.
- **Don't** ever send a resume blind. A cover letter should always accompany a resume and that letter should always be directed to a specific person.
- **Don't** have any typos. Your resume must be perfect—proofread everything as many times as necessary to catch any misspellings, grammatical errors, strange hyphenations, or typos.
- **Do** use the spell check feature on your personal computer to find errors, and also try reading the resume backwards—you'll be surprised at how errors jump out at you when you do this. Finally, have a friend proof your resume.
- **Do** use your resume as your sales tool. It is, in many cases, as close to you as an employer will ever get. Make sure it includes the information necessary to sell yourself the way you want to be sold!
- **Do** spend the money for good printing. Soiled, tattered or poorly reproduced copies speak poorly of your own self- image. Spend the money and take the time to make sure your resume is the best presentation you've ever made.

- **Do** help the reader, by organizing your resume in a clear-cut manner so key points are easily gleaned.
- **Don't** have a cluttered resume. Leave plenty of white space, especially around headings and all four margins.
- **Do** use bullets, asterisks, or other symbols as "stop signs" that the reader's eye will be naturally drawn to.

On the following pages, I've included a "fill-in-the-blanks" resume form so you can construct your own resume right away, plus one example each of a chronological, functional, and targeted resume.

EMPLOYMENT DATA INPUT SHEET

Employer name: ____

Address: ____

Phone: __________ Dates of employment: ______________________

Hours per week: ________ Salary/Pay: ______________________

Supervisor's name and title: ______________________________

Duties: ____

____

____

Skills utilized: ____

____

____

____

Accomplishments/Honors/Awards: ______________________________

____

____

____

Other important information: ______________________________

____

____

____

____

VOLUNTEER WORK DATA INPUT SHEET

Organization name: ____________________

Address: ____________________

Phone: __________ Dates of activity: ____________________

Hours per week: ____________________

Supervisor's name and title: ____________________

Duties: ____________________

____

____

Skills utilized: ____________________

____

____

____

Accomplishments/Honors/Awards: ____________________

____

____

____

Other important information: ____________________

____

____

____

____

HIGH SCHOOL DATA INPUT SHEET

School name: ______________________________

Address: ______________________________

Phone: __________ Years attended: ______________________________

Major studies: ______________________________

GPA/Class rank: ______________________________

Honors: ______________________________

Important courses: ______________________________

____

____

____

OTHER SCHOOL DATA INPUT SHEET

School name: ______________________________

Address: ______________________________

Phone: __________ Years attended: ______________________________

Major studies: ______________________________

GPA/Class rank: ______________________________

Honors: ______________________________

Important courses ______________________________

____

____

____

____

COLLEGE DATA INPUT SHEET

College: ____________________

Address: ____________________

Phone: __________ Years attended: ____________________

Degrees earned: __________ Major: ______Minor: ____________________

Honors: ____________________

Important courses: ____________________

____

____

____

____

GRADUATE SCHOOL DATA INPUT SHEET

College: ____________________

Address: ____________________

Phone: __________ Years attended: ____________________

Degrees earned: __________ Major: ______Minor: ____________________

Honors: ____________________

Important courses: ____________________

____

____

____

____

____

MILITARY SERVICE DATA INPUT SHEET

Branch: ______________________________

Rank (at discharge): ______________________________

Dates of service: ______________________________

Duties and responsibilities: ______________________________

____

____

____

Special training and/or school attended: ______________________________

____

____

____

Citations or awards: ______________________________

____

____

____

Specific accomplishments: ______________________________

____

____

____

____

____

ACTIVITIES DATA INPUT SHEET

Club/activity: ______________________ Office(s) held: ______________

Description of participation: ______________________________________

____

____

Duties/responsibilities: ____

____

Club/activity: ______________________ Office(s) held: ______________

Description of participation: ______________________________________

____

____

Duties/responsibilities: ____

____

Club/activity: ______________________ Office(s) held: ______________

Description of participation: ______________________________________

____

____

Duties/responsibilities: ____

____

____

____

____

AWARDS AND HONORS DATA INPUT SHEET

Name of Award or Citation: ______________________________

From Whom Received: ______________Date:______________

Significance: ______________________________

____

Other pertinent information: ______________________________

____

Name of Award or Citation: ______________________________

From Whom Received: ______________Date: ______________

Significance: ______________________________

____

Other pertinent information: ______________________________

____

Name of Award or Citation: ______________________________

From Whom Received: ______________Date:______________

Significance: ______________________________

____

Other pertinent information: ______________________________

____

____

LANGUAGE DATA INPUT SHEET

Language: ____

___Read ___Write ___Converse

Background (number of years studied, travel, etc.) ________________

____

____

____

Language: ____

___Read ___Write ___Converse

Background (number of years studied, travel, etc.) ________________

____

____

____

Language: ____

___Read ___Write ___Converse

Background (number of years studied, travel, etc.) ________________

____

____

____

____

FILL-IN-THE-BLANKS RESUME OUTLINE

Name: ____

Address: ____

City, state, ZIP Code: ______________________________________

Telephone number: ______________________________________

OBJECTIVE: ____

____

____

____

____

SUMMARY OF QUALIFICATIONS: ______________________________

____

____

____

EDUCATION

GRADUATE SCHOOL: ______________________________________

Address: ____

City, state, ZIP Code: ______________________________________

Expected graduation date:______________Grade Point Average: __________

Degree earned (expected):______________Class Rank: __________________

Important classes, especially those related to your career: ____________

____

____

____

____

____

____

____

COLLEGE: ____________

Address: ____________

City, state, ZIP Code: ____________

Expected graduation date:____________Grade Point Average: ____________

Class rank:____________Major:____________Minor:____________

Important classes, especially those related to your career: ____________

____

____

____

____

____

____

____

____

____

____

HIGH SCHOOL: ______________________________

Address: ______________________________

City, state, ZIP Code: ______________________________

Expected graduation date: ____________ Grade Point Average: __________

Class rank: ______________________________

Important classes, especially those related to your career: ______________

HOBBIES AND OTHER INTERESTS (OPTIONAL) ______________

EXTRACURRICULAR ACTIVITIES (Activity name, dates participated, duties and responsibilities, offices held, accomplishments): ____________

AWARDS AND HONORS (Award name, from whom and date received, significance of the award and any other pertinent details): ____________

WORK EXPERIENCE. Include job title, name of business, address and telephone number, dates of employment, supervisor's name and title, your major responsibilities, accomplishments, and any awards won. Include volunteer experience in this category. List your experiences with the most recent dates first, even if you later decide not to use a chronological format.

REFERENCES. Though you should *not* include references in your resume, you do need to prepare a separate list of at least three people who know you fairly well and will recommend you highly to prospective employers. For each, include job title, company name, address, and telephone number. Before you include anyone on this list, make sure you have their permission to use their name as a reference and confirm what they intend to say about you to a potential employer.

1. ______________________________

____

____

2. ______________________________

____

____

3. ______________________________

____

____

4. ______________________________

____

____

5. ______________________________

____

____

____

SAMPLE RESUME - CHRONOLOGICAL

AMY C. CHRISTIAN

Local	Permanent
E. Quad #346	904 N. Apache
Boulder, CO 80303	Littleton, CO 80120
(303) 845-0012	(303) 875-3490

EDUCATION

Bachelor of Science in **Forestry Studies**
University of Colorado Boulder, CO
May, 1994
Overall GPA: 2.9 Major GPA: 3.6
Senior Project entitled: *Agroforestry, the Greening of the Third World*

Associate Degree in **Natural Resources Management**
Colorado College Colorado Springs, CO
June, 1992

SKILLS

•Environmental Management
•Disease Control
•Public Education Programs

EMPLOYMENT

9/93 - Present
9/92 - 4/93

Helene's Cafe Boulder, CO
Waitress/Assistant Manager
Promoted for dependable and reliable service.
Served clientele.
Scheduled and monitored staff of five.

9/90 - 5/92

Hostess
Monitored seating arrangement.
*Partially subsidized education by employment.

Summer, 1993

Deep Lake Catskills, NY
Park Attendant
Assisted rangers in summer programming, including nature walks and conservation displays.

Summer, 1992

Fresh Air Fund Fishkill, NY
Camp Counselor
Responsible for activities and safety for three groups of 12 grade school girls; organized and supervised overnight excursions.

EXTRA-CURRICULAR

•Ecology Club, Co-Founder/President
•Intramural Sports
•Quetico Wilderness Trip
•Mountain Biking
•First Aid and CPR certification

SAMPLE RESUME - FUNCTIONAL

MARGARET E. PEARL
4422 Kensington
Cleveland Heights, OH 44118
(216) 001-8932

OBJECTIVE A position in the **Environmental Area.**

EDUCATION

Bachelor of Chemical Engineering
Case Western Reserve Cleveland, OH
Concentration: Environmental Studies
May, 1994 GPA: 3.6

Lab/Field Skills

Knowledge of tar analysis and data reduction.
Liquid-liquid equilibrium data and coalescing tests.
Sampling for environmental violations.

Communications Ability

Presented co-op findings to Departmental Committee.
Ability to effectively utilize computer software for report writing and data analysis.
Successfully completed Dale Carnegie Course.

PROFESSIONAL EXPERIENCE

DuPont Houston, TX
1/93 - 4/93 Co-op
5/92 - 8/92 Rotated to three different business units at two plant sites. Exposed to working with polymers.

EMPLOYMENT

Quinn and McKnight Law Firm Cleveland, OH
5/93 - Present Clerk
9/92 - 12/92 Responsible for billing clients, researching legal issues, and
9/91 - 4/9 preparing/organizing files.

AFFILIATIONS Society of Women Engineers, Student Chapter Vice President
Sierra Club Member
Afro American Association

REFERENCES Furnished Upon Request

SAMPLE RESUME - TARGETED

CHRISTOPHER D. FRANCIS

Apt. #18 Cass Street Detroit, MI 48202 (313) 894-2341

CAREER GOAL **Microbiologist**

EDUCATION

Bachelor of Science in Microbiology
University of Detroit Mercy
Detroit, MI
May, 1994 GPA: 3.9

ACCOMPLISHMENTS

Experience in water pollutant testing.
Extensive background in Chemistry and Biological Sciences.
Transformation of fungal cells via plasmids.
Sequencing of recovered plasmid DNA.
Computer training includes BASIC, PASCAL, Excel, WordPerfect.
Basic understanding of verbal and written Spanish.

PROFESSIONAL EXPERIENCE

University of Detroit Mercy 9/93 - Present
Detroit, MI
Biology Laboratory Assistant/Intern
Key Results: Learned proper lab procedures and handling of materials Assist in preparing cultures and performing biochemical and special serological tests to identify bacterial and fungal isolates.

Bay Municipal Utility District Summer, 1992
San Francisco, CA
Intern
Key Results: Tested water for pollutants and researched possible dam site.

Cranbrook Upward Bound Program Summer, 1991
Birmingham, MI
Project Intern
Key Results: Set-up program dealing with biological study of crayfish; students achieved average overall score of B+ in program.

EMPLOYMENT

Detroit Parks and Recreation Summer 1990
Detroit, MI
Playground Instructor
Instructed approximately 30-40 elementary aged children in athletic and academic activities.

AWARDS/ACHIEVEMENTS

Allied Health Science Award
NRM Eligible May, 1995

CHAPTER TWENTY-ONE

Writing Better Letters

Stop for a moment and review your resume draft. It is undoubtedly (by now) a near-perfect document that instantly tells the reader the kind of job you want and why you are qualified. But does it say anything personal about you? Any amplification of your talents? Any words that are ideally "you?" Any hint of the kind of person who stands behind that resume?

If you've prepared it properly, the answers should be a series of ringing "no's"—your resume should be a mere sketch of your life, a bare-bones summary of your skills, education, and experience.

To the general we must add the specific. That's what your letters must accomplish—adding the lines, colors, and shading that will help fill out your self-portrait. This chapter will cover the kinds of letters you will most often be called upon to prepare in your job search. There are essentially nine different types you will utilize again and again, based primarily on what each is trying to accomplish. One well-written example of each is included at the end of this chapter.

Answer these Questions

Before you put pencil to paper to compose any letter, there are five key questions you must ask yourself:

- **Why** are you writing it?
- To **Whom**?
- **What** are you trying to accomplish?
- **Which** lead will get the reader's attention?
- **How** do you organize the letter to best accomplish your objectives?

Why?

There should be a single, easily definable reason you are writing any letter. This reason will often dictate what and how you write—the tone and flavor of the letter—as well as what you include or leave out.

Have you been asked in an ad to amplify your qualifications for a job and provide a salary history and college transcripts? Then that (minimally) is your objective in writing. Limit yourself to following instructions and do a little personal selling—but very little. Including everything asked for and a simple, adequate cover letter is better than writing a "knock 'em, sock 'em" letter and omitting the one piece of information the ad specifically asked for.

If, however, you are on a networking search, the objective of your letter is to seek out contacts who will refer you for possible informational or job interviews. In this case, getting a name and address—a referral—is your stated purpose for writing. You have to be specific and ask for this action.

You will no doubt follow up with a phone call, but be certain the letter conveys what you are after. Being vague or oblique won't help you. You are after a definite yes or no when it comes to contact assistance. The recipient of your letter should know this. As they say in the world of selling, at some point you have to ask for the order.

Who?

Using the proper "tone" in a letter is as important as the content—you wouldn't write to the owner of the local meat market using the same words and style as you would employ in a letter to the director of personnel of a major company. Properly addressing the person or persons you are writing to is as important as what you say to them.

Always utilize the recipient's job title and level (correct title and spelling are a **must**). If you know what kind of person they are (based on your knowledge of their area of involvement) use that knowledge to your advantage as well. It also helps if you know his or her hiring clout, but even if you know the letter is going through a screening stage instead of to the actual person you need to contact, don't take the easy way out. You have to sell the person doing the screening just as convincingly as you would the actual contact, or else you might get passed over instead of passed along! Don't underestimate the power of the person doing the screening.

For example, it pays to sound technical with technical people—in other words, use the kinds of words and language which they use on the job. If you have had the opportunity to speak with them, it will be easy for you. If not, and you have formed some opinions as to their types then use these as the basis of the language you employ. The cardinal rule is to say it in words you think the recipient will be comfortable hearing, not in the words you might otherwise personally choose.

What?

What do you have to offer that company? What do you have to contribute to the job, process or work situation that is unique and/or of particular benefit to the recipient of your letter.

For example, if you were applying for a sales position and recently ranked number one in a summer sales job, then conveying this benefit is logical and desirable. It is a factor you may have left off your resume. Even if it was listed in the skills/accomplishment section of the resume, you can underscore and call attention to it in your letter. Repetition, when it is properly focused, can be a good thing.

Which?

Of all the opening sentences you can compose, which will immediately get the reader's attention? If your opening sentence is dynamic, you are already 50 percent of the way to your end objective—having your entire letter read. Don't slide into it. Know the point you are trying to make and come right to it. One word of caution: your first sentence **must** make mention of what led you to write—was it an ad, someone at the company, a story you saw on television? Be sure to give this point of reference.

How?

While a good opening is essential, how do you organize your letter so that it is easy for the recipient to read in its entirety? This is a question of *flow*—the way the words and sentences naturally lead one to another, holding the reader's interest until he or she reaches your signature.

If you have your objective clearly in mind, this task is easier than it sounds: Simply convey your message(s) in a logical sequence. End your letter by stating what the next steps are—yours and/or the reader's.

One More Time

Pay attention to the small things. Neatness still counts. Have your letters typed. Spend a few extra dollars and have some personal stationery printed.

And most important, make certain that your correspondence goes out quickly. The general rule is to get a letter in the mail during the week in which the project comes to your attention or in which you have had some contact with the organization. I personally attempt to mail follow-up letters the same day as the contact; at worst, within 24 hours.

When to Write

- To answer an ad
- To prospect (many companies)
- To inquire about specific openings (single company)
- To obtain a referral
- To obtain an informational interview
- To obtain a job interview
- To say "thank you"
- To accept or reject a job offer
- To withdraw from consideration for a job

In some cases, the letter will accompany your resume; in others, it will need to stand alone. Each of the above circumstance is described in the pages that follow. I have included at least one sample of each type of letter at the end of this chapter.

Answering an Ad

Your eye catches an ad in the Positions Available section of the Sunday paper for a microbiologist. It tells you that the position is with a pollution control firm and that, though some experience would be desirable, it is not required. Well, you possess *those* skills. The ad asks that you send a letter and resume to a Post Office Box. No salary is indicated, no phone number given. You decide to reply.

Your purpose in writing—the objective (why?)—is to secure a job interview. Since no person is singled out for receipt of the ad, and since it is a large company, you assume it will be screened by Human Resources.

Adopt a professional, formal tone. You are answering a "blind" ad, so you have to play it safe. In your first sentence, refer to the ad, including the place and date of publication and the position outlined. (There is a chance that the company is running more than one ad on the same date and in the same paper, so you need to identify the one to which you are replying.) Tell the reader what (specifically) you have to offer that company. Include your resume, phone number, and the times it is easiest to reach you. Ask for the order—tell them you'd like to have an appointment.

Blanket Prospecting Letter

In June of this year you will graduate from a four-year college with a degree in microbiology. You seek a position (internship or full-time employment) at a pollution control company. You have decided to write to 50 top companies, sending each a copy of your resume. You don't know which, if any, have job openings.

Such blanket mailings are effective given two circumstances: 1) You must have an exemplary record and a resume which reflects it; and 2) You must send out a goodly number of packages, since the response rate to such mailings is very low.

A blanket mailing doesn't mean an impersonal one—you should always be writing to a specific executive. If you have a referral, send a personalized letter to that person. If not, do not simply mail a package to the Human Resources department; identify the department head and *then* send a personalized letter. And make sure you get on the phone and follow up each letter within about ten days. Don't just sit back and wait for everyone to call you. They won't.

Just Inquiring

The inquiry letter is a step above the blanket prospecting letter; it's a "cold-calling" device with a twist. You have earmarked a company (and a person) as a possibility in your job search based on something you have read about them. Your general research tells you that it is a good place to work. Although you are not aware of any specific openings, you know that they employ entry-level personnel with your credentials.

While ostensibly inquiring about any openings, you are really just "referring yourself" to them in order to place your resume in front of the right person. This is what I would call a "why not?" attempt at securing a job interview. Its effectiveness depends on their actually having been in the news. This, after all, is your "excuse" for writing.

Networking

It's time to get out that folder marked "Contacts" and prepare a draft networking letter. The lead sentence should be very specific, referring immediately to the friend, colleague, etc. "who suggested I write you about..." Remember: Your objective is to secure an informational interview, pave the way for a job interview, and/or get referred to still other contacts.

This type of letter should not place the recipient in a position where a decision is necessary; rather, the request should be couched in terms of "career advice." The second paragraph can then inform the reader of your level of experience. Finally, be specific about seeking an appointment.

Unless you have been specifically asked by the referring person to do so, you will probably not be including a resume with such letters. So the letter itself must highlight your credentials, enabling the reader to gauge your relative level of experience. For entry-level personnel, education, of course, will be most important.

For an Informational Interview

Though the objectives of this letter are similar to those of the networking letter, they are not as personal. These are "knowledge quests" on your part and the recipient will most likely not be someone you have been referred to. The idea is to convince the reader of the sincerity of your research effort. Whatever selling you do, if you do any at all, will arise as a consequence of the meeting, not beforehand. A positive response to this type of request is in itself a good step forward. It is, after all, exposure, and amazing things can develop when people in authority agree to see you.

Thank-You Letters

Although it may not always seem so, manners do count in the job world. But what counts even more are the simple gestures that show you actually care—like writing a thank-you letter. A well-executed, timely thank-you note tells more about your personality than anything else you may have sent, and it also demonstrates excellent follow-through skills. It says something about the way you were brought up—whatever else your resume tells them, you are, at least, polite, courteous and thoughtful.

Thank-you letters may well become the beginning of an all-important dialogue that leads directly to a job. So be extra careful in composing them, and make certain that they are custom made for each occasion and person.

The following are the primary situations in which you will be called upon to write some variation of thank-you letter:

1. After a job interview
2. After an informational interview
3. Accepting a job offer

4. Responding to rejection: While optional, such a letter is appropriate if you have been among the finalists in a job search or were rejected due to limited experience. Remember: Some day you'll *have* enough experience; make the interviewer want to stay in touch.
5. Withdrawing from consideration: Used when you decide you are no longer interested in a particular position. (A variation is usable for declining an actual job offer.) Whatever the reason for writing such a letter, it's wise to do so and thus keep future lines of communication open.

IN RESPONSE TO AN AD

10 E. 89th Street
New York, NY 10028
October 22, 1993

The New York Times
PO Box 7520
New York, NY 10128

Dear Sir or Madam:

This letter is in response to your advertisement for an ecologist which appeared in the October 18th issue of the *New York Times.* I have the qualifications you are seeking.

I graduated from American University with a B.S. in earth science with a minor in biology and an M.S. in ecology. I worked as an intern for two summers at the Raleigh Wildlife Refuge and as a volunteer for the International Wildlife Mission throughout Latin America. For the past year, I have been studying soil erosion in abandoned farmland in the Northwest area of the country. I am also a member of the National Soil and Water Conservation Group.

My resume is enclosed. I would like to have the opportunity to meet with you personally to discuss your requirements for the position. I can be reached at (212) 785-1225 between 8:00 a.m. and 5:00 p.m. and at (212) 785-4221 after 5:00 p.m. I look forward to hearing from you.

Sincerely,

Karen Weber

Enclosure: Resume

PROSPECTING LETTER

Kim Kerr
8 Robutuck Hwy.
Hammond, IN 54054
555-875-2392
October 22, 1993

Mr. Fred Jones
Personnel Director
Universal Solid Waste Corp.
Chicago, Illinois 91221

Dear Mr. Jones:

The name of Universal continually pops up in our classroom discussions of solid waste management companies. Given my interest in the waste services industry as a career and recycling as a specialty, I've taken the liberty of enclosing my resume.

As you can see, I have just completed a very comprehensive educational program at Warren University, majoring in environmental engineering with a minor in management. Though my resume does not indicate it, I will be graduating in the top 10% of my class, with honors.

I will be in the Chicago area on November 29 and will call your office to see when it is convenient to arrange an appointment.

Sincerely yours,

Kim Kerr

INQUIRY LETTER

42 7th Street
Ski City, Vermont 85722
October 22, 1993

Dr. Michael Maniaci
Executive Director
Pinnacle Geoscience Center
521 West Elm Street
Indianapolis, IN 83230

Dear Dr. Maniaci:

I just completed reading the article in the January issue of *Fortune* on your company's record-breaking quarter. Congratulations!

Your innovative approach to recruiting minorities is of particular interest to me because of my background in geosciences and minority recruitment. I am interested in learning more about your work as well as the possibilities of joining your firm.

My qualifications include:

- B.S. in Geology
- Research on minority recruitment
- Geosciences Seminar participation (Univ. of Virginia)
- Reports preparation on marine geology, paleontology and minority recruitment

I will be in Indiana during the week of November 22 and hope your schedule will permit us to meet briefly to discuss our mutual interests. I will call your office next week to see if such a meeting can be arranged.

I appreciate your consideration.

Sincerely yours,

Ronald W. Sommerville

NETWORKING LETTER

Rochelle A. Starky
42 Bach St.,
Musical City, MO 20202
317-555-1515
October 22, 1993

Dr. Michelle Fleming
Executive Director
Heights Conservatory
42 Jenkins Avenue
Fulton, Missouri 23232

Dear Dr. Fleming:

Sam Kinney suggested I write you. I am interested in an ecology position in a nature conservatory. Sam felt it would be mutually beneficial for us to meet and talk.

I have a B.S. from Musical City University in biology and an M.S. from the University of Kettering School of Environmental Science. While working on my postgraduate degree, I volunteered with an independent conservation organization to help clean up the Florida coastline. I also worked as an intern for a year at the Parnell County Zoo in Jefferson City.

I know from Sam how similar our backgrounds are—the same training, the same interests. And, of course, I am aware of how successful you have managed your career—three promotions in four years!

As I begin my job search during the next few months, I am certain your advice would help me. Would it be possible for us to meet briefly? My resume is enclosed.

I will call your office next week to see when your schedule would permit such a meeting.

Sincerely,

Rochelle A. Starky

TO OBTAIN AN INFORMATIONAL INTERVIEW

16 NW 128th Street
Raleigh, NC 757755
October 22, 1992

Ms. Jackie B. McClure
General Manager
Golden County Fish Hatchery
484 Smithers Road
Awkmont, North Carolina 76857

Dear Ms. McClure:

I'm sure a good deal of the credit for your facility's success last year is attributable to the highly-motivated and knowledgeable staff you have recruited during the last three years. I hope to obtain a fisheries management position with a facility just as committed to growth.

I have two years of fishery and wildlife experience, which I acquired while working as an intern at the Bode County Fish and Wildlife Service. I graduated from Gresham University with a B.S. in biology and a minor in environmental health. I believe that my experience and education have properly prepared me for a career in fisheries management.

As I begin my job search, I am trying to gather as much information and advice as possible before applying for positions. Could I take a few minutes of your time next week to discuss my career plans? I will call your office on Monday, October 29, to see if such a meeting can be arranged.

I appreciate your consideration and look forward to meeting you.

Sincerely,

Karen R. Burns

AFTER AN INFORMATIONAL INTERVIEW

Lazelle Wright
921 West Fourth Street
Steamboat, Colorado 72105
303-310-3303

November 22, 1993

Dr. James R. Payne
Managing Director
Finch County Park
241 Snowridge
Ogden, Utah 72108

Dear Dr. Payne:

Jinny Bastienelli was right when she said you would be most helpful in advising me on a career in parks and recreation.

I appreciated your taking the time from your busy schedule to meet with me. Your advice was most helpful and I have incorporated your suggestions into my resume. I will send you a copy next week.

Again, thanks so much for your assistance. As you suggested, I will contact Joe Simmons at Cregskill County Park next week in regard to a possible opening.

Sincerely,

Lazelle Wright

AFTER A JOB INTERVIEW

1497 Lilac Street
Old Adams, MA 01281
November 22, 1993

Mr. Rudy Delacort
Director of Personnel
Grace Environmental Consultants
175 Boylston Avenue
Ribbit, Massachusetts 02857

Dear Mr. Delacort:

Thank you for the opportunity to interview yesterday for the air quality control specialist position. I enjoyed meeting with you and Dr. Cliff Stoudt and learning more about Grace.

Your facility appears to be growing in a direction which parallels my interests and goals. The interview with you and your staff confirmed my initial positive impressions of Grace, and I want to reiterate my strong interest in working for you.

I am convinced that my prior experience as an intern with the Fellowes Conservatory in Old Adams, B.S. in environmental engineering and M.S. in air quality control from the University of Adams would enable me to progress steadily through your training program and become a productive member of your staff.

Again, thank you for your consideration. If you need any additional information from me, please feel free to call.

Yours truly,

Harold Beaumont

cc: Dr. Cliff Stoudt

ACCEPTING A JOB OFFER

1497 Lilac Street
Old Adams, MA 01281
November 22, 1993

Mr. Rudy Delacort
Director of Personnel
Grace Environmental Consultants
175 Boylston Avenue
Ribbit, Massachusetts 01281

Dear Mr. Delacort:

I want to thank you and Dr. Stoudt for giving me the opportunity to work for Grace. I am very pleased to accept the position as an air quality control specialist. The position entails exactly the kind of work I want to do, and I know that I will do a good job for you.

As we discussed, I shall begin work on January 5, 1994. In the interim, I shall complete all the necessary employment forms, obtain the required physical examination and locate housing.

I plan to be in Ribbit within the next two weeks and would like to deliver the paperwork to you personally. At that time, we could handle any remaining items pertaining to my employment. I'll call next week to schedule an appointment with you.

Sincerely yours,

Harold Beaumont

cc: Dr. Cliff Stoudt

WITHDRAWING FROM CONSIDERATION

1497 Lilac Street
Old Adams, MA 01281
October 22, 1993

Mr. Rudy Delacort
Director of Personnel
Grace Environmental Consultants
175 Boylston Avenue
Ribbit, Massachusetts 01281

Dear Mr. Delacort:

It was indeed a pleasure meeting with you and Dr. Stoudt last week to discuss your needs for an air quality control specialist. Our time together was most enjoyable and informative.

As I discussed with you during our meetings, I believe one purpose of preliminary interviews is to explore areas of mutual interest and to assess the fit between the individual and the position. After careful consideration, I have decided to withdraw from consideration for the position.

I want to thank you for interviewing me and giving me the opportunity to learn about your needs. You have a fine staff and I would have enjoyed working with them.

Yours truly,

Harold Beaumont

cc: Dr. Cliff Stoudt

IN RESPONSE TO REJECTION

1497 Lilac Street
Old Adams, MA 01281
November 22, 1993

Mr. Rudy Delacort
Director of Personnel
Grace Environmental Consultants
175 Boylston Avenue
Ribbit, Massachusetts 01281

Dear Dr. Delacort:

Thank you for giving me the opportunity to interview for the air quality control specialist position. I appreciate your consideration and interest in me.

Although I am disappointed in not being selected for your current vacancy, I want to you to know that I appreciated the courtesy and professionalism shown to me during the entire selection process. I enjoyed meeting you, Dr. Cliff Stoudt, and the other members of your staff. My meetings confirmed that Grace would be an exciting place to work and build a career.

I want to reiterate my strong interest in working for you. Please keep me in mind if a similar position becomes available in the near future.

Again, thank you for the opportunity to interview and best wishes to you and your staff.

Sincerely yours,

Harold Beaumont

cc: Dr. Cliff Stoud

CHAPTER TWENTY-TWO

Questions for You, Questions for Them

You've finished your exhaustive research, contacted everyone you've known since kindergarten, compiled a professional-looking and sounding resume, and written brilliant letters to the dozens of companies your research has revealed are perfect matches for your own strengths, interests, and abilities. Unfortunately, all of this preparatory work will be meaningless if you are unable to successfully convince one of those firms to hire you.

If you were able set up an initial meeting at one of these companies, your resume and cover letter obviously piqued someone's interest. Now you have to traverse the last minefield—the job interview itself. It's time to make all that preparation pay off.

This chapter will attempt to put the interview process in perspective, giving you the "inside story" on what to expect and how to handle the questions and circumstances that arise during the course of a normal interview—and even many of those that surface in the bizarre interview situations we have all experienced at some point.

Why Interviews Shouldn't Scare You

Interviews shouldn't scare you. The concept of two (or more) persons meeting to determine if they are right for each other is a relatively logical idea. As important as research, resumes, letters, and phone calls are, they are inherently impersonal. The interview is your chance to really see and feel the company firsthand, so think of it as a positive opportunity, your chance to succeed.

That said, many of you will still be put off by the inherently inquisitive nature of the process. Though many questions *will* be asked, interviews are essentially experiments in chemistry. Are you right for the company? Is the company right for you? Not just on paper—*in the flesh.*

If you decide the company is right for you, your purpose is simple and clear-cut—to convince the interviewer that you are the right person for the job, that you will fit in, and that you will be an asset to the company now and in the future. The interviewer's purpose is equally simple—to decide whether he or she should buy what you're selling.

This chapter will focus on the kinds of questions you are likely to be asked, how to answer them, and the questions you should be ready to ask of the interviewer. By removing the workings of the interview process from the "unknown" category, you will reduce the fear it engenders.

But all the preparation in the world won't completely eliminate your sweaty palms, unless you can convince yourself that the interview is an important, positive life experience from which you will benefit—even if you don't get the job. Approach it with enthusiasm, calm yourself, and let your personality do the rest. You will undoubtedly spend an interesting hour, one that will teach you more about yourself. It's just another step in the learning process you've undertaken.

What to Do First

Start by setting up a calendar on which you can enter and track all your scheduled appointments. When you schedule an interview with a company, ask them how much time you should allow for the appointment. Some require all new applicants to fill out numerous forms and/or complete a battery of intelligence or psychological tests—all before the first interview. If you've only allowed an hour for the interview—and scheduled another at a nearby firm 10 minutes later—the first time you confront a three-hour test series will effectively destroy any schedule.

Some companies, especially if the first interview is very positive, like to keep applicants around to talk to other executives. This process may be planned or, in a lot of cases, a spontaneous decision by an interviewer who likes you and wants you to meet some other key decision makers. Other companies will tend to schedule such a series of second interviews on a separate day. Find out, if you can, how the company you're planning to visit generally operates. Otherwise, a schedule that's too tight will fall apart in no time at all, especially if you've traveled to another city to interview with a number of firms in a short period of time.

If you need to travel out-of-state to interview with a company, be sure to ask if they will be paying some or all of your travel expenses. (It's generally expected that you'll be paying your own way to firms within your home state.) If they don't offer—and you don't ask—presume you're paying the freight.

Even if the company agrees to reimburse you, make sure you have enough money to pay all the expenses yourself. While some may reimburse you immediately, the majority of firms may take from a week to a month to send you an expense check.

Research, Research, and More Research

The research you did to find these companies is nothing compared to the research you need to do now that you're beginning to narrow your search. If you followed our detailed suggestions when you started targeting these firms in the first place, you've already amassed a great deal of information about them. If you didn't do the research *then,* you sure better decide to do it *now.* Study each company as if you were going to be tested on your detailed knowledge of their organization and operations. Here's a complete checklist of the facts you should try to know about each company you plan to visit for a job interview:

The Basics

1. The address of (and directions to) the office you're visiting
2. Headquarters location (if different)
3. Some idea of domestic and international branches
4. Relative size (compared to other similar companies)
5. Annual billings, sales, and/or income (last two years)
6. Subsidiary companies and/or specialized divisions
7. Departments (overall structure)
8. Major accounts, products, or services

The Subtleties

1. History of the firm (specialties, honors, awards, famous names)
2. Names, titles, and backgrounds of top management
3. Existence (and type) of training program
4. Relocation policy
5. Relative salaries (compared to other companies in field or by size)
6. Recent developments concerning the company and its products or services (from your trade magazine and newspaper reading)
7. Everything you can learn about the career, likes, and dislikes of the person(s) interviewing you

The amount of time and work necessary to be this well prepared for an interview is considerable. It will not be accomplished the day before the interview. You may even find some of the information you need is unavailable on short notice.

Is it really so important to do all this? Well, somebody out there is going to. And if you happen to be interviewing for the same job as that other, well-prepared, knowledgeable candidate, who do you think will impress the interviewer more?

As we've already discussed, if you give yourself enough time, most of this information is surprisingly easy to obtain. In addition to the reference sources covered in the Career Resources chapter, the company itself can probably supply you with a great deal of data. A firm's annual report—which all publicly-owned companies must publish yearly for their stockholders—is a virtual treasure trove of information. Write each company and request copies of their last two annual reports. A comparison of sales, income, and other data over this period may enable you to discover some interesting things about their overall financial health and growth potential. Many libraries also have collections of annual reports from major corporations.

Attempting to learn about your interviewer is hard work, the importance of which is underestimated by most applicants (who then, of course, don't bother to do it). Being one of the exceptions may get you a job. Find out if he or she has written any articles that have appeared in the trade press or, even better, books on his or her area(s) of expertise. Referring to these writings during the course of an interview, without making it too obvious a compliment, can be very effective. We all have egos and we all like people to talk about us. The interviewer is no different from the rest of us. You might also check to see if any of your networking contacts worked with him or her at his current (or a previous) company and can help fill you in.

Selection vs. Screening Interviews

The process to which the majority of this chapter is devoted is the actual **selection interview,** usually conducted by the person to whom the new hire will be reporting. But there is another process—the **screening interview**—which many of you may have to survive first.

Screening interviews are usually conducted by a member of the human resources department. Though they may not be empowered to hire, they are in a position to screen out or eliminate those candidates they feel (based on the facts) are not qualified to handle the job. These decisions are not usually made on the basis of personality, appearance, eloquence, persuasiveness, or any other subjective criteria, but rather by clicking off yes or no answers against a checklist of skills. If you don't have the requisite number, you will be eliminated from further consideration. This may seem arbitrary, but it is a realistic and often necessary way for corporations to minimize the time and dollars involved in filling even the lowest jobs on the corporate ladder.

Remember, screening personnel are not looking for reasons to *hire* you; they're trying to find ways to *eliminate* you from the job search pack. Resumes sent blindly to the personnel department will usually be subjected to such screening; you will be eliminated without any personal contact (an excellent reason to construct a superior resume and not send out blind mailings).

If you are contacted, it will most likely be by telephone. When you are responding to such a call, keep these four things in mind: 1) It is an interview, be on your guard; 2) Answer all questions honestly; 3) Be enthusiastic; and 4) Don't offer any more information than you are asked for. Remember, this is another screening step, so don't say anything that will get you screened out before you even get in. You will get the standard questions from the interviewer—his or her attempts to "flesh out" the information included on your resume and/or cover letter. Strictly speaking, they are seeking out any negatives which may exist. If your resume is honest and factual (and it should be), you have no reason to be anxious, because you have nothing to hide.

Don't be nervous—be glad you were called and remember your objective: to get past this screening phase so you can get on to the real interview.

The Day of the Interview

On the day of the interview, wear a conservative (not funereal) business suit—*not* a sports coat, *not* a "nice" blouse and skirt. Shoes should be shined, nails cleaned, hair cut and in place. And no low-cut or tight-fitting clothes.

It's not unusual for resumes and cover letters to head in different directions when a company starts passing them around to a number of executives. If you sent them, both may even be long gone. So bring along extra copies of your resume and your own copy of the cover letter that originally accompanied it.

Whether or not you make them available, we suggest you prepare a neatly-typed list of references (including the name, title, company, address, and phone number of each person). You may want to bring along a copy of your high school or college transcript, especially if it's something to brag about. (Once you get your first job, you'll probably never use it—or be asked for it—again, so enjoy it while you can!)

On Time Means Fifteen Minutes Early

Plan to arrive fifteen minutes before your scheduled appointment. If you're in an unfamiliar city or have a long drive to their offices, allow extra time for the unexpected delays that seem to occur with mind-numbing regularity on important days.

Arriving early will give you some time to check your appearance, catch your breath, check in with the receptionist, learn how to correctly pronounce the interviewer's name, and get yourself organized and battle ready.

Arriving late does not make a sterling first impression. If you are only a few minutes late, it's probably best not to mention it or even excuse yourself. With a little luck, everybody else is behind schedule and no one will notice. However, if you're more than fifteen minutes late, have an honest (or at least serviceable) explanation ready and offer it at your first opportunity. Then drop the subject as quickly as possible and move on to the interview.

The Eyes Have It

When you meet the interviewer, shake hands firmly. People notice handshakes and often form a first impression based solely on them.

Try to maintain eye contact with the interviewer as you talk. This will indicate you're interested in what he or she has to say. Eye contact is important for another reason—it demonstrates to the interviewer that you are confident about yourself and your job skills. That's an important message to send.

Sit straight. Body language is also another important means of conveying confidence.

Should coffee or a soft drink be offered, you may accept (but should do so only if the interviewer is joining you).

Keep your voice at a comfortable level, and try to sound enthusiastic (without

> **You Don't Have to Say a Word**
>
> "Eighty percent of the initial impression you make is nonverbal," asserts Jennifer Maxwell Morris, a New York-based image consultant, quoting a University of Minnesota study. Some tips: walk tall, enter the room briskly while making eye contact with the person you're going to speak to, keep your head up, square your shoulders and keep your hand ready for a firm handshake that involves the whole hand but does not pump.
>
> Source: *Working Woman*

imitating Charleen Cheerleader). Be confident and poised and provide direct, accurate, and honest answers to the trickiest questions.

And, as you try to remember all this, just be yourself, and try to act like you're comfortable and almost enjoying this whole process!

Don't Name Drop...Conspicuously

A friendly relationship with other company employees may have provided you with valuable information prior to the interview, but don't flaunt such relationships. The interviewer is interested only in how you will relate to him or her and how well he or she surmises you will fit in with the rest of the staff. Name dropping may smack of favoritism. And you are in no position to know who the interviewer's favorite (or least favorite) people are.

On the other hand, if you have established a complex network of professionals through informational interviews, attending trade shows, reading trade magazines, etc., it is perfectly permissible to refer to these people, their companies, conversations you've had, whatever. It may even impress the interviewer with the extensiveness of your preparation.

Fork on the Left, Knife on the Right

Interviews are sometimes conducted over lunch, though this is not usually the case with entry-level people. If it does happen to you, though, try to order something in the middle price range, neither filet mignon nor a cheeseburger.

Do not order alcohol—ever! If your interviewer orders a carafe of wine, politely decline. You may meet another interviewer later who smells the alcohol on your breath, or your interviewer may have a drinking problem. It's just too big a risk to take after you've come so far. Just do your best to maintain your poise, and you'll do fine.

The Importance of Last Impressions

There are some things interviewers will always view with displeasure: street language, complete lack of eye contact, insufficient or vague explanations or answers, a noticeable lack of energy, poor interpersonal skills (i.e., not listening or the basic inability to carry on an intelligent conversation), and a demonstrable lack of motivation.

Every impression may count. And the very *last* impression an interviewer has may outweigh everything else. So, before you allow an interview to end, summarize why you want the job, why you are qualified, and what, in particular, you can offer their company.

Then, take some action. If the interviewer hasn't told you about the rest of the interview process and/or where you stand, ask him or her. Will you be seeing other people that day? If so, ask for some background on anyone else with whom you'll be interviewing. If there are no other meetings that day, what's the next step? When can you expect to hear from them about coming back?

Ask for a business card. This will make sure you get the person's name and title right when you write your follow-up letter. You can staple it to the company file for easy reference as you continue networking. When you return home, file all the business cards, copies of correspondence, and notes from the interview(s) with each company in the appropriate files. Finally, but most importantly, ask yourself which firms you really want to work for and which you are no longer interested in. This will quickly determine how far you want the process at each to develop before you politely tell them to stop considering you for the job.

Immediately send a thank-you letter to each executive you met. These should, of course, be neatly typed business letters, not handwritten notes (unless you are most friendly, indeed, with the interviewer and want to stress the "informal" nature of your note). If you are still interested in pursuing a position at their company, tell them in no uncertain terms. Reiterate why you feel you're the best candidate and tell each of the executives when you hope (expect?) to hear from them.

On the Eighth Day God Created Interviewers

Though most interviews will follow a relatively standard format, there will undoubtedly be a wide disparity in the skills of the interviewers you meet. Many of these executives (with the exception of the human resources staff) will most likely not have extensive interviewing experience, have limited knowledge of interviewing techniques, use them infrequently, be hurried by the other duties, or not even view your interview as critically important.

Rather than studying standardized test results or utilizing professional evaluation skills developed over many years of practice, these nonprofessionals react intuitively—their initial (first five minutes) impressions are often the lasting and over-riding factors they remember. So you must sell yourself—fast.

The best way to do this is to try to achieve a comfort level with your interviewer. Isn't establishing rapport—through words, gestures, appearance common interests, etc.—what you try to do in *any* social situation? It's just trying to know one another better. Against this backdrop, the questions and answers will flow in a more natural way.

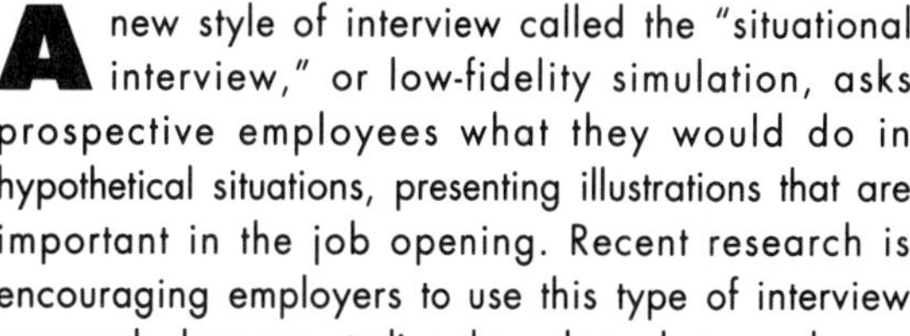

A new style of interview called the "situational interview," or low-fidelity simulation, asks prospective employees what they would do in hypothetical situations, presenting illustrations that are important in the job opening. Recent research is encouraging employers to use this type of interview approach, because studies show that what people say they would do is pretty much what they will do when the real-life situation arises.

Source: *Working Woman*

The Set Sequence

Irrespective of the competence levels of the interviewer, you can anticipate an interview sequence roughly as follows:

- Greetings
- Social niceties (small talk)
- Purpose of meeting (let's get down to business)
- Broad questions/answers
- Specific questions/ answers
- In-depth discussion of company, job, and opportunity
- Summarizing information given & received
- Possible salary probe (this should only be brought up at a second interview)

• Summary/indication as to next steps

When you look at this sequence closely, it is obvious that once you have gotten past the greeting, social niceties and some explanation of the job (in the "getting down to business" section), the bulk of the interview will be questions—yours and the interviewer's. In this question and answer session, there are not necessarily any right or wrong answers, only good and bad ones.

Be forewarned, however. This sequence is not written in stone, and some interviewers will deliberately **not** follow it. Some interviewers will try to fluster you by asking off-the-wall questions, while others are just eccentric by nature. Be prepared for anything once the interview has started.

It's Time to Play Q & A

You can't control the "chemistry" between you and the interviewer—do you seem to "hit it off" right from the start or never connect at all? Since you can't control such a subjective problem, it pays to focus on what you *can* control—the questions you will be asked, your answers and the questions you had better be prepared to ask.

Not surprisingly, many of the same questions pop up in interview after interview, regardless of company size, type, or location. I have chosen the 14 most common—along with appropriate hints and answers for each—for inclusion in this chapter. Remember: There are no right or wrong answers to these questions, only good and bad ones.

Substance counts more than speed when answering questions. Take your time and make sure that you listen to each question—there is nothing quite as disquieting as a lengthy, intelligent answer that is completely irrelevant to the question asked. You wind up looking like a programmed clone with stock answers to dozens of questions who has, unfortunately, pulled the wrong one out of the grab bag.

Once you have adequately answered a specific question, it is permissible to go beyond it and add more information if doing so adds something to the discussion and/or highlights a particular strength, skill, course, etc. But avoid making lengthy speeches just for the sake of sounding off. Even if the interviewer asks a question that is right up your "power alley", one you could talk about for weeks, keep your answers short. Under two minutes for any answer is a good rule of thumb.

Study the list of questions (and hints) that follow, and prepare at least one solid, concise answer for each. Practice with a friend until your answers to these most-asked questions sound intelligent, professional and, most important, unmemorized and unrehearsed.

"Why do you want to be in this field?"

Using your knowledge and understanding of the particular field, explain why you find the business exciting and where and what role you see yourself playing in it.

"Why do you think you will be successful in this business?"

Using the information from your self-evaluation and the research you did on that particular company, formulate an answer which marries your strengths to their's and to the characteristics of the position for which you're applying.

"Why did you choose our company?"

This is an excellent opportunity to explain the extensive process of education and research you've undertaken. Tell them about your strengths and how you match up with their firm. Emphasize specific things about their company that led you to seek an interview. Be a salesperson—be convincing.

"What can you do for us?"

Construct an answer that essentially lists your strengths, the experience you have which will contribute to your job performance, and any other unique qualifications that will place you at the head of the applicant pack. Use action-oriented words to tell exactly what you think you can do for the company—all your skills mean nothing if you can't use them to benefit the company you are interviewing with. Be careful: This is a question specifically designed to *eliminate* some of that pack. Sell yourself. Be one of the few called back for a second interview.

"What position here interests you?"

If you're interviewing for a specific position, answer accordingly. If you want to make sure you don't close the door on other opportunities of which you might be unaware, you can follow up with your own question: "I'm here to apply for your microbiologist opening. Is there another position open for which you feel I'm qualified?"

If you've arranged an interview with a company without knowing of any specific openings, use the answer to this question to describe the kind of work you'd like to do and why you're qualified to do it. Avoid a specific job title, since they will tend to vary from firm to firm.

If you're on a first interview with the human resources department, just answer the question. They only want to figure out where to send you.

"What jobs have you held and why did you leave them?"

Or the direct approach: "Have you ever been fired?" Take this opportunity to expand on your resume, rather than precisely answering the question by merely recapping your job experiences. In discussing each job, point out what you liked about it, what factors led to your leaving, and how the next job added to your continuing professional education. If you have been fired, say so. It's very easy to check.

"What are your strengths and weaknesses?"

Or **"What are your hobbies (or outside interests)?"** Both questions can be easily answered using the data you gathered to complete the self-evaluation process. Be wary of being too forthcoming about your glaring faults (nobody expects you to volunteer every weakness and mistake), but do not reply, "I don't have any." They won't believe you and, what's worse, you won't believe you. After all, you did the evaluation—you know it's a lie!

Good answers to these questions are those in which the interviewer can identify benefits for him or herself. For example: "I consider myself to be an excellent planner. I am seldom caught by surprise and I prize myself on being able to anticipate problems and schedule my time to be ahead of the game. I devote a prescribed number of hours each week to this activity. I've noticed that many people just react. If you plan ahead, you should be able to cut off most problems before they arise."

You may consider disarming the interviewer by admitting a weakness, but doing it in such a way as to make it relatively unimportant to the job function. For example: "Physics has never been my strong suit. In this industry, though, I haven't found this to be a liability."

"Do you think your extracurricular activities were worth the time you devoted to them?"

This is a question often asked of entry-level candidates. One possible answer: "Very definitely. As you see from my resume, I have been quite active in the Student Government and French Club. My language fluency allowed me to spend my junior year abroad as an exchange student, and working in a functioning government gave me firsthand knowledge of what can be accomplished with people in the real world. I suspect my marks would have been somewhat higher had I not taken on so many activities outside of school, but I feel the balance they gave me contributed significantly to my overall growth as a person."

"What are your career goals?"

Interviewers are always seeking to probe the motivations of prospective employees. Nowhere is this more apparent than when the area of ambition is discussed. The key answer to this question might be; "Given hard work, company growth, and personal initiative, I'd look forward to being in a top executive position by the time I'm 35. I believe in effort and the risk/reward system—my research on this company has shown me that it operates on the same principles. I would hope it would select its future leaders from those people who displaying such characteristics."

"At some future date would you be willing to relocate?"

Pulling up one's roots is not the easiest thing in the world to do, but it is often a fact of life in the corporate world. If you're serious about your career (and such a move often represents a step up the career ladder), you will probably not mind such a move. Tell the interviewer. If you really *don't* want to move, you may want to say so, too—though I would find out how probable or frequent such relocations would be before closing the door while still in the interview stage.

Keep in mind that as you get older, establish ties in a particular community, marry, have children, etc., you will inevitably feel less jubilation at the thought of moving once a year or even "being out on the road." So take the opportunity to experience new places and experiences while you're young. If you don't, you may never get the chance.

"How did you get along with your last supervisor?"

This question is designed to understand your relationship with (and reaction to) authority. Remember: Companies look for team players, people who will fit in with their hierarchy, their rules, their ways of doing things. An answer might be: "I prefer to work with smart, strong people who know what they want and can express themselves. I learned in the military that in order to accomplish the mission, someone has to be the leader and that person has to be given the authority to lead. Someday I aim to be that leader. I hope then my subordinates will follow me as much and as competently as I'm ready to follow now."

"What are your salary requirements?"

If they are at all interested in you, this question will probably come up, though it is more likely at a second interview. The danger, of course, is that you may price yourself too low or, even worse, right out of a job you want. Since you will have a general idea of industry figures for that position (and may even have an idea of what that company tends to pay new people for the position), why not refer to a range of salaries, such as $25,000 - $30,000?

If the interviewer doesn't bring up salary at all, it's doubtful you're being seriously considered, so you probably don't need to even bring the subject up. (If you know you aren't getting the job or aren't interested in it if offered, you may try to nail down a salary figure in order to be better prepared for the next interview.)

"Tell me about yourself"

Watch out for this one! It's often one of the first questions asked. If you falter here, the rest of the interview could quickly become a downward slide to nowhere. Be prepared, and consider it an opportunity to combine your answers to many of the previous questions into one concise description of who you are, what you want to be, and why that company should take a chance on you. Summarize your resume—briefly—and expand on particular courses or experiences relevant to the firm or position. Do not go on about your hobbies or personal life, where you spent your summer vacation, or anything that is not relevant to securing that job. You may explain how that particular job fits in with your long-range career goals and talk specifically about what attracted you to their company in the first place.

"Do you have any questions?"

It's the last fatal question on our list, often the last one an interviewer throws at you after an hour or two of grilling. Even if the interview has been very long and unusually thorough, you *should* have questions—about the job, the company, even the industry. Unfortunately, by the time this question off-handedly hits the floor, you are already looking forward to leaving and may have absolutely nothing to say.

Preparing yourself for an interview means more than having answers for some of the questions an interviewer may ask. It means having your own set of questions—at least five or six—for the interviewer. The interviewer is trying to find the right person for the job. You're trying to find the right job. So you should be just as curious about him or her and the company as he or she is about you. Be careful with any list of questions prepared ahead of time. Some of them were probably answered during the course of the interview, so to ask that same question at this stage would demonstrate poor listening skills. Listening well is becoming a lost art, and its importance cannot be stressed enough. (See the box on this page for a short list of questions you may consider asking on any interview).

Your Turn to Ask the Questions

1. What will my typical day be like?
2. What happened to the last person who had this job?
3. Given my attitude and qualifications, how would you estimate my chances for career advancement at your company?
4. Why did you come to work here? What keeps you here?
5. If you were I, would you start here again?
6. How would you characterize the management philosophy of your company?
7. What characteristics do the successful employees at your company have in common?
8. What's the best (and worst) thing about working here?

The Not-So-Obvious Questions

Every interviewer is different and, unfortunately, there are no rules saying he or she has to use all or any of the "basic" questions covered above. But we think the odds are against his or her avoiding all of them. Whichever of these he or she includes, be assured most interviewers do like to come up with questions that are "uniquely theirs." It may be just one or a whole series—questions developed over the years that he or she feels help separate the wheat from the chaff.

You can't exactly prepare yourself for questions like, "What would you do if...(fill in the blank with some obscure occurrence)?," "What do you remember about kindergarten?," or "What's your favorite ice cream flavor?" Every interviewer we know has his or her favorites and all of these questions seem to come out of left field. Just stay relaxed, grit your teeth (quietly), and take a few seconds to frame a reasonably intelligent reply.

The Downright Illegal Questions

Some questions are more than inappropriate—they are illegal. The Civil Rights Act of 1964 makes it illegal for a company to discriminate in its hiring on the basis of race, color, religion, sex, or national origin. It also means that any interview questions covering these topics are strictly off-limits. In addition to questions about race and color, what other types of questions can't be asked? Some might surprise you:

- Any questions about marital status, number and ages of dependents, or marriage or child-bearing plans.
- Any questions about your relatives, their addresses, or their place of origin.
- Any questions about your arrest record. If security clearance is required, it can be done after hiring but before you start the job.

A Quick Quiz to Test Your Instincts

After reading the above paragraphs, read through the 10 questions below. Which ones do you think would be legal to ask at a job interview? Answers provided below.

1. Confidentially, what is your race?
2. What kind of work does your spouse do?
3. Are you single, married, or divorced?

4. What is your native language?
5. Who should we notify in case of an emergency?
6. What clubs, societies, or organizations do you belong to?
7. Do you plan to have a family?
8. Do you have any disability?
9. Do you have a good credit record?
10. What is your height and weight?

The answer? Not a single question out of the 10 is legal at a job interview, because all could lead to a discrimination suit. Some of the questions would become legal once you were hired (obviously a company would need to know who to notify in an emergency), but none belong at an interview.

Now that you know what an interviewer can't ask you, what if he or she does? Well, don't lose your cool, and don't point out that the question may be outside the law—the nonprofessional interviewer may not realize such questions are illegal, and such a response might confuse, even anger, him or her.

Instead, whenever any questions are raised that you feel are outside legal boundaries, politely state that you don't understand how the question has bearing on the job opening and ask the interviewer to clarify his or herself. If the interviewer persists, you may be forced to state that you do not feel comfortable answering questions of that nature. Bring up the legal issue as a last resort, but if things reach that stage, you probably don't want to work for that company after all.

Testing and Applications

Though not part of the selection interview itself, job applications, skill tests, and psychological testing are often part of the pre-interview process. You should know something about them.

The job application is essentially a record-keeping exercise—simply the transfer of work experience and educational data from your resume to a printed application form. Though taking the time to recopy data may seem like a waste of time, some companies simply want the information in a particular order on a standard form. One difference: Applications often require the listing of references and salary levels achieved. Be sure to bring your list of references with you to any interview (so you can transfer the pertinent information), and don't lie about salary history; it's easily checked.

Many companies now use a variety of psychological tests as additional mechanisms to screen out undesirable candidates. Although their accuracy is subject to question, the companies that use them obviously believe they are effective at identifying applicants whose personality makeups would preclude their participating positively in a given work situation, especially those at the extreme ends of the behavior spectrum.

Their usefulness in predicting job accomplishment is considered limited. If you are normal (like the rest of us), you'll have no trouble with these tests and may even find them amusing. Just don't try to outsmart them—you'll just wind up outsmarting yourself.

Stand Up and Be Counted

Your interview is over. Breathe a sigh of relief. Make your notes—you'll want to keep a file on the important things covered for use in your next interview. Some people consider one out of 10 (one job offer for every 10 interviews) a good score—if you're keeping score. We suggest you don't. It's virtually impossible to judge how others are judging you. Just go on to the next interview. Sooner than you think, you'll be hired. For the right job.

Job Opportunities Databank

CHAPTER TWENTY-THREE

Job Opportunities Databank

The Job Opportunities Databank contains listings for more than 225 chemical companies, paper mills, metal and mining companies, consumer product manufacturers, and energy companies, that offer entry-level hiring and/or internships. It is divided into two sections: Entry-Level Job and Internship Listings, which provides full descriptive entries for companies in the United States; and Additional Companies, which includes name, address, and telephone information only for companies that did not respond to our inquiries. For complete details on the information provided in this chapter, please consult "How to Use the Job Opportunities Databank" at the front of this directory.

Entry-Level Job and Internship Listings

Air Products & Chemicals Inc.
7201 Hamilton Blvd.
Allentown, PA 18195-1501
Phone: (215)481-4911

Business Description: An international producer and distributor of chemicals and natural gases, and a manufacturer of industrial process equipment, serving 4,000 customers in 29 countries. Through a joint undertaking with Browning-Ferris Industries, it designs, owns, and operates waste-to-energy facilities.

Officers: James H. Agger, VP & General Counsel; Ronald D. Barclay, VP & Treasurer; P.L. Thibaut Brian, VP of Engineering; Leon C. Holt, Jr., Chief Acctg. Officer; Joseph J. Kaminski, VP of Corp. Planning; Brian M. Rushton, VP of Research & Development; Harold A. Wagner, CEO & Pres.

Benefits: Benefits include a stock option plan for executives and key employees and an employee pension plan.

Human Resources: Lois Marrisey.

Application Procedures: Accepts unsolicited resumes. Applications can be filled out on site, or send resume and cover letter to the attention of Personnel Department.

Alcan Aluminum Corp.
100 Erie View
Cleveland, OH 44114
Phone: (216)523-6800

Business Description: Engaged in flat rolling

aluminum or aluminum-base alloys to produce sheets, plates or foil. Engaged in manufacturing miscellaneous structural metal work.

Officers: Jacques Bougie, Pres. & COO; David Morton, CEO & Chairman of the Board; Estella Taylor, Contact.

Human Resources: Joseph Szafraniec.

Application Procedures: Send resume and cover letter to the attention of Joseph Szafraniec.

▶ Internships

Type: The company does not offer an internship program.

Allegheny Power System Inc.

320 Park Ave.
New York, NY 10022
Phone: (212)752-2121
Fax: (212)836-4340

Business Description: A holding company engaged in the generation, transmission, and distribution of electricity, supplying 1.3 million customers in a service area of 29,100 square miles in portions of Pennsylvania, West Virginia, Maryland, Virginia, and Ohio.

Officers: K. Bergman, CEO & Pres.

Application Procedures: Places newspaper advertisements for certain openings. Applications can be filled out on site, or send resume and cover letter to the attention of Personnel.

▶ Internships

Type: The company does not offer an internship program.

AMAX Inc.

200 Park Ave.
New York, NY 10166
Phone: (212)856-4200

Business Description: Producer of aluminum and manufactured aluminum products. It also has substantial interests in domestic energy and in gold production.

Officers: Dennis Arrouet, Treasurer; Douglas H. Ashby, CEO & Pres. AMAX Coal Industries Inc.; Malcolm B. Bayliss, Exec. VP & General Counsel; Allen Born, CEO, Pres. & Chairman of the Board; Paul E. Drack, CEO & Pres. Alumax Inc.; Helen M. Feeney, Secretary; Timothy J. Haddon, CEO & Pres. AMAX Gold Inc.; Stephen M. Johnson, CEO & Pres. Climax Metals Co.; Richard A. Kalaher, VP & Assoc. General Counsel; Stephen C. Knup, Sr. VP & CFO; Thomas A. McKeever, Exec. VP; Lloyd L. Parks, CEO & Pres. AMAX Oil & Gas Inc.; H. Michael Simeon, Vice Pres.; Charles Toder, Controller; William R. Wahl, Vice Pres.

Benefits: Benefits include post-retirement health and life insurance, an employee pension plan and a 401(k) plan.

Human Resources: Tricia Graf.

Application Procedures: Places newspaper advertisements for certain openings. Accepts unsolicited resumes. Send resume and cover letter to the attention of Tricia Graf.

▶ Internships

Type: The company does not offer an internship program at present.

Amerada Hess Corp.

1185 Avenue of the Americas
New York, NY 10036
Phone: (212)997-8500

Business Description: Engaged in the production of oil and natural gas, and the refining of oil.

Officers: Leon Hess, CEO & Chairman of the Board; H.W. McCollum, CFO.

Benefits: Benefits include medical insurance, savings plan, stock option plan, and tuition assistance.

Application Procedures: Applications can be filled out on site. Accepts unsolicited resumes. Places newspaper advertisements for certain openings. Send resume and cover letter to the attention of Human Resources. Will keep resumes on file for one year.

▶ Internships

Type: The company does not offer an internship program at present.

American Cyanamid Co.

1 Cyanamid Plaza
Wayne, NJ 07470
Phone: (201)831-2000
Fax: (201)831-3473

Business Description: A research-based biotechnology and life science company that develops medical and agricultural products and manufactures and markets them throughout the world.

Officers: Larry Ellberger, Vice Pres.; Frank V. Atlee, President; William Stiller, Vice Pres.; Albert J. Costello, CEO; Paul W. Wood, Vice Pres.; Joseph McAuliffe, Vice Pres.; Darryl D. Fry, Exec. VP; Terence D. Martin, Vice Pres.; Robert D. Reisman, Controller.

Average Entry-Level Hiring: 80.

Benefits: Benefits include medical, dental, life, and short- and long-term disability insurances; an employee pension plan; a savings plan; tuition assistance; paid holidays; vacation days; maternity leave; an employee counseling program; an employee cafeteria; and training programs.

Human Resources: Bronwin Kelly Agricultural Business; George Renton, Medical Research; Melvin Roberts, International; James Sands, Davis & Geck; Donald Wagner, Lederle Laboratories.

Application Procedures: Accepts unsolicited resumes. Send resume and cover letter to the attention of the appropriate personnel director.

▶ Internships

Contact: Lisa Magliano, Assistant.

Type: Offers summer internships in various departments.

Qualifications: Must be a college student.

American Electric Power Company Inc.

1 Riverside Plaza
Columbus, OH 43215
Phone: (614)223-1000
Fax: (614)223-1823

Business Description: An electric utility company that operates 20 coal-fired plants and one nuclear plant. The plants are located in Michigan, Indiana, Ohio, Kentucky, Tennessee, West Virginia, and Virginia.

Officers: Peter J. DeMaria, Treasurer; Richard E. Disbrow, President; A. Joseph Dowd, Secretary; Gerald P. Maloney, Vice Pres.; W.S. White, Jr., CEO & Chairman of the Board.

Benefits: Benefits include medical insurance, life insurance, dental insurance, 401(k), and a retirement plan.

Human Resources: L.M. Feck.

Application Procedures: Send resume and cover letter to the attention of the Human Resources Department.

▶ Internships

Contact: Mrs. Elaine Strutner, Internship Coordinator.

Type: The company typically offers a co-op/internship program which has been suspended for the 1993 year. The company normally awards internships to college students who maintain a 2.8 GPA or above. For more information, please contact Mrs. Elaine Strutner.

> According to a 1991 study by the U.S. Department of the Interior, only an estimated 103.3 million acres of wetland remain intact in the lower 48 states, out of an estimated original total of 221 million acres. Losses continue at an estimated rate of 200,000 to 300,000 acres each year.
>
> Source: *Environment*

American Petrofina Inc.

Fina Plaza
8350 N. Central Expy.
Dallas, TX 75206
Phone: (214)750-2400

Business Description: American Petrofina, Inc., through its main operating subsidiary, Fina Oil and Chemical Co., engages in crude oil and natural gas exploration, production, and marketing; petroleum products refining, supply and transportation, and marketing; and chemicals manufacturing and marketing. American Petrofina, Inc. is part of an international group of about 200 companies in 33 countries affiliated with Petrofina S.A., which is headquartered in Brussels, Belgium.

Officers: Christian Buggenhout, VP & CFO; Michael J. Couch, Vice Pres.; Ron W. Haddock, CEO & Pres.

Benefits: Company offers a full benefits program including a stock option plan.

Human Resources: Paula Green, Employee Manager.

Application Procedures: Send resume and cover letter to the attention of Paula Green,

Employee Manager, PO Box 2159, Dallas, TX 75206.

▶ Internships

Type: The company does not offer an internship program.

Amoco Corp.

200 E. Randolph Dr.
Chicago, IL 60601
Phone: (312)856-6111

Business Description: Involved in the exploration, production, and refining of oil; also develops industrial chemicals.

Officers: Frederick S. Addy, Exec. VP & CFO; Ronald E. Callahan, Secretary; Robert C. Carr, VP & Controller; Richard L. Fischer; William R. Hutchinson, VP & Treasurer; Rady A. Johnson, VP of Public & Government Affairs; John R. Lyman, VP of Planning & Economics; Keith W. McHenry, Sr. VP of Technology; William J. Montgomery, VP of Supply; Richard M. Morrow, CEO & Chairman of the Board; Walter R. Quanstrom, VP of Environmental Affairs & Safety; George S. Spindler, VP & General Counsel.

Human Resources: R. Wayne Anderson.

Application Procedures: Send resume and cover letter to the attention of PO Box 87703, Chicago, IL 60680-0703.

▶ Internships

Type: The company does not offer an internship program.

Arcadian Corp.

6750 Poplar Ave., Ste. 600
Memphis, TN 38138
Phone: (901)758-5200

Business Description: Manufactures fertilizers and industrial chemicals, with plants in LaPlatte, Nebraska; Clinton, Iowa; and Geismer, Louisiana.

Benefits: The company offers a complete flex benefit package with 401(k), an HMO plan, and employee stock purchase plan.

Human Resources: Jerre Harris; Cathy Norris.

Application Procedures: The company advertises employment opportunities in classified newspaper advertisements. Interested candidates should forward resumes to Claudine Peters, Employee Relations Coordinator.

▶ Internships

Type: The company does not offer any internship programs.

ARCO Chemical Co.

3801 W. Chester Pike
Newtown Square, PA 19073
Phone: (215)359-2000

Business Description: "ARCO Chemical Company is a leading multinational manufacturer and marketer of intermediate chemicals and specialty products used in a broad range of consumer goods."(Arco Chemical Company 1989 Annual Reports.)

Officers: Alan R. Hirsig, Sr. VP; John G. Johnson, Jr., Sr. VP; Marvin O. Schlanger, Sr. VP & CFO; Harold A. Sorgenti, CEO & Pres.; Donald W. Wood, Sr. VP.

Benefits: Benefits include retirement plans and an employee pension plan.

Human Resources: Frank W. Welsh; Cheryl Simmons.

Application Procedures: Send resume and cover letter to the attention of Human Resources.

Aristech Chemical Corp.

600 Grant St.
Pittsburgh, PA 15219-2704
Phone: (412)433-2747

Business Description: Aristech is engaged in chemical operations including dibasics, alcohols, unsaturated polyester resins, and plasticizers.

Officers: T. Marshall, CEO & Chairman of the Board.

Benefits: Benefits include medical insurance, dental insurance, vision insurance, and savings plan.

Human Resources: Saudra Cillo.

Application Procedures: Places newspaper advertisements for certain openings. Send resume and cover letter to the attention of Michael J. Prendergast, 600 Grant St., Rm. 1160, Pittsburgh, PA 15219-0250.

▶ Internships

Type: Offers summer internships.

Application Procedure: Call Human Resources for application information.

Arkla Inc.
PO Box 751
Little Rock, AR 72203
Phone: (501)377-4659

Business Description: Arkla is a balanced natural gas company, geographically concentrated, with strong and mutually supportive positions in the three main phases of the natural gas industry: transmission, distribution, and exploration/production.

Officers: Michael B. Bracy, Exec. VP; Jack W. Ellis, II, VP & Controller; James G. Ivey, Treasurer; Bradford G. Keithley, Sr. VP & General Counsel; William H. Kelly, Sr. VP & CFO; Thomas F. McLarty, III, CEO & Chairman of the Board; Jim O. Wilhite, Vice Chairman of the Board.

Benefits: Benefits include medical, dental, life, and short- and long-term disability insurances; pension and savings plans; tuition assistance; selected bonuses; paid holidays; personal/sick days; vacation days; counseling; training programs; and company-sponsored sports teams.

Human Resources: Karen Murph.

Application Procedures: Applications are processed by the State Employment Security Division, which then makes employment referrals. Does not accept unsolicited resumes.

▶ **Internships**

Type: The company does not offer an internship program.

Armco Inc.
300 Interpace Pkwy.
Parsippany, NJ 07054-0324
Phone: (201)316-5200

Business Description: Armco is a producer of stainless, electrical, and carbon steels and steel products.

Officers: Wallace B. Askins, Exec. VP & CFO; Julio R. Bartol, Vice Pres.; Robert E. Boni, CEO & Chairman of the Board; G. Rylander, VP of Mktg. & Sales.

Benefits: Benefits include an employee pension plan, health care, and life insurance.

Human Resources: John M. Bilich.

Application Procedures: Send resume and cover letter to the attention of Personnel Services Manager.

▶ **Internships**

Type: The company does not offer an internship program.

Asarco Inc.
180 Maiden Ln.
New York, NY 10038
Phone: (212)510-2000

Business Description: Producer of nonferrous metals, primarily copper, silver, lead, zinc and gold, specialty chemicals, and minerals. The company operates mines in the United States, Australia, Canada, Mexico, and Peru. The company also provides environmental services and produces crushed stone, ready-mix concrete, agricultural limestone, and asphalt. In addition to its wholly-owned subsidiaries, it has holdings in Mexico, Peru, and Australia.

Officers: George W. Anderson, Exec. VP; William A. Bennis, VP of Admin.; Robert J. Bothwell, Jr., VP of Sales; Ronald J. O'Keefe, Controller; Richard Osborne, CEO, Pres. & Chairman of the Board; Thomas C. Osborne, Exec. VP.

Benefits: Benefits include medical insurance, dental insurance, vision insurance, life insurance, and an employee pension plan.

Human Resources: Madeline Fotopulos; Christine Perrotta.

Application Procedures: Send resume and cover letter.

> The area of greatest employment growth within the past decade has been that of the small organizations—companies with fewer than 500 employees.
>
> Source: *Journal of Career Planning & Employment*

▶ **Internships**

Type: The company does not offer an internship program.

Ashland Chemical Co.
General Polymers Div.
12001 Toepfer Rd.
Warren, MI 48089
Phone: (313)755-1100

Business Description: Wholesaler of miscellaneous chemicals or allied products.

Officers: Bob Beers, Dir. of Systems; Daniel W. McGuire, Vice Pres.

Human Resources: Joe Welsh; Coleen O'Connell.

Application Procedures: Interested candidates should contact the Ohio office at (614)889-3333.

Ashland Oil Inc.
PO Box 391
Ashland, KY 41169
Phone: (606)329-3333

Business Description: A diversified energy corporation based in Kentucky. Operations include refining, supplying petroleum products, marketing motor oil, distributing chemicals, and contracting highways. Inter-company relationships provide Ashland operating companies guaranteed markets and suppliers.

Officers: John R. Hall, CEO & Chairman of the Board; Charles J. Luellen, Pres. & Chairman of the Board.

Benefits: Benefits include an employee pension plan, thrift plan, post-retirement health and life insurance, employee stock ownership plan, and incentive stock plan. Employee's children are eligible for educational scholarships, pension plans, thrift plans, post-retirement health care and life insurance, stock ownership, and stock incentives.

Human Resources: Philip W. Block.

Application Procedures: The company accepts unsolicited resumes and cover letters (send to the attention of Human Resources). Provides a job hotline at (606) 329-4328.

▶ **Internships**

Type: Offers a summer program during which students are usually employed as law clerks.

Qualifications: Students who have completed at least one year of college and have a related major (typically engineering, chemistry, or accounting).

Application Procedure: Applications are available after Christmas. Write for an application to the attention of Personnel: Summer Program.

Application Deadline: March 1.

Atlanta Gas and Light Co.
PO Box 4569
Atlanta, GA 30302
Phone: (404)584-4000

Business Description: A natural gas distribution company serving more than 1.1 million customers in 225 cities and communities in Georgia. As a public utility, it is regulated regarding areas served, rates, service, accounting, and safety standards. General offices are in Atlanta, while 6 operating units are located in the region.

Officers: David R. Jones, CEO & Pres.

Benefits: Benefits include medical insurance, dental insurance, an employee pension plan, a retirement savings plan, and an employee stock purchase plan.

Human Resources: Charles B. Seymour.

Application Procedures: Advertises in the *Atlanta Journal.* Maintains a job hotline at (404) 584-4705 for application information and available positions. Does not accept unsolicited resumes.

▶ **Internships**

Type: Offers a co-op program with five area schools.

Qualifications: Engineering students.

Application Procedure: Contact the school's co-op coordinator.

Atlantic Richfield Co.
515 S. Flower St.
Los Angeles, CA 90071
Phone: (213)486-3511

Business Description: Atlantic Richfield Company engages in the development, production, and sale of petroleum and natural gas. The company also mines and sells coal.

Officers: Ronald J. Arnault, Exec. VP; George H. Babikian, Sr. VP; H.L. Bilhartz, Sr. VP; Mike R. Bowlin, Sr. VP; Lodwrick M. Cook, CEO & Chairman of the Board; Camron Cooper, Sr. VP & Treasurer; Kent E. Damon, Jr., Sr. VP; Kenneth R. Dickerson, Sr. VP; Anthony G. Fernandes, Sr. VP; Marie L. Knowles, Sr. VP &

Controller; Francis X. McCormack, Sr. VP of Legal Affairs; James A. Middleton, Exec. VP; James S. Morrison, Exec. VP & CFO; William C. Rusnack, Sr. VP; William E. Wade, Jr., Sr. VP; Robert E. Wycoff, Pres. & Chairman of the Board.

Benefits: Benefits include health care and life insurance, long-term disability, short-term disability, an employee pension plan, a savings plan, profit sharing, tuition assistance, bonuses/incentives, paid holidays, flexible holidays, vacation days, maternity leave, counseling, flex time, and a smoke-free environment.

Human Resources: Donald A. Murray; Myrta Rodrigiuez.

Application Procedures: Send resume and cover letter to the attention of Donald A. Murray.

Avon Products Inc.

9 W. 57th St.
New York, NY 10019
Phone: (212)546-6015

Business Description: An international company comprised of two industry segments: the sale of beauty products through independent sales representatives and the sale of fragrance products to retail stores. Avon has operations in North and South America, Europe, and Asia.

Officers: Robert J. Conologue, VP & Controller; James E. Preston, CEO & Chairman of the Board; Edward J. Robinson, Exec. VP & CFO.

Benefits: Benefits include retirement plans, post-retirement health and life insurance, and life insurance.

Human Resources: Marcia L. Worthing.

Application Procedures: Send resume and cover letter to the attention of Human Resources.

Baltimore Gas & Electric Co.

Gas & Electric Bldg.
Charles Center
Baltimore, MD 21201
Phone: (410)234-5000

Business Description: Baltimore Gas and Electric (BG & E) is an investor-owned utility that produces and sells natural gas and electricity to customers in the Baltimore, Maryland, area. BG & E operates the Calvert Cliffs nuclear power plant, and several coal-fired generating plants. The company plans to increase its energy supply through construction of new generators by 1995.

Officers: George V. McGowan, CEO & Chairman of the Board; Charles W. Shivery, VP of Finance & Treasurer; E.W. Skoglin, Mktg. Mgr.

Benefits: Offers employees medical, dental, life, and short- and long-term disability insurances. Other benefits include an employee pension plan, a savings plan, tuition assistance, national and flexible holidays, personal and vacation days, and maternity leave. The company also provides an employee counseling program, company-sponsored sports teams, an employee cafeteria, flextime, and a smoke-free environment.

Human Resources: Barb Cannon; W. E. Johnson; L. D. Miller.

Application Procedures: Send resume and cover letter to the attention of W. E. Johnson. Attn: Employment, Rm. 706, PO Box 1475, Baltimore, MD 21203-1475.

Barringer Laboratories Inc.

15000 W. 6th Ave., Ste. 300
Golden, CO 80401
Phone: (303)277-1687

Business Description: Analytical testing for the environmental and mineral exploration industries.

Officers: Robert H. Walker, CEO; Stanley S. Binder, CFO.

Opportunities: Hires degreed and experienced lab technicians.

Benefits: Benefits include medical insurance, life insurance, dental insurance, tuition assistance, profit sharing, and child-care programs.

Application Procedures: Send resume and samples to the Laboratory Director.

▶ Internships

Type: Offers paid and college credit internships.

Qualifications: Requirements vary with position being sought, but previous experience is generally required.

Application Procedure: Applications are available either at the students' schools or through the company.

Bemis Company Inc.
222 S. 9th St., Ste. 2300
Minneapolis, MN 55402
Phone: (612)376-3000

Business Description: Manufacturer of flexible packaging products and specialty coated and graphics products, primarily for the food industry.

Officers: Ceroy F. Bazany, VP & Controller; Howard Curler, Chairman of the Board; Jeffrey H. Curler, Exec. VP; Leona A. Droll, Exec. VP; Benjamin R. Field, III, VP & Treasurer; Scott W. Johnson, VP, General Counsel & Sec.; Lisa D. Locken, Dir. of Communications; Edwin S. McBride, Exec. VP; Robert F. Minarik, Exec. VP; John H. Roe, CEO & Pres.

Benefits: Benefits include an employee pension plan.

Human Resources: Marilyn Pearson; Lawrence E. Schwanke.

Application Procedures: Send resume and cover letter to the attention of Marilyn Pearson.

Whether you are using file cards or a computer, the trick to your job search is developing a discipline to your efforts. As you begin to send out your resume, you should automatically assign yourself a follow-up date. The idea is to realize that you are now marketing a product that you know very well: yourself.

Source: *H & MM*

Bethlehem Steel Corp.
701 E. 3rd St.
Bethlehem, PA 18016-7699
Phone: (215)694-2424

Business Description: Engages primarily in the manufacture and sale of a variety of steel mill products. Also produces and sells coal and other raw materials; repairs ships and offshore drill rigs; and manufactures forgings, castings, railroad cars, and trackwork.

Officers: Lonnie A. Arnett, VP & Controller Accounting; D. Sheldon Arnot, Exec. VP Steel Commercial; Curtis H. Barnette, Sr. VP, General Counsel & Sec.; Stephen G. Donches, Vice Pres. State & Community Affairs; George T. Fugere VP, Operations Services; John A. Jordon, Jr. Sr. VP of Corporate Development; John L. Kluttz, Vice Pres. Union Relations; Gary L. Millenbruch, Sr. VP & CFO; Walter F. Williams, CEO.

Benefits: Benefits include an employee pension plan and profit sharing.

Human Resources: Benjamin C. Boylston; John A. Jordan, Jr.; James F. Sinnwell.

Application Procedures: Send resume and cover letter to the attention of James F. Sinnwell.

Betz Laboratories Inc.
4636 Somerton Rd.
Trevose, PA 19047
Phone: (215)355-3300

Business Description: Engages in the engineered chemical treatment of water, wastewater, and process systems operating in a wide variety of industrial and commercial applications, with particular emphasis on the chemical, petroleum refining, paper, automotive, electrical utility, and steel industries. Also produces and markets a wide range of specialty chemical products, including the technical and laboratory services necessary to utilize Betz products effectively. Chemical treatment programs are applied for use in boilers, cooling towers, heat exchangers, paper and petroleum process streams, and both influent and effluent systems. Operates 15 production plants in the United States and 7 in foreign countries. With additional engineering and laboratory backup from product management and research functions, Betz monitors changing water, process, and plant operating conditions so as to prescribe the appropriate treatment program to solve such customer problems as scale, corrosion, and deposit formation, resulting in the preservation or enhancement of productivity, reliability, and efficiency in customer plant operations.

Officers: William R. Cook, Pres. & COO; John F. McCaughan, CEO & Chairman of the Board; R. Dale Voncanon, VP of Finance & Treasurer.

Benefits: Benefits include retirement plans; profit sharing; an employee pension plan; a 401(k) plan; a domestic pension plan; a foreign pension plan; medical, dental, life, and short- and long-term disability insurances; tuition assistance; bonuses/incentives; paid holidays; flexible holidays; personal/sick days; vacation days;

counseling; sports teams; a cafeteria; a smoke-free environment; and training programs.

Application Procedures: Send resume and cover letter to the attention of Christine Becker.

Boise Cascade Corp.

1 Jefferson Sq.
PO Box 50
Boise, ID 83728-0001
Phone: (208)384-6161
Fax: (208)384-4841

Business Description: Manufactures and distributes paper and paper products, office products, and owns and manages timberland to support these operations.

Officers: J. Randolph Ayre, VP & Legal Counsel; J. Ray Barbee, VP of Sales White Paper; John C. Bender, VP of Sales Timber & Wood Products; Alex P. Boormann, Vice Pres. Paper Engineering; William Bridenbaugh, Sr. VP; John E. Clute, Sr. VP & General Counsel; Peter G. Danis, Jr., Exec. VP Office & Building Products; Rex L. Dorman, Vice Pres. Control & Information Services; E. Thomas Edquist, Office Products; Charles E. Faries, VP of Manufacturing White Paper; John B. Fery, CEO & Chairman of the Board; John A. Haase, Sr. VP Paper Technical Resources; George J. Harad, Exec. VP & CFO; Alice E. Hennessey, Sr. VP Corp. Relations & Corp. Secty.; Stephen C. Larson, Sr. VP & General Mgr. Coated Paper; Irving Littman, VP & Treasurer; Terry R. Lock, Sr. VP & General Mgr. White Paper; Jon H. Miller, Pres. & Chairman of the Board; Richard B. Parrish, Sr. VP & General Mgr. Timber & Wood Products; D. Ray Ryden, Vice Pres. Transportation & Procurement; Donald F. Smith, Vice Pres. Timberland Resources; Jerry P. Soderberg, VP of Sales Publishing & Packaging Paper; N. David Spence, Vice Pres. Southern Operations; J. Kirk Sullivan, Vice Pres. Governmental & Environmental Affairs; John H. Wasserlein, Sr. VP & General Mgr. Publishing & Packaging Paper.

Benefits: Benefits include an employee stock ownership plan; medical, dental, life, and short- and long-term disability insurances; an employee pension plan; a savings plan; tuition assistance; national and flexible holidays; personal and vacation days; maternity leave; an employee counseling program, company-sponsored sports teams, an employee cafeteria, flextime, and a smoke-free environment; and training programs.

Human Resources: John E. Clute; J. Michael Gwartney; John Shewmake; Kay Strand.

Application Procedures: Does not accept unsolicited resumes. Maintains a job hotline at (208)384-4900. If qualified for a listed job, send resume and cover letter to the attention of JoAnn Walston.

▶ Internships

Contact: JoAnn Walston, Human Resources.

Type: Offers paid summer internships in the legal, internal auditing, and information services departments.

Qualifications: College students entering their senior year who are majoring in a subject appropriate for the position.

Boston Edison Co.

800 Boylston St.
Boston, MA 02199
Phone: (617)424-2000

Business Description: This electric power utility generates a third of its electricity from residual oil, a third from natural gas, and the other third from Pilgrim Nuclear Power Station. Recent projects include substation development in order to meet future load growth, installation of fault indicator and Radio Controlled Sectionalizing Switches, along with advances in substation insulation and underground cables.

Officers: Marc S. Alpert, VP & Treasurer; Arthur P. Phillips Jr., VP of Info. Systems; Stephen J. Sweeney, CEO & Chairman of the Board.

Benefits: Benefits include 401(k), medical insurance and disability insurance.

Human Resources: John J. Higgins.

Application Procedures: Send resume and cover letter to the attention of Jerome McKinnon.

▶ Internships

Contact: Jerome McKinnon, Contact.

Type: Offers an internship program.

Qualifications: Communication specialists.

Application Procedure: Interested candidates should contact Mr. McKinnon.

Bowater Inc.

PO Box 1028
Greenville, SC 29602
Phone: (803)271-7733

Business Description: Produces newsprint, coated publication paper, and market pulp. The company is also the leading converter of continuous stock computer paper in the United States.

Officers: Donald J. D'Antuono, VP of Investor Relations; John P. Fucigna, VP & Treasurer; Anthony P. Gammie, CEO, Pres. & Chairman of the Board; Richard McDonough, Sr. VP & CFO.

Benefits: Benefits include medical insurance, dental insurance, life insurance, and long-term disability insurance.

Human Resources: Ronald E. Gustafson.

Application Procedures: Send resume and cover letter to the attention of Patty Garrison.

▶ Internships

Type: The company offers no internship program.

BP Chemicals America Inc.

PO Box 628
Lima, OH 45802
Phone: (419)226-1200

Business Description: Manufacturer of miscellaneous industrial inorganic chemicals.

Officers: W.B. Powell, Mgr. of Finance; J.W. Walpole, CEO.

Human Resources: J.E. Jacobi.

Application Procedures: Interested candidates should forward resumes to Ms. Duvall.

▶ Internships

Type: The company offers co-op internships.

Qualifications: Students enrolled in a four-year college or university.

Brooklyn Union Gas Co.

195 Montague St.
Brooklyn, NY 11201
Phone: (718)403-2000

Business Description: In addition to the distribution of natural gas to consumers and businesses in Brooklyn, Queens, and Staten Island, the company is engaged in such unregulated businesses as gas exploration, natural gas vehicles, cogeneration, and replacing electric air conditioning with gas-powered air conditioning.

Officers: Robert B. Catell, COO; Craig G. Matthews, Sr. VP & CFO; Maurice K. Shaw, Sr. VP of Mktg.

Benefits: The company offers full benefits including medical insurance, dental insurance, vision insurance, sick leave, and vacation days. Employees become eligible two weeks after one year of service.

Human Resources: Jerelyn Cronk.

Application Procedures: The company intends to hire 7 engineering majors, 2-3 computer science majors, and 2-3 business majors in 1993. Qualified applicants are encouraged to apply. Candidates with bachelor's and/or master's degrees are wanted, as well as candidates with chemical engineering, civil engineering, computer science, and mechanical engineering degrees. Interested applicants should forward resumes and cover letters to the attention of Management Recruitment Administrators.

▶ Internships

Type: The company does not offer an internship program.

Cabot Corp.

75 State St.
Boston, MA 02109
Phone: (617)345-0100

Business Description: Manufactures products made from carbon black (used in printing inks, tires, and plastics), sells tantalum and fumed silica, produces protective earplugs through its Cabot Safety subsidiary, operates a natural gas terminal in Massachusetts and has a growing European recycling business.

Officers: Samuel W. Bodman, CEO & Chairman of the Board; John D. Curtin Jr., Exec. VP & CFO.

Benefits: Benefits include medical insurance, dental insurance, life insurance, 401(k), profit sharing, retirement plan, long and short-term disability insurance, and vacation days.

Human Resources: Mr. Gary Weiss.

Application Procedures: Send resume and cover letter to the attention of the human resource department.

▶ Internships

Type: The company does not offer any internship programs.

Cameron Industries Inc.

P.O. Box 1212
Houston, TX 77251
Phone: (713)939-2311
Fax: (713)939-2620

Business Description: Manufacturer of oil field machinery, iron forging, valves and pipe fittings.

Officers: Norman D. Shahan, President.

Benefits: Benefits include medical insurance, dental insurance, and paid vacation days.

Human Resources: Stan Howard.

Application Procedures: Send resume and cover letter to the attention of Employment Relations.

▶ Internships

Type: The company does not offer internships.

Cargill Inc.

15407 McGinty Rd. W.
Minnetonka, MN 55345
Phone: (612)475-7575
Fax: (612)475-7785

Business Description: Grain brokers and manufacturers of soybean oil. Processes, markets, and exports grains, fruit juices, peanuts, meat and poultry products, vegetable oils and meals, corn starches and syrups, Nutrena feeds, hybrid seed, oil-based chemicals, steel products, and bulk commodities such as salt, molasses, and fertilizers. Also engages in corn and flour milling, leases equipment, and provides bulk transportation service.

Officers: Gene Gross, Dir. of Systems; Whitney Macmillan, CEO & Chairman of the Board.

Benefits: Cargill offers a competitive compensation and benefits package.

Human Resources: Karolyn Karsell.

Application Procedures: The company intends to hire 35 engineering majors in 1993 and 1994. The company has expressed specific interest in agricultural engineers, chemical engineers, mechanical engineers, and metallurgical engineers; as well as computer science majors, business majors, and liberal arts majors. Career development and management training are intricate parts of employment for the company. Typically promotions are made from within and employees can expect to relocate during their career. Interested candidates should contact College Programs Manager, P.O. Box 9300, Minneapolis, MN 55440.

▶ Internships

Type: The company does not offer an internship program.

> Your next job need not be at another company. Pay attention to the special skills of people newly hired or recently promoted by your current employer. That will give you an indication of what talents are valued so you can upgrade your skills and re-invent your job to make sure it stays relevant to your company's needs.
>
> Source: *Money*

Carolina Power & Light Co.

411 Fayetteville St.
P.O. Box 1551
Raleigh, NC 27602
Phone: (919)546-6111

Business Description: Provides electric power to customers in a region covering 30,000 square miles of North and South Carolina. The company has a generating capacity of 9,654 megawatts.

Officers: Charles D. Barham, Jr., Sr. VP; Lynn W. Eury, Exec. VP; William E. Graham, Jr., Vice Chairman of the Board; Edward G. Lilly, Jr., Exec. VP & CFO; Sherwood H. Smith, Jr., Chairman of the Board, Pres., CEO & COO.

Benefits: Benefits include an employee pension plan, medical insurance for retirees, life insurance for retirees, vacation, and sick leave.

Human Resources: Cecil L. Goodnight.

Application Procedures: The company anticipates hiring employees for entry-level positions primarily from North Carolina. The company also recruits from the Midwest and Southeastern United States. The company has expressed interest in all engineering majors. Interested candidates should contact the Director of Corporate Recruiting, P.O. Box 1551, Raleigh, NC 27602.

▶ Internships

Type: The company does not offer an internship program.

Carter-Wallace Inc.

1345 Avenue of the Americas
New York, NY 10105
Phone: (212)339-5000
Fax: (212)339-5100

Business Description: Manufactures, markets, and distributes toiletry items, pet products, pharmaceuticals, and specialty diagnostic equipment.

Officers: Henry H. Hoyt, Jr., CEO & Chairman of the Board; Paul A. Veteri, VP & CFO.

Application Procedures: Send resume and cover letter to the attention of Tina Schuder.

▶ Internships

Type: The company does not offer any internships.

CBI Industries Inc.

800 Jorie Blvd.
Oak Brook, IL 60522-7001
Phone: (708)572-7000

Business Description: CBI Industries has subsidiaries operating in the construction of metal plate structures and other contracting services, industrial gases, oil transport and storage, and other investments.

Officers: Lewis E. Akin, Exec. VP; Beth A. Bailey, Dir. of Info. Systems; Robert J. Daniels, Exec. VP; John E. Jones, CEO, Pres. & Chairman of the Board; George L. Schueppert, Exec. VP & CFO.

Benefits: Benefits include an employee pension plan, post-retirement benefits, and an employee stock ownership plan.

Human Resources: Susan Marks.

Application Procedures: Some hiring is done through an employment agency. Send resume and cover letter to the attention of Jim Morgan.

▶ Internships

Type: The company does not offer a formal internship program, but is currently seeking individuals with an MBA degree in marketing for intern positions.

Centerior Energy Corp.

PO Box 94661
Cleveland, OH 44101-4661
Phone: (216)447-3100

Business Description: Consolidated electric utility system serving 2.6 million people in a combined service area of 4,200 square miles in northern Ohio.

Officers: Robert J. Farling, President; Edgar H. Maugans, Sr. VP & Finance Officer; Richard A. Miller, CEO & Chairman of the Board.

Benefits: Benefits include medical insurance and dental insurance.

Application Procedures: Send resume and cover letter to the attention of Human Resource Department.

▶ Internships

Type: The company does not offer any internship programs.

Central & South West Corp.

1616 Woodall Rodgers Fwy.
PO Box 660164
Dallas, TX 75266-0164
Phone: (214)754-1000

Business Description: A public utility holding company with four electric subsidiary companies. These four subsidiaries provide electricity to more than four million people in a widely diversified service area covering 152,000 square miles. In addition to its four electric subsidiary companies, Central and South West owns six other subsidiaries, two of which are described in detail below; the other four subsidiaries are diversification ventures.

Officers: E.R. Brooks, CEO, Pres. & Chairman of the Board; Verla R. Campbell, Asst. Sec.; Frederic L. Frawley, Corp. Sec.; Harry D. Mattison, COO & Exec. VP; Stephen J. McDonnell, Treasurer; Fred C. Meyer, Jr., Sr. VP & General Counsel; Rocky R. Miracle, Asst. Treasurer; Glenn D. Rosilier, Sr. VP & CFO; Thomas V. Shockley, III, Exec. VP; Michael D. Smith, Controller.

Benefits: Benefits include an employee pension plan, medical insurance, and post-retirement benefits.

Human Resources: Walt Ratcliff.

Application Procedures: Send resume and cover letter to the attention of Brett Blair.

▶ Internships

Contact: Brett Blair.

Type: The company offers internships to students in different areas.

Application Procedure: Interested candidates should contact Brett Blair, Employee Relations for more information.

CF Industries Inc.

1 Salem Lake Dr.
Long Grove, IL 60047
Phone: (708)438-9500

Business Description: An interregional cooperative owned by and serving 13 regional cooperatives. Manufactures nitrogen, phosphate, and potash fertilizer products. Plants are located in Donaldsonville, Louisiana; Medicine Hat, Alberta, Canada; and Bartow and Plant City, Florida. Phosphate mining operations are in Hardee County, Florida. The phosphate port terminal is in Tampa, Florida. The Engineering & Projects Office is in Bartow, Florida. The Public Affairs Office is in Washington, D.C. Warehouses and terminals are in 25 locations in Illinois, Nebraska, Ohio, Iowa, Indiana, Minnesota, North Dakota, Missouri, Michigan, and Washington.

Officers: Wayne E. Brown, Dir. of Systems; Lawrence H. Devereaux, Sr. VP & CFO; Robert C. Liuzzi, CEO & Pres.; Paul R. Obert, VP, General Counsel & Sec.; John H. Sultenfuss, VP of Mktg.

Benefits: Benefits include medical, dental, life, and short- and long-term disability insurances; pension and savings plans, profit sharing, tuition assistance, and selected bonuses; paid holidays; vacation days; employee assistance program; an employee cafeteria; company-sponsored sports teams; a smoke-free environment; training programs; and fitness center access. The company's benefits package is a flexible plan.

Human Resources: William Eppel; Clarence E. Lynn.

Application Procedures: The company intends to hire five people in 1993. Positions vary but may include agricultural engineering. Interested candidates should contact Mrs. William Eppel.; Carolyn H. Taylor, Supervisor, Corporate Placement.

▶ Internships

Type: The company does not offer an internship program.

> What is underway in the 1990s is more than a massive corporate restructuring or a one-time adjustment. It's an overhaul of the U.S. labor force, a sea of change in the kinds of jobs and the type of work that will be available. Workers in this new era will have to be more flexible, more willing to move cross-country for a job, more willing to go back to school. Today's college graduate can expect 12 to 13 jobs in three to four different careers over her or his lifetime.
>
> Source: *USA Today*

Champion International Corp.

1 Champion Plaza
Stamford, CT 06921
Phone: (203)358-7000

Business Description: Worldwide manufacturer of printing and writing papers, publication papers, newsprint, kraft, pulp, and forest products. Operates plants in ten states and in Brazil and Canada.

Officers: L.C. Heist, Pres. & COO; Andrew C. Sigler, CEO & Chairman of the Board.

Benefits: Benefits include medical insurance, dental insurance, vision insurance, and paid vacation after six months.

Human Resources: Tom Brown; Richard L. Porterfield; Donna White Recruiting System Administrator.

Application Procedures: Interested candidates should forward resumes to Donna White, Recruiting System Administrator.

▶ Internships

Contact: Donna White.

Type: The company offers internships to college students who have completed their sophomore year in accounting and engineering.

Qualifications: Students must carry at least a 3.0 GPA.

Application Procedure: Interested candidates should contact Donna White, Recruiting System Administrator.

Chevron Corp.

PO Box 7318
San Francisco, CA 94120-7318
Phone: (415)894-7700

Business Description: An international petroleum company whose operations include exploration and production, manufacturing, marketing, distribution, and research and technology. The company is also involved in chemicals, minerals, and real estate industries. Facilities are worldwide, with most United States locations in the South and West.

Officers: Kenneth T. Derr, CEO & Chairman of the Board.

Benefits: Benefits include retirement plans, a savings plan, profit sharing, health care and life insurance, dental insurance, post-retirement health and life insurance, and a management recognition plan.

Human Resources: Louis Fernandez, Jr.

Application Procedures: Send resume and cover letter to the attention of Louise Lowry.

▶ Internships

Contact: Louise Lowry.

Type: Offers engineering internships.

Qualifications: College students between their junior and senior years.

Application Procedure: Interested candidates should forward applications to Louise Lowry.

Church & Dwight Company Inc.

469 N. Harrison St.
Princeton, NJ 08543-5297
Phone: (609)683-5900

Business Description: Manufactures sodium bicarbonate and related products.

Officers: Anthony P. Deasey, VP & CFO; Dwight C. Minton, CEO & Chairman of the Board; Albert R. Nicusanti, Jr., VP of Sales.

Benefits: Benefits include medical, dental, life, and short- and long-term disability insurances, medical insurance, dental insurance, 401(k), pension and savings plans, profit sharing, tuition assistance, and selected bonuses, an employee counseling program, company-sponsored sports teams, an employee cafeteria, flextime, and a smoke-free environment, and national and flexible holidays, personal and vacation days, and maternity leave.

Human Resources: Kathy Marino.

Application Procedures: Interested candidates should forward resume to the personnel office.

▶ Internships

Type: The company offers internships in many areas.

Application Procedure: For more information, contact the personnel office.

Cincinnati Gas & Electric Co.

139 E. 4th St.
Cincinnati, OH 45202
Phone: (513)381-2000

Business Description: Provides electricity and gas to customers in southwestern Ohio and the bordering areas of Indiana and Kentucky. In addition to its electric and gas subsidiaries, the company operates a real estate development subsidiary and a rail and barge terminal subsidiary.

Officers: Donald R. Blum, Secretary; Earl A. Borgmann, Sr. VP; Terry E. Bruck, Vice Pres.; Robert E. Byrnes, Sr. VP; C. Robert Everman, Sr. VP & Finance Officer; R. Gregory Graham, Vice Pres.; Daniel R. Herche, Controller; James J. Mayer, General Counsel; Jackson H. Randolph, CEO & Pres.; Stephen G. Salay, Vice Pres.; C. Larry Schmidt, Vice Pres.; William L. Sheafer, Treasurer; M.L. Van Schoik, VP of Info. Systems; W.D. Waymire, Mktg. Mgr.; Robert P. Wiwi, Sr. VP.

Benefits: The company offers a benefits package including an employee pension plan and life insurance for retirees.

Application Procedures: Send resume and cover letter to the attention of Dave Crale.

▶ Internships

Type: The company offers an internship program.

Application Procedure: Interested candidates should contact the employment division.

Citgo Petroleum Corp.
PO Box 3758
Tulsa, OK 74102
Phone: (918)495-4826

Business Description: A petroleum refining, marketing, and transportation company. CITGO manfactures and markets transportation fuels, lubricants, refined waxes, petrochemical feedstocks, and other industrial products.

Officers: Peer L. Anderson, VP & General Counsel; L.H. Brittain, Jr., VP of Mktg.; Ronald E. Hall, CEO & Pres.; Eddie R. Humphrey, Controller; M.A. Johnson, Sr. VP of Advertising; Jerry E. Thompson, Vice Pres.

Benefits: Benefits include an employee pension plan.

Human Resources: Tom G. Richardson.

Application Procedures: The company advertises vacant positions in the newspaper. Interested candidates should forward resumes to the company per published instructions.

▶ **Internships**

Type: The company does not offer an internship program.

Clorox Co.
1221 Broadway
Oakland, CA 94612
Phone: (510)271-7000

Business Description: A diversified international company whose principal business is developing, manufacturing, and marketing premium quality household products sold in grocery stores and other retail outlets.

Officers: William F. Ausfahl, VP & CFO; N. Wheeler, Vice Pres. Health, Safety and Environment.

Benefits: Benefits include a pension and savings plans, profit sharing, tuition assistance, and selected bonuses, as well as medical, dental, life, and short- and long-term disability insurances. In 1989, the full-benefit vesting period was reduced from ten to five years.

Human Resources: John J. Calderini.

Application Procedures: Interested candidates should forward resumes or completed applications to the company.

▶ **Internships**

Type: The company offers internships in marketing research and government affairs to junior students. Interested candidates should contact the human resource department.

CMS Energy Corp.
Fairlane Plaza S.
330 Town Center Dr., Ste. 1100
Dearborn, MI 48126
Phone: (313)436-9200

Business Description: The company's principal subsidiary, Consumers Power Co., provides electricity and natural gas to customers in Michigan's lower peninsula. Through its other subsidiaries, the company is engaged in oil and gas exploration and production worldwide, tires-to-energy projects, nuclear plant conversion projects, and natural gas storage and marketing.

Officers: John W. Clark, Sr. VP of Corp. Communications; Victor J. Fryling, President; Preston D. Hopper, VP, Controller & Chief Acctg. Officer; William T. McCormick, Jr., CEO & Chairman of the Board; Thomas A. McNish, Treasurer & Sec.; S. Kinnie Smith, Jr., Vice Chairman of the Board; Alan M. Wright, Sr. VP & CFO.

Benefits: Benefits include medical, dental, life, and short- and long-term disability insurances; an employee pension plan; a savings plan; tuition assistance; and selected bonuses. The company also offers an employee counseling program, company-sponsored sports teams, an employee cafeteria, flextime, and a smoke-free environment.

Application Procedures: Interested applicants should forward resumes to Anne Childs.

▶ **Internships**

Type: The company does not offer any formal internships.

Coastal Corp.
Coastal Tower
9 Greenway Plaza
Houston, TX 77046-0995
Phone: (713)877-1400

Business Description: The Coastal Corporation and its subsidiaries are involved in energy concerns, including natural gas refining, marketing, exploration, and production, as well as coal, chemicals, and power production and marketing. The company participates in exploration and production of gas and oil in major reserve basins; mines, processes, and markets low-sulfur coal from extensive owned reserves; and operates major interstate pipeline systems that produce, purchase, transport, store, and sell natural gas.

Officers: David A. Arledge, Exec. VP & CFO; Michael L. Beatty, Exec. VP & General Counsel; James F. Cordes, Exec. VP; Dan J. Hill, Sr. VP of Mktg.; Dennis F. Juren, Exec. VP; James R. Paul, CEO & Pres.; Oscar S. Wyatt, Jr., Chairman of the Board & Chairman of the Exec. Committee.

Benefits: Benefits include medical, dental, life, and short- and long-term disability insurances.

Human Resources: Lloyd Healy.

Application Procedures: Interested candidates should forward resumes to the attention of the Personnel Department.

How do you define a field biologist? Presumably he or she is not merely a person who views a trip to the wilderness as a refreshing interval, a touch of scientific ecotourism. One test of authenticity might be the length of time this biologist lives afield: someone who suffers from culture shock not when settling into a project, but on returning home.

Source: George B. Schaller in *Wildlife Conservation*

▶ Internships

Type: The company doesn't offer any internships, but does offer a training program.

Columbia Gas Systems Inc.

20 Montchanin Rd.
Wilmington, DE 19807-0020
Phone: (302)429-5000
Fax: (302)429-5730

Business Description: A holding company whose subsidiaries are engaged in natural gas and oil exploration, production, transmission, storage, and distribution, and in other energy-related ventures. Oil and gas production are concentrated in the Gulf of Mexico area, the Appalachians, and Canada. The products are then transported to markets in 14 northeastern, middle Atlantic, midwestern, and southern states.

Officers: Larry J. Bainter, Treasurer; Daniel L. Bell, Jr., Sr. VP, Legal Counsel & Sec.; Tejinder S. Bindra, Asst. Sec.; John H. Croom, CEO, Pres. & Chairman of the Board; Joyce K. Hayes, Asst. Sec.; Richard E. Lowe, VP & Controller; Alexander P. McCann, Asst. Sec. & Asst. Treasurer; Michael W. O'Donnell, Sr. VP & Asst. CFO; Robert A. Oswald, Exec. VP & CFO.

Benefits: Benefits include an employee pension plan, a long-term incentive plan, medical insurance, dental insurance, life insurance, short-term disability, long-term disability, a savings plan, tuition assistance, paid holidays, maternity leave, employee activities, an employee cafeteria, flex time, a smoke-free environment, and training programs.

Human Resources: Lois Hubbs; Mary Wong.

Application Procedures: Interested candidates should forward resumes to Mary Wong.; Lois Hubbs, Placement Manager.

▶ Internships

Type: The company does not offer any internship programs.

Commonwealth Edison Co.

PO Box 767
Chicago, IL 60690-0767
Phone: (312)394-4321
Toll-free: 800-950-2377

Business Description: Engaged in the production, transmission, distribution, and sale of electricity to wholesale and retail customers. The company provides retail service across one-fifth of the State of Illinois including the metro Chicago area.

Officers: John C. Bukovski, Vice Pres.; Dennis F. O'Brien, Treasurer; Bide L. Thomas, President.

Benefits: Benefits include an employee pension plan and certain post-retirement health care benefits for retirees and their dependents.

Application Procedures: The company is currently not accepting any applications, but may in the future. For more information please contact the Human Resource Department.

▶ Internships

Type: The company is not currently offering an

internship program, but expects to offer a summer internship program in the future.

Consolidated Edison Company of New York Inc.

4 Irving Pl.
New York, NY 10003
Phone: (212)460-4600

Business Description: Provider of electric and other utility services. Engaged in the production and/or distribution of steam, heated air or cooled air for sale.

Officers: Arthur Hauspurg, CEO & Chairman of the Board; Raymond J. McCann, Exec. VP & CFO.

Human Resources: Kevin Morgan.

Application Procedures: The company is not accepting any applications or resumes until January 1994. For further information, please contact the company.

▶ Internships

Type: The company offers an internship program.

Application Procedure: For availability and application information, please contact the company address, Room 952S.

Consolidated Papers Inc.

PO Box 8050
Wisconsin Rapids, WI 54495-8050
Phone: (715)422-3111

Business Description: A producer of enamel papers for the printed communications industry.

Officers: Patrick F. Brennan, COO & Pres.; Gorton M. Evans, Jr., VP of Mktg.; Richard J. Kenney, VP of Finance & Treasurer; Carl R. Lemke, Asst. Sec.; J.R. Matsch, Asst. Treasurer; Duane R. Mayer, Asst. Controller; George W. Mead, CEO & Chairman of the Board; Philip G. Meyers, Sec. & Legal Counsel; William P. Orcutt, VP of Manufacturing; Gary L. Philips, Asst. Controller; Roy E. Schulz, VP of Manufacturing; James E. Shewchuk, Controller; Donald L. Stein, Vice Pres.; John D. Steinberg, Asst. Treasurer; Carl H. Wartman, Asst. Sec.

Benefits: Benefits include an employee pension plan.

Human Resources: Mary E. Krekowski.

Application Procedures: Send resume and cover letter to the attention of Mary Polivaa.

▶ Internships

Type: The company typically offers internships to process engineers and electrical engineers.

Qualifications: Requirements vary for positions.

Application Procedure: Interested candidates should contact either the Personnel Office or the Human Resource Department.

Consolidation Coal Co.

Consol Plaza
Pittsburgh, PA 15241
Phone: (412)831-4000

Business Description: Engaged in the development of underground mines containing bituminous coal and/or the production of bituminous coal in underground mines.

Officers: R.B. Atwater, Exec. VP of Mktg.; B.R. Brown, CEO & Pres.; W.G. Karis, Exec. VP of Finance.

Application Procedures: Interested candidates should forward application to Gary Walton.

▶ Internships

Contact: Gary Walton, Contact.

Type: The company offers engineering and computer internships.

Qualifications: Must be a college student going into the sophomore year.

Application Procedure: Interested applicants should forward an application to Gary Walton.

Crown Central Petroleum Corp.

PO Box 1168
Baltimore, MD 21203
Phone: (410)539-7400
Fax: (410)659-4730

Business Description: Producer, refiner, and marketer of petroleum products.

Officers: Charles L. Dunlap, Pres. & COO; Paul J. Ebner, Vice Pres. Marketing Support Services; Phillip F. Hodges, Asst. Sec.; Stephen A. Noll, Asst. Sec.; Thomas L. Owsley, VP & Legal Counsel Legal; Dolores B. Rawlings, Secretary; Frank B. Rosenberg, Vice Pres. Marketing; Edward L. Rosenberg, Vice Pres. VP, Corporate Dev. and Asst. Treasurer; Henry A. Rosenberg

Jr., CEO & Chairman of the Board; Kajal Roy, Asst. Sec.; David J. Shade, Asst. Sec.; George R. Sutherland, Jr., Vice Pres. Supply and Transportation; Randall M. Trembly, Vice Pres. Refining; John E. Wheeler, Jr., VP, Treasurer & Controller; Peter G. Wolfhagen, Asst. Sec.; William A. Wolters, Asst. Sec.; J. Gregory Yawman, Asst. Sec.

Benefits: Benefits include medical insurance, dental insurance, life insurance, and a savings plan.

Human Resources: J. Michael Mims.

Application Procedures: Interested candidates should forward resumes with cover letters to the Human Resource Department.

▶ Internships

Type: The company offers an internship program.

Application Procedure: Interested candidates should forward resumes or applications to the Human Resources department.

Cyprus Minerals Co.

9100 E. Mineral Circle
PO Box 3299
Englewood, CO 80155
Phone: (303)643-5000
Fax: (303)643-5049

Business Description: A diversified mining company producing copper, zinc, lithium, coal, molybdenum, talc, gold, and iron ore. Cyprus has 31 mines in 10 states, including four copper mines located in Nevada, Oregon, and Arizona. The company produces other minerals concurrent with the copper at its mines.

Officers: Calvin Campbell, CEO & Chairman of the Board; Gerald J. Malys, Sr. VP & CFO; John Taraba, VP & Controller.

Benefits: Benefits include medical insurance, dental insurance, life insurance, and disability insurance.

Human Resources: Sharon Kinser; Gerard H. Peppard.

Application Procedures: Applications can be filled out on site, or applications will be mailed upon request. Accepts unsolicited resumes. Send resume and cover letter to the attention of Tom LeBlanc.

▶ Internships

Type: The company offers internships through the "In Roads" program.

Qualifications: Requirements vary, but may include a 3.0 GPA, 800 SAT score, 20 ACT score, a business, engineering, or computer science major.

Application Procedure: Interested applicants should contact the Human Resources department.

Detroit Edison Co.

2000 2nd Ave.
Detroit, MI 48226
Phone: (313)237-8000
Fax: (313)596-6530

Business Description: Engaged in the generation, transmission and/or distribution of electricity.

Officers: John E. Lobbia, Pres. & COO; Leslie L. Loomans, VP & Treasurer; Walter J. McCarthy, Jr., CEO & Chairman of the Board.

Benefits: Benefits include an employee pension plan, retirement plans, and health care and life insurance. Also offers medical insurance, dental insurance, life insurance, tuition assistance, free parking, and 2 weeks vacation after a year.

Human Resources: Malcolm G. Dade, Jr.

Application Procedures: Advertises in in newspapers. Send resume and cover letter to the attention of the Human Resources staff.

▶ Internships

Type: The company does not offer an internship program.

Dexter Corp.

1 Elm St.
Windsor Locks, CT 06096
Phone: (203)627-9051
Fax: (203)627-9713

Business Description: Provides specialty materials and supporting services to customers in six markets: aerospace, automotive, electronics, food packaging, industrial assembly and finishing, and medical.

Officers: Kathleen Burdett, Exec. VP & Controller; Robert E. McGill III, Exec. VP of Finance; K. Grahame Walker, CEO & Pres.

Benefits: Benefits include employee pensions,

deferred profit sharing, some health care and life insurance benefits for retired and active employees, and a stock option plan.

Application Procedures: Interested candidates should forward resumes to Michelle Vinkler, Recruiter.

▶ Internships

Contact: Kevin Lake, Contact.

Type: Offers paid internships.

Qualifications: College students.

Application Procedure: Interested candidates should contact Kevin Lake.

Dial Corp.

Dial Tower
Phoenix, AZ 85077
Phone: (602)207-2800
Fax: (602)201-7121

Business Description: Manufacturer of soap or detergents, and/or producer of crude or refined glycerin. Wholesaler of miscellaneous grocery products.

Benefits: Offers employees a full benefits package.

Human Resources: Bernhard J. Welle.

Application Procedures: Send resume and cover letter to the attention of Tom Wymer.

▶ Internships

Contact: Rosalie Robinson.

Type: Offers a college internship program in customer service, research and development, international marketing, and finance. Offers marketing or accounting internships for 12 weeks from May to August.

Qualifications: MBA students.

Application Procedure: Apply to Rosalie Robinson.

Diamond Shamrock Inc.

9830 Colonnade Blvd.
San Antonio, TX 78230
Phone: (210)641-6800
Fax: (210)641-8670

Business Description: Regional refiner of petroleum products. The company markets gasoline through its Diamond Shamrock outlets. Diamond Shamrock R & M operates major divisions in Dallas, Houston, and San Antonio, Texas. The company staffs the following major departments: accounting, engineering, information systems, and marketing.

Officers: Robert C. Becker, VP & Treasurer; Roger R. Hemminghaus, CEO & Chairman of the Board; J. Robert McHall, Sr. VP; A.W. O'Donnell, Sr. VP; J.E. Prater, Sr. VP.

Opportunities: Annually, the company hires five full-time, summer, and co-op/intern chemical engineers with bachelor of sciences degree in chemical engineering; two mechanical engineers with bachelor of sciences degree in business or marketing; two DOT qualified truck drivers with three to five years experience; two systems analysts with bachelor of sciences degree in computer science and two years of MIS experience; two accountants with bachelor of sciences degree in accounting; and 1,000 full- and part-time store operators with retail experience.

Benefits: Benefits include medical, dental, life, and short- and long-term disability insurances, vision insurance, an employee stock purchase plan, an employee stock ownership plan, an employee pension plan, tuition assistance, 10 paid holidays and five personal/sick days per year, and 10 vacation days after one year. Other benefits include an employee counseling program, company-sponsored sports teams, and funeral leave.

Human Resources: Donna Clerk; Kim Griffin.

Application Procedures: Recruits at Texas A & M University, Texas Technical University, Auburn University, and career fairs. Advertises in the *Wall Street Journal, San Antonio Express,* and *Houston Chronicle.* Send resume and cover letter to the attention of Kim Griffin, PO Box 696000, San Antonio, TX 78269-6000.

▶ Internships

Contact: Kim Griffin.

Type: Offers a college internship program to engineering students.

Application Procedure: Send application to Kim Griffin.

DP & L Inc.

PO Box 8825
MacGregor Park
Dayton, OH 45401
Phone: (513)224-6000

Business Description: Holding company

whose principal subsidiary is The Dayton Power and Light Company, which sells electricity and natural gas in a 6,000 square mile area of West Central Ohio. Electricity is generated at seven power plants. DP&L also provides steam service in downtown Dayton.

Officers: Peter H. Forster, CEO & Chairman of the Board; Thomas M. Jenkins, VP & Treasurer; Stephen F. Koziar, Group VP.

Benefits: Benefits include medical insurance, dental insurance, a 401(k) plan, sick pay, vacation, holidays, and an employee pension plan.

Human Resources: Darlene Mullin.

Application Procedures: Send resume and cover letter to the attention of the Human Resources Department.

▶ Internships

Contact: Jill Klaser.

Type: Offers a college internship program.

> If complacency is bad for your career, thinking into the future will keep you ahead of change. To others, it will seem as if you are moving effortlessly into the better jobs in the successful department or company. In fact, it will be because you worked hard, planned well and prepared yourself.
>
> Source: *Business Monday/Detroit Free Press*

DQE Inc.

1 Oxford Center
301 Grant St.
Pittsburgh, PA 15279
Phone: (412)393-6059
Fax: (412)393-4059

Business Description: Provider of electric and other utility services. Holding company engaged in holding or owning the securities of companies in order to exercise some degree of control over the companies' activities.

Officers: Gary L. Schwass, VP & Treasurer; Wesley W. von Schack, CEO, Pres. & Chairman of the Board.

Benefits: Benefits include medical insurance, dental insurance, a 401(k) plan, an employee pension plan, long and short-term disability, tuition assistance, and a smoke-free environment.

Human Resources: Maureen Lison, Director of Employment.

Application Procedures: Bring in a resume in person or send resume and cover letter to the attention of Maureen Lison, Director of Employment.

▶ Internships

Contact: Maureen Lison, Director of Employment.

Type: Offers various summer internships to college students.

Application Procedure: Send applications to Maureen Lison, Director of Employment.

Dresser Industries Inc.

1600 Pacific Bldg.
Dallas, TX 75201
Phone: (214)740-6000
Fax: (214)740-6584

Business Description: A global supplier of products and services primarily utilized in two core business areas: upstream and downstream energy activities. The company also produces equipment for selected industrial markets, including mining, construction, and general industry.

Officers: William E. Bradford, Sr. VP of Operations; James J. Corboy, Sr. VP; David P. McElvain, VP of Finance; John J. Murphy, Chairman of the Board, Pres., CEO & COO; Bill D. St. John, Exec. VP of Admin.; Ralph W. Ytterberg, Sr. VP of Operations.

Benefits: Benefits include medical insurance, dental insurance, vision insurance, an employee stock purchase plan, an employee pension plan, a 401(k) plan, and membership in various clubs.

Human Resources: Richard E. Hauslein; Danny Sanchez.

Application Procedures: Send resume and cover letter to the attention of Danny Sanchez, PO Box 718, Dallas, TX 75221.

▶ Internships

Type: The company does not offer an internship program.

Drummond Company Inc.
530 Beacon Pkwy. W.
PO Box 10246
Birmingham, AL 35202
Phone: (205)945-6500
Fax: (205)945-6557

Business Description: Drummond is one of the largest independent, privately owned coal companies in the United States and one of the nation's largest coal exporters. The Coal Division operates seven surface mines and four underground mines throughout the 5100-square-mile Warrior Coal Basin near Birmingham, Alabama. The nation's merchant producer of foundry coke, the ABC Coke Division of Drummund Company Inc., is a natural extension of the company's coal operation. Drummond produces nine million tons of coal annually, and owns over one billion tons of coal reserves.

Officers: Garry N. Drummond, CEO; Walter Johnsey, CFO.

Benefits: Benefits include medical insurance, dental insurance, life insurance, retirement plans, a 401(k) plan, paid holidays, vacation days, tuition assistance, and a smoke-free environment.

Human Resources: Mr. Joseph B. Bilich.

Application Procedures: Send resume and cover letter to the attention of Cindy Cook.

▶ **Internships**

Contact: Cindy Cook.

Type: Offers the "In-Roads" internship program for business and engineering.

Application Procedure: Send applications to the attention of Cindy Cook.

Duke Power Co.
422 S. Church St.
Charlotte, NC 28242-0001
Phone: (704)373-4011

Business Description: Duke Power is "the nation's seventh-largest investor-owned electric utility." Headquartered in Charlotte, North Carolina, the company serves 4.5 million people in a 20,000 square-mile service in North Carolina and South Carolina. Duke Power supplies electricity to more than 1.6 million residential, commercial and industrial customers in that area.

Officers: Sue A. Becht, Treasurer; Donald H. Denton Jr., Sr. VP of Mktg.; Excell O. Ferrell, III, VP of Operations; William S. Lee, Pres. & Chairman of the Board; Richard J. Osborne, VP of Finance.

Benefits: Benefits include an employee pension plan, a non-contributory, defined benefit retirement plans, holiday pay, vacation, and sick leave.

Human Resources: James R. Bavis.

Application Procedures: Job applications can be filled out on site only on Mondays, Wednesdays, and Fridays 9-4 pm. Places newspaper advertisements for certain openings. Send resume and cover letter to the attention of Personnel Department.

Thirty years after the Equal Pay Act was passed, women are still earning only 70 cents for every dollar a man makes.

Source: *Working Woman*

Eimco
Wemco
669 W. 2nd St.
Salt Lake City, UT 84101
Phone: (801)526-2000

Business Description: Manufacturer of mining machinery and equipment. Manufacturer of machinery and equipment for oil and gas fields, or for drilling water wells. Manufacturer of pumps and pumping equipment.

Human Resources: James R. Burns.

Application Procedures: Send resume and cover letter to the attention of Human Resources.

▶ **Internships**

Contact: Peggy Stone.

Type: The company offers an internship program.

Engelhard Corp.
101 Wood Ave.
Iselin, NJ 08818
Phone: (908)205-6000

Business Description: Manufacturer of petroleum, chemical, and environmental catalysts and pigments.

Officers: Nick Bayacher, Mktg. Mgr.; R. Keith Elliott, Sr. VP & CFO; Stephen I. Pook, Dir. of Info. Systems; Orin R. Smith, CEO & Pres.

Human Resources: William M. Dugle.

Application Procedures: The company does not accept unsolicited resumes.

▶ Internships

Type: Company offers engineering and research internships on an as needed basis.

Application Procedure: Applications should be forwarded to the Human Resources Department.

Enron Corp.

1400 Smith St.
Houston, TX 77002-7369
Phone: (713)853-6161

Business Description: An integrated natural gas energy company, from reservoir to the burner tip, and natural gas-fired generation of electricity. Through Enron Oil & Gas, natural gas is explored for and produced. Liquids in the natural gas stream are processed, marketed, and transported by Enron's liquid fuels companies. Natural gas is purchased, sold, and transported for residential, commercial, electric utility, and industrial markets by the natural gas pipeline group. The company's power subsidiary is participating in the expansion of electric power generation. Enron Corp. through its subsidiaries has a 38,000-mile pipeline network, an 84 percent interest in Enron Oil & Gas Company, and involvement in the liquid fuel businesses and four groups which have a total of 16 subsidiaries.

Officers: Ronald J. Burns, Sr. VP; Richard D. Kinder, Vice Chairman of the Board; Kenneth L. Lay, CEO, Pres. & Chairman of the Board; Jack I. Tompkins, Sr. VP & CFO.

Benefits: The company offers full benefits.

Human Resources: James G. Barnhart.

Application Procedures: The company intends to hire entry level staff in 1993 and 1994. Interested candidates should forward resumes to the attention of the Personnel Department. Graduates with two or more years of experience are encouraged to apply.

▶ Internships

Type: The company does not offer any internship programs.

Enserch Corp.

Enserch Center
300 S. St. Paul St.
Dallas, TX 75201
Phone: (214)651-8700

Business Description: Engaged in the operation of oil and/or gas field properties. Engaged in drilling oil and/or gas wells. Engaged in the transmission and distribution of natural gas.

Officers: William C. McCord, CEO, Pres. & Chairman of the Board; Sanford R. Singer, Sr. VP & CFO.

Benefits: Benefits include medical insurance, dental insurance, vision insurance, life insurance, short-term disability, long-term disability, an employee pension plan, a savings plan, tuition assistance, paid holidays, vacation days, maternity leave, employee activities, training programs, a 401(k) plan, and a stock purchase plan.

Application Procedures: Send resume and cover letter to the attention of the Employment Office, 1817 Wood St., Dallas, TX 75201.

▶ Internships

Type: The company does not offer an internship program.

Entergy Corp.

PO Box 61000
New Orleans, LA 70161
Phone: (504)529-5262

Business Description: An electric utility holding company. Its subsidiaries provide electricity to 1.7 million customers along the Mississippi River in Missouri, Arkansas, Mississippi, and Louisiana. They operate both nuclear power plants and fossil fuel plants.

Officers: James M. Cain, Sr. VP; Edwin Lupberger, Pres. & Chairman of the Board; Jerry L. Maulden, Sr. VP; Alan M. Wright, VP of Finance.

Benefits: Benefits include HMO's, a 401(k), an employee stock purchase plan, stock option plan, savings plan, credit unions, and long and short-term disability.

Application Procedures: The company only accepts resumes or applications when specific job openings are available. Phone: (504)569-4661.

▶ Internships

Contact: Henry Ryan, Contact.

Type: The company offers internships through the In-Roads program. Additionally, the company offers a program directed to minority college students.

Qualifications: Interns are paid according to grade average. Applicants must be college sophomores.

Application Procedure: Interested candidates should contact Henry Ryan.

Estee Lauder Inc.

767 5th Ave.
New York, NY 10153
Phone: (212)572-4200
Fax: (212)572-6745

Business Description: Manufactures cosmetics, perfumes, and other toiletries.

Officers: Robert Aquilina, Sr. VP & CFO; Leonard Lauder, CEO & Pres.; Saul Magram, Sr. VP.

Benefits: Benefits include 401(k), savings plan, health insurance, pension plan, and disability insurance.

Human Resources: Ed Callahan.

Application Procedures: Send resume and cover letter to the attention of the human resources department.

▶ Internships

Type: The company does not offer any internship programs.

Ethyl Corp.

330 S. 4th St.
PO Box 2189
Richmond, VA 23217
Phone: (804)788-5000

Business Description: Manufactures and markets chemicals for the petroleum and plastics industries, and chemical intermediates for detergents, electronics, agricultural chemicals, and pharmaceuticals. The company's four divisions are Industrial Chemicals, Electronic Materials, Performance Products, and Petroleum Additives. Manufacturing plants are located in Elgin, South Carolina; Feluy, Belgium; Houston, Texas; Magnolia, Arkansas; Orangeburg, South Carolina; Sarnia, Ontario, Canada; and Sauget, Illinois. Research and development facilities are located in Baton Rouge, Louisiana; Bracknell, Berkshire, England; Elgin and Orangeburg, South Carolina; Elk Grove Village, Illinois; Houston, Texas; and Magnolia, Arkansas.

Officers: Bruce C. Gottwald, Pres. & Chairman of the Board; Floyd D. Gottwald, Jr., CEO & Chairman of the Board; Charles B. Walker, Exec. VP & CFO.

Benefits: Benefits include HMO's and retirement plans with 50% company matched contributions.

Human Resources: Henry C. Page, Jr.

Application Procedures: The company accepts positions when employees are needed. Jobs and promotions are considered internally first. Job vacancies are advertised in newspapers. Interested candidates should contact the Human Resource Department.

▶ Internships

Type: The company does not offer any internship programs.

Federal Paper Board Company Inc.

75 Chestnut Ridge Rd.
Montvale, NJ 07645
Phone: (201)391-1776

Business Description: Manufactures and distributes paperboard products used by the folding carton and commercial printing industries. The company also produces market pulp, white lumber and specialty packaging. Federal Paper Board uses recycled paper in several of its facilities and maintains international sales offices in London, Tokyo, and Zurich.

Officers: Robert D. Baldwin, Sr. VP of Mktg.; Thomas L. Cox, Treasurer; J.R. Kennedy, CEO & Pres.; Quentin J. Kennedy, Exec. VP & Sec.

Human Resources: Donald J. Gardner.

▶ Internships

Type: The company does not offer an internship program.

Ferro Corp.

1000 Lakeside Ave.
Cleveland, OH 44114-1183
Phone: (216)641-8580

Business Description: Producer of specialty materials for industrial use.

Officers: Kenneth R. Barr, Group VP; Albert

Bersticker, Pres. & COO; Adolph Posnick, CEO & Chairman of the Board.

Benefits: Benefits include life insurance, medical insurance, health care and life insurance, dental insurance and an employee stock ownership plan.

Human Resources: Paul Richard.

Application Procedures: Send resume and cover letter to the attention of Human Resources.

▶ Internships

Type: Offers internships in engineering and codings.

Qualifications: College students.

Application Procedure: Contact the Human Resources department.

> Like your appearance, your attitude can deteriorate from bad habits you develop. Just as you can let the heels of your shoes run down, you can let your attitude run down. And, like your shoes, your attitude can reach a point of where it is so run down that you might as well throw it away and start fresh.
>
> Source: *Business Monday/Detroit Free Press*

First Mississippi Corp.

PO Box 1249
Jackson, MS 39215-1249
Phone: (601)948-7550

Business Description: Engaged in the development, manufacture, and marketing of specialty chemicals; the manufacture and marketing of industrial chemicals; the manufacture, marketing, and brokerage of fertilizer; the exploration for development, and production of natural gas and oil; the mining and marketing of coal; and the mining of and exploration for gold. In addition, the company is starting such operations as steel melting and casting; manufacturing combustion and incineration equipment; manufacturing industrial insulation products; and biotechnology research.

Officers: Charles M. McAuley, Group VP; R. Michael Summerford, VP & CFO; J.Kelly Williams, CEO & Chairman of the Board.

Benefits: Benefits include a 401(k) plan and a savings plan, health maintenance organizations, long-term disability, and sick benefits.

Human Resources: Del Oliver.

Application Procedures: The company accepts resumes for vacant positions only.

▶ Internships

Type: The company's subsidiaries offer internship progrms.

Florida Progress Corp.

PO Box 33042
St. Petersburg, FL 33733-8042
Phone: (813)824-6400

Business Description: Florida Progress is a holding company whose seven subsidiaries are engaged in utilities, energy and technology, real estate development, building products, financial services, and life insurance. The company's primary subsidiary, Florida Power, is an electric company with an annual customer growth rate of 4.1 percent, over twice the national average.

Officers: Dr. Jack B. Critchfield, CEO & Pres.; Andrew H. Hines, Jr., Chairman of the Board; Richard Korpan, Exec. VP & CFO.

Benefits: Benefits include an employee pension plan, health care programs, and life insurance.

Application Procedures: Send resume and cover letter.

▶ Internships

Type: The company does not offer an internship program.

FMC Corp.
Agricultural Chemical Group

2000 Market St.
Philadelphia, PA 19103
Phone: (215)299-6000

Business Description: Manufacturer of miscellaneous pesticides or agricultural chemicals.

Officers: David B. Cassidy, Dir. of Mktg.; David D. Eckert, Manager; Peter Laempitte, Controller; John Lowry, Dir. of Systems.

Benefits: Benefits include employee pension plan, 401(k), dental insurance, medical insurance, vacation days, and sick leave.

Human Resources: B. Russell Lockridge.

Application Procedures: Interested candidates should forward resumes with cover letters to the attention of Human Resources Department.

▶ **Internships**

Type: The company does not offer any internship programs.

Fort Howard Corp.
1919 S. Broadway
PO Box 19130
Green Bay, WI 54307-9130
Phone: (414)435-8821
Fax: (414)435-3703

Business Description: Manufacturer of paper tissue products for businesses, institutions, and homes. Fort Howard Corp. produces the steam and electricity, and some of the chemicals, needed for its manufacturing and recycling operations; performs in-house maintenance on machines; and operates a fleet of trucks to distribute its products. The company's manufacturing plants are located in Green Bay, Wisconsin; Muskogee, Oklahoma; Rincon, Georgia; and Fort Sterling, Manchester, England. In addition, the company has two subsidiaries. Harmon Associates buys, sells, and exports wastepaper. Ecosource sorts wastepaper.

Benefits: Benefits include medical insurance, 401(k), long and short-term disability insurance, paid vacation and holidays.

Human Resources: Gary Umhoeffer.

Application Procedures: Interested candidates should contact the local job service office for application information. Resumes are accepted only when a job is available. Direct resumes to the attention of the Human Resources Department.

▶ **Internships**

Type: The company offers an internship program.

Qualifications: Must be a college student in good standing.

Application Procedure: Interested candidates should contact the Personnel Department.

FPL Group Inc.
Golden Bear Plaza
PO Box 088801
North Palm Beach, FL 33408-8801
Phone: (407)694-6300

Business Description: A holding company providing electric service to approximately three million customers in the coastal regions of Florida. Its principal subsidiary is Florida Power & Light Co. Other activities include non-utility energy production, agriculture, real estate, technical services, and cable television.

Officers: James L. Broadhead, CEO & Pres.; Dennis P. Coyle, VP & General Counsel; J.L. Howard, VP & CFO.

Benefits: Benefits include medical insurance, life insurance, dental insurance, vision insurance, tuition assistance, 401(k), short and long term disability, family leave, maternity leave, and a pension plan.

Human Resources: Kammi Yates.

Application Procedures: Send resume and cover letter to the attention of Kammi Yates, P.O. Box 078768, West Palm Beach, FL 33407.

▶ **Internships**

Contact: Kammi Yates, Employment Coordinator.

Type: The company offers summer internships.

Qualifications: Candidates for internships must be college students.

Freeport-McMoRan Copper Company Inc.
6110 Plumas St.
Reno, NV 89509
Phone: (702)826-3000

Business Description: Engaged in mining or preparing copper ores.

Officers: G.A. Mealy, President.

Human Resources: Todd Graver, Employee Relations Specialist.

Application Procedures: Interested candidates should forward resumes and cover letters to Todd Graver, Employee Relations Specialist.

▶ **Internships**

Contact: Karen Coughlan, Employee Relations Supervisor.

Type: The company offers summer internships.

Qualifications: Applicants must be college seniors.

H.B. Fuller Co.

1200 West County Rd. E
Arden Hills, MN 55112
Phone: (612)481-4610
Fax: (612)481-0014

Business Description: Manufactures specialty chemicals. The company has the following major divisions: adhesive sealant coatings; Linear; Monarch; and TEC building products.

Officers: Vartkes H. Ehramjian, Sr. VP & CFO; Walter Kissling, Sr. VP of Intl. Operations; Rolf Schubert, VP of Research & Development.

Opportunities: Annually hires ten co-op/intern chemists and five full-time chemists with masters of science PhDs in chemistry or polymer science.

Benefits: Benefits include medical, dental, life, and short- and long-term disability insurances; vision insurance; an employee pension plan, a savings plan, profit sharing, bonuses/incentives, and tuition assistance; and 10 paid holidays per year, flexible holidays, 10 personal/sick days per year, and 10 vacation days at entry level. Other benefits include an employee counseling program, company-sponsored sports teams, and a smoke-free environment.

Human Resources: Leo Johnson.

Application Procedures: Recruits at Howard University, North Carolina State University and Purdue University. Also recruits at the Illinois Minority Career Fair. Places newspaper advertisements for certain openings in the *Minneapolis Tribune* and the *St. Paul Pioneer Press.* Send resume and cover letter to the attention of Lco Johnson, 1200 W. County Rd. E., Auden Hills, MN 55110.

▶ Internships

Contact: Tom Walters, Staffing Administrator.

Type: The company offers year round internships.

Qualifications: Applicants must be either high school or college students.

GAF Corp.

1361 Alps Rd.
Wayne, NJ 07470
Phone: (201)628-3000

Business Description: Manufactures specialty chemicals, roofing material, and glass fiber.

Officers: Richard Olsen, VP of Finance; Heinn F. Tomfohrde, President.

Average Entry-Level Hiring: Hiring levels are expected to increase during the next year.

Opportunities: Types of employees typically hired by the company include: executives, administrators, and managers; engineers, systems analysts, scientists, research chemists, and lawyers; paralegals and research lab technicians; marketing and sales staff; benefits and compensation administrators; and electricians and machinists.

Benefits: Benefits include: medical, dental, life, and short- and long-term disability insurances; vision insurance; 401(k); cafeteria; tuition assistance; health club.

Human Resources: A.M. Litzenberger; James Strupp.

Application Procedures: Advertises in *The New York Times* and trade journals. Some hiring is done through an employment agency. Faxed resumes are accepted at (201)628-3577. Send resume and cover letter to the attention of A.M. Litzenberger.

Gaylord Container Corp.

500 Lake Cook Rd., Ste. 400
Deerfield, IL 60015-4965
Phone: (708)405-5500

Business Description: Manufactures paper products which include corrugated containers (boxes), containerboard, unbleached kraft paper (from which brown paper grocery bags are made), and multiwall bags. Owns and operates four containerboard and paper mills, 23 converting facilities, and a kraft mill and multiwall bag manufacturing plant located in Pine Bluff, Arkansas.

Officers: Dan P. Casey, Sr. VP & Finance Officer; Marvin A. Pomerantz, CEO & Chairman of the Board; Harry R. Struthers, VP of Mktg. & Sales.

Average Entry-Level Hiring: Hiring levels are expected to increase.

Opportunities: Future positions will include full- and part-time jobs and freelance assignments.

Benefits: Benefits include medical, dental, life, and short- and long-term disability insurances, vision insurance, pension and savings plans, profit sharing, tuition assistance, and selected bonuses, 11 paid holidays, 2 flexible holidays, 9 personal/sick days, cumulative vacation plan, and maternity leave. Offers employees counseling, sports teams, cafeteria, smoke-free environment, training programs, credit union membership, and automatic banking.

Human Resources: Sue Dammann; Lawrence G. Rogna.

Application Procedures: Send resume and cover letter to the attention of Sue Dammann.

▶ Internships

Type: The company does not offer any internship programs.

General Public Utilities Corp.

100 Interpace Pkwy.
Parsippany, NJ 07054-1149
Phone: (201)263-6500

Business Description: Provides about 39 billion kilowatt hours of electricity for approximately 1.8 million customers. The company's service territories encompass about half the land area of Pennsylvania and New Jersey. The operating companies are: Jersey Central Power & Light Company in New Jersey; Metropolitan Edison Company and Pennsylvania Electric Company, both in Pennsylvania. General Portfolios Corporation (GPC), organized in 1988, is a holding company for non-utility business and investments. The only GPC subsidiary is Energy Initiatives, Inc., which was established to allow General Public Utilities to invest in cogeneration and other qualifying facilities. GPU Service Corporation provides integrated system plans and policies, along with a broad range of professional services to the operating companies and GPC. GPU Nuclear Corporation is responsible for the operation, maintenance, and management of the company's nuclear facilities.

Officers: Mary L. Breslin, Asst. Sec.; F. Allen Donofrio, VP & Comptroller; John G. Graham, Sr. VP & CFO; Standley H. Hoch, CEO, Pres. & Chairman of the Board; Ira H. Jolles, Sr. VP & General Counsel; Michael P. Morrell, VP & Treasurer; Mary A. Nalewako, Secretary.

Benefits: Benefits include a 401(k), dental insurance, vision insurance, tuition assistance, employee pension plan, post-retirement health and life insurance, short- and long-term disability, family leave, a smoke-free workplace, paid vacation days, personal/sick days, and credit union membership.

Application Procedures: Send resume and cover letter to the attention of Richard J. Postweiler.

▶ Internships

Type: The company does not have an internship program but may occasionally hire summer help.

> To make yourself more attractive to international employers, you might start with simple things: brushing up on your foreign languages or even learning a new one; seizing opportunities to travel abroad, whether for business or pleasure; cultivating overseas friends; or just reading widely about other cultures.
>
> Source: *Money*

Georgia Gulf Corp.

400 Perimeter Center Terrace, Ste. 595
Atlanta, GA 30346
Phone: (404)395-4500
Fax: (404)395-4529

Business Description: Georgia Gulf is a manufacturer of several highly integrated lines of commodity and polymer chemicals, including electrochemical, aromatic, and natural gas products.

Officers: Dennis M. Chorba, VP, General Counsel & Sec.; James R. Kuse, CEO & Chairman of the Board; Richard B. Marchese, VP of Finance & Treasurer; Jerry R. Satrum, Pres. & COO; Edwin S. Schiffer, Vice Pres.; Thomas G. Swanson, Vice Pres.

Benefits: Benefits include a 401(k).

Human Resources: Ronald M. Finley.

Application Procedures: The company advertises job vacancies through newspapers and private employment services. Interested candidates should forward applications with cover letters to James Worrell.

▶ Internships

Type: The company does not offer an internship program.

Georgia-Pacific Corp.
133 Peachtree St., NE
Atlanta, GA 30303
Phone: (404)521-4000

Business Description: Manufacturer and wholesale distributor of building products, industrial wood products, pulp, paper, packaging, and related chemicals. Georgia-Pacific is one of the world's largest manufacturers of forest products. It has facilities in 48 states, Brazil, Canada, and the United Kingdom.

Officers: A.D. Correll, Exec. VP; Diane Durgin, Sr. VP; Donald L. Glass, Sr. VP; T. Marshall Hahn, Jr., CEO & Chairman of the Board; Ronald P. Hogan, Pres. & COO; Davis K. Mortensen, Exec. VP; Carroll T. Tolar, Sr. VP of Engineering; James C. Van Meter, Exec. VP of Finance & CFO.

Benefits: Benefits include an employee pension plan, a savings plan, and an employee stock purchase plan.

Human Resources: David W. Reynolds.

Application Procedures: Send resume and cover letter to the attention of Human Resources, PO Box 105605, Atlanta, GA 30348.

▶ Internships

Type: The company offers communications and engineering internships to junior and senior college students. Internships are compensated by credit or by pay. Interested candidates should contact the Human Resources Department for more information.

Gillette Co.
Prudential Tower Bldg.
Boston, MA 02199
Phone: (617)421-7000

Business Description: Develops, manufactures, and markets personal care products, stationery supplies, and small appliances. Operates 54 manufacturing facilities in 26 countries. The company's products are sold worldwide. Gillette blades and razors lead the market in many countries, as do Oral-B toothbrushes. In addition, Gillette "is the world's top seller of writing instruments."

Officers: Gaston R. Levy, Exec. VP; Colman M. Mockler, Jr., CEO & Chairman of the Board; Lloyd B. Swaim, VP & Treasurer; John W. Symons, Exec. VP; Lorne R. Waxlax, Exec. VP.

Benefits: Benefits include medical insurance, health care and life insurance, short-term disability, long-term disability, tuition assistance, dental insurance, vision insurance, a 401(k) plan, an employee pension plan and an employee stock ownership plan.

Human Resources: Jan Roiter.

Application Procedures: Send resume and cover letter to the attention of Jan Roiter.

▶ Internships

Contact: Jan Roiter, Employment Mgr.

Type: Offers summer internships.

Qualifications: Seniors and college students.

Application Procedure: Send application to Jan Roiter.

P.H. Glatfelter Co.
228 S. Main St.
Spring Grove, PA 17362
Phone: (717)225-4711

Business Description: A manufacturer of printing papers and tobacco and other specialty papers at paper mills located in Spring Grove, Pennsylvania; Pisgah Forest, North Carolina; and Neenah, Wisconsin.

Officers: W.F. Boswell, III, Vice Pres.; D. F. Grady, Comptroller; M.A. Johnson, II, Exec. VP, CFO & Treasurer; J.F. Myers, Vice Pres.; T.C. Norris, CEO, Pres. & Chairman of the Board; R.W. Wand, VP of Admin.; R.S. Wood, Sec. & Asst. Treasurer.

Benefits: Benefits include medical insurance, life insurance, vision insurance, dental insurance, and a pension plan.

Human Resources: Thomas Buckovich; Thomas H. Crawford.

Application Procedures: Send resume and cover letter to the attention of Kenneth Ross, Training and Personnel Manager ; Thomas Crawford.

▶ Internships

Type: There is no formal internship program, but the company does occasionally offer summer positions to students. These positions are advertised in the newspaper.

W.R. Grace & Co.

1 Town Center Rd.
Boca Raton, FL 33486
Phone: (407)362-2000

Business Description: Manufactures industrial chemicals, flexible packaging, water treatment, and construction products that are marketed globally. Its diverse interests include cocoa, energy services, textiles, agricultural feed, and book and cassette distribution. It employs 24,000 at 400 facilities in 42 countries.

Officers: J. Peter Grace, CEO & Chairman of the Board; Brian J. Smith, Exec. VP & CFO.

Benefits: Benefits include, medical insurance, dental insurance, life insurance, short- and long-term disability, pension plan, and a 401k plan.

Human Resources: Christine Hilker; William L. Monroe.

Application Procedures: Send resume and cover letter to the attention of Christine Hilker.

▶ Internships

Contact: Christine Hilker, Contact.

Type: The offering of summer internships varies according to departmental needs.

Qualifications: Candidates for internships must be college students.

Great Lakes Chemical Corp.

PO Box 2200
West Lafayette, IN 47906
Phone: (317)497-6100

Business Description: Great Lakes Chemical Corporation is a producer of bromine, brominated specialty chemicals, and furfural derivatives. Based in West Lafayette, Indiana, it has more than 50 sales, production, and distribution facilities in the U.S., Europe, and Japan.

Officers: William P. Blake, Vice Pres.; David A. Hall, VP of Development; Lowell C. Horwedel, Vice Pres.; Robert T. Jeffares, VP of Finance & CFO; Emerson Kampen, CEO, Pres. & Chairman of the Board; Robert B. McDonald, Sr. VP; B.G McGuire, Sr. VP; John B. Talpas, VP & Mgr.; Dennis R. Venters, Vice Pres.; Frank H. Wheeler, Sr. VP.

Benefits: Benefits include an employee pension plan, medical insurance, dental insurance, life insurance, tuition assistance, and long-term disability insurance.

Human Resources: Gayle Hardison.

Application Procedures: Send resume and cover letter to the attention of Gayle Hardison.

▶ Internships

Contact: Gayle Hardison.

Type: The company offers summer internships to college students. Opportunities fluctuate depending upon different department's needs.

The National Association of Environmental Educators estimates that, nationwide, there are 125 to 200 environmental programs at four-year universities. Enrollment has doubled or tripled at environmental-studies programs at University of Colorado at Boulder, Southern Vermont College, Colorado School of Mines, and many other universities.

Source: *Garbage*

Gulf States Utilities Co.

350 Pine St.
Beaumont, TX 77701
Phone: (409)838-6631

Business Description: Generates, transmits, and sells electricity to more than 563,000 customers in a 28-thousand square mile area that stretches from Baton Rouge, Louisiana, to Austin, Texas. The company also supplies steam and electricity to a large industrial customer through a cogeneration facility in Baton Rouge, and is a partner in a cogeneration project, Nelson Industrial Steam Co., near Lake Charles. Gulf States owns and operates a natural gas retail distribution system serving about 83,000 customers in the Baton Rouge area.

Officers: James C. Deddens, Sr. VP; Joseph L. Donnelly, Sr. Exec. VP & CFO; E. Linn Draper, Jr., CEO, Pres. & Chairman of the Board; Calvin J. Hebert, Sr. VP; Edward M. Loggins, Sr. Exec. VP of Operations; James E. Moss, VP of Mktg.

Benefits: Benefits include an employee pension plan, 401(k), and post-retirement health and life insurance.

Human Resources: J. Lee Miller.

Application Procedures: Send resume and cover letter to the attention of Human Resources, though the company is currently engaged in a hiring freeze.

▶ Internships

Type: The company does not offer an internship program.

Halliburton Co.

500 N. Acker St.
Dallas, TX 75201-3391
Phone: (214)978-2600

Business Description: Diversified oil field services and engineering and construction company with international interests and a work force of 77,000 worldwide. The company also provides insurance services.

Officers: Jerry H. Blurton, VP & Controller; Lester L. Coleman, Exec. VP of Finance; Thomas H. Cruikshank, CEO & Chairman of the Board; C. Robert Fielder, VP & Treasurer; Dale P. Jones, President; Susan S. Keith, VP & Sec.; Robert M. Kennedy, VP & Legal Counsel; Guy T. Marcus, VP of Investor Relations; Jack R. Skinner, VP of Taxes.

Benefits: Benefits include an employee pension plan, medical insurance, dental insurance, and life insurance. Also offers a 401(k) plan.

Human Resources: Karen S. Stuart.

Application Procedures: Places newspaper advertisements for certain openings. Send resume and cover letter to the attention of Karen S. Stuart.

▶ Internships

Type: Offers an internship program.

Application Procedure: Contact the company for more information.

Handy & Harman

555 Theodore Frend
New York, NY 10022
Phone: (212)661-2400
Fax: (914)925-4497

Business Description: Engaged in the primary smelting and refining of nonferrous metals other than copper and aluminum. Engaged in the secondary smelting and refining of nonferrous metals. Engaged in rolling, drawing or extruding nonferrous metals other than copper and aluminum.

Officers: George G. Cimini, Vice Pres.; Donald A. Corrigan, VP of Research & Development; Richard N. Daniel, Pres. & Chairman of the Board; Philip G. Deuchler, Group VP; George P. Ekern, VP, General Counsel & Sec.; Frank E. Grzelecki, Vice Chairman of the Board; William H. Martinson, Controller; Stephen B. Mudd, VP & Treasurer; Joseph M. O'Donnell, Group VP; Robert M. Thompson, Group VP; Barry Wayne, Vice Pres.

Benefits: Benefits include an employee pension plan.

Human Resources: Mary Sullivan.

Application Procedures: Send resume and cover letter to the attention of Human Resources.

▶ Internships

Type: The company does not offer an internship program.

M.A. Hanna Co.

1301 E. 9th St., Ste. 3600
Cleveland, OH 44114-1860
Phone: (216)589-4000
Fax: (216)589-4109

Business Description: The company is made up of 16 business units operating in the formulated polymers, natural resources, insurance, marine services, and metallurgical research industries. In the formulated polymers segment, those subsidiaries engaged in the custom compounding of polymers are Burton Rubber Processing, Inc. (with four plants), Colonial Rubber Works, Inc. (two plants), and Southwest Chemical Services. Those engaged in producing custom formulated colorants for plastics are Allied Color Industries, Inc. (3 plants), Avecor, Inc. (4 plants), and PMS Consolidated. Those engaged in the distribution of plastic shapes, films, and resins are Cadillac Plastic Group (141 branches worldwide) and Bruck Plastics Co. (six branches). Those engaged in the manufacture of polymer products are Colonial Rubber Works, Inc. (producing rubber roofing membrane and automotive sponge products), Day International Printing Products (producing polymer printing blankets and operating four plants), and Day International Textile Products (producing polymer consumables for the textile industry at two plants). In the natural resources segment, M.A. Hanna Co. is a joint venture partner in a Colorado surface coal mine; holds a 28 percent interest in and manages an iron ore operation in Canada; and owns interests in oil and gas production operations in the U.S.

Officers: Ronald G. Fountain, VP of Finance & CFO; Douglas J. McGregor, Pres. & COO; Martin D. Walker, CEO & Chairman of the Board.

Benefits: Benefits include insurance plans and a savings plan.

Human Resources: Thomas E. Wilson.

Application Procedures: Resumes kept on file for one year. Send resume and cover letter to the attention of Thomas E. Wilson.

▶ **Internships**

Contact: Thomas E. Wilson.

Type: Internships are offered on an "as needed" basis.

Application Procedure: Send applications to Thomas E. Wilson or other specific department heads. Any education or experience is helpful.

Hawaiian Electric Industries Inc.
PO Box 2750
Honolulu, HI 96840
Phone: (808)543-5662
Fax: (808)543-7966

Business Description: An electric utility holding company with diverse holdings.

Officers: Robert F. Clarke, Group VP; Robert F. Mougeot, VP & CFO; C. Dudley Pratt, Jr., CEO & Pres.; Harwood D. Williamson, Group VP.

Benefits: Benefits include medical insurance, dental insurance, and accidental death and dismemberment insurance. Also offers retirement benefits, a savings plan, and a 401(k) plan.

Application Procedures: Send resume and cover letter to the attention of Joan Diamond, PO Box 2750, Honolulu, HI 96840.

▶ **Internships**

Type: Offering internships again in 1994.

Application Procedure: Apply to the Employment Office.

Application Deadline: Apply no later than Nov. 30, 1994.

Helene Curtis Industries Inc.
325 N. Wells St.
Chicago, IL 60610
Phone: (312)661-0222

Business Description: Develops and manufactures personal care products.

Officers: Lewis D. Duberman, VP, CFO & Treasurer; Ronald J. Gidwitz, CEO & Pres.

Benefits: Benefits include medical insurance, life insurance, disability insurance, profit sharing, and employee stock options.

Human Resources: Mary Wilson.

Application Procedures: Send resume and cover letter to the attention of Mary Wilson.

▶ **Internships**

Contact: Mary Wilson, Human Resources Mgr.

Type: Offers internships through the "In Roads" program.

Helmerich & Payne Inc.
Utica & 21st St.
Tulsa, OK 74114
Phone: (918)742-5531

Business Description: A diversified, energy-oriented company engaged in contract drilling, oil and gas exploration and production, chemicals manufacturing, and real estate development and management. The company also holds substantial equity investments in several other publicly-owned corporations.

Officers: Allen S. Braumiller, Vice Pres.; Douglas E. Fears, VP of Finance; Robert G. Gambrell, Treasurer; Hans Helmerich, Pres. & CEO; W.H. Helmerich, III, Chairman of the Board; W.R. Horkey, Sr. VP; Steven R. Mackey, VP & General Counsel; Ray Marsh, Vice Pres.; Steven R. Shaw, VP of Production.

Benefits: Benefits include employee pension plan, medical insurance, and dental insurance.

Human Resources: Todd Sprague.

Application Procedures: Places newspaper advertisements for certain openings. Send resume and cover letter to the attention of Todd Sprague.

▶ **Internships**

Type: Offers internships when needed.

Hercules Inc.
Hercules Plaza
1313 N. Market
Wilmington, DE 19894
Phone: (302)594-5000
Fax: (302)594-7097

Business Description: Manufactures fragrance and food ingredients at plants in Harbor

Beach, Michigan; Middletown, New York; and Safety Harbor and Vero Beach, Florida. Manufactures chemicals for paper in Brunswick and Savannah, Georgia; Chicopee, Massachusetts; Franklin, Virginia; Hattiesburg, Mississippi; Kalamazoo, Michigan; and Milwaukee, Wisconsin. Resins are manufactured in Brunswick, Georgia; Burlington and Gibbstown, New Jersey; Hattiesburg, Mississippi; and Jefferson, Pennsylvania. The Advanced Materials and Systems segment manufactures carbon fiber and composite structures fabricated from carbon fiber products, and is developing technologies for liquid molding resin systems, advanced ceramics, and performance coatings. These plants are located in Clearfield and Magna, Utah; Culver City and San Jose, California; Deer Park, Texas; and Middletown, Delaware. The Aerospace segment manufactures solid rocket motor systems and ordnance, and is involved in missile programs. These plants are in Cedar Knolls, Chester, and Kenvil, New Jersey; Rocket Center, West Virginia; Clearwater, Florida; Magna, Utah; McGregor, Texas; Norwich, New York; Vergennes, Vermont; Radford, Virginia; and Lawrence, Kansas. Polypropylene fiber products are manufactured in Deer Park, Texas, and Oxford, Georgia. Packaging films for candy, snacks, and tobacco products are made in Covington, Virginia, and Terre Haute, Indiana. Water-soluble polymers are manufactured by Aqualon Co. in Hopewell, Virginia; Kenedy, Texas; Louisiana; Missouri; and Parlin, New Jersey. Sales offices are located in Agawam, Massachusetts; Atlanta, Georgia; Beaverton, Oregon; Chicago, Illinois; Cincinnati, Ohio; Dallas, Texas; Detroit, Michigan; Green Bay, Wisconsin; Kalamazoo, Michigan; Los Angeles, California; Mobile, Alabama; Richmond, Maryland; San Francisco, California; Savannah, Georgia; Shreveport, Louisiana; Waterville, Maine; and Wilmington, Delaware. In addition, 37 other plants and offices are located throughout Europe and in Canada, Mexico, and Brazil.

Officers: Fred L. Buckner, Pres. & COO; Eugene D. Crittenden, Jr.; Sr. VP; Arden B. Engebretsen, VP & CFO; Thomas L. Gossage, CEO & Chairman of the Board.

Benefits: Benefits include an employee pension plan.

Human Resources: Thomas J. McCarthy.

Application Procedures: The company generally accepts mailed resumes to the attention of Fred Lequenta.

▶ Internships

Contact: Fred Lequenta.

Type: The company has established an internship program for chemical engineers with specific universities.

Qualifications: Interested candidates should have completed two or more years of college.

Application Procedure: For application information, please contact Fred Lequenta.

Homestake Mining Co.

650 California St., 9th Fl.
San Francisco, CA 94108-2788
Phone: (415)981-8150

Business Description: Homestake is an international gold mining company. It has gold interests, as well as other natural resource interests, in the United States, Australia, Chile, and Canada.

Officers: Harry M. Conger, CEO & Chairman of the Board; David K. Fagin, Pres. & COO; Richard W. Stumbo, Jr., VP & CFO.

Benefits: Benefits include medical insurance, dental insurance, and life insurance. Also offers a 401(k) plan and a retirement plan.

Human Resources: Richard R. Hinkel.

Application Procedures: Send resume and cover letter to the attention of Richard R. Hinkel.

▶ Internships

Type: Offers internships through the McCoughlin program.

Houston Industries Inc.

5 Post Oak Park
2700 Post Oak Pkwy.
PO Box 4567
Houston, TX 77210
Phone: (713)629-3000

Business Description: Houston Industries, Inc.'s core business is Houston Lighting & Power Co., an electric utility using coal, lignite, gas, and uranium. This utility company serves a 5,000 square-mile area along Texas' Gulf Coast, including Houston. Houston Industries Inc. has five other subsidiaries. KBLCOM Inc. is a cable television operator serving 559,000 customers in

Texas, Minnesota, Oregon, and California. It operates a 50 percent partnership with Paragon Cable, which serves 865,000 customers. Utility Fuels, Inc. supplies, transports, and handles coal for Houston Lighting & Power Co. and for other businesses. Innovative Controls, Inc. manufactures outdoor lights. Houston Industries Finance, Inc. purchases and finances accounts receivable for Houston Lighting & Power Co. and KBLCOM Inc. Development Ventures, Inc. is a venture capital company, assisting service and manufacturing businesses.

Officers: William A. Cropper, VP & Treasurer; Hollis R. Dean, Exec. VP & CFO; Don D. Jordan, CEO & Pres.

Benefits: Benefits include employee pensions.

Human Resources: Ross E. Doan; Paul Pierce.

Application Procedures: Send resume and cover letter to the attention of Paul Pierce.

▶ Internships

Type: The company does not offer an internship program.

Idaho Power Co.

1221 West Idaho
PO Box 70
Boise, ID 83702
Phone: (208)383-2200

Business Description: An independent, investor-owned utility. At the end of 1989, it supplied electric energy to over 284,000 general business customers in a 20,000 square-mile area, encompassing parts of southern Idaho, eastern Oregon and northern Nevada. The company is a combination hydro-thermal utility with 16 hydro power plants and part ownership in three coal-fired generating plants.

Officers: Wayne W. Anderson, Pres. & COO; Clifford E. Bissell, Sr. VP of Power Supply; Daniel K. Bowers, VP & Treasurer; Larry R. Gunnoe, VP of Distribution; DuWayne D. Hammond, Jr., VP & CFO; J. Lamont Keen, Controller; Logan E. Lanham, Sr. VP of Public Affairs; Joseph W. Marshall, CEO & Chairman of the Board; Jan B. Packwood, Vice Pres. Power Supply; Robert W. Stahman, VP, General Counsel & Sec.

Benefits: Benefits include employee pension plan, medical insurance, dental insurance, vision insurance, life insurance, long-term disability, tuition assistance, paid holidays, personal/sick days, vacation days, counseling, sports teams, cafeteria, flex time, smoke-free environment, and training programs.

Human Resources: Paul L. Jauregui; Dan Minor; Jim Lambert; Richard Wearier.

Application Procedures: Applications can be picked up from receptionist. Application must accompany resume. Send resume and cover letter to the attention of Human Resources Department.

▶ Internships

Type: Offers internships mostly in engineering.

Application Procedure: Send applications to Human Resources. Recruits from schools and looks for experience.

> A myriad of possibilities for volunteer service are available in the United States and abroad, ranging from community service to education to development projects. . . In addition to the personal rewards volunteer service offers, volunteering can actually be a step toward a future career goal.
>
> Source: *Journal of Career Planning & Employment*

Illinois Power Co.

500 S. 27th St.
Decatur, IL 62525
Phone: (217)424-6600

Business Description: A public utility principally engaged in the generation, transmission, distribution, and sale of electric energy and the distribution and sale of natural gas solely in the state of Illinois. The company's territory is approximately 15,000 square miles, or one-quarter of the state and serves approximately 549,000 customers.

Officers: Larry F. Altenbaumer, Controller; Larry S. Brodsky, Vice Pres. Technical Services; Wilfred Connell, Vice Pres. Fossil Power Generation; Larry D. Haab, President; Larry L. Idleman, Vice Pres. Corporate Services; Wendell J. Kelley, CEO & Chairman of the Board; Paul L. Lang, Vice Pres.; Ann H. McEvoy, Asst. Sec.; J. Stephen Perry, Vice Pres. Nuclear Power Generation; Robert A. Schultz, Treasurer; Gary L. Secor, Asst. Treasurer; Rodney A. Smith, Vice

Pres.; Leah Manning Stetzner, General Counsel & Sec.; Charles W. Wells, Exec. VP; Porter J. Womeldorff, Vice Pres. Gas Resources & Planning Activities.

Benefits: Benefits include an employee pension plan, medical insurance, savings plan, and a 401(k) plan. Also offers an employee assistance program.

Human Resources: Veta Rudolph, Professional Recruiting Specialist.

Application Procedures: Keeps applications on file for one year. Send resume and cover letter to the attention of Veta Rudolph, Professional Recruiting Specialist.

▶ Internships

Contact: Veta Rudolph, Professional Recruiting Specialist.

Type: Offers internships when needed.

IMC Fertilizer Group Inc.

2100 Sanders Rd.
Northbrook, IL 60062
Phone: (708)272-9200

Business Description: Produces phosphatic fertilizer, phosphate rock, and industrial organic chemicals. Engages in strip-mining to remove surface contamination by phosphates.

Benefits: Benefits include medical, dental, life, and short- and long-term disability insurances, an employee pension plan, a savings plan, paid holidays, personal/sick days, vacation days, maternity leave, an employee counseling program, company-sponsored sports teams, an employee cafeteria, a smoke-free environment, and training programs.

Human Resources: Sandra Tippet.

Application Procedures: After Human Resources reviews resumes, candidates are contacted to fill out an application, and then called for an interview. Send resume and cover letter to the attention of Sandra Tippet, 2100 Sanders Rd., Northbrook, IL 60062.

▶ Internships

Type: The company does not offer an internship program.

Inland Steel Industries Inc.

30 W. Monroe St.
Chicago, IL 60603
Phone: (312)346-0300

Business Description: A holding company operating through its three subsidiaries in the steel industry. Inland Steel Co. is the fourth-largest producer of steel in the U.S., and is located at the Indiana Harbor Works in East Chicago. The company operates a research and development facility and maintains a Great Lakes fleet and railroad hopper cars. Joseph T. Ryerson & Son Inc. and J.M. Tull Metals Co. Inc. are steel service center companies. They operate 28 and 18 service centers, respectively, across the country. In addition, Inland Steel Industries Inc. is involved in two joint ventures with Nippon Steel Corp. I/N Tek operates a cold rolling facility near New Carlisle, Indiana, and I/N Kote plans to build two galvanized coating lines nearby.

Officers: Paul M. Anderson, VP of Finance; Robert J. Darnall, Pres. & COO; Frank W. Luerssen, CEO & Chairman of the Board; Robert E. Powell, VP of Mktg.

Benefits: Benefits include an employee pension plan, 401(k), an employee stock ownership plan, an HMO, and a credit union.

Human Resources: Judd R. Cool.

Application Procedures: The company is not currently accepting resumes or applications at the moment. The company posts job vacancies. Interested candidates should contact the human resources department.

▶ Internships

Type: The company is not currently offering any internships.

International Flavors & Fragrances Inc.

521 W. 57th St.
New York, NY 10019
Phone: (212)765-5500

Business Description: Develops and manufactures fragrances for personal products such as soups, detergents, and shampoos, and flavors needed to improve food and beverage products, including microwave and fast foods.

Officers: Ronald D. Anderson, Sr. VP; Eugene P. Gresanti, Pres. & Chairman of the Board; John P. Winandy, VP of Finance & Treasurer.

Benefits: Benefits include 401(k) and an HMO.

Application Procedures: The company accepts unsolicited resumes and keeps them on file for a limited time. Available positions are advertised in the newspapers and are posted on bulletin boards. The company does not use employment agencies.

▶ **Internships**

Contact: Shirley Dawkins, Employment Managers.

Type: The company offers marketing internships. Interested candidates should forward resumes to Shirley Dawkins.

International Paper Co.

2 Manhattanville Rd.
Purchase, NY 10577
Phone: (914)397-1500

Business Description: Manufactures wood pulp; reprographic, writing, coated, and fine paper; paperboard and packaging; photographic products; panel products; nonwoven fabric products; rosins and resins; and wood products. Operates manufacturing plants in 25 countries and exports to over 130. In the United States alone, it enjoys annual revenues of nearly $3 billion from its approximately 250 wholesale and retail outlets. It employs over 60,000 worldwide.

Officers: Robert C. Butler, Sr. VP & CFO; John A. Georges, CEO & Chairman of the Board.

Benefits: Benefits include tuition assistance and short term disability.

Human Resources: Robert M. Byrnes.

Application Procedures: The company does not accept unsolicited resumes. Job vacancies are filled through classified ads or private recruiting companies.

▶ **Internships**

Type: The company offers summer internships for investment and corporate communications to college students from participating schools only.

IPALCO Enterprises Inc.

PO Box 1595
Indianapolis, IN 46206
Phone: (317)261-8261

Business Description: IPALCO is a holding company of which Indianapolis Power & Light Co. and Mid-America Capital Resources Inc. are subsidiaries. Mid-America was formed as a holding company for nonutility activities. IPL serves more than 380,000 residential, commercial, and industrial customers in a 528 square mile area in central Indiana.

Officers: John R. Brehm, VP & Treasurer; Robert W. Hill, Pres. & Chairman of the Board; John R. Hodowal, Pres. & Chairman of the Board.

Benefits: Benefits include maternity leave, vacation days, personal/sick days, compensatory time, extended leave, employee parking, flex time, medical insurance, dental insurance, recreational programs, floating holidays, and a leave of absence program.

Application Procedures: The company does not accept resumes unless submitted in response to external postings or advertised on the job line (317)261-8515. If interested, candidates should forward resumes to the employment department with cover letters expressing interest in a specific position in order for their resumes to be considered.

▶ **Internships**

Type: The company is no longer offering internships.

> Your future in the world of work will depend at least in part on your ability to express yourself in groups. One thing you can do in the near future is sign up for a class in public speaking. There you can get practice and guidance in speaking in front of a group.
>
> Source: *Business Monday/Detroit Free Press*

Island Creek Corp.

PO Box 11430
Lexington, KY 40575-1430
Phone: (606)288-3000

Business Description: Engaged in the development of underground mines containing bituminous coal and/or the production of bituminous coal in underground mines.

Officers: Joellen E. Drisko, VP of Finance; D. Moore, Dir. of Info. Systems; Sylvester O. Ogden, CEO; R. S. Woolard, Dir. of Mktg.

Benefits: Benefits include medical insurance,

dental insurance, tuition assistance, savings plan, and retirement plans.

Human Resources: David La Belle.

Application Procedures: The company is currently experiencing a hiring freeze, but the company accepts resumes with cover letters only. Interested candidates should contact Joyce Lloyd for further information.

▶ Internships

Contact: Joyce Lloyd, Contact.

Type: The company offers internships in accounting and data processing to college students. Interested candidates should contact Joyce Lloyd.

ITT Rayonier Inc.

1177 Summer St.
Stamford, CT 06904
Phone: (203)348-7000
Fax: (203)964-4528

Business Description: Produces chemical cellulose, fluff pulps, specialty pulps, logs, lumber, chemicals, and grows and harvests trees. Provides forest management services. The company has four pulp mills, two lumber mills, three chemical manufacturing facilities, and 1.26 million acres of timberland.

Officers: Macdonald Auguste, Treasurer; Roman Balzar, Vice Pres.; William S. Berry, Sr. VP; James R. Bland, Vice Pres.; John B. Canning, Corp. Sec. & Assoc. General Counsel; Ronald L. Casebier, Vice Pres.; Jerome D. Gregoire, Vice Pres.; Ronald M. Gross, CEO, Pres. & Chairman of the Board; Grant J. Munro, Vice Pres.; Leroy D. Nott, Vice Pres.; W. Lee Nutter, Exec. VP; Kevin S. O'Brien, Sr. VP; Gerald J. Pollack, VP & CFO; Ronald K. Rogstad, Vice Pres.; Dennis C. Snyder, Vice Pres.; Michael E. Zaleski, Vice Pres.

Opportunities: Entry level positions depend on specific job openings, but may include accounting, finance, engineering, and marketing.

Benefits: Benefits include medical insurance, dental insurance, life insurance, short-term disability, an employee pension plan, a savings plan, tuition assistance, ten paid holidays and two flexible holidays per year, unlimited personal/sick days, ten vacation days per year, an employee counseling program, a smoke-free environment, a 401(k) plan, an employee stock ownership plan, and 50 percent off rooms at Sheraton hotels.

Human Resources: Geoffrey R. Broom; Thomas J. Gildea; Cynthia Kabbe.

Application Procedures: Recruits at the University of Georgia and Emory University. Advertises in *New York Times, Wall Street Journal,* and various local papers. Send resume and cover letter to the attention of Cynthia Kabbe.

▶ Internships

Type: Internship availability varies from year to year but usually includes accounting and/or MIS positions.

Application Procedure: Interested candidates should contact Human Resources to inquire about availability.

James River Corp.

PO Box 2218
Richmond, VA 23217
Phone: (804)644-5411

Business Description: Produces communication papers, consumer-hygienics products, coated films, Dixie products, packaging materials, specialty papers, and disposable foodservice products. Encompasses 160 manufacturing facilities located in the United States, Canada, Mexico, and ten European countries. It employs over 38,000 worldwide.

Officers: Robert C. Williams, CEO & Pres.

Benefits: Offers full-range corporate benefits.

Human Resources: Barbara Lanier.

Application Procedures: Accepts unsolicited resumes. Send resume and cover letter to the attention of Barbara Lanier.

▶ Internships

Contact: Barbara Lanier, Mgr. of Recruitment Services.

Type: Offers an internship program.

Application Procedure: Contact Barbara Lanier for information.

Jefferson Smurfit Corp.

8182 Maryland Ave.
St. Louis, MO 63105
Phone: (314)746-1100
Fax: (314)746-1276

Business Description: Operator of paperboard

mills. Manufacturer of corrugated and solid fiber boxes and related products. Manufacturer of folding paperboard boxes.

Officers: John R. Funke, CFO; Michael W.J. Smurfit, CEO & Chairman of the Board; Ron L. Yates, VP of Mktg. & Sales.

Benefits: Benefits include tuition assistance and maternity leave.

Human Resources: Thomas W. Hardy.

Application Procedures: Advertises in in newspapers. Send resume and cover letter to the attention of Personnel Departmemt.

▶ Internships

Type: The company does not offer an internship program.

S.C. Johnson and Son Inc.

1525 Howe St.
Racine, WI 53403
Phone: (414)631-2000
Fax: (414)631-4483

Business Description: Manufactures laundry aids, cleaners, air fresheners, wall products, insecticides and personal care products under consumer product names such as Pledge, Raid, Edge, and Agree. Other company ventures include insurance and real estate services. It maintains operations in 48 countries.

Officers: Larry L. Beebe, VP of Sales; Richard M. Carpenter, CEO; William D. George, Jr., COO & Pres.; Donald A. Houselander, Dir. of Info. Systems; S.C. Johnson, Chairman of the Board; Larry K. Switzer, Sr. VP & CFO.

Benefits: Benefits include child care programs, an elder care account program, maternity leave, flextime, job-sharing and part-time work for some employees, an employee assistance program, a fitness center program, on-site medical care, recreational facilities, tuition assistance, scholarships for the children of employees, profit sharing, an employee pension plan, and a 401(k) plan.

Human Resources: M. Garvin Shantster.

Application Procedures: Send resume and cover letter to the attention of M. Garvin Shantster.

▶ Internships

Type: Offers a college internship program.

Qualifications: Research and development, finance, marketing, and engineering students.

Application Procedure: Apply to the Human Resources staff.

Kentucky Utilities Co.

1 Quality St.
Lexington, KY 40507
Phone: (606)255-1461
Fax: (606)288-1125

Business Description: Engages in the production and sale of electricity in Kentucky. State's largest electric utility, serving 77 of its 120 counties. Also provides service to 5 counties in southwestern Virginia.

Officers: John T. Newton, CEO, Pres. & Chairman of the Board; Lynwood Schrader, Sr. VP of Customer Services Info. & Field Operations; Michael R. Whitley, Sr. VP & CFO.

Benefits: Benefits include medical insurance, life insurance, dental insurance, a 401(k) plan, vacation and all major holidays.

Human Resources: Wayne Jackson.

Application Procedures: Look for posted jobs in the lobby or send resume and cover letter to the attention of Wayne Jackson.

▶ Internships

Type: The company does not offer an internship program.

Kerr-McGee Corp.

Kerr-McGee Center
PO Box 25861
Oklahoma City, OK 73125
Phone: (405)270-1313

Business Description: A diversified energy and chemical company.

Officers: Ray A. Freels, Sr. VP; John C. Linehan, Sr. VP & CFO; Jere W. McKenny, Pres. & COO; Frank A. McPherson, CEO & Chairman of the Board.

Benefits: Benefits include an employee pension plan, employee stock ownership plan, and noncontributory retirement plans.

Human Resources: Linda Chape; Jean B. Wallace.

Kimberly-Clark Corp.

PO Box 619100
Dallas, TX 75261-9100
Phone: (214)830-1200

Business Description: Kimberly-Clark is "principally engaged in the manufacturing and marketing throughout the world of a wide range of products for personal, business and industrial uses." Most of these products are made from natural and synthetic fibers using advanced technologies in absorbency, fiber-forming and related fields. The company's national products are sold under a variety of brand names including Kleenex, Huggies, Pull-Ups, Kotex, New Freedom, Lightdays, Depend, Hi-Dri, Delsey, Spenco, Kimguard, Kimwipes and Classic. The company's products and services are segmented into three classes. Class I includes tissue products for household, commercial, institutional, and industrial uses; infant, child, feminine, and incontinence care products; industrial and commercial wipers; health care products; and related products. Class II includes newsprint, printing papers, premium business and correspondence papers, tobacco industry papers and products, technical papers, and related products. Class III includes aircraft services, commercial air transportation, and other products and services.

Officers: Donald M. Crook, Corp. Sec.; Brendan M. O'Neill, Sr. VP & Finance Officer; Wayne R. Sanders, President; Darwin E. Smith, CEO & Chairman of the Board; Randy J. Vest, Controller.

Benefits: Benefits include medical insurance, life insurance, dental insurance, a 401(k) plan, tuition assistance, and defined benefit retirement plans.

Human Resources: Eva Powell.

Application Procedures: Resumes are kept on file. Promotes from within the company. Apply through the Local Employment Commission.

▶ Internships

Type: Offers internships in the Tax Department.

Qualifications: Applicants must be college juniors.

Application Procedure: The Company contacts schools with internship opportunities.

Loctite Corp.

Hartford Sq. N.
10 Columbus Blvd.
Hartford, CT 06106
Phone: (203)520-5000
Fax: (203)520-5073

Business Description: Develops and manufactures industrial and household adhesives and sealants. Has subsidiaries in Latin America (Argentina, Brazil, Chile, Columbia, Costa Rica, Mexico, and Venezuela); Canada; Europe (Yugoslavia, Austria, Belgium, Germany, Spain, Ireland, Italy, England, France, and the Netherlands); Asia (Hong Kong, Japan, and Korea); Australia; and South Africa.

Officers: Robert L. Aller, VP of Finance; Kenneth W. Butterworth, CEO & Chairman of the Board; David Freeman, Exec. VP & COO.

Benefits: Benefits include an employee stock ownership plan, a thrift plan, and profit sharing.

Human Resources: Don Atencio.

Application Procedures: Send resume and cover letter to the attention of Bill Mastrianna.

▶ Internships

Type: The company offers an internship program.

Long Island Lighting Co.

175 E. Old Country Rd.
Hicksville, NY 11801
Phone: (516)933-4590
Fax: (516)937-3180

Business Description: Provider of electric and other utility services.

Officers: William J. Catacosinos, CEO & Chairman of the Board; George J. Sideris, Sr. VP & CFO.

Benefits: Benefits include medical insurance, dental insurance, life insurance, short-term disability, long-term disability, a pension plan, a savings plan, tuition assistance, paid holidays, flexible holidays, personal days, vacation days, maternity leave, an employee counseling program, employee activities, a cafeteria, and training programs.

Human Resources: Lynn Oneota; Robert X. Kelleher.

Application Procedures: Send resume and cover letter to the attention of the Employment Office.

▶ **Internships**

Type: The company does not offer an internship program.

Longview Fibre Co.
PO Box 639
Longview, WA 98632
Phone: (206)425-1550
Fax: (206)425-3116

Business Description: Owns and operates tree farms in Washington and Oregon. Produces paper, containerboard, containers, and bags in Longview, Seattle, and Yakima, Washington; Oakland, California; Twin Falls, Idaho; Spanish Fork, Utah; Milwaukee, Wisconsin; Cedar Rapids, Iowa; Minneapolis, Minnesota; Rockford, Illinois; Amsterdam, New York; and Springfield and Waltham, Massachusetts.

Officers: Raymund G. McDermott, Sr. VP of Finance, Treasurer & Sec.; George E. Schwartz, Exec. VP & Asst. Sec.; Robert E. Wertheimer, Exec. VP; Richard P. Wollenberg, CEO, Pres. & Chairman of the Board.

Benefits: Benefits include medical, dental, life, and short- and long-term disability insurances, vision insurance, tuition assistance, vacation, an employee pension plan and a 401(k).

Human Resources: Jerry Dow.

Application Procedures: Interested candidates can fill out an application for clerical positions. Technical positions are advertised in newspapers. Send resume and cover letter to the attention of Jerry Dow.

▶ **Internships**

Contact: Jerry Dow.

Type: Offers a college internship program.

Qualifications: Forestry, engineering, and chemistry students.

Application Procedure: Apply to Jerry Dow.

Louisiana Land & Exploration Co.
PO Box 60350
New Orleans, LA 70160
Phone: (504)566-6500
Fax: (504)566-6575

Business Description: Explores for and produces petroleum and natural gas, and manufactures refined petroleum products.

Officers: Richard A. Bachmann, Exec. VP & CFO; H. Leighton Steward, CEO & Chairman of the Board.

Benefits: Benefits include medical insurance, dental insurance, vision insurance, and long-term disability and short-term disability. Also offers an employee pension plan, a 401(k) plan, tuition assistance, a smoke-free workplace, a fitness center, and service awards.

Human Resources: Linda Jones.

Application Procedures: Places newspaper advertisements for certain openings. Some hiring is done through an employment agency. Send resume and cover letter to the attention of Linda Jones.

▶ **Internships**

Type: Offers a college internship program through "In-Roads".

Qualifications: Accounting students.

Application Procedure: Apply to Human Resources.

Students with the luxury of a couple of years until graduation should start plotting for that first job and snagging some experience *now*. But with many employers reluctant to pay even the modest salary of an internship, getting actual business experience is increasingly difficult. One strategy: Try a so-called externship, typically a one-week, unpaid stint at a company that provides a snapshot of various careers and a chance to network with insiders. Externships can be particularly useful for liberal-arts majors without a clear career track.

Source: *U.S. News and World Report*

Louisiana-Pacific Corp.
111 SW 5th Ave.
Portland, OR 97204
Phone: (503)221-0800

Business Description: Manufacturer of building materials and pulp.

Officers: John C. Hart, VP of Finance & Treasurer; Harry A. Merlo, Pres. & Chairman of the Board.

Human Resources: Gary Maffel.

Application Procedures: Places newspaper advertisements for certain openings in local papers. Interested persons can apply for specific openings through the Oregon Job Service.

▶ Internships

Type: The company does not offer an internship program.

A powerful combination of workers who equip themselves to be competitive and employers who provide them with challenging jobs can help businesses stay on top. But to mesh these elements managers must give employees a voice in their jobs and enable workers to develop new skills throughout their careers. Workers must get as much schooling as possible, demand broader duties on the job, and take on more responsibility for the company's success.

Source: *Business Week*

Lubrizol Corp.

29400 Lakeland Blvd.
Wickliffe, OH 44092-2298
Phone: (216)943-4200
Fax: (216)943-9009

Business Description: A specialty chemical company that applies chemical, mechanical, and biological technologies to create high-performance products used in world transportation, industry, and agricultural markets. Operates a network of 18 manufacturing plants, three technical centers, and 50 sales offices. Plants are located in Ohio, Texas, Georgia, Australia, Brazil, Canada, England, France, India, Japan, Mexico, Saudi Arabia, Singapore, South Africa, and Venezuela. Conducts chemical research and mechanical testing in Wickliffe, Ohio; Hazelwood, England; and Atsugi, Japan. Pursues biotechnological research in Madison, Wisconsin. The Specialty Chemicals Segment develops, produces, and sells chemical additives for transportation and industrial lubricants and functional fluids, fuel additivies, and diversified specialty chemical products. The Agribusiness Segment develops, produces, and markets planting seeds for agricultural and oilseed crops, as well as specialty vegetable oils. The Agribusiness Segment also conducts strategic activities, including biotechnology research and development directed toward developing new products for the agricultural, food, and chemical industries.

Officers: John R. Ahern, Controller; Ray A. Andreas, VP & CFO; W.G. Bares, COO & Pres.; L.E. Coleman, CEO & Chairman of the Board; George R. Hill, Sr. VP; K.H. Hopping, Vice Pres.; Roger Y.K. Hsu, Sr. VP; William R. Jones, Treasurer; Philip L. Krug, Exec. VP; William D. Manning, Sr. VP; Robert W. Scher, Sr. VP; R. John Senz, Vice Pres.; John A. Studebaker, Vice Pres.

Benefits: Benefits include an employee pension plan.

Human Resources: J. Cody Davis.

Application Procedures: Send resume and cover letter to the attention of the Personnel Dept.

▶ Internships

Type: The company offers chemistry internships.

Qualifications: College students.

Application Procedure: Interested applicants should contact the personnel department in February or March.

Magma Copper Co.

PO Box M
San Manuel, AZ 85631
Phone: (602)385-3100
Fax: (602)385-3299

Business Description: Produces copper ores, copper rolling, and copper drawing. The company has three operations in Arizona.

Officers: J. Burgess Winter, CEO & Pres.

Benefits: Benefits include medical, dental, life, and short- and long-term disability insurances, pension and savings plans, profit sharing, tuition assistance, and selected bonuses, national and flexible holidays, personal and vacation days, and maternity leave, an employee counseling program, a smoke-free environment, and training programs.

Human Resources: J. Michael Benson.

Application Procedures: Applications will be mailed to those requesting them by phone or fill out an application in person. Send resume and cover letter to the attention of J. Michael Benson.

▶ Internships

Contact: J. Michael Benson.

Type: Offers a college internship program to engineering students and for labor and clerical positions.

Application Procedure: Apply directly to J. Michael Benson.

Marathon Petroleum Co.

539 S. Main St.
Findlay, OH 45840
Phone: (419)422-2121

Business Description: Engaged in petroleum exploration, production, refining, and distribution worldwide. Also engaged in the distribution and marketing of crude oil, natural gas, and petroleum products.

Officers: Victor G. Beghini, President; G. Jerry Kramer, Info. Systems Mgr.; James Low, VP of Finance; Richard E. White, VP of Mktg.

Benefits: Benefits include medical insurance, dental insurance, retirement plans, a 401(k) plan, tuition assistance, and a smoke-free environment.

Human Resources: K.L. Matiney.

Application Procedures: Send resume and cover letter to the attention of Corporate Recruitment.

▶ Internships

Type: Offers a college internship program.

Qualifications: Environmental and safety engineering and computer science students.

Application Procedure: Apply to Corporate Recruitment.

Mary Kay Cosmetics Inc.

8787 Stemmons Fwy.
Dallas, TX 75247
Phone: (214)630-8787

Business Description: Manufacturer of cosmetics, perfumes or other toilet preparations. Retailer of products through the use of direct selling methods.

Officers: Richard Bartlett, CEO & Pres.; Barbara Beasley, Exec. VP of Sales; Gary Bishop, VP of Info. Systems; John P. Rochon, CFO.

Human Resources: Betty Bessler.

Application Procedures: Fill out an application in person or send resume and cover letter to the attention of Human Resources.

Maxus Energy Corp.

717 N. Harwood St.
Dallas, TX 75201
Phone: (214)953-2000

Business Description: Maxus Energy Corp. is one of the largest independent oil and gas exploration and production companies in North America.

Officers: Charles J. Blackburn, CEO, Pres. & Chairman of the Board; Donald C. Mielke, Sr. VP & CFO.

Human Resources: George W. Pasley.

Application Procedures: Send resume and cover letter to the attention of Karen Gibson.

▶ Internships

Type: The company offers no formal internship program.

Maxxam Inc.

5847 San Felipe, Ste. 2600
Houston, TX 77057
Phone: (713)975-7600
Fax: (713)267-3703

Business Description: Engages in aluminum production, forest products operations, and real estate development.

Officers: Charles E. Hurwitz, CEO; James V. Iaco, Jr., Sr. VP of Finance & Treasurer; William C. Leone, President; Barry Munitz, Vice Chairman of the Board.

Benefits: Benefits include medical insurance, dental insurance, life insurance, an employee pension plan, tuition assistance, a smoke-free environment, and free parking.

Human Resources: Sharon Romere.

Application Procedures: Recruits through employment agencies and advertises in local newspapers. Send resume and cover letter to the attention of the Human Resources Department.

▶ Internships

Type: The company does not offer an internship program.

MCN Corp.
500 Griswold St.
Detroit, MI 48226
Phone: (313)256-5500
Toll-free: 800-548-4655

Business Description: A natural gas distribution, transmission and storage company.

Officers: Stephen E. Ewing, Pres. & COO; Alfred R. Glancy, CEO & Chairman of the Board; William K. McCrackin, Vice Chairman of the Board, Treasurer & CFO; Daniel L. Schiffer, VP, General Counsel & Sec.

Benefits: Benefits include employee pension plan.

Application Procedures: Send resume and cover letter to the attention of Employment Department.

▶ Internships

Type: The company offers a variety of co-op programs. Requirements vary. For further information, please contact the employment department.

In point of fact there are 700 different job categories represented in the membership of the Society of American Foresters.

Source: *The Conservationist*

Mead Corp.
Courthouse Plaza, NE
Dayton, OH 45463
Phone: (513)222-6323

Business Description: Manufacturer of paper products. Through its school and office products and paper divisions, Mead manufactures the products for which it is best known. Also engaged in the electronic information industry. One of the largest makers of beverage packaging materials.

Officers: William A. Enouen, Sr. VP & CFO; J.K. Langenbahn, VP of Info. Systems; Wallace O. Nugent, VP of Mktg.; Burnell R. Roberts, CEO & Chairman of the Board.

Human Resources: Lisa Hone; C.J. Mazza.

Application Procedures: Send resume and cover letter to the attention of Donna Chapman.

▶ Internships

Type: The company does not offer an internship program.

Mennen Co.
Hanover Ave.
Morristown, NJ 07962-1928
Phone: (201)631-9000
Fax: (201)292-6117

Business Description: Manufacturer of cosmetics, perfumes or other toilet preparations.

Officers: L. Donald Horne, President.

Human Resources: Jeff Lund.

Application Procedures: The company is currently not accepting any resumes.

▶ Internships

Type: The company does not offer any internship programs.

Mobil Corp.
3225 Gallows Rd.
Fairfax, VA 22037
Phone: (703)846-3000

Business Description: Involved in refining, exploration, and production of gas and oil supplies, lubricants, and motor-fuel additives.

Officers: R. Hartwell Gardner, Treasurer; Allen E. Murray, CEO, Pres. & Chairman of the Board.

Application Procedures: Send resume and cover letter to the attention of Fran Cody.

Monsanto Co.
800 N. Lindbergh Blvd.
St. Louis, MO 63167
Phone: (314)694-1000

Business Description: Manufacturer of synthetic resins, plastics materials and/or nonvulcanizable elastomers. Engaged in manufacturing, fabricating and/or processing drugs in pharmaceutical preparations. Manufacturer of miscellaneous pesticides or agricultural chemicals. Manufacturer of instruments which measure, display, transmit or control process variables in industrial establishments.

Officers: Earl H. Harbison, Jr., Pres. & COO; Richard J. Mahoney, CEO & Chairman of the Board; Nicholas L. Reding, Exec. VP.

Human Resources: Joe Kohlberg.

Application Procedures: Send resume and cover letter to the attention of Patty Jones.

Montana Power Co.

40 E. Broadway
Butte, MT 59701-9989
Phone: (406)723-5421

Business Description: Montana Power Co. provides electrical utilty services to its residential and commercial customers.

Officers: W. Paul Schmechel, CEO & Chairman of the Board; Frank V. Woy, Exec. VP of Finance.

Benefits: Benefits include medical insurance, dental insurance, life insurance, and a payroll savings plan.

Human Resources: Bill Caine.

Application Procedures: Apply through the State Job Service.

▶ Internships

Type: The company does not offer an internship program.

Morton International Inc.

100 N. Riverside Plaza
Chicago, IL 60606-1596
Phone: (312)807-2000

Business Description: Manufactures and markets specialty chemicals, salt, and inflatable automotive restraint systems.

Officers: John R. Bowen, Sr. VP & CFO; Robert B. Covalt, Exec. VP; Stephen A. Gerow, Group VP; Perry R. Grace, Group VP; Kenneth D. Holmgren, Group VP; William E. Johnston, Jr., Group VP; Donald L. Kidd, VP of Info. Systems; Richard B. Kron, Group VP; Charles S. Locke, CEO & Chairman of the Board; Thomas F. McDevitt, VP of Finance & Controller; P. Michael Phelps, VP & Sec.; Thomas S. Russell, Group VP; Bruce G. Wolfe, Treasurer.

Opportunities: Hires accountants, purchasing agents, human resources personnel, chemical engineers, chemists, systems analysts, patent attorneys, technical sales representatives, and secretaries.

Benefits: Benefits include medical, dental, life, and short- and long-term disability insurances; an employee pension plan; a 401(k) plan; a smoke-free environment; and tuition assistance. Most international subsidiaries also have retirement plans.

Human Resources: John C. Hadley; Patricia S. Hanna.

Application Procedures: Phone calls not accepted. Send resume and cover letter to the attention of Barbara Martin.

▶ Internships

Type: The company offers health and safety internships to qualified applicants.

Application Procedure: Interested candidates should forward resumes to Patricia S. Hanna in the Human Resources department. If no internships are available, resumes are kept on file.

Murphy Oil Corp.

200 Peach St.
El Dorado, AR 71730
Phone: (501)862-6411

Business Description: Engaged in the operation of oil and/or gas field properties. Engaged in logging. Engaged in petroleum refining. Holding company engaged in holding or owning the securities of companies in order to exercise some degree of control over the companies' activities.

Officers: Jack W. McNutt, CEO & Pres.; B. David Richardson, Treasurer.

Benefits: Benefits include medical insurance and dental insurance, and a thrift plan.

Human Resources: Dana Green.

Application Procedures: Pick up an application or send resume and cover letter to the attention of Dana Green.

▶ Internships

Type: The company does not offer an internship program.

Nalco Chemical Co.

1 Nalco Center
Naperville, IL 60563-1198
Phone: (708)305-1000

Business Description: Produces chemicals and services for water and waste treatment, pollution control, petroleum production and refining, papermaking, mining, steelmaking, metalworking, and other industrial processes. The company's products are marketed in nearly 130 countries.

Officers: W.H. Clark, CEO & Chairman of the Board; Edward J. Mooney, President.

Benefits: Benefits include retirement plans, medical insurance, dental insurance, a 401(k) plan, and an employee stock ownership plan.

Human Resources: James F. Lambe.

Application Procedures: Send resume and cover letter to the attention of Human Resources.

▶ Internships

Type: Offers a co-op program.

Qualifications: Students.

Application Procedure: Apply to the Human Resources Department.

According to the Bureau of Labor Statistics, the rapid growth of women entering the workforce—about 2.3% per year from 1975 to 1990—is expected to slow, growing at a rate of 1.6% per year in the next fifteen years. By 2005, minorities are expected to account for more than 25% of all working people in the US, with the fastest growth occurring among Hispanics, who will make up over 11% of the workforce by 2005.

Source: *Forbes*

National Fuel Gas Co.

30 Rockefeller Plaza
New York, NY 10112
Phone: (212)541-7533

Business Description: Engaged in the business of owning and holding all of the securities of National Fuel Gas Supply Corporation (Supply Corporation), National Fuel Gas Distribution Corporation (Distribution Corporation), Penn-York Energy Corporation (Penn-York), Seneca Resources Corporation (Seneca Resources), Empire Exploration, Inc. (Empire Exploration), Utility Constructors, Inc. (UCI), Highland Land and Minerals, Inc. (Highland), and Data-Track Account Services, Inc. (Data-Track).

Officers: Philip C. Ackerman, Sr. VP; John M. Brown, Vice Chairman of the Board; Richard M. DiValerio, Secretary; Bernard J. Kennedy, CEO, Pres. & Chairman of the Board; Joseph P. Pawlowski, Treasurer; Gerald T. Wehrlin, Controller.

Benefits: Benefits include retirement plans, medical insurance, an employee stock plan, and life insurance for retirees.

Human Resources: Thomas Hodick.

Application Procedures: Send resume and cover letter to the attention of Thomas Hodick, 10 Lafayette Sq., Buffalo, NY 14203.

▶ Internships

Type: Offers an internship program.

NCH Corp.

PO Box 152170
Irving, TX 75015
Phone: (214)438-0211

Business Description: Manufacturer of polishes, waxes, disinfectants, or other sanitation preparations. Manufacturer of metal plumbing fixture fittings and trim. Wholesaler of miscellaneous chemicals or allied products.

Officers: I.L. Levy, President.

Benefits: Benefits include medical insurance, dental insurance, life insurance, and a 401(k) plan.

Application Procedures: Send resume and cover letter to the attention of the Employment Manager.

▶ Internships

Type: The company does not offer an internship program.

Nerco Inc.

500 NE Multnomah St., No. 1500
Portland, OR 97232-2045
Phone: (503)731-6600
Fax: (503)230-9045

Business Description: NERCO, Inc., a diversified mining and resource development company, is one of the largest producers of coal, gold, and silver in North America and a significant producer of gas and oil in the Gulf Coast region of the United States. The company is also engaged in the exploration for and development of precious metals, gas and oil.

Officers: Thomas Albanese, Sr. VP; Peter J. Craven, VP & Controller; Gerard K. Drummond, CEO & Chairman of the Board; William W. Lyons, Sr. VP; William Glasgow, President;

Rodney D. Erskine, Vice Pres.; Clynton R. Nauman, Vice Pres.; Nicholas P. Moros, Sr. VP; Richard T. O'Brien, Sr. VP; Kenneth E. Rohan, Vice Pres.; John P. Shepherd, VP & Asst. Sec.

Benefits: Benefits include an employee pension plan, retirement plans, an employee stock ownership plan and a savings plan.

Human Resources: Rick Dols.

Application Procedures: Send resume and cover letter.

▶ Internships

Type: The company does not offer an internship program.

New England Electric System

25 Research Dr.
Westborough, MA 01582
Phone: (508)366-9011

Business Description: Public utility holding company that operates subsidiaries in six states, and provides services to more than 1.2 million customers.

Officers: Alfred D. Houston, Sr. VP & CFO; John F. Kaslow, Exec. VP & COO; John V. Rowe, CEO & Pres.

Benefits: Offers health benefits.

Application Procedures: Send resume and cover letter to the attention of Susan Reynolds.

▶ Internships

Contact: Susan Reynolds.

Type: Offers co-op positions to engineering and computer science students.

Application Procedure: Apply to Susan Reynolds.

New York State Electric & Gas Corp.

PO Box 287
Ithaca, NY 14851
Phone: (607)347-4131

Business Description: Provider of electric and other utility services.

Officers: James A. Carrigg, CEO & Chairman of the Board; Orlin W. Darrach, VP of Mktg.; Richard A. Jacobson, Exec. VP & CFO.

Application Procedures: Send resume and cover letter to the attention of Patricia Wilkins.

▶ Internships

Type: Offers an internship program.

Newmont Gold Co.

1 United Bank Center
1700 Lincoln St.
Denver, CO 80203
Phone: (303)863-7414

Business Description: Engaged in gold mining. The company has fifteen deposits with measured gold resources, and ten of these have mineable reserves of 20.7 million ounces. Newmont Gold operates along a 38-mile stretch of the Carlin Trend in Nevada. Its property is encompassed by approximately 380 square miles owned or controlled by Newmont Mining Corporation, which holds 90.1 percent of Newmont Gold's common stock.

Officers: P.L. Maroni, VP & Treasurer; G.R. Parker, CEO & Chairman of the Board; T. Peter Philip, Pres. & COO; Ronald Vance, VP of Mktg.

Average Entry-Level Hiring: The company expects hiring levels will increase over the next few years.

Benefits: Benefits include pension plans, medical insurance, dental insurance, life insurance, short-term disability, long-term disability, tuition assistance, bonuses/incentives, 10 paid holidays per year, and two weeks vacations after one year of service. Special benefits include training programs, a smoke-free environment, banking facilities on the premises, and reimbursement of health club membership fees.

Human Resources: George Jackson.

Application Procedures: Interested candidates should forward resumes to the Employee Relations Department.

▶ Internships

Type: The company does not offer any internship programs.

Newmont Mining Corp.

1700 Lincoln St.
Denver, CO 80203
Phone: (303)837-6113

Business Description: A gold exploration company. Also operates, manages, and finances its gold properties in the United States. The company mines gold through Newmont Gold

Company and conducts worldwide exploration through its subsidiary, Newmont Exploration Limited (NEL). NEL operates an advanced metallurgical research laboratory in Utah. It is also developing and using geophysical techniques for mapping near-surface and deep-structures.

Human Resources: George Jackson.

Application Procedures: Send resume and cover letter to the attention of George Jackson.

▶ Internships

Type: The company does not offer an internship program.

Niagara Mohawk Power Corp.

300 Erie Blvd. W.
Syracuse, NY 13202
Phone: (315)474-1511

Business Description: Provides energy, including natural gas, to 1.5 million customers in upper New York state. The company's U.S. and Canadian subsidiaries are engaged in the construction of power production facilities, the marketing of advanced instrumentation systems to the utility industry, and in exploration. In the early 1990s, Niagara Mohawk underwent a corporate restructuring and redefined its natural gas business as a separate operating unit.

Officers: Lawrence Burkhardt, III, Exec. VP Nuclear Operations; William J. Donlon, CEO & Chairman of the Board; John M. Endries, President; Arthur W. Roos, Treasurer.

Benefits: Benefits include an employee pension plan, medical insurance, dental insurance, and life insurance. Also offers workman's compensation, disability insurance, and a 401(k) plan.

Human Resources: Carol Byrne.

Application Procedures: Send resume and cover letter to the attention of Carol Byrne.

▶ Internships

Type: Offers an internship program.

Application Procedure: Apply to Employee Relations.

Nicor Inc.

PO Box 190
Aurora, IL 60507
Phone: (708)983-8888

Business Description: Engaged in the operation of oil and/or gas field properties. Engaged in activities directly related to the loading and unloading of marine cargo. Engaged in the distribution of natural gas. Holding company engaged in holding or owning the securities of companies in order to exercise some degree of control over the companies' activities.

Officers: R.G. Cline, Pres. & Chairman of the Board.

Benefits: Benefits include medical insurance, dental insurance, vision insurance, life insurance, a savings and thrift plan, vacation, free parking, a smoke-free environment, an employee pension plan, a stock option plan, and an exercise room.

Application Procedures: Applications accepted for openings only. Submit applications to the attention of Tamara Saunaitis.

▶ Internships

Contact: Toni Hill.

Type: Offers internships through the Minority Scholarship Achievement Award.

Qualifications: College sophomores.

NIPSCO Industries Inc.

5265 Hohman Ave.
Hammond, IN 46320
Phone: (219)853-5200
Toll-free: 800-348-6466

Business Description: An energy-based holding company whose primary subsidiaries are Northern Indiana Public Service Co., a natural gas and electric utility serving the northern third of Indiana; NIPSCO Capital Markets Inc., a funding agent for all non-regulated ventures; NIPSCO Development Company Inc., engaged in real estate and other development investments; NIPSCO Energy Services Inc., involved in the sale of services to other utilities and customers; NIPSCO Energy Trading Corp. Inc., engaged in gas brokering for gas transportation customers; NIPSCO Fuel Company Inc., which invests in gas and oil exploration and development projects; and NI-TEX Inc., a natural gas transmission and supply company. Northern Indiana Public Service Co. is the core business for NIPSCO Industries, providing electric service to more than 377,000 customers and gas service to about 585,000 customers across northern Indiana.

Officers: John W. Dunn, Sr. VP; Gary L. Neale, Exec. VP; Edmund A. Schroer, CEO, Pres. &

Chairman of the Board.

Benefits: Benefits include a non-contributory employee pension plan, health care programs, and life insurance for retirees.

Human Resources: Gene Freen.

Application Procedures: Send resume and cover letter.

▶ Internships

Type: Offers an internship program.

Qualifications: Business and engineering students.

Application Procedure: Apply to the Employment and Development Department.

Noble Affiliates Inc.

110 W. Broadway
PO Box 1967
Ardmore, OK 73402
Phone: (405)223-4110

Business Description: An oil and natural gas company. Its subsidiary, Samedan Oil Corp., is engaged in exploration and production in the Gulf of Mexico, offshore California, several western states, Canada, Tunisia, and Indonesia. Noble Natural Gas Inc. is another subsidiary.

Officers: William D. Dickson, VP of Finance & Treasurer; Robert Kelley, CEO & Pres.; Orville Walraven, Corp. Sec.

Benefits: Benefits include medical insurance, dental insurance, life insurance, a thrift plan, and an employee pension plan.

Human Resources: Calvin Burton.

Application Procedures: Can fill out applications on Mondays and Wednesdays between 9-11 a.m.

▶ Internships

Type: The company does not offer an internship program.

Northeast Utilities

174 Brush Hill Ave.
PO Box 2010
West Springfield, MA 01089
Phone: (413)785-5871

Business Description: Northeast Utilities is the parent company of the NU system, the largest utilities in the country, and the largest in New England. It serves 1.25 million customers in Connecticut and western Massachusetts.

Officers: Robert E. Busch, Sr. VP & CFO; William B. Ellis, CEO & Chairman of the Board; Bernard M. Fox, Pres. & COO.

Benefits: Benefits include medical insurance, dental insurance, life insurance, and an employee pension plan. Also offers paid vacation, holidays, a stock purchase plan, and a 401(k) plan.

Human Resources: Maurice Nichols.

Application Procedures: Fill out an application or send resume and cover letter to the attention of Maurice Nichols.

▶ Internships

Type: The company does not offer an internship program.

> Every resume should pass the "so what?" test. It's not enough to simply list your accomplishments. You need to demonstrate the impact of your actions on your department or the company at large. Beverly Robsham, president of Robsham & Associates, an outplacement firm in Boston, MA, advocates the "PAR" approach when delineating accomplishments: "Specify the *problem*, the *actions* you took, and the *results* for the company."
>
> Source: *Working Woman*

Northern States Power Co.

414 Nicollet Mall
Minneapolis, MN 55401
Phone: (612)330-5500

Business Description: Distributes electric power and gas, and provides telephone and nuclear energy services. Serves more than 994,000 retail electric customers in Minnesota.

Officers: James D. Doudiet, Sr. VP & CFO; Ed Theisen, COO & Pres.

Human Resources: John A. Noer.

Application Procedures: Send resume and cover letter to the attention of Employment Office.

▶ Internships

Type: The company does not offer an internship program.

Noxell Corp.
11103 Pepper Rd.
Hunt Valley, MD 21031
Phone: (410)785-7300

Business Description: Manufacturer of cosmetics, toiletries and household cleaning products. In late 1989, Noxell agreed to merge with the Proctor and Gamble Company. The Proctor and Gamble take-over allows Noxell to increase its research and development budget, and obtain greater distribution and advertising for its products.

Human Resources: Cindy Volacawizz.

Application Procedures: Can fill out an application Monday through Friday from 9-4 or send resume and cover letter to the attention of Cindy Volacawizz.

▶ Internships

Type: The company does not offer an internship program.

Nucor Corp.
2100 Rexford Rd.
Charlotte, NC 28211
Phone: (704)366-7000
Fax: (704)362-4208

Business Description: A manufacturer of steel and steel products. Products include structural steel such as I-beams, and stainless steel wire. Nucor, a low-cost producer using scrap metal, remains profitable at a time when other structural steel manufacturers are leaving the market.

Officers: Hugh D. Aycoch, Pres. & COO; F. Kenneth Iverson, CEO & Chairman of the Board; Samuel Siegel, Exec. VP & CFO.

Benefits: Benefits include medical insurance and dental insurance.

Human Resources: James Coblin.

Application Procedures: Send resume and cover letter to the attention of Employee Relations.

▶ Internships

Type: The company does not offer an internship program.

Occidental Petroleum Corp.
10889 Wilshire Blvd.
Los Angeles, CA 90024
Phone: (310)208-8800

Business Description: Currently ranked as one of the best oil and gas finders in the world, Occidental continues to have low finding costs and a high reserve-replacement record. From 1986 to 1991, Occidental replaced 112 percent of its production on an energy-equivalent basis. In 1992, the company increased its worldwide exploration budget for international operations to support drilling approximately 50 wells in Albania, Argentina, Gabon, Indonesia, Malaysia, Oman, Pakistan, the Philippines, Syria, and Yemen.

Officers: David A. Hentschel, Exec. VP; J. Roger Hirl, Exec. VP; Dr. Ray R. Irani, CEO, Pres. & Chairman of the Board; Dr. Dale R. Laurance, Exec. VP of Operations; Anthony R. Leach, Exec. VP; Angelo Leparulo, Exec. VP; Gerald M. Stern, Exec. VP & Sec. & Sen. Gen. Counsel.

Benefits: Benefits include medical insurance and an employee pension plan for salaried employees.

Human Resources: Ronald H. Asquith; Patrick Dailey.

Application Procedures: Does not accept unsolicited resumes. Call to inquire about job openings.

▶ Internships

Type: The company does not offer an internship program.

Ohio Edison Co.
76 S. Main St.
Akron, OH 44308
Phone: (216)384-5100

Business Description: Engaged in the generation, transmission and distribution of electricity.

Officers: Justin T. Rogers, Jr., President; Kenneth J. Verbic, Treasurer.

Benefits: Benefits include medical insurance, dental insurance, life insurance, employee pension plan, and sick leave.

Human Resources: Thomas Kayula.

Application Procedures: Send resume and cover letter to the attention of Thomas Kayula.

▶ Internships

Type: Offers an internship program.

Oklahoma Gas & Electric Co.

PO Box 321
Oklahoma City, OK 73101-0321
Phone: (405)272-3000

Business Description: Owns and operates an interconnected electric production, transmission, and distribution system. The system includes seven active generating stations with a total capability of 5,691,300 kilowatts. The company furnishes retail electric service in 270 communities, in addition to rural and suburban areas in Oklahoma and western Arkansas.

Officers: Bob G. Bunce, Sr. VP; Richard C. Day, VP of Mktg.; Irma B. Elliot, Secretary; James G. Harlow, Jr., CEO, Pres. & Chairman of the Board; Steven E. Moore, VP of Public Affairs and Law; Patrick J. Ryan, Exec. VP & COO; Al M. Strecker, VP & Treasurer; Don L. Young, Controller.

Benefits: Benefits include medical insurance, free parking, an employee pension plan, and health and life insurance for retired employees.

Human Resources: A. Dwain Howard.

Application Procedures: Send resume and cover letter to the attention of Mail Code 108.

▶ Internships

Type: Offers a college internship program.

Application Procedure: Send application to Mail Code 108.

Olin Corp.

120 Long Ridge Rd.
Stamford, CT 06904-1355
Phone: (203)356-2000

Business Description: Olin's business is primarily in chemicals, metals, and applied physics, with an emphasis on electronic materials and services and defense/aerospace. The company is divided into three operating units: chemicals, metals, and materials; defense; and ammunition. These divisions produce such diverse products as pool products and rocket engines.

Officers: John W. Johnstone, Jr., CEO & Pres.

Benefits: Benefits include health maintenance organization, dental insurance, an employee pension plan, post-retirement benefits, including health care and life insurance, and an employee stock ownership plan.

Human Resources: Michael E. Campbell.

Application Procedures: Send resume and cover letter or fill out an application in person.

▶ Internships

Type: The company does not offer an internship program at this time, but internships may be offered in the future.

> Trade and professional associations are good sources of information about jobs in your target field. Look for associations in *The Encyclopedia of Associations.*
>
> Source: *Executive Female*

Oryx Energy Co.

13155 Noel Rd.
Dallas, TX 75240
Phone: (214)715-4000

Business Description: Engaged in the operation of oil and/or gas field properties. Provides geophysical, geological or other exploration services to oil and gas fields.

Officers: Donald E. Burns, VP of Mktg.; Robert P. Hauptfuhrer, CEO & Chairman of the Board; Robert Keiser, VP of Systems; James E. McCormick, Pres. & COO; Edward W. Moneypenny, VP & CFO.

Benefits: Benefits include medical, dental, life, and short- and long-term disability insurances, an employee pension plan, and a 401(k) plan.

Human Resources: Harold R. Ashby.

Application Procedures: Send resume and cover letter to Harold R. Ashby.

▶ Internships

Type: Offers an internship program.

Qualifications: College juniors.

Application Procedure: Apply to the Personnel Department.

Owens-Illinois Inc.

1 Seagate Ave.
Toledo, OH 43666
Phone: (419)247-5000

Business Description: Owens-Illinois is a major manufacturer of glass containers for the food and beverage industry. Its plastics products include bottles and packaging items such as container closures and can carriers. Through its subsidiaries and affiliates, the diversified company produces cardboard boxes, glass television parts, and has interests in the health care field, primarily rest homes and facilities.

Officers: J.A. Bohland, VP of Finance; W. Laimbeer, Exec. VP; Joseph H. Lemieux, CEO & Pres.

Human Resources: B.B. Jones.

▶ Internships

Type: The company does not offer an internship program.

Pacific Enterprises

801 S. Grand Ave.
Los Angeles, CA 90017
Phone: (213)895-5000

Business Description: Utility engaged in the exploration for, production, and distribution of natural gas and oil. Also owns retail operations. The company has lost money through its retail operations, but hopes recent restructuring will cause a turnaround.

Officers: Thomas H. Kenney, Secretary; Lloyd A. Levitin, Exec. VP; James R. Ukropina, CEO & Chairman of the Board; Paul A. Williams, II, VP & Treasurer; Willis B. Wood, Jr., President.

Benefits: Benefits include an employee pension plan.

Human Resources: Carolyn Sims.

Application Procedures: Send resume and cover letter to the attention of Carolyn Sims, PO Box 60043, Los Angeles, CA 90060-0043.

▶ Internships

Type: The company does not offer an internship program.

Pacific Gas & Electric Co.

77 Beale St.
San Francisco, CA 94106
Phone: (415)972-7000

Business Description: Provides customers with natural gas and electricity, on-site energy management, supply and price forecasts, and a range of conservation programs. PG&E operates in the Sacramento Valley, San Joaquin Valley, San Jose, San Mateo, San Rafael, Red Bluff, Diablo Canyon, and the central coastal area of California.

Officers: Richard A. Clarke, CEO & Chairman of the Board; Jack F. Jenkins-Stark, Treasurer; Thomas R. O'Connor, VP of Mktg.

Benefits: Benefits include an early retirement program for qualified employees and medical packages for each level of employees.

Human Resources: Russell Cunningham.

Application Procedures: Send resume and cover letter to the attention of Russell Cunningham.

▶ Internships

Type: Offers an internship program.

Qualifications: Offers the James B. Black internship to high school seniors and career scholarships to college students.

Application Procedure: Must submit GPA and SAT scores for internships. The company targets major schools for the career scholarships.

PacifiCorp

920 SW 6th Ave.
Portland, OR 97204
Phone: (503)464-6000

Business Description: A diversified electric utility company operating in seven western states. The company also provides services in telecommunications, bituminous coal and lignite surface mining, and crude petroleum and natural gas distribution. PacifiCorp runs four of the nation's lowest-cost coal-fired generating plants.

Officers: Jacqueline S. Bell, Controller; David F. Bolender, President Electric Operations; Gerard K. Drummond, Exec. VP Chairman and CEO of NERCO; William J. Glasgow, CEO, Pres. & Chairman of the Board PacifiCorp Financial Services Inc.; A.M. Gleason, CEO & Pres.; Lawrence E. Heiner, President NERCO; Robert F. Lanz, VP & Treasurer; Robert W. Moench, President Pacific Power; Sally A. Nofziger, VP & Sec.; Charles E. Robinson, CEO & Chairman of the Board Pacific Telecom; Daniel L. Spalding, Vice Pres.; Verl R. Topham, President Utah Power.

Benefits: Benefits include medical insurance, dental insurance, and vision insurance. Also offers a stock purchase plan, a 401(k) plan, personal time, holiday pay, and employee discounts.

Human Resources: Ms. Francis Thompson.

Application Procedures: Send resumes or applications for job openings only. Maintains a job hotline at (503)464-6848. Send resume and cover letter to the attention of Ms. Francis Thompson, 920 SW 6th Ave., Portland, OR 97204. Phone: (503)464-6861.

▶ Internships

Type: The company does not offer an internship program.

Panhandle Eastern Corp.

PO Box 1642
Houston, TX 77251-1642
Phone: (713)627-5400

Business Description: Panhandle Eastern Corp. (PEC) is a holding company whose subsidiaries own and operate interstate natural gas transmission systems. Panhandle Eastern Pipe Line Company, Trunkline Gas Company, Texas Eastern Transmission Corporation, and Algonquin Gas Transmission Company are the principal transmission units. These subsidiaries operate an interconnected, 27,500-mile pipeline system.

Officers: Dennis Hendrix, President & Chairman of the Board; Charles E. Lasseter, VP & CFO.

Benefits: Benefits include pension, employee stock plans, medical insurance, dental insurance, and vision insurance. Also offers a 401(k) plan and childcare referrals.

Application Procedures: Places newspaper advertisements for certain openings. Send resume and cover letter to the attention of Human Resources. May also leave resumes with receptionist. Applications are taken by appointment only.

▶ Internships

Contact: Gretchen Castro or Mark Scuzzarella.

Type: Offers an internship program for several departments.

Application Procedure: Apply to Gretchen Castro or Mark Scuzzarella.

Peabody Coal Co.

PO Box 1990
Henderson, KY 42420-1990
Phone: (502)827-0800

Business Description: Engaged in the development of underground mines containing bituminous coal and/or the production of bituminous coal in underground mines.

Officers: John E. Kappler, VP of Mktg.; R. Quenon, President; John P. Wolk, VP & Treasurer.

Benefits: Offers a comprehensive benefit program.

Human Resources: Betty Jones.

Application Procedures: Accepts applications and resumes for newspaper advertisements. May also apply in person.

▶ Internships

Type: The company does not offer an internship program, but does offer a co-op program for college students.

Pennsylvania Power & Light Co.

2 N. 9th St.
Allentown, PA 18101
Phone: (215)774-5151

Business Description: Provides electric service to more than 1.1 million homes and businesses throughout a 10,000-square-mile area in 29 counties of central eastern Pennsylvania. Among the company's operations is a nuclear power plant in Susquehanna.

Officers: John T. Kauffman, CEO & Chairman of the Board; Grayson E. McNair, VP of Mktg.; Charles E. Russoli, Exec. VP & CFO.

Benefits: Benefits include medical insurance, health maintenance organizations, dental insurance, vacation pay, sick pay, an employee pension plan, an employee stock ownership plan, life insurance for retirees, and medical insurance for retirees.

Human Resources: Robert S. Gombos; Janice Williams.

Application Procedures: Places newspaper advertisements for certain openings. Other openings listed through internal bulletins and through universities. Send resume and cover letter to the attention of Janice Williams.

▶ Internships

Type: Offers an internship program.

Pennzoil Co.
Pennzoil Pl.
Box 2967
Houston, TX 77252-2967
Phone: (713)546-4000
Fax: (713)546-6589

Business Description: Conducts business through four operating divisions that manufacture and market a range of refined petroleum products and sulfur. The company is best known for its Pennzoil Motor Oil, which is sold internationally. Pennzoil also holds domestic real estate and foreign gold mining interests.

Officers: James L. Pate, CEO & Pres.

Benefits: Benefits include retirement plans and post-retirement health and life insurance.

Human Resources: Sheila Garza.

Application Procedures: Call to get job listings and the job number for specific positions at (713) 546-4000. Send resume with job number to the attention of the Human Resources department at 700 Milan, 1st Fl., Pennzoil Place Bldg., Houston, TX 77232.

To gain more control over your career, develop strong communications skills, both listening and talking. This means understanding and being able to translate what corporate goals are, and being able to talk to management. Actively solicit feedback.

Source: *Dallas Morning News*

Peoples Energy Corp.
122 S. Michigan Ave.
Chicago, IL 60603-9942
Phone: (312)431-4000
Fax: (312)431-4220

Business Description: Holding company which operates through its two natural gas utilities, The Peoples Gas Light and Coke Company, and North Shore Gas Company. These utility companies serve over 900,000 customers in Chicago and northeast Illinois.

Officers: J. Bruce Hasch, Exec. VP; Michael S. Reeves, Exec. VP; Richard E. Terry, Pres. & COO; Eugene A. Tracy, CEO & Chairman of the Board.

Benefits: Benefits include medical insurance, a 401(k) plan, and a thrift plan.

Human Resources: John Iback.

Application Procedures: Accepts applications or can contact the Personnel Department by phone.

▶ Internships

Type: Summer internship programs are available.

Qualifications: Applicants must be college students.

Petroleum Information Corp.
PO Box 2612
Denver, CO 80201-2612
Phone: (303)740-7100

Business Description: Provider of miscellaneous computer-related services.

Officers: L. Doughty, Controller; Les Doughty, Sr. VP of Info. Systems; R.G. Harston, President; Mike Keller, VP of Mktg.; Nora McClintock, Contact.

Benefits: Benefits include dental insurance, medical insurance, 401(k), and life insurance.

Human Resources: S. Johnson.

Application Procedures: Send resume and cover letter to the attention of Kathy McMahan.

▶ Internships

Type: The company does not offer any internship programs.

Pfizer Inc.
235 E. 42nd St.
New York, NY 10017
Phone: (212)573-2323

Business Description: A diversified, worldwide healthcare company. Although 80 percent of its sales are in health-related categories, Pfizer also produces intermediates, such as food ingredients, minerals for paper production, and refractory products for the production of glass and steel.

Officers: William E. Mullin, VP of Info. Systems; Edmund T. Pratt, Jr., CEO & Chairman of the Board; Jean-Paul Valles, VP of Finance.

Benefits: The company offers full benefits for full-time employees only.

Human Resources: Bruce R. Ellig.

Application Procedures: Interested applicants should forward resumes to Liz Ramos. Resumes will be held on file for six months.

▶ Internships

Type: The company offers a summer internship in various departments, including marketing, sales, human resources, and finance.

Qualifications: Applicants must have some college course work or experience.

Application Procedure: Interested candidates should send resumes to Liz Ramos and the company will contact you if qualified.

Phelps Dodge Corp.

2600 N. Central Ave.
Phoenix, AZ 85004-3014
Phone: (602)234-8100
Fax: (602)234-8337

Business Description: International mining and manufacturing concern that operates mines and plants in 23 countries. Phelps Dodge Mining Company, the mining division, is one of North America's largest producers of copper. It produces silver, gold, and molybdenum as by-products of its copper operations, and fluorspar, gold, silver, lead, zinc, and copper from mines abroad; it also explores for metals and minerals in the U.S. and abroad. Phelps Dodge Industries, the corporation's manufacturing and specialty chemicals division that serves the transportation and electrical markets, is one of the largest international producers of carbon black, a basic raw material for the rubber industry and other industrial applications; a major North American producer of wheels and rims for medium and heavy trucks and trailers; a major domestic producer of magnet wire and specialty conductors; and has various interests in and manages companies that manufacture wire and cable products in 14 countries around the world.

Officers: Leonard R. Judd, Pres. & COO; Arthur R. Miele, VP of Mktg.; Thomas M. St. Clair, Sr. VP & CFO; Douglas C. Yearley, CEO & Chairman of the Board.

Benefits: Benefits include an employee pension plan, life insurance for retirees, and medical insurance for retirees.

Human Resources: John C. Replogle; Jean Smith.

Application Procedures: Places newspaper advertisements for certain openings. Maintains a job hotline at (602)234-8281. Send resume and cover letter to the attention of the Human Resource representative.

▶ Internships

Type: The company does not offer an internship program.

Philadelphia Electric Co.

2301 Market St.
PO Box 8699
Philadelphia, PA 19101
Phone: (215)841-4000

Business Description: An electric and gas utility provider. The company operates in northeastern Maryland and the greater Philadelphia area. Philadelphia Electric and utility partners Delmarva Power and Light Company, Atlantic City Electric Company, and Public Service Electric and Gas Company, own the Peach Bottom nuclear power plant on the Susquehanna River.

Officers: Richard G. Gilmore, Sr. VP & CFO; Raymond F. Holman, Sr. VP; Corbin A. McNeill, Jr., Exec. VP of Nuclear Products; Joseph F. Paquette, Jr., CEO, Pres. & Chairman of the Board.

Opportunities: Hires legal assistants, human resources staff, and clerical staff. Requirements differ according to the position. May require a college degree, previous experience, or specific skills.

Benefits: Benefits include retirement plans.

Human Resources: William Deihm.

Application Procedures: Maintains a job hotline at (215)841-4340. Send resume and cover letter.

▶ Internships

Type: Company offers internships as needed on an informal basis. Most are clerical in nature.

Pittston Co.

100 1st Stamford Pl., 7th Fl.
Stamford, CT 06092-0700
Phone: (203)978-5200
Fax: (203)978-5210

Business Description: Operates an air freight service; installs home security equipment; provides security transportation services (armored car); and currency processing and coin wrapping services in the U.S. and several foreign countries; and operates coal mines and markets coal. Much of its black ore and coal is sold overseas.

Officers: Paul W. Douglas, CEO & Chairman of the Board; Robert D. Duke, Sr. VP & General Counsel; Joseph C. Farrell, Exec. VP; David L. Marshall, Exec. VP & CFO.

Benefits: Benefits include an employee pension plan and retirement plans.

Human Resources: Ed Cox.

Under present estimates, the U.S. will be spending $185 billion per year on cleaning up toxic and radioactive waste by the year 2000.

Source: *E Magazine*

Potlatch Corp.

1 Maritime Plz.
San Francisco, CA 94111
Phone: (415)576-8800

Business Description: A diversified forest products company with 1.5 million acres of timberland in Arkansas, Idaho and Minnesota. Converts wood fiber into two main product lines: bleached fiber products (bleached kraft pulp, paperboard, packaging, printing papers and consumer tissue) and wood products (lumber, plywood, oriented strand board, particleboard and wood specialties).

Officers: Harold W. Arnold, VP & Dir. of Taxes; F. Andrew Bayer, VP of Industrial Relations; Terry L. Carter, Controller; Richard N. Congreve, Group VP Pulp, Paperboard & Packaging; Harry A. Cooper, Vice Pres. Consumer Products Division; Brian W. Davis, Secretary; Frances M. Davis, VP & General Counsel; Edwin F. Erickson, Vice Pres. Northwest Paper Division; Richard B. Madden, CEO & Chairman of the Board; George E. Pfautsch, Sr. VP of Finance; Sandra T. Powell, Treasurer; John M. Richards, Pres. & COO; L. Pendleton Siegel, Group VP Wood Products; Hubert D. Travaille, Vice Pres.

Benefits: Benefits include retirement, incentive, and 401(k) savings plans, as well as company insurance and student loans.

Human Resources: Barbra M. Failing; Lois Sequin.

Application Procedures: Advertises in newspapers. Hires through employment agencies. Resumes are kept on file for 6 months. Contact Lois Seguin, PO Box 8162, Walnut Creek, CA 94596.

▶ Internships

Type: Offers an internship program.

Qualifications: College and high school students.

Application Procedure: Apply to the Personnel Department.

Public Service Company of Colorado

PO Box 840
Denver, CO 80255
Phone: (303)571-7511

Business Description: Provides electric, natural gas, and steam heat utility services for approximately 75 percent of Colorado's residents, including metropolitan Denver and the Cheyenne, Wyoming area. Public Service Company of Colorado also provides bulk electricity to rural electric associations.

Officers: James N. Bumpus, Sr. VP of Finance & Admin.; D.D. Hock, Chairman of the Board, Pres., CEO & COO.

Benefits: Benefits include medical insurance, dental insurance, life insurance, stock option plan and tuition assistance.

Human Resources: Marilyn E. Taylor.

Application Procedures: The company lists position openings on its Job Hotline (303) 571-7563. Interested candidates may apply between 9am and 2pm. 1400 Glenarm, Denver, CO 80202.

▶ Internships

Contact: Val Kline, Contact.

Type: The company offers an internship program.

Application Procedure: Interested candidates should contact Val Kline.

Public Service Enterprise Group Inc.
80 Park Plaza
PO Box 570
Newark, NJ 07101-1171
Phone: (201)430-7000

Business Description: Public Service Enterprise Group is a diversified public utility holding company that provides electric and gas power to three-quarters of New Jersey.

Officers: E. James Ferland, CEO, Pres. & Chairman of the Board; Richard E. Hallett, VP & Comptroller; Everett L. Morris, Vice Pres.; Francis J. Riepl, Treasurer; R. Edwin Selover, VP & General Counsel; Robert S. Smith, Secretary.

Benefits: Benefits include an employee pension plan and medical insurance and life insurance for active and retired employees.

Application Procedures: Places newspaper advertisements for certain openings. The company has a recorded employment information message. Applications can be filled out on site, or applications will be mailed upon request. Accepts unsolicited resumes. Send resume and cover letter to the attention of Payroll Administration.

▶ **Internships**

Type: The company offers a summer employment program.

Qualifications: Must be a college student.

Application Procedure: Interested applicants should apply between September and May. For more information, please contact the company.

Puget Sound Power & Light Co.
Puget Power Bldg.
411 108th Ave. NE
Bellevue, WA 98004
Phone: (206)454-6363

Business Description: Puget Sound Power & Light is an investor-owned electric utility, which serves 1.6 million people in a 4,500 square mile service area in Washington. The company also is engaged in developing new power-generating resources using natural gas and clean-coal technology.

Officers: John W. Ellis, CEO & Chairman of the Board; Richard R. Sonstelie, Pres. & CFO.

Benefits: Benefits include tuition assistance, medical insurance, dental insurance, life insurance, and savings plan.

Application Procedures: Send resume and cover letter to the attention of Personnel. For job vacancies, please call (206)462-3540.

▶ **Internships**

Type: The company does not offer any internship programs.

Quaker State
255 Elm St.
PO Box 989
Oil City, PA 16301
Phone: (814)676-7676

Business Description: Produces Quaker State brand name motor oil and other auto care products. Operates in the petroleum, coal, and insurance industries. Also conducts vehicular lighting and docking and chemical products operations. Owns and operates 450 fast lube facilities in 26 states and the province of Ontario.

Officers: James D. Berry, III, Exec. VP; Conrad A. Conrad, Pres. & COO; Jack W. Corn, CEO; R. Scott Keefer, VP of Finance & Treasurer.

Benefits: Benefits include tuition assistance, savings plan, medical insurance, dental insurance, and life insurance.

Human Resources: Wanda Weaver.

Application Procedures: Interested applicants should forward resumes to the Employee Relations Department.

▶ **Internships**

Type: The company offers an internship program.

Quantum Chemical Corp.
11500 North Lake Dr.
PO Box 429550
Cincinnati, OH 45249
Phone: (513)530-6500

Business Description: Engages in chemical manufacturing and petroleum refining.

Officers: Francis L. Brophy, VP of Corp. Development; David W. Lodge, VP, CFO & Treasurer; Paul W. Morris, VP of Info. Systems; John Hoyt Stookey, Chairman of the Board & Dir.

Human Resources: H. Weston Clarke, Jr.; Michael Keating.

Application Procedures: Send resume and cover letter to the attention of Michael Keating.

▶ Internships

Type: The company intends to offer internships in the near future.

Revlon Group Inc.

725 Madison Ave.
New York, NY 10022
Phone: (212)527-4000

Business Description: Manufactures cosmetics, perfumes and other toiletries, as well as drugs for pharmaceutical preparations.

Officers: D.G. Drapkin, Vice Chairman of the Board; H Gittis, Vice Chairman of the Board; R.O. Perelman, CEO & Chairman of the Board; B Slovin, President.

Human Resources: F.L. Tepperman.

Application Procedures: Interested candidates should direct their submission to the Human Resources Department.

▶ Internships

Type: Offers internship programs.

Application Procedure: Interested candidates should forward resumes with cover letters to 625 Madison Ave., New York, NY 10022 to the attention of Personnel.

The US Congress's Office of Technology Assessment estimated in 1990 that US companies spent $30 billion to $40 billion annually on training, mostly in programs for executives, salespeople, and technical workers.

Source: *Business Week*

Rexene Products Co.

5005 Lyndon B. Johnson Fwy.
Dallas, TX 75224
Phone: (214)450-9000
Fax: (214)450-9077

Business Description: Manufacturer of synthetic resins, plastics materials and/or nonvulcanizable elastomers.

Officers: Herm Rosenman, Vice Chairman of the Board & CFO; James M. Ruberto, Exec. VP of Mktg.; Andrew J. Smith, CEO & Pres.

Application Procedures: Contact the company for more information.

Reynolds Metals Co.

PO Box 27003
Richmond, VA 23261
Phone: (804)281-2000

Business Description: Produces aluminum and aluminum products such as foil, sheet, cans, and wire. They are a manufacturer of consumer goods, including plastic wrap, plastic film packaging, and paper products for homes and the food service industry. Reynolds holds interest in two Australian gold mines and is involved in real estate development. The company is also involved in manufacturing and marketing an aluminum alloy and products used for aerospace systems.

Officers: William O. Bourke, CEO & Chairman of the Board; R. Bern Crowl, Exec. VP & CFO; James T. Matsey, Dir. of Info. Systems.

Benefits: Benefits include medical insurance, life insurance, and dental insurance.

Human Resources: John R. McGill; Dave Thorne.

Application Procedures: Interested candidates should forward resumes to the company.

▶ Internships

Type: The company offers an internship program.

Application Procedure: Interested candidates should contact Robert Mayo.

Rohm and Haas Co.

Independence Mall W.
Philadelphia, PA 19105
Phone: (215)592-3000

Business Description: A manufacturer of specialty chemicals and plastics.

Officers: John J. Doyle, Jr., Vice Pres.; Gail P. Granoff, Secretary; John P. Mulroney, Pres. & COO; Fred W. Shaffer, VP & CFO; Angus F. Smith, Treasurer; David A. Stitely, Controller; John T. Subak, VP & General Counsel; J. Lawrence Wilson, CEO & Chairman of the Board.

Benefits: Offers employees medical insurance, life insurance, savings plan, tuition assistance, vision insurance, and dental insurance.

Human Resources: Mark Feck.

Application Procedures: Interested candidates should forward resumes to the company or complete an application in person.

▶ Internships

Contact: Rose Lepra.

Type: The company offers a co-op program to qualified applicants.

Application Procedure: Interested candidates should contact Rose Lepra.

Rowan Companies Inc.

5450 Transco Tower
2800 Post Oak Blvd.
Houston, TX 77056-6196
Phone: (713)621-7800

Business Description: An international offshore drilling contractor with operations and rigs in Alaska, eastern Canada, Venezuela, Europe, and the Pacific Rim. The company also operates charter aviation services.

Officers: A.G. Holt, Treasurer; C.R. Palmer, CEO, Pres. & Chairman of the Board.

Benefits: Benefits include dental insurance, savings plan, a comprehensive insurance package, a pension plan, a savings bond, traveler's insurance, and stocks.

Human Resources: Robert Tedrett.

Application Procedures: Interested candidates should forward completed application and/or resumes to the Industrial Relations Department.

St. Joe Paper Co.

PO Box 1380
Jacksonville, FL 32201
Phone: (904)396-6600

Business Description: Operator of paperboard mills. Manufacturer of corrugated and solid fiber boxes and related products. Manufacturer of miscellaneous products made from converted paper or paperboard.

Officers: Jacob C. Belin, CEO & Chairman of the Board; Edward C. Brownlie, Treasurer.

Benefits: Benefits include 401(k), employee pension plan, and a stock option plan.

Human Resources: Ronald Anderson.

Application Procedures: Interested candidates should forward resumes to Mr. E.C. Brownlie, Administration.

▶ Internships

Type: The company does not offer any internship programs.

San Diego Gas & Electric Co.

101 Ash St.
PO Box 1831
San Diego, CA 92101
Phone: (619)696-2000

Business Description: San Diego Gas & Electric is an investor-owned energy management company founded in 1881. About 80 percent of the company's revenues are generated from its utility businesses. "SDG&E owns two subsidiaries: Pacific Diversified Capital, an independently operated holding company that owns companies serving utility, environmental and real estate markets; and Califia Company, a subsidiary used for general corporate purposes such as holding real estate."

Officers: Donald E. Felsinger, Exec. VP; R. Lee Haney, Sr. VP of Customer Services Mktg.; Thomas A. Page, CEO & Chairman of the Board; Jack E. Thomas, Pres. & COO; Stephen Baum, Exec. VP.

Opportunities: Positions typically filled which require previous related experience are custodian, gardener, laborer, helper, messenger, secretary, and accounting clerk. Openings which require a degree include associate accountant and associate engineer. The requirements for positions of financial analyst, paralegal, economic analyst, and information system professionals, are a degree and previous related experience.

Benefits: Benefits include medical insurance, dental insurance, vision insurance, life insurance, 401(k), and educational assistance.

Human Resources: Margot Kyd.

Application Procedures: The company advertises job vacancies through its job hotline (619)654-1600. Interested candidates should forward resumes to the company. 8306 Century Park Ct., No. 4100, San Diego, CA 92123.

▶ Internships

Type: The company does not offer any internship programs.

SCANA Corp.
Palmetto Center
1426 Main St.
Columbia, SC 29201
Phone: (803)748-3000

Business Description: SCANA provides electric service through steam, hydro, internal combustion, and nuclear generation. The company also provides natural gas service.

Officers: Barbara D. Blair, Secretary; R.L. Cohen, VP of Corp. Development; L.M. Gressette, Jr., CEO, Pres. & Chairman of the Board; B.T. Horton, Jr., Treasurer; Cathy B. Novinger, Sr. VP of Admin. & Governmental Affairs; W.B. Timmerman, Sr. VP, Controller & CFO.

Benefits: Benefits include medical insurance, dental insurance, and life insurance.

Human Resources: Nancy Brazell.

Application Procedures: For job vacancy information, please call (803) 748-3001. Interested applicants should forward resumes to the company or fill out an application between 9 AM and 4 PM.

▶ **Internships**

Type: The company does not offer a formal internship program.

SCEcorp
2244 Walnut Grove Ave.
Rosemead, CA 91770
Phone: (818)302-2222
Fax: (818)302-4815

Business Description: A holding company for Southern California Edison Company and The Mission Group. Southern California Edison provides electric service to 4.1 million customers in central and southern California. The Mission Group's subsidiaries include Mission Energy Company, Mission First Financial, and Mission Land Company. These subsidiaries provide energy-related services throughout the United States and in nondomestic markets.

Officers: David N. Barry, III, Vice Pres.; John E. Bryson, CEO & Chairman of the Board; Richard K. Bushey, Vice Pres.; Alan J. Fohrer, Vice Pres.; Michael R. Peevey, President; Diana L. Peterson-More, Secretary.

Opportunities: The company is currently in a hiring freeze.

Benefits: Benefits include medical insurance, dental insurance, vision insurance, life insurance, long-term disability, short-term disability, an employee pension plan, bonuses/incentives, a savings plan, tuition assistance, paid holidays, two flexible holidays per year, personal/sick days, vacation days, and maternity leave. Offers employees a counseling program, company-sponsored sports teams, and training programs.

Human Resources: Al Cain; Ron Juliff.

Application Procedures: Send resume and cover letter.

▶ **Internships**

Type: The company does not offer an internship program.

Schlumberger Ltd.
277 Park Ave.
New York, NY 10172
Phone: (212)350-9400

Business Description: Schlumberger, through its divisions and subsidiaries, provides oilfield services to help locate and define oil and gas reservoirs; acquires, processes, and interprets seismic data; manufactures data analysis and transmission products; and offers engineering hardware and software products. The company has two main divisions; Oilfield Services and Measurement and Systems. The company also operates the following as subsidiaries: GECO; Sedco Forex; Anadrill; Schlumberger Industries; and Schlumberger Technologies.

Officers: Euan Baird, CEO & Chairman of the Board; Roland Genin, Vice Chairman of the Board; Arthur Lindenauer, Exec. VP & CFO.

Application Procedures: Send resume and cover letter.

▶ **Internships**

Type: The company does not offer any internship programs.

A. Schulman Inc.
3550 W. Market St.
PO Box 1710
Akron, OH 44309-1710
Phone: (216)666-3751

Business Description: A. Schulman Inc. is a supplier of high performance plastic compounds and resins used by product manufacturers around the world. A. Schulman Inc. operates eight manufacturing facilities in North America and Europe.

Officers: James H. Berick, Secretary; Brian R. Colbow, Treasurer; Terry L. Haines, Pres. & COO; Robert A. Stefanko, Exec. VP of Finance & Admin.; William C. Zekan, CEO & Chairman of the Board.

Benefits: Benefits include employee pension plan.

Human Resources: Terry Haines.

Application Procedures: Send resume and cover letter.

Shaffer A. Varco Co.
Shaffer

PO Box 1473
Houston, TX 77251-1473
Phone: (713)937-5000

Business Description: Manufacturer of machinery and equipment for oil and gas fields, or for drilling water wells.

Officers: K. Barrett, VP of Finance; T. Bishop, Dir. of Mktg. & Sales; J. Compoflice, President.

Human Resources: L. Howe.

Shell Oil Co.

1 Shell Plaza
Houston, TX 77002
Phone: (713)241-6161

Business Description: Shell Oil is "a leading U.S. oil, gas and petrochemical company." The company's three principal businesses are domestic exploration and production, oil products, and chemical products.

Officers: Phillip J. Carroll, Exec. VP; J.C. Jacobsen, VP of Finance; Steve Miller, VP of Mktg.; Frank H. Richardson, CEO & Pres.

Benefits: The Shell Pension Plan covers employees of the company and certain subsidiaries. Shell Oil also has a Benefit Restoration Plan and a Senior Staff Plan.

Application Procedures: The company is currently not hiring, but for information pertaining hiring status or application procedure, please contact The Shell Oil Recruitment, PO Box 2463, Houston, TX 77252-2463.

▶ Internships

Type: For more information, please contact the company.

Sherwin-Williams Co.

101 Prospect Ave. NW
Cleveland, OH 44115-1075
Phone: (216)566-2000

Business Description: Sherwin-Williams is engaged in the manufacture, distribution, and retail sale of paint and other coating products. The company operates 1,981 paint and wallcovering stores in 48 states and Canada.

Officers: John G. Breen, CEO & Chairman of the Board; Thomas R. Miklich, Sr. VP & CFO.

Benefits: Benefits include training programs.

Human Resources: Susan Szekeres, Employment Admin.

Application Procedures: Send resume and cover letter to the attention of Susan Szekeres, Employment Admin.

▶ Internships

Contact: Susan Szekeres.

Type: The company offers an internship and co-op program.

Application Procedure: Interested candidates should contact Susan Szekeres.

> The methods advocated by W. Edwards Deming and other such quality gurus are more about changes in organization and attitude than about the statistical control charts they are often associated with. Two recent books about Deming: *Deming Management at Work*, by Mary Walton, and *The Man Who Discovered Quality: How W. Edwards Deming Brought the Quality Revolution to America—the Stories of Ford, Xerox, and GM*, by Andrea Gabor.
>
> Source: *The New York Times Book Review*

Sonat Inc.

PO Box 2563
Birmingham, AL 35202-2563
Phone: (205)325-3800

Business Description: Worldwide energy company involved in natural gas transmission and marketing, oil and gas exploration and production, and oil services.

Officers: J. Robert Doody, Vice Chairman of the Board & CFO; Duane J. Kerper, VP of Info. Systems; Ronald L. Kuehn, Jr., CEO, Pres. &

Chairman of the Board; William E. Matthews, IV, Sr. VP.

Benefits: Benefits include an employee pension plan, medical insurance for retirees, and life insurance for retirees.

Human Resources: David Hopper; Beverly T. Krannich.

Application Procedures: Send resume and cover letter to the attention of David Hopper.

▶ Internships

Contact: Don Demetz, Contact.

Type: Internships are offered in different areas including accounting, engineering, computers, and human resources.

Application Procedure: Interested candidates should contact Don Demetz.

"Eighty percent of the initial impression you make is nonverbal," asserts Jennifer Maxwell Morris, a New York-based image consultant, quoting a University of Minnesota study. Some interview tips: walk tall, enter the room briskly while making eye contact with the person you're going to speak to, keep your head up, square your shoulders and keep your hand ready for a firm handshake that involves the whole hand but does not pump.

Source: *Working Woman*

Sonoco Products Co.

N. 2nd St.
PO Box 29551
Hartsville, SC 29550
Phone: (803)383-7000

Business Description: Manufacturer of packaging products for both consumer and industrial markets. Maintains over 200 operations located around the world.

Officers: Charles W. Coker, President; Thomas C. Coxe, Jr., Exec. VP; Charles J. Hupfer, Treasurer; Russell C. King, Jr., Sr. VP; F. Bennett Williams, Sr. VP.

Benefits: Benefits include an employee pension plan.

Human Resources: Robert C. Eimers.

Application Procedures: Send resume and cover letter to the attention of Robert C. Eimers.

▶ Internships

Contact: Glenda Gilbert, Contact.

Type: The company offers summer internships, especially in business.

Qualifications: College seniors.

Application Procedure: Interested candidates should contact Glenda Gilbert.

The Southern Co.

64 Perimeter Center E.
Atlanta, GA 30346
Phone: (404)393-0650

Business Description: Engaged in the generation, transmission, and distribution of electricity. The company serves approximately 11 million customers in Georgia and Alabama and parts of Florida and Mississippi.

Officers: Edward L. Addison, President; W.L. Westbrook, VP of Finance.

Benefits: Benefits include basic health care coverage, stock option plan, tuition assistance, vision insurance and a retirement program.

Application Procedures: The company advertises position openings on its job hotline (404) 668-3464. Interested candidates should forward resumes to the company.

▶ Internships

Type: The company only awards internships through school programs.

Southwest Gas Corp.

5241 Spring Mountain Rd.
Las Vegas, NV 89102
Phone: (702)876-7011

Business Description: Southwest Gas Corporation is a diversified natural gas and financial services organization. The company serves more than 800,000 customers in Nevada, California, and Arizona. In addition, it provides gas for resale to almost 100,000 customers of Sierra Pacific Power Company and CP National Corporation. PriMerit Bank, representing the financial services segment of the company, operates principally in the thrift industry. It is a federally chartered savings bank that markets a wide variety of consumer financial products and services through branches in Nevada and Arizona.

Officers: George C. Biehl, Sr. VP & CFO; Kenny C. Guinn, CEO & Chairman of the Board; Michael O. Maffie, Pres. & COO; John L. Mayo, Exec. VP of Operations; Marvin R. Shaw, Exec. VP.

Benefits: The company offers different benefit plans which may include a tuition assistance.

Application Procedures: The company advertises available positions on its Job Line (702) 365-2085. Send resume and cover letter to the attention of Personnel.

▶ Internships

Type: The company offers engineering and accounting internships.

Sterling Chemicals Inc.

PO Box 1311
Texas City, TX 77592-1311
Phone: (409)945-4431
Fax: (409)942-3448

Business Description: Producer of seven intermediate petrochemical products.

Officers: George W. Bostick, Info. Systems Mgr.; Douglas W. Metten, VP & CFO; Robert W. Roten, VP of Mktg.; J. Virgil Waggoner, CEO & Pres.

Human Resources: Ms. Tonie Gower; Norman G. Higgins.

Application Procedures: Send resume and cover letter to the attention of Ms. Tonie Gower.

▶ Internships

Type: The company does not offer any internship programs.

Stone Container Corp.

150 N. Michigan Ave.
Chicago, IL 60601
Phone: (312)346-6600

Business Description: A multinational paper company that produces and sells commodity pulp, paper, and packaging products. Maintains production facilities in Alabama, Arizona, Arkansas, California, Colorado, Connecticut, Florida, Georgia, Illinois, Indiana, Iowa, Kansas, Kentucky, Louisiana, Maryland, Massachusetts, Michigan, Minnesota, Mississippi, Missouri, Montana, New Jersey, New Mexico, New York, North Carolina, North Dakota, Ohio, Oklahoma, Oregon, Pennsylvania, South Carolina, South Dakota, Tennessee, Texas, Utah, Virginia, West Virginia, and Wisconsin. The company also has plants across Canada, and in Germany, Great Britain, The Netherlands, Mexico, and Costa Rica.

Officers: Arnold F. Brookstone, Sr. VP & CFO; Thomas P. Cutilletta, VP & Corp. Controller; James Doughan, Exec. VP; William J. Klaisle, VP of Mktg.; Leslie T. Lederertta, VP, Counsel & Sec.; Roger W. Stone, CEO, Pres. & Chairman of the Board.

Benefits: Benefits include an employee pension plan, medical insurance, life insurance, medical insurance for retirees, and life insurance for retirees.

Application Procedures: Send resume and cover letter to the attention of Sherry Rezonca.

▶ Internships

Type: The company does not offer an internship program.

Sun Company Inc.

1801 Market St.
Philadelphia, PA 19103
Phone: (215)977-3000

Business Description: A supplier of energy. Sun explores for, develops, produces, and markets crude oil and natural gas internationally, primarily in Canada and the North Sea. The company mines coal in the eastern and western regions of the U.S., produces synthetic crude oil in Western Canada, refines crude oil, and markets a full range of petroleum products. Sun is also involved in real estate development, equipment leasing, and secured lending.

Officers: Robert McClements, Jr., CEO, Pres. & Chairman of the Board.

Benefits: Benefits include health maintenance organizations, medical insurance, dental insurance, life insurance, travel accident insurance, accidental death and dismemberment insurance, and an employee pension plan.

Human Resources: Bill N. Rutherford.

Application Procedures: Send resume and cover letter to the corporate headquarters.

▶ Internships

Type: Offers a summer internship program and a co-op program.

Tambrands Inc.

777 Westchester Ave.
White Plains, NY 10604
Phone: (914)696-6060

Business Description: Manufactures and markets the Tampax line of feminine protection products, as well as other lines of these products. The company has operating subsidiaries in Brazil, Canada, France, Ireland, Mexico, and the United Kingdom. Its products are marketed worldwide in over 135 countries.

Officers: Charles J. Chapman, Exec. VP; R. Kent Doss, VP of Sales; Martin F.C. Emmett, CEO & Chairman of the Board; Paul E. Konney, Sr. VP, General Counsel & Sec.; Raymond F. Wright, Sr. VP, CFO & Treasurer.

Human Resources: Helen G. Goodman.

Application Procedures: Send resume and cover letter.

▶ Internships

Contact: Agnes Canale.

Type: Company offers an internship program.

Qualifications: Qualified applicants include local high school students.

Application Procedure: Applications should be forwarded to Agnes Canale.

TECO Energy Inc.

PO Box 111
Tampa, FL 33601
Phone: (813)228-4111

Business Description: Distributes electric power and provides water transportation of coal and grain.

Officers: Timothy L. Guzzle, CEO & Pres.; Alan D. Oak, Sr. VP of Finance & Treasurer.

Human Resources: Ray Mead, Mgr. of Recruitment and Staffing; Keith S. Surgenor.

Application Procedures: Send resume and cover letter to the attention of Ray Mead, Mgr. of Recruitment and Staffing.

▶ Internships

Type: Offers an internship-like program.

Duties: Students can attend school in the mornings and work in the evenings in "student clerk" positions.

Qualifications: High school students.

Temple-Inland Inc.

PO Drawer N
Diboll, TX 75941
Phone: (409)829-1313

Business Description: Temple-Inland is a financial investment company whose early years were centered in the production of timber and paper.

Officers: Clifford J. Grum, CEO & Pres.; W. Wayne McDonald, Exec. VP & CFO.

Opportunities: Hires for full- and part-time positions, freelance assignments, and foreign postings.

Benefits: Benefits include medical, dental, life, and short- and long-term disability insurances; an employee pension plan; a savings plan; profit sharing; bonuses/incentives; paid holidays; personal/sick days; vacation days; and maternity leave. Other benefits include a scholarship program, an employee counseling program, a cafeteria, flex time, a smoke-free environment, and training programs.

Human Resources: P.J. Caldwell; Jim Havard.

Application Procedures: Send resume and cover letter. Accepts walk-in applicants.

▶ Internships

Contact: Wanda Weeks.

Type: Offers an internship program.

Application Procedure: Send applications to Wanda Weeks, Personnel.

Texaco Inc.

2000 Westchester Ave.
White Plains, NY 10650
Phone: (914)253-4000

Business Description: Texaco is a producer, refiner and distributor of petroleum and petroleum products.

Officers: James W. Kinnear, CEO & Pres.; Allen J. Krowe, Sr. VP & CFO.

Human Resources: John D. Ambler; Denise Roseubeck.

Application Procedures: Send resume and cover letter to the attention of Denise Roseubeck.

▶ **Internships**

Contact: Lisa Nilson.

Type: Offers internships.

Qualifications: College students. Grade point averages are considered.

Application Procedure: Interested candidates should contact Lisa Nilson.

Texas Utilities Co.
2001 Bryan Tower
Dallas, TX 75201
Phone: (214)812-4600

Business Description: Engaged in the generation, purchase, transmission, distribution, and sale of electric energy in Texas, with a customer population estimated at 5,220,000.

Officers: Jerry Farrington, CEO & Chairman of the Board; W.H. Goodenough, Treasurer; Erle Nye, President.

Benefits: Benefits include retirement plans, an early retirement plan, and post-retirement healthcare and life insurance.

Human Resources: Ron Keenwy.

Application Procedures: Send resume and cover letter to the attention of Ron Keenwy.

▶ **Internships**

Type: The company offers an engineering internship program that is arranged through colleges.

Transco Energy Co.
PO Box 1396
Houston, TX 77251
Phone: (713)439-2000

Business Description: This energy company is primarily engaged in natural gas transmission via pipelines to markets in the East and Midwest. Also engaged in oil and gas exploration and production, and coal production and transportation. Transco is currently enacting a plan to improve profitability that calls for the sale of non-core assets, including its oil and gas exploration operations, the early retirement and voluntary severance of employees, and the reduction of capital expenditures. A Transco affiliate, Tren-Fuels Inc., is currently opening public natural gas refueling stations, developing a mobile refueling system, and operating the Alternative Fuel Technology Center, which is a natural gas vehicle center.

Officers: Bob Best, Sr. VP; John DesBarres, CEO & Pres.

Benefits: Benefits include health maintenance organizations, an employee pension plan, a savings plan, and a cafeteria program.

Human Resources: Thomas W. Spencer.

Application Procedures: Accepts walk-in applicants. Advertises in newspapers. Send resume and cover letter to the attention of Personnel Staffing Department.

▶ **Internships**

Contact: Mike Dale.

Type: Offers a college internship program.

Qualifications: Engineering students.

Application Procedure: Recruits for internships through campus interviews. Interested candidates should contact Mike Dale.

Between positions job-seekers do best when they create a daily schedule, establishing structure for what will be done each day. Setting non-job goals to attain achievements outside job-related activities helps maintain self-confidence. Flexibility is essential; a willingness to consider alternatives can lead to opportunities in new fields and offer a chance to explore something new.

Source: *Working Woman*

Unilever United States Inc.
390 Park Ave.
New York, NY 10022
Phone: (212)888-1260

Business Description: Manufacturer of miscellaneous prepared foods or specialty foods. Manufacturer of soap or detergents, and/or producer of crude or refined glycerin. Manufacturer of cosmetics, perfumes or other toilet preparations. Holding company engaged in holding or owning the securities of companies in order to exercise some degree of control over the companies' activities.

Officers: David Kellie-Smith, VP of Finance; Morris Tabaksblat, CEO.

Opportunities: Hires for full- and part-time

positions, freelance assignments, and foreign postings.

Benefits: Benefits include medical insurance, dental insurance, life insurance, long-term disability, short-term disability, an employee pension plan, a savings plan, tuition assistance, bonuses/incentives for management employees, vacation days, personal/sick days, maternity leave, an employee counseling program, summer flex time, an employee cafeteria, a family plan, a well baby plan, and training programs.

Application Procedures: Send resume and cover letter to the attention of Susan Jenkins.

▶ Internships

Contact: Beryl Matsheiqi.

Type: Offers a college internship program for management training.

Union Camp Corp.

1600 Valley Rd.
Wayne, NJ 07470
Phone: (201)628-2000

Business Description: Operates in five business segments: paper and paperboard production; packaging production; chemicals production; building products production; and wood and land resources. Paper operations are located in Eastover, South Carolina; Franklin, Virginia; Prattville, Alabama; Savannah, Georgia; and Normal, Illinois. Bags, corrugated containers, and cartons are produced at 40 plants located in Texas, Pennsylvania, Virginia, Missouri, Georgia, Indiana, South Carolina, Maine, Ohio, Illinois, Arkansas, Alabama, Colorado, Florida, Mississippi, North Carolina, Michigan, Louisiana, Tennessee, Connecticut, California, and New Jersey. Plastics products are made in Griffin and LaGrange, Georgia; Shelbyville, Kentucky; and Tomah, Wisconsin. School supplies and stationery are made in Birmingham, Alabama; Franklin, Ohio; and Houston, Texas. Lumber, plywood, and particleboard are made in Chapman, Alabama; Folkston, Georgia; Franklin, Virginia; Meldrim, Georgia; Opelika, Alabama; Seaboard, North Carolina; and Thorsby, Alabama. Chemicals are produced in Dover, Ohio; Jacksonville, Florida; Savannah, Georgia; and Valdosta, Georgia. The Corporate Research Center is in Princeton, New Jersey. Operates a forestry research center in Rincon, Georgia, and seedling nurseries in Belleville, Georgia; Capron, Virginia, and Union Springs, Alabama. Operates subsidiaries worldwide.

Officers: Jerry H. Ballengee, Exec. VP; Donald W. Barney, Treasurer; Raymond E. Cartledge, CEO & Chairman of the Board; W. Craig McClelland, Pres. & COO; John D. Munford, Exec. VP.

Benefits: Benefits include medical insurance, an employee pension plan, and extra spending accounts.

Human Resources: Sidney Phin.

Application Procedures: Send resume and cover letter to the attention of Gary Scott.

▶ Internships

Contact: Christine Dyer.

Type: Offers "In-Roads" internships each summer.

Qualifications: Minority high school students.

Union Carbide Corp.

39 Old Ridgebury Rd.
Danbury, CT 06817-0001
Phone: (203)794-2000

Business Description: A major manufacturer of industrial chemicals, plastics and gases.

Officers: Joseph S. Byck, Vice Pres. Strategic Planning; John A. Clerico, VP, CFO & Treasurer; Joseph E. Geoghan, VP & General Counsel; William H. Joyce, Exec. VP of Operations; Robert D. Kennedy, CEO, Pres. & Chairman of thc Board; H. William Lichtenberger, President & COO; Gilbert E. Playford, VP, Treasurer & CFO; O. Jules Romary, Vice Pres. Public Affairs & Investor Relations; Ronald Van Mynen, Vice Pres. Health, Safety & Environmental Affairs; John K. Wulff, VP & Controller.

Benefits: Benefits include an employee pension plan and a noncontributory defined benefit retirement program.

Application Procedures: Send resume and cover letter.

▶ Internships

Type: Interested candidates should contact the company for more information.

Union Electric Co.
PO Box 149
St. Louis, MO 63166
Phone: (314)554-3502
Toll-free: 800-255-2237

Business Description: A utility company supplying electric service to three central states.

Officers: Donald E. Brandt, Sr. VP & Finance Officer; William E. Cornelius, CEO & Chairman of the Board; Earl K. Dille, President.

Human Resources: Herbert W. Loeh; Joe Nesselhauf; Jan Heitman; Johnetta Carver.

Application Procedures: Send resume and cover letter to the attention of Jan Heitman.

▶ **Internships**

Contact: Johnetta Carver, Employment Supervisor.

Type: Offers internships.

Qualifications: Third-year engineering students.

Application Procedure: Interested parties should send applications to Johnetta Carver, Employment Supervisor.

Union Texas Petroleum Holdings Inc.
PO Box 2120
Houston, TX 77252-2120
Phone: (713)623-6544
Fax: (713)968-2771

Business Description: Engaged in oil and natural gas processing worldwide. The company conducts exploration and production programs in Indonesia, the North Sea, Pakistan, and elsewhere. Near Baton Rouge, Louisiana, Union Texas operates a jointly-owned ethylene manufacturing plant.

Officers: William J. Cepica, VP of Mktg.; A. Clark Johnson, CEO & Chairman of the Board; Michael N. Markowitz, VP & Treasurer.

Benefits: Benefits include medical insurance, dental insurance, life insurance, a 401(k) plan, long- and short-term disability, an employee pension plan, an indemnity plan, and an employee stock purchase plan.

Human Resources: N.W. Wilson III.

Application Procedures: The company hires through an agency and accepts resumes. Send resume and cover letter to the attention of Personnel.

▶ **Internships**

Type: Offers a summer internship program.

Qualifications: College and high school students.

Application Procedure: Apply to Human Resources/Personnel. Must meet specific GPA requirement.

USX Corp.
600 Grant St.
Pittsburgh, PA 15219
Phone: (412)433-1121

Business Description: USX is a diversified company that conducts business in three major industry segments: Energy, Steel, and Diversified Businesses. The Energy segment includes Marathon Oil Co. and its subsidiaries, which are involved in natural gas exploration and production, transportation, domestic refining, and marketing of crude oil and petroleum products; and Texas Oil and Gas Corp. and its subsidiaries, which are engaged primarily in domestic oil and gas exploration and production, natural gas gathering, transportation, marketing and distribution, gas liquids extraction and contract drilling. The Steel business consists of USS, which is a domestic integrated steel producer engaged in the production and sale of a wide range of steel mill products, coke, and taconite pellets. Diversified Businesses include the U.S. Diversified Group, which consists of management of mineral resources; real estate; engineering and consulting services; technology licensing; fencing projects; and agricultural chemicals. Also included are domestic and international mining and leasing and financial services.

Officers: Charles A. Corry, CEO & Chairman of the Board; W. Bruce Thomas, Vice Chairman of the Board & CFO.

Benefits: Benefits include medical insurance, life insurance, sick days, and accident insurance.

Human Resources: Mr. Richard Schinagl.

Application Procedures: Advertises in newspapers and bulletins. Send resume and cover letter to the attention of Personnel.

▶ **Internships**

Contact: Porter Jarble, Personnel Representative.

Type: Offers a summer internship program.

Qualifications: College students.

Application Procedure: Interested candidates should apply to Porter Jarble.

Valhi Inc.

3 Lincoln Centre
5430 LBJ Fwy., Ste. 1700
Dallas, TX 75240-2697
Phone: (214)233-1700

Business Description: Manufactures and markets chemical products, petroleum services, sugar and its by-products, timber and wood items, fiberboard, locks and metal products, and fast food. The corporation is active throughout the world, with major operations in the United States, Canada, and Europe. Its subsidiaries include: NL Industries, Inc.; Baroid Corp.; The Amalgamated Sugar Co.; Medford Corp.; Medite Corp.; Sybra Inc. and the Hardware Division.

Officers: Michael A. Setzer, President; Harold C. Simmons, CEO & Chairman of the Board; William C. Timm, VP of Finance.

Benefits: Offers medical benefits.

Application Procedures: Send resume and cover letter to the attention of Personnel.

▶ Internships

Type: The company does not offer an internship program.

There are over 100 public-access environmental and scientific bulletin boards out there right now, containing special databases and electronic conferences on everything from animal rights group newsletters to extensive listings of products made of recycled material.

Source: *Buzzworm: The Environmental Journal*

Valspar Corp.

1101 S. 3rd St.
Minneapolis, MN 55415
Phone: (612)332-7371

Business Description: Manufacturer of paintings and coatings.

Officers: R.E. Pajor, Pres. & COO; P.C. Reyelts, VP of Finance; C.A. Wurtele, CEO & Chairman of the Board.

Benefits: Benefits include an health maintenance organization, a 401(k) plan, life insurance, dental insurance. Also offers tuition assistance, direct deposit, union protection, healthcare and day care reimbursement.

Human Resources: Gary Gardner.

Application Procedures: Advertises in newspapers. Apply in person or send resume and cover letter to the attention of Paul Mason.

▶ Internships

Contact: Paul Mason.

Type: Offers a college internship program in lab positions and other departments.

Application Procedure: Interested candidates should contact Paul Mason.

Vista Chemical Co.

900 Threadneedle
PO Box 19029
Houston, TX 77224-9029
Phone: (713)588-3000
Fax: (713)588-3236-37

Business Description: Vista Chemical Co. is an integrated producer of commodity and specialty chemicals. Products are sold into such markets as household laundry detergents, shampoos, cosmetics and other personal care products, auto interior trim and fittings.

Officers: John D. Burns, CEO, Pres. & Chairman of the Board; R. Debs Gamblin, Sr. VP of Operations; Bruce E.A. Larsen, VP of Mktg.; John J. Weidner, Sr. VP & CFO; Virgil W. Weiss, VP of Research & Development; Robert R. Whitlow, Treasurer.

Benefits: Benefits include medical insurance, dental insurance, hospitalization, vision insurance, a 401(k) plan, paid vacation, sick pay, and an employee pension plan.

Human Resources: Wanda Clements; Maureen Herzog, Employee Relations.

Application Procedures: Some hiring is done through an employment agency. Recruits at college campuses. Send resume and cover letter to the attention of Maureen Herzog, Employee Relations.

▶ Internships

Contact: Maureen Herzog, Supervisor Employee Relations.

Type: Offers a summer internship program.

Qualifications: College sophomores.

Application Procedure: Recruits at college campuses. Contact Maureen Herzog for information.

Warner-Lambert Co.

201 Tabor Rd.
Morris Plains, NJ 07950
Phone: (201)540-2000

Business Description: Develops, markets, and manufactures health care and consumer products, including ethical and non-prescription pharmaceuticals, chewing gum, breath mints, shaving products, and empty hard gelatin capsules. The company has focused its research on cognitive disorders, central nervous system conditions such as Alzheimer's disease, schizophrenia, and cardiovascular diseases such as congestive heart failure.

Officers: Ernest J. Lavini, Exec. VP & CFO; Lodewijk deVink, Pres. & COO; Melvin R. Goodes, CEO & Chairman of the Board.

Benefits: Benefits include family leave, vacation days, personal/sick days, overtime pay, child-care referrals, elder-care referrals, telecommuting, extended leave, part-time employment, job sharing, employee parking, 401(k), flex time, summer hours, on-site services such as a credit union, dry cleaners, sick pay, health insurance, and long-term disability, oil change and vehicle inspections and company store.

Human Resources: Raymond M. Fino.

Application Procedures: Interested candidates should forward resumes to the corporate human resources department.

▶ Internships

Contact: Robert Hoffman, Human Resources Dir.

Type: Provides paid internships during the summer (10 to 12 weeks). **Number Available Annually:** 12-15. **Applications Received:** 150-200.

Duties: Tasks vary depending on job. Most positions offer general project work.

Qualifications: Accepts candidates with master's degrees in Business Administration only.

Application Procedure: Campus recruiting only.

Weirton Steel Corp.

400 Three Springs Dr.
Weirton, WV 26062-4989
Phone: (304)797-2000

Business Description: Manufactures and markets steel. The company's Weirton Technology Center conducts research on can-making technology, steel-making processes, and corrosion resistance. Weirton Steel Corp. is the nation's seventh largest steelmaker.

Officers: W.E. Bartel, Exec. VP of Operations; Herbert Elish, CEO, Pres. & Chairman of the Board; R.K. Riederer, VP & CFO.

Benefits: Benefits include medical, dental, life, and short- and long-term disability insurances, vision insurance, an employee pension plan, profit sharing, paid holidays, vacation days, maternity leave, training programs, an employee counseling program, company-sponsored sports teams, an employee cafeteria, flextime, and a smoke-free environment, and child-care referrals.

Human Resources: William C. Brenneisen.

Application Procedures: Send resume and cover letter to the attention of Gene Gillison.

▶ Internships

Contact: Jeff Robinson.

Type: Offers an internship program.

Application Procedure: Send applications to Jeff Robinson.

Wellman Inc.

1040 Broad St., Ste. 302
Shrewsbury, NJ 07702-4318
Phone: (908)542-7300
Fax: (908)542-9344

Business Description: Recycler of reclaimed plastic, soft drink bottles, fibre and film wastes.

Officers: William Bazemore, Vice Pres.; Clifford J. Christenson, VP, CFO & Treasurer; John L. Dings, Vice Pres.; Thomas M. Duff, CEO & Pres.; David K. Duffell, Secretary.

Benefits: Benefits include employee pension plan.

Human Resources: Dal Auant; Jim Carraway.

Application Procedures: Send resume and cover letter to the attention of Jim Carraway, Hwys. 41/51 N., PO Box 188, Johnsonville, SC 29555.

▶ Internships

Type: The company does not offer an internship program.

Western Resources
PO Box 889
Topeka, KS 66601
Phone: (913)296-6300
Fax: (913)575-6523

Business Description: A major supplier of natural gas to customers in Kansas, Missouri, Oklahoma, and Nebraska. The company operates as KPL Gas Service.

Human Resources: Helen Gaschen.

Application Procedures: Send resume and cover letter to the attention of Vicki Pritchard.

▶ Internships

Contact: Vicki Pritchard, Contact.

Type: The company offers an internship program to students.

Application Procedure: Interested candidates should contact Vicki Pritchard or forward resumes indicating the applicant desires an internship position.

Westmoreland Coal Co.
200 S. Broad St., 7th Fl.
Philadelphia, PA 19102
Phone: (215)545-2500

Business Description: A Pennsylvania-based supplier of coal generated power.

Officers: Pemberton Hutchinson, CEO & Pres.; E.B. Leisenring, Jr., Chairman of the Board; Christopher K. Seglem, Sr. VP & General Counsel; Larry Zalkin, Sr. VP & CFO.

Benefits: Benefits include life insurance, a savings plan plan, a retirement plan, a company-matched 401(k) plan, disability insurance, dental insurance, travel and accident insurance, and an employee pension plan.

Human Resources: Glen Pierce; Thomas M. Spangler.

Application Procedures: Some hiring is done through an employment agency. Apply in person or send resume and cover in attention to Irene Meeks.

▶ Internships

Contact: Tom Spangler.

Type: Offers a college internship program in marketing.

Qualifications: Applicants must be college students.

Application Procedure: Send applications to Tom Spangler.

Westvaco Innovation Corp.
299 Park Ave.
New York, NY 10171
Phone: (212)688-5000
Toll-free: 800-255-3548

Business Description: Manufacturer of paper products for reproduction, consumer and industrial packaging, and specialty chemicals for industrial and environmental applications. Maintains operating divisions in Illinois, Massachusetts, South Carolina, and Virginia. Westvaco manages 1.5 million acres of timberland and markets its products internationally.

Officers: John A. Luke, CEO & Pres.

Benefits: Benefits include retirement plans, life insurance, health maintenance organizations, disability insurance, a 401(k) plan, and a restricted stock plan.

Application Procedures: Some hiring is done through networking or employee referrals. Can also apply in person. Send resume and cover letter to the attention of Marianne DiGregoril.

▶ Internships

Contact: Marianne DiGregoril.

Type: Offers an internship program.

Qualifications: MBA candidates.

Weyerhaeuser Co.
33663 32nd Dr. S.
Tacoma, WA 98477
Phone: (206)924-2345

Business Description: Engaged in making forest products, including building materials, printing and writing papers, and paperboard and containerboard. Weyerhaeuser also has U.S. real estate development operations and mortgage banking and financial services companies. Maintains operations in California, Indiana, Michigan, Minnesota, New Jersey, New York, Washington, and Wisconsin.

Officers: John W. Creighton, Jr., President; Robert L. Schuyler, Exec. VP & CFO; George H. Weyerhaeuser, CEO & Chairman of the Board.

Benefits: Benefits include health maintenance organizations, disability plans, and a 401(k) plan.

Human Resources: Dian Joseph.

Application Procedures: Can apply in person. Send resume and cover letter to the attention of Dian Joseph.

▶ Internships

Type: Offers an internship program.

Qualifications: High school and college students.

Application Procedure: Apply to the Recruiting and Staffing Committee.

Wheeling-Pittsburgh Steel Corp.

1134 Market St.
Wheeling, WV 26003
Phone: (304)234-2400

Business Description: Manufacturer of steel and primary steel products.

Officers: Frederick G. Chbosky, VP & CFO; James D. Hesse, VP of Mktg.; Pat J. Meneely, Vice Pres.; William J. Scharffenberger, CEO & Chairman of the Board; James Wareham, President.

Benefits: Benefits include medical insurance, dental insurance, and disability insurance.

Human Resources: James Bronchik; Anthony F. Verdream.

Application Procedures: Places newspaper advertisements for certain openings. Send resume and cover letter to the attention of Mr. Wallace, Human Resources Department.

▶ Internships

Type: The company does not offer an internship program.

Willamette Industries Inc.

3800 1st Interstate Tower
1300 5th Ave.
Portland, OR 97201
Phone: (503)227-5581

Business Description: A forest products company with 71 plants in 71 states. It manufactures containerboard, fine paper, bleached hardwood market pulp, corrugated containers, business forms, and fiberboard. The company owns approximately 1 million acres of forestland.

Officers: William P. Kinnune, Exec. VP; Michael R. Onustock, Exec. VP of Mktg.; J.A. Parsons, Exec. VP & CFO; William Swindells, CEO, Pres. & Chairman of the Board.

Benefits: Benefits include health maintenance organizations, accidental death and dismemberment insurance, an employee pension plan, disability insurance, savings plan plans, and a 401(k) plan.

Human Resources: David W. Morthland.

Application Procedures: Interested candidates should forward application or resumes to David W. Morthland.

▶ Internships

Type: The company does not offer an internship program.

> H. Wayne Huizenga co-founded Waste Management, Inc., now the world's largest handler of waste materials, then started a bottled-water business that he sold to concentrate on creating Blockbuster Entertainment. He counsels budding entrepreneurs to plan their products around logical, foreseeable developments.
>
> Source: *Forbes*

Williams Companies Inc.

1 Williams Center
Tulsa, OK 74172
Phone: (918)588-2000

Business Description: Engaged in the operation of gas and petroleum pipelines, and through a subsidiary, the telecommunications industry.

Officers: Jack D. McCarthy, VP & Treasurer; Joseph H. Williams, CEO & Chairman of the Board.

Benefits: Offers employees a smoke-free environment. The company helps employees quit smoking.

Human Resources: John C. Fischer.

Application Procedures: The company's employment hot line is (918)588-3050. Send resume and cover letter to the attention of Personnel Department-Employment Office, PO Box 2400, Tulsa, OK 74102.

▶ Internships

Type: Offers paid internships.

Qualifications: College students selected from the company's "adopted schools."

Application Procedure: For more information, please contact the Human Resources Department.

Wisconsin Energy Corp.

231 W. Michigan St.
Milwaukee, WI 53203
Phone: (414)221-2345

Business Description: Wisconsin Energy Corp. is a holding company with subsidiaries in utility and nonutility businesses. Its principal subsidiaries are Wisconsin Electric Power Co. and Wisconsin Natural Gas Co. Wisconsin Energy is also the parent of five nonutility subsidiaries.

Officers: Richard A. Abdoo, CEO, Pres. & Chairman of the Board; John W. Boston, Vice Pres.; Francis S. Brzezinski, Vice Pres.; John H. Goetsch, Secretary; Ann Marie Brady, Asst. Sec.; Jerry G. Remmel, Treasurer; Gordon A. Willis, Asst. Treasurer.

Benefits: Offers full corporate benefits to regular employees, including medical insurance, dental insurance, vision insurance, a 401(k) plan, and savings plan.

Human Resources: Bob Cutler.

Application Procedures: Send resume and cover letter.

▶ Internships

Contact: Vivian Krenzke, College Relations Officer.

Type: Offers a college internship program.

Qualifications: Engineering students.

Application Procedure: Send applications to Vivian Krenzke, College Relations Officer.

Witco Corp.

520 Madison Ave.
New York, NY 10022
Phone: (212)605-3800
Fax: (212)605-3660

Business Description: Develops and manufactures specialty chemicals, specialty petroleum products, and engineered materials. Chemical manufacturing facilities are located in Los Angeles and Santa Fe Springs, California; Portland, Connecticut; Blue Island and Chicago, Illinois; Taft, Louisiana; Detroit, Michigan; Brainards, Newark, Paterson, and Perth Amboy, New Jersey; Brooklyn, New York; Cleveland, Ohio; Memphis, Tennessee; Houston, LaPorte, and Marshall, Texas; and Quincy, Washington. Petroleum products plants are in Phenix City, Alabama; Compton, Los Angeles, Oildale, and Richmond, California; Jacksonville, Florida; Spencer, Iowa; Olathe, Kansas; Gretna, Louisiana; Omaha, Nebraska; Ponca City, Oklahoma; Bakerstown, Bradford, Petrolia, and Trainer, Pennsylvania; and Houston and Sunray, Texas. Engineered materials facilities are located in City of Industry, California; Indianapolis, Indiana; Philadelphia, Mississippi; and Beacon, New York. The company also operates facilities in Canada, Denmark, England, France, Israel, Mexico, and The Netherlands.

Officers: Denis Andreuzzi, Pres. & COO; William R. Toller, Vice Chairman of the Board & CFO; William Wishnick, CEO & Chairman of the Board.

Benefits: Benefits include health care programs, dental insurance, vision insurance, a retirement and employee pension plan, full- and short-term disability, and a 401(k) plan.

Application Procedures: Send resume and cover letter to the attention of Human Resources. Some hiring is done through an employment agency. Advertises in in newspapers.

▶ Internships

Type: The company does not offer an internship program.

Witco Corp.

PO Box 23523
Harahan, LA 70183
Phone: (504)733-7777

Business Description: Manufacturer of miscellaneous industrial inorganic chemicals. Manufacturer of soap or detergents, and/or producer of crude or refined glycerin.

Officers: L. Waasdorp, General Mgr.

Benefits: Benefits include medical, dental, life, and short- and long-term disability insurances, pension and savings plans, profit sharing, tuition assistance, and selected bonuses, paid holidays, maternity leave, vacation days, counseling and training programs.

Application Procedures: Send resume and

cover letter to the attention of Human Resources.

▶ Internships

Type: The company does not offer an internship program.

Worthington Industries Inc.

1205 Dearborn Dr.
Columbus, OH 43085
Phone: (614)438-3210

Business Description: Producer of steel, pressure cylinders, suspension ceilings, custom plastic and precision metals, and steel castings. The company operates 24 manufacturing facilities in 10 states and Canada. The company also has seven distribution centers located throughout the United States and participates in two joint ventures.

Officers: Robert J. Klein, Exec. VP; Donald H. Malenick, COO & Pres.; John H. McConnell, CEO & Chairman of the Board.

Benefits: Benefits include health care programs, dental insurance, a 401(k) plan, profit sharing, and an employee pension plan.

Human Resources: Dwight Kelly.

Application Procedures: Send resume and cover letter to the attention of Ike Kellie.

▶ Internships

Type: Offers paid internships.

Application Procedure: Send resume to the attention of the Human Resources Department.

Additional Companies

Dow Chemical USA

PO Box 994
Midland, MI 48686
Phone: (517)496-4000

Exxon Corp.

225 E. Carpenter Fwy.
Irving, TX 75062
Phone: (214)444-1000

Career Resources

CHAPTER TWENTY-FOUR

Career Resources

The Career Resources chapter covers additional sources of job-related information that will aid you in your job search. It includes full, descriptive listings for sources of help wanted ads, professional associations, employment agencies and search firms, career guides, professional and trade periodicals, and basic reference guides and handbooks. Each of these sections is arranged alphabetically by organization, publication, or service name. For complete details on the information provided in this chapter, consult the introductory material at the front of this directory.

Sources of Help Wanted Ads

AAPG Bulletin
American Association of Petroleum Geologists
1444 S. Boulder Ave.
PO Box 979
Tulsa, OK 74101
Phone: (918)584-2555

Monthly. $135.00/year; $160.00/year for foreign subscribers; $8.00/issue for members; $12.00/issue for others.

AAPG Explorer
American Association of Petroleum Geologists
1444 S. Boulder Ave.
PO Box 979
Tulsa, OK 74101
Phone: (918)584-2555
Fax: (918)584-0469

Monthly. $15.00/year.

Advanced Composites
Edgell Communications, Inc.
120 W. 2nd St.
Duluth, MN 55802
Phone: (218)723-9253
Fax: (218)723-9445

Bimonthly. $4.00/single issue.

AEG Newsletter
Association of Engineering Geologists
62 King Phillip Rd.
Sudbury, MA 01776-2363

Agbiotechnology News
Freiberg Publishing
PO Box 7
Cedar Falls, IA 50613
Phone: (319)277-3599
Fax: (319)277-3783

Bimonthly. $75.00/year; $12.50/single issue.

Agricultural Engineering
2950 Niles Rd.
St. Joseph, MI 49085
Phone: (616)429-0300

Bimonthly. $36.50/year.

According to Mack Hanan, author of *Tomorrow's Competition: The Next Generation of Growth Strategies*, in the new order of global business, success will depend on alliances that strengthen the customer, thus securing a company's value in the marketplace. In his book Hanan offers advice on how to compete on value rather than price or performance, how to drive markets, and how to "sell without selling" by co-managing customer operations. The goal is to prosper in a new world where "competition is cooperative, and 3 suppliers are obsolete."

AISES Newsletter
American Indian Science and Engineering Society (AISES)
1630 30th St., Ste. 301
Boulder, CO 80301
Phone: (303)492-8658
Fax: (303)492-3400

Quarterly. Free. Includes calendar of events and employment opportunities.

American Association of Botanical Gardens and Arboreta—Internship Directory
American Association of Botanical Gardens and Arboreta
786 Church Rd.
Wayne, PA 19087
Phone: (215)688-1120

Lists available summer internships in public horticulture and private estates.

American Biotechnology Laboratory
International Scientific Communications, Inc.
PO Box 870
30 Controls Dr.
Shelton, CT 06484-0870
Phone: (203)926-9300
Fax: (203)926-9310

Ten times/year.

American City and County
Communication Channels, Inc.
6255 Barfield Rd.
Atlanta, GA 30328
Phone: (404)256-9800

Monthly. $48.00/year.

American Horticulturist
American Horticultural Society
7931 E. Boulevard Dr.
Alexandria, VA 22308
Phone: (703)768-5700
Fax: (703)768-7533

Monthly. Lists job openings for horticulturists.

American Industrial Hygiene Association Journal
American Industrial Hygiene Association
PO Box 8390
345 White Pond Dr.
Akron, OH 44320
Phone: (216)873-2442

Monthly. $75.00/year; $90.00/year for foreign subscribers.

American Journal of Public Health
American Public Health Association (APHA)
1015 15th St., NW
Washington, DC 20005
Phone: (202)789-5600
Fax: (202)789-5681

Monthly. Free to members; $80.00/year for nonmembers. Includes annual membership directory and news briefs.

American Laboratory News
International Scientific Communications, Inc.
30 Controls Dr.
PO Box 870
Shelton, CT 06484-0870
Phone: (203)926-9300
Fax: (203)926-9310

Bimonthly.

AMS Newsletter
American Meteorological Society (AMS)
45 Beacon St.
Boston, MA 02108
Phone: (617)227-2425
Fax: (617)742-8718

Periodic. $20.00/year for members; $60.00/year for nonmembers. Includes employment opportunities, contracts and grants listings, member news, promotions, and calendar of events. Contains brief reports on the affairs of government, industry, schools, and national and international bodies as they affect the atmospheric and hydrospheric sciences.

Appalachian Trailway News
PO Box 807
Harpers Ferry, WV 25425
Phone: (304)535-6331

Five times/year. $18.00/year. Magazine about Appalachian Trail protection.

Applied Occupational and Environmental Hygiene
Applied Industrial Hygiene, Inc.
Bldg. D-7
Cincinnati, OH 45211-4438
Phone: (513)661-7881

Monthly. $70.00/year. Magazine covering issues in occupational and environmental hygiene.

APWA Reporter
Magazine of American Public Works Association
1313 E. 60th St.
Chicago, IL 60637
Phone: (312)667-2200

Monthly. $1.00/single issue.

Membership in a cross-departmental problem-solving group provides a greater understanding of other business units and a broader perspective on issues. You'll need this broader perspective, because lateral moves will be increasingly common in any organization, and may play a part in your job search. "Middle managers must look sideways—not just up—if they want to increase their marketability in the 1990s," notes Beverly Robsham, president of Robsham & Associates, an outplacement firm in Boston, MA. On your resume be sure to mention any cross-departmental activities you've undertaken.

Source: *Working Woman*

ASHS Newsletter
American Society for Horticultural Science (ASHS)
113 S. West St., Ste. 400
Alexandria, VA 22314-2824
Phone: (703)836-4606
Fax: (703)836-2024

Monthly. Free for members. Includes employment listings, society activities, horticultural science, news of people in the field, calendar of events, and new publications.

ASM News
American Society for Microbiology (ASM)
1325 Massachusetts Ave., NW
Washington, DC 20005
Phone: (202)737-3600

Monthly. Free to members; $24.00/year for nonmembers in the U.S. Journal including employment listings, articles on a wide range of nonscientific as well as scientific topics, reports on legislative activity affecting microbiology, news of ASM activities, book reviews, and calendar of events.

ASPP Newsletter
American Society of Plant Physiologists (ASPP)
15501 Monona Dr.
Rockville, MD 20855
Phone: (301)251-0560
Fax: (301)279-2996

Bimonthly. Free to members; $30.00/year for nonmembers. Includes employment listings, calendar of events, regional section news, and book reviews.

Many job-placement experts agree that in any career situation, especially one in the environmental field, a balance must be played between well-rounded generalism and marketable specialization. At a minimum, you should have a skill to show for your years in school. Quite a few high-minded generalists with ecology degrees can't find a job.

Source: *Garbage*

AWWA Journal
American Water Works Association
6666 W. Quincy Ave.
Denver, CO 80235
Phone: (303)794-7711

Monthly.

Better Roads
PO Box 558
Park Ridge, IL 60068
Phone: (708)693-7710

Monthly. $15.00/year; $90.00/year for foreign subscribers. Magazine serving manufacturers, consultants, and federal, state, city, or county officials involved in road building.

Bio Science
American Institute of Biological Sciences (AIBS)
730 11th St., NW
Washington, DC 20001-4521
Phone: (202)628-1500
Fax: (202)628-1509

Eleven times/year. Free to members; $99.50/year for institutions; $9.00 copy for nonmembers. Journal covering employment listings, institute news, book reviews, calendar of events, and personnel appointments and distinctions.

Bio Technology
Nature Publishing Company
65 Bleecker St.
New York, NY 10012-2467
Phone: (212)477-9600

Monthly. $98.00/year.

BioCycle
The JG Press
419 State Ave.
Emmaus, PA 18049
Phone: (215)967-4135

Monthly. Focuses on management of city and industrial wastes by recycling and composting. Lists several environmental positions, generally focusing on recycling.

Biomedical Instrumentation & Technology
Association for the Advancement of Medical Instrumentation (AAMI)
3330 Washington Blvd., Ste. 400
Arlington, VA 22201-4598
Phone: (703)525-4890
Fax: (703)276-0793

Bimonthly. Free to members; $60.00 for nonmembers. Peer-reviewed journal which lists employment opportunities and includes association news, book reviews, advertisers and annual subject indexes, and statistics.

Bioworld Magazine
IO Publishing, Inc.
217 South B St.
San Mateo, CA 94401
Phone: (415)696-6555

Bimonthly.

Bulletin of the American Meteorological Society
American Meteorological Society (AMS)
45 Beacon St.
Boston, MA 02108
Phone: (617)227-2425
Fax: (617)742-8718

Monthly. Free to members; $60.00/year for nonmembers. Includes reports on employment opportunities, contents of AMS journals, annual meeting, and science fairs. Contains calendar of events, chapter news, book reviews, new publications, member news, professional directory, and obituaries.

Cell
50 Church St.
Cambridge, MA 02138
Phone: (617)661-7057

Biweekly. $275.00/year; $95.00/year for individuals. Journal on molecular and cell biology.

Chemical and Engineering News
American Chemical Society
1155 16th St., NW
Washington, DC 20036
Phone: (202)872-4600
Fax: (202)872-8727

Michael Heylin, editor. Weekly. Free to members; $95.00/year for nonmembers. Chemical process industries trade journal.

Chemical Business
Schnell Publishing Company
80 Broad St.
New York, NY 10004
Phone: (212)248-4177

Monthly.

Chemical Engineering
McGraw-Hill, Inc.
1221 Avenue of the Americas
New York, NY 10020
Phone: (212)512-2921
Fax: (212)512-4762

Richard Zanetti, editor. Biweekly. $27.50/year. Chemical process industries magazine.

Chemical Engineering Progress
American Institute of Chemical Engineers
353 E. 47th St.
New York, NY 10017
Phone: (212)705-7576

Monthly. $48.00/year.

Chemical Equipment
Gordon Publications, Inc.
301 Gibraltar Dr.
PO Box 650
Morris Plains, NJ 07950-0650
Phone: (201)292-5100

Monthly.

Chemical Week
810 7th Ave., 9th Fl.
New York, NY 10019
Phone: (212)586-3430

Weekly. $89.00/year.

The Chemist
American Institute of Chemists (AIC)
7315 Wisconsin Ave., NW
Bethesda, MD 20814
Phone: (301)652-2447

Eleven times/year. Free to members; $30.00/year for nonmembers. Includes employment opportunities, demographic/salary survey, book reviews, and calendar of events. Six issues per year published in magazine form, five issues as a newsletter.

Companies are foregoing the old five-year plan method of strategic planning for a new, everyday outlook: strategic thinking. This describes what a company does in becoming smart, targeted, and nimble enough to prosper in an era of constant change. The key words for the 1990s are focus and flexibility.

Source: *Fortune*

Chemtech
American Chemical Society
Centcom Ltd.
500 Post Rd. E.
PO Box 231
Westport, CT 06881-0231
Phone: (203)226-7131
Fax: (203)454-9939

Monthly. $24.00/single issue.

The City-County Recruiter and The State Recruiter
PO Box 2400
Station B
Lincoln, NE 68502
Phone: (402)476-9120

Biweekly. $18.00/year. Covers job openings within municipal, county, and state government at all levels.

Civil Engineering
American Society of Civil Engineers
345 E. 47th St.
New York, NY 10017
Phone: (212)705-7514
Fax: (212)705-7712

Monthly. $72.00/year; $9.00/issue.

"Paradigm" has become the hottest new thing in business buzzwords. It means a dominant pattern, a set of rules and regulations that both establishes boundaries and dictates behavior within those boundaries. When a paradigm shifts, you suddenly face a brand-new ball game, on a new playing field, with a new set of rules. Probably a whole new team, too. These are revolutionary changes, not incremental ones, and handling them successfully demands a radical break with tradition.

Source: *Working Woman*

Community Jobs
ACCESS: Networking in the Public Interest
1601 Connecticut Ave., NW, 6th Fl.
Washington, DC 20009
Phone: (202)667-0661
Fax: (202)387-7915

Monthly. $45.00/year to institutions; $25.00/year to nonprofit organizations; $20.00/year to individuals; $3.95/issue. Covers: Jobs and internships available with nonprofit organizations active in issues such as the environment, foreign policy, consumer advocacy, housing, education, etc. Entries include: Position title, name, address, and phone of contact; description, responsibilities, requirements, salary. Arrangement: Geographical.

Consulting/Specifying Engineer
Cahners Publishing Co.
PO Box 5080
Cahners Plaza
1350 Touhy Ave.
Des Plaines, IL 60018
Phone: (708)635-8800
Fax: (708)299-8622

Monthly. $69.95/year.

Energy User News
Fairchild Publications
7 E. 12th St.
New York, NY 10003
Phone: (212)741-4428

Quarterly. Magazine exploring industrial and commercial uses of energy.

Engineering & Mining Journal
Maclean Hunter Publishing Co.
29 N. Wacker Dr.
Chicago, IL 60606
Phone: (312)726-2802

Monthly. $50.00/year. Magazine focusing on metal and non-metallic mining.

Engineering News Record
1221 Avenue of the Americas
New York, NY 10020
Phone: (212)512-2000

Weekly. $42.00/year; $2.00/issue.

Engineering Times
National Society of Professional Engineers
1420 King St.
Alexandria, VA 22314
Phone: (703)684-2875

Monthly.

Environmental Action Magazine
Environmental Action, Inc.
6930 Carroll Ave., No. 600
Tacoma Park, MD 20912
Phone: (301)891-1106
Fax: (301)891-2218

Barbara Ruben and Hawley Truax, editors. Quarterly. Covers employment opportunities in various environmental fields.

Environmental Job Opportunities
Institute for Environmental Studies
University of Wisconsin-Madison
550 N. Park St.
15 Science Hall
Madison, WI 53706

Ten issues/year. $10.00/year.

Environmental Opportunities

Environmental Opportunities
PO Box 4957
Arcata, CA 95521
Phone: (802)253-9336

Monthly. $44.00/year; $24.00/six months; $4.50/copy. Lists full-time openings in environmental positions as well as short-term opportunities and internships.

Environmental Protection

Stevens Publishing Corp.
225 N. New Rd.
Waco, TX 76710
Phone: (817)776-9000
Fax: (817)776-9016

Nine times/year.

Environmental Science & Technology

American Chemical Society
1155 16th St., NW
Washington, DC 20036
Phone: (202)872-4581

Monthly. $30.00/year for members; $192.00/year for nonmembers.

Environmental Waste Management

243 West Main St.
Kutztown, PA 19530
Phone: (215)683-5098
Fax: (215)683-3171

Twelve times/year.

EOS

American Geophysical Union (AGU)
2000 Florida Ave., NW
Washington, DC 20009
Phone: (202)462-6900
Fax: (202)328-0566

Weekly. Free to members; $180.00/year for institutions. Newspaper; contains employment opportunities, meeting reports, book reviews, calendar of events, and announcements of grants and fellowships.

Farm Journal

230 W. Washington Sq.
Philadelphia, PA 19105
Phone: (215)829-4700

Fourteen times/year. $14.00/year. Agricultural news magazine.

Farmland News

PO Box 7305
Dept. 178
Kansas City, MO 64116
Phone: (816)459-6000

Monthly. $5.00/year.

Squeezed by foreign competition and a slowing economy, employers are increasingly shunning fixed raises in favor of pay plans where employees can enrich themselves only by enriching the company. From hourly workers to managers in pin stripes, those who boost earnings, productivity, or other results prosper. Those who turn in a lackluster performance take home less.

Source: *US News & World Report*

FASEB Journal

Federation of American Societies for Experimental Biology (FASEB)
9650 Rockville Pike
Bethesda, MD 20814
Phone: (301)530-7000
Fax: (301)571-1855

Periodic. Free to members; $95.00/year for nonmembers; $225.00/year for institutions. Includes employment opportunities, research communications, book lists, calendar of events, and current literature.

Federal Career Opportunities

Federal Research Service, Inc.
243 Church St. NW
Vienna, VA 22183
Phone: (703)281-0200

Biweekly. $160.00/year; $75.00/six months; $38.00/three months; $7.50/copy. Provides information on more than 4,200 current federal job vacancies in the United States and overseas; includes permanent, part-time, and temporary positions. Entries include: Position title, location, series and grade, job requirements, special forms, announcement number, closing date, application address. Arrangement: Classified by federal agency and occupation.

Federal Jobs Digest
Federal Jobs Digest
325 Pennsylvania Ave., SE
Washington, DC 20003
Phone: (914)762-5111

Biweekly. $110.00/year; $29.00/three months; $4.50/issue. Covers over 20,000 specific job openings in the federal government in each issue. Entries include: Position name, title, General Schedule grade and Wage Grade, closing date for applications, announcement number, application address, phone, and name of contact. Arrangement: By federal department or agency, then geographical.

As much as half of the impression you make on a prospective employer may have to do with your general knowledge of issues in your profession as well as issues in the industry in which you currently work or the industry in which you want to work. Subscribe to the journals in your field and industry, and don't forget to stay on top of the broader picture of the national and world economies.

Source: *Working Woman*

Feedstuffs
12400 Whitewater Dr.
Minnetonka, MN 55343
Phone: (612)931-0211

Weekly. $75.00/year.

Fisheries
American Fisheries Society
5400 Grosvenor Ln.
Bethesda, MD 20814-2198
Phone: (301)897-8720
Fax: (301)897-3690

Magazine covering fisheries management and aquatic resource issues. Includes job listings.

Geology
The Geological Society of America
3300 Penrose Pl.
PO Box 9140
Boulder, CO 80301
Phone: (303)447-2020

Monthly. $90.00/year.

Geotimes
American Geological Institute (AGI)
4220 King St.
Alexandria, VA 22302
Phone: (703)379-2480
Fax: (703)379-7563

Monthly. $22.95/year. Includes employment listings, book and map reviews, calendar of events, and geoscience consultants listings. Professional magazine covering geologic events, research, scientific meetings, education developments, government policies, and activities of the AGI and other geologic societies.

Ground Water
Association of Ground Water Scientists and Engineers (AGWSE)
6375 Riverside Dr.
Dublin, OH 43017
Phone: (614)761-1711
Fax: (614)761-3446

Bimonthly. Free to members; $63.00/year for nonmembers. Lists employment opportunities. Includes bibliographical listing of groundwater papers and reports, book reviews, and calendar of events; includes new publications on groundwater topics, and personnel promotions and job changes. Also contains state groundwater association news and student section of abstracts or summaries of Master's theses and Ph.D. dissertations.

GSA News Today
Geological Society of America (GSA)
PO Box 9140
3300 Penrose Pl.
Boulder, CO 80301-9140
Phone: (303)447-2020
Fax: (303)447-1133

Monthly. Free to members; $36.00/year for nonmembers in North America; $46.00/year for nonmembers outside North America. Membership and society activities newsletter. Includes employment listings, meeting announcements, new member information, and general earth science data.

Hazardous Materials Control
HMCRI
7237 Hanover Pkwy.
Greenbelt, MD 20070-3602
Phone: (301)587-9390

Bimonthly. $30.00/year; $3.50/single issue.

Hazmat World
Tower-Borner Publishing, Inc.
800 Roosevelt Rd.
Bldg. C, Ste. 206
Glen Ellyn, IL 60137
Phone: (708)858-1888
Fax: (708)858-1957

Monthly. $30.00/year; $3.00/single issue.

High Technology Careers
Westech Publishing Company
4701 Patrick Henry Dr., No. 1901
Santa Clara, CA 95054
Phone: (408)970-8800

Bimonthly. Free. Publication containing employment opportunity information for the engineering and technical community.

IJAPCA - International Journal of Air Pollution Control and Hazardous Waste Management
PO Box 2861
Pittsburgh, PA 15230
Phone: (412)232-3444

Monthly. $175.00/year.

Industrial Hygiene News
Rimbach Publishing, Inc.
8650 Babcock Blvd.
Pittsburgh, PA 15237
Phone: (412)364-5366

Bimonthly.

InTech
Instrument Society of America (ISA)
PO Box 12277
67 Alexander Dr.
Research Triangle Park, NC 27709
Phone: (919)549-8411
Fax: (919)549-8288

Monthly. Free to members; $60.00/year for non-members. Includes employment listings, advertisers' index, book reviews, calendar of events, new members, and new products and literature.

ITE Journal
Institute of Transportation Engineers
525 School St., SW, Ste. 410
Washington, DC 20024-2729
Phone: (202)554-8050

Monthly. $50.00/year; $65.00/year for foreign subscribers. Technical publication focusing on the plan, design, and operation of highway systems.

> An important task of environmental analysts is identifying natural resources that need to be protected—or at least, considered—during development. . . Information about the environmental setting of a proposed project is vital to successful environmental analysis, and environmental analysts increasingly draw on state-of-the-art information tools.
>
> Source: *The Conservationist*

Job Bank
Water Pollution Control Federation (WPCF)
601 Wythe St.
Alexandria, VA 22314-1994
Phone: (703)684-2400
Fax: (703)684-2492

Biweekly.

Job Scan
Student Conservation Association, Inc.
Box 550
Charleston, NH 03603
Phone: (603)826-5206

Monthly. $29.95/year; $6.00/copy.

Jobs Available
PO Box 1222
Newton, IA 50208-1222
Phone: (515)791-9019

Biweekly. $18.00/year. Lists a wide range of employment opportunities in the public sector. Published in Midwest/Eastern and Western editions.

Journal of Agricultural and Food Chemistry
American Chemical Society
1155 16th St., NW
Washington, DC 20036
Phone: (202)872-4600

Bimonthly. $24.00/year for members; $126.00/year for nonmembers.

Techniques for winning people over to your team when you're new on the job and change is in your program: make sure those who work for you see your vision as clearly as you do; listen to your critics—if you respect their work, they probably have good advice; make it clear that you're not on a power trip—be honest and don't promise what you can't deliver; get people involved in different aspects of the business so they know how everything works.

Source: *Working Woman*

Journal of Bacteriology
1325 Massachusetts Ave. NW
Washington, DC 20005
Phone: (202)737-3600

Monthly. $360.00/year.

Journal of Environmental Health
National Environmental Health Association (NEHA)
720 S. Colorado Blvd., Ste. 970, South Tower
Denver, CO 80222
Phone: (303)756-9090
Fax: (303)691-9490

Bimonthly. Free to members; $40.00/year for nonmembers. Contains listings of employment and educational opportunities, peer-reviewed articles on environmental issues, news on association activities, special columns, and annual index.

Journal of Forestry
Society of American Foresters
5400 Grosvenor Ln.
Bethesda, MD 20814
Phone: (301)897-8720

Monthly. $20.00/year; $90.00/year for institutions.

Journal of Range Management
Society for Range Management (SRM)
1839 York St.
Denver, CO 80206
Phone: (303)355-7070

Bimonthly. Free to members; $56.00/year for nonmembers. Includes list of employment opportunities, book reviews, and indexes.

Journal of the Air and Waste Management Association
Air and Waste Management Association (AWMA)
PO Box 2861
Pittsburgh, PA 15230
Phone: (412)232-3444
Fax: (412)232-3450

Monthly. Free to members; $165.00/year for nonmembers; $75.00/year for nonprofit organizations. Lists employment opportunities, personnel changes, and continuing education programs. Includes annual index, calendar of events, microcomputer software reviews, new product information, bibliographies, and legislative reports.

Lab World
401 N. Broad St.
Philadelphia, PA 19108

Management of World Wastes
6255 Barfield Rd.
Atlanta, GA 30328
Phone: (404)256-9800

Monthly. $35.00/year. Wastes, removal, and disposal magazine.

Minority Engineer
Equal Opportunity Publications
44 Broadway
Greenlawn, NY 11740
Phone: (516)261-8899

Quarterly. $17.00/year. Affirmative action magazine serving college graduating and minority professional engineers.

Modern Plastics
1221 Avenue of the Americas
New York, NY 10020
Phone: (212)512-6241

Monthly. $41.75/year.

The Municipality
122 W. Washington Ave., Rm. 301
Madison, WI 53703-2757
Phone: (608)267-2380

Monthly. $12.00/year.

Natural Science Center News
Natural Science for Youth Foundation (NSYF)
130 Azalea Dr.
Roswell, GA 30075
Phone: (404)594-9367
Fax: (404)594-7738

Quarterly. Includes employment opportunities and training courses in museum and nature center management. Reports on natural science centers, junior nature museums, native animal parks, and trailside museums.

Nature: International Weekly Journal of Science
1137 National Press Building
Washington, DC 20045
Phone: (202)737-2355

Weekly. $350.00/year for institutions; $135.00/year for individuals. Magazine covering the field of science and technology, serving the fields of biology, biochemistry, genetics, medicine, earthsciences, physics, pharmacology, and behavioral sciences.

Northeast Oil World
1900 Grant St., Ste. 400
Denver, CO 80203
Phone: (303)837-1917

Monthly. $36.00/year.

NSBE Magazine
NSBE Publications
344 Commerce St.
Alexandria, VA 22314
Phone: (703)549-2207

Five times/year. $10.00/year; $2.00/issue. Provides information on engineering careers, self-development, and cultural issues for recent graduates with technical majors.

Occupational Hazards
Penton Publishing
1100 Superior Ave.
Cleveland, OH 44114-2543
Phone: (216)696-7000

Monthly. $45.00/year.

The Oil & Gas Journal
PennWell Publishing Co.
1421 S. Sheridan Rd.
Tulsa, OK 74112
Phone: (918)835-3161

Weekly. $48.50/year. Trade magazine serving engineers and managers in international petroleum operations.

The optimum time for follow-up calls after job interviews is from 9 to 11 am, Tuesday through Friday, according to Jeffrey G. Allen, author of *The Perfect Follow-Up Method to Get the Job*. The book provides a suggested script for follow-up calls or letters, gives tips on handling an interview while dining, and covers typical questions raised in a follow-up interview.

Source: *Career Opportunities News*

Operations Forum
Water Environment Federation
601 Wythe St.
Alexandria, VA 22314
Phone: (703)684-2400

Monthly. $10.00/year; $2.50/single issue. Magazine covering water/wastewater technology for industry professionals.

Opportunities
Natural Science for Youth Foundation (NSYF)
130 Azalea Dr.
Roswell, GA 30075
Phone: (404)594-9367
Fax: (404)594-7738

Bimonthly. Newsletter listing job opportunities for employers and employees.

Opportunities in Non-Profit Organizations
ACCESS/Networking in the Public Interest
96 Mt. Auburn St.
Cambridge, MA 02138

Monthly. Lists opportunities in many fields, including public interest law.

Options
Project Concern
PO Box 85323
San Diego, CA 92186

Bimonthly. $10.00/year. Aimed at health services professionals. Lists international openings.

> In a crowded job market, employers become more selective. With more applicants to choose from, they're not just looking for those who do what's expected. They look for those who take the initiative to exceed designated objectives or to improve the status quo in some way. Any instances you can point to in which you've reduced expenditures or staffing requirements, customer complaints, or product defects will tend to improve your chances. Examples of enhanced revenue, productivity, or customer satisfaction you've managed to produce will also tend to impress employers looking for ways to compete and survive.
>
> Source: *Newark Star-Ledger*

Park Maintenance and Grounds Management
PO Box 1936
Appleton, WI 54913-1936
Phone: (414)733-2301

Monthly. $16.00/year; $2.50/issue.

Photogrammetric Engineering and Remote Sensing
American Society for Photogrammetry and Remote Sensing (ASPRS)
5410 Grosvenor Ln., Ste. 210
Bethesda, MD 20814-2160
Phone: (301)493-0290
Fax: (301)493-0208

Monthly. Free to members; $120.00/year for nonmembers. Includes employment listings, news of ASPRS, calendar of events, list of sustaining members, news of individual members, new products guide, and annual directory. Provides technical information about the applications of photogrammetry, remote sensing, and geographic information systems.

The Physiologist
American Physiological Society (APS)
9650 Rockville Pike
Bethesda, MD 20814
Phone: (301)530-7164
Fax: (301)571-1814

Bimonthly. Free to members; $25.00/year for nonmembers. Newsletter containing employment opportunity listings, book reviews, obituaries, statistics, and abstracts of annual meetings.

PM Network
Project Management Institute
PO Box 43
Drexel Hill, PA 19026
Phone: (215)622-1796
Fax: (215)622-5640

Eight times/year.

PM/USA The Green Sheet
Marketing Handbooks, Inc.
7094 Skyline Dr.
Delray Beach, FL 33446-2212
Phone: (407)498-7660
Fax: (407)495-5278

Monthly. $25.00/year; $5.00/single issue.

Pollution Engineering
Cahners Publishing Co.
Cahners Plaza
1350 East Touhy Ave.
PO Box 5080
Des Plaines, IL 60017-5080
Phone: (708)498-9846

Monthly. $18.00/year. Magazine focusing on pollution control, air, water, solid waste, and toxic/hazardous waste.

Pollution Equipment News
Rimbach Publishing, Inc.
8650 Babcock Blvd.
Pittsburgh, PA 15237
Phone: (412)364-5366

Six times/year.

Powder and Bulk Engineering
CSC Publishing, Inc.
1300 E. 66th St.
Minneapolis, MN 55423
Phone: (612)866-2242
Fax: (612)866-1939

Monthly.

Power
11 W. 19th St.
New York, NY 10011
Phone: (212)337-4060

Monthly. $19.00/year; $5.00/single issue. Magazine for engineers in electric utilities, process and manufacturing industries, commercial and service establishments, and consulting engineering firms working in the power technology.

Public Works
200 S. Broad St.
Ridgewood, NJ 07451
Phone: (201)445-5800

Monthly. Free to qualified subscribers; $30.00/year for others. Trade magazine covering city, county, and state improvement.

Rangelands
Society for Range Management (SRM)
1839 York St.
Denver, CO 80206
Phone: (303)355-7070

Bimonthly. $30.00/year for nonmembers in the U.S. Journal containing lists of current employment opportunities, annual index, legislative updates, and nontechnical articles.

The Rhodes Report
PO Box 1205
New Port Richey, FL 34291

SCA Listing of Volunteer Positions
Student Conservation Association (SCA)
Box 550
Charlestown, NH 03603
Phone: (603)826-4301
Fax: (603)826-7755

Annual.

Science
American Association for the Advancement of Science
1333 H St., NW
Washington, DC 20005
Phone: (202)326-6500

Weekly. $75.00/year; $120.00/year for institutions; $3.50/single issue. Magazine devoted to science, scientific research, and public policy.

> Greenpeace, which has grown to become the largest environmental organization ever in the world (with over 2 million contributors in 1990) and has the most U.S. supporters, has managed to accomplish something none of the other big groups has: maintaining its staff's radical-amateur image, while taking in big bucks.
>
> Source: *Buzzworm: The Environmental Journal*

Science and Engineering Newsletter
National Consortium for Black Professional Development
PO Box 18308
Louisville, KY 40218-0038

Quarterly. Free to members. Seeks to publicize the opportunities for black professionals in the fields of business administration, communications, applied and natural sciences, engineering, and law. Provides a clearinghouse for information concerning placement in these fields.

The Scientist
The Scientist, Inc.
3501 Market St.
Philadelphia, PA 19104
Phone: (215)386-0100
Fax: (215)387-7542

Biweekly. $58.00/year.

Solid Waste & Power
HCI Publications
410 Archibald St., Ste. 100
Kansas City, MO 64111
Phone: (816)931-1311
Fax: (816)931-2015

Seven times/yr. Lists job vacancies in all aspects of solid waste management.

Technology Review
Massachusetts Institute of Technology
MIT W59-200
Cambridge, MA 02139
Phone: (617)253-8250

Eight times/year (during the academic year). $24.00/year; $30.00/year for Canada; $36.00/year for foreign subscribers; $3.00/issue.

Some handy books to help you contemplate the job-change process: *Switching Gears: How to Master Career Change and Find the Work That's Right for You,* by Carole Hyatt; *Congratulations! You've Been Fired* , by Emily Knoltnow; and *How to Get the Job You Want,* by Melvin Danaho and John L. Meyer.

Source: *Better Homes and Gardens*

Teratology: The International Journal of Abnormal Development
Teratology Society (TS)
c/o Alexandra Ventura
9650 Rockville Pike
Bethesda, MD 20814
Phone: (301)571-1841
Fax: (301)530-7133

Monthly. Free to members. Includes listing of employment opportunities, reports on studies in all areas of abnormal development and related fields, abstracts of papers presented at annual meeting (indexed), book reviews, and obituaries.

US Women Engineer
Society of Women Engineers
345 E. 47th St.
New York, NY 10017
Phone: (212)705-7855

Bimonthly. $20.00/year.

Waste Age
1730 Rhode Island Ave., NW, Ste. 1000
Washington, DC 20036
Phone: (202)861-0708

Monthly. $45.00/year.

Waste Tech News
Schouweiler Communications Group
131 Madison St.
Denver, CO 80206
Phone: (303)394-2905
Fax: (303)394-3011

Biweekly. $25.00/year; $2.00/single issue.

Water & Wastes Digest
Scranton Gillette Communications, Inc.
380 Northwest Hwy.
Des Plaines, IL 60016
Phone: (708)298-6622
Fax: (708)390-0408

Bimonthly. $10.00/year; $2.00/single issue.

Water Engineering and Management
380 Northwest Hwy.
Des Plaines, IL 60016
Phone: (708)298-6622

Monthly. $19.00/year; $26.50/year for foreign subscribers.

Water, Environment, and Technology
Water Environment Federation
601 Wythe St.
Alexandria, VA 22314
Phone: (703)684-2400

Monthly. $144.00/year; $14.00/single issue.

Water Well Journal
6375 Riverside Dr.
Dublin, OH 43017
Phone: (614)761-3222

Monthly. Free to qualified subscribers. $12.00/year.

Weatherwise
4000 Albermarle St., NW
Washington, DC 20016
Phone: (202)362-6445

Bimonthly. $25.00/year; $42.00/year for institutions; $9.00 additional for foreign subscribers. Popular meteorology journal.

Western City
1400 K St.
Sacramento, CA 95814
Phone: (916)444-8960

Monthly. $24.00/year.

The Woman Engineer
44 Broadway
Greenlawn, NY 11740

Four times/year. $17.00/year. Recruitment magazine; includes a resume service.

Professional Associations

Air and Waste Management Association
PO Box 2861
Pittsburgh, PA 15230
Phone: (412)232-3444
Fax: (412)232-3450

Researchers, industrialists, educators, and others who are dedicated to seeking economical answers to the problems of air pollution and hazardous waste management. Publishes a directory and a journal that provides information on job openings, new products, and continuing education programs.

American Academy of Clinical Toxicology (AACT)
Kansas State University
Comparative Toxicology Laboratories
Manhattan, KS 66506-5606
Phone: (913)532-4334
Fax: (913)532-4481

Membership: Physicians, veterinarians, pharmacists, research scientists, and analytical chemists. Activities: Maintains placement services. Objectives are to: unite medical scientists and facilitate the exchange of information; encourage the development of therapeutic methods and technology; establish a mechanism for the certification of medical scientists in clinical toxicology. Conducts workshops and professional training in poison information and emergency service personnel. Maintains speakers' bureau. Bestows awards.

American Academy of Environmental Engineers (AAEE)
130 Holiday Ct., No. 100
Annapolis, MD 21401
Phone: (301)266-3311

Membership: Environmentally-oriented registered professional engineers certified by examination as diplomates of the academy. Activities: Identifies potential employment candidates through Talent Search Service. Purposes are: to improve the standards of environmental engineering; to certify those with special knowledge of environmental engineering; to furnish lists of those certified to the public. Requires written and oral examinations for certification. Works with other professional organizations on environmentally oriented activities. Bestows awards; maintains speakers' bureau.

Most often-cited corporate restructuring goals

1. Reduce expenses
2. Increase profits
3. Improve cash flow
4. Increase productivity
5. Increase shareholder return on investment
6. Increase competitive advantage
7. Reduce bureaucracy
8. Improve decision making
8. Increase customer satisfaction
10. Increase sales

Source: *The Wall Street Journal*

American Association of Blacks in Energy (AABE)
801 Pennsylvania Ave. SE, Ste. 250
Washington, DC 20003
Phone: (202)547-9378

Membership: Blacks in energy-related professions, including engineers, scientists, consultants, academicians, and entrepreneurs; government officials and public policymakers; interested students. Activities: Offers information on current job openings. Represents blacks and other minorities in matters involving energy use and research, the formulation of energy policy, the ownership of energy resources, and the development of energy technologies. Seeks to increase the knowledge, understanding, and awareness of the minority community in energy issues by serving as an energy information source for policymakers, recommending blacks and other minorities to appropriate energy officials and executives, encouraging students to pursue professional careers in the energy industry, and advocating the participation of blacks and other minorities in energy programs and policymaking activities. Updates members on key legislation and regulations being developed by the Department of Energy, the Department of Interior, the Department of Commerce, the Small Business Administration, and other federal and state agencies. Provides a scholarship program for higher education students; maintains speakers' bureau; holds seminars for minority energy professionals. Operates archive; bestows awards. Maintains computerized membership data base.

Strategies for "jump-starting" stalled job searches are included in *Parting Company: How To Survive the Loss of a Job and Find Another Successfully*, co-authored by William J. Morin, chairman of Drake Beam Morin Inc., the world's largest career-management consulting firm. Other chapters cover such timely topics as: assessing your skills and interests, making career decisions, financial planning, exploring different options such as early retirement, starting a business, consulting, targeting your job search, resumes and references, marketing strategy, job interviews, negotiating an offer, starting a new job.

American Association of Botanical Gardens and Arboreta (AABGA)
786 Church Rd.
Wayne, PA 19087
Phone: (215)688-1120

The AABGA is made up of directors and staffs of botanical gardens, arboreta, institutions maintaining or conducting horticultural courses, and others. It bestows awards of merit to individuals and organizations for outstanding contributions to horticulture. The group also acts as a resource center for information on garden management jobs.

American Association of Engineering Societies (AAES)
1111 19th St., NW, Ste. 608
Washington, DC 20036
Phone: (202)296-2237

Membership: Societies representing over one-half million engineers. **Purpose:** To advance the knowledge and practice of engineering in the public interest; act as an advisory, communication, and information exchange agency for member activities, especially regarding public policy issues. Conducts studies sponsored by Engineering Manpower Commission. Bestows National Engineering Award, Chairman's Award, Kenneth Andrew Roe Award, and Palladium Medal in conjunction with National Audubon Society; compiles statistics. **Publication(s):** *AAES Update*, quarterly. • *Directory of Engineering Societies*, biennial. • *Engineering and Technology Degrees*, annual. • *Engineering and Technology Enrollments*, annual. • *Engineers Salary Survey*, annual. • *Who's Who in Engineering*, biennial. • Also publishes *EMC Bulletins*.

American Association of Zoological Parks and Aquariums
Oglebay Park
Rte. 88
Wheeling, WV 26003
Phone: (304)242-2160
Fax: (304)242-2283

The association is made up of zoological park and aquarium personnel; and individuals interested in promoting zoos and aquariums for educational and scientific interpretation of nature and animal conservation and for public recreation and cultural pursuits. Publishes its annual conference proceedings and a monthly newsletter containing such information as employment listings and a calendar of events.

American Chemical Society (ACS)
1155 16th St., NW
Washington, DC 20036
Phone: (202)872-4600
Fax: (202)872-6067

Membership: Scientific and educational society of chemists and chemical engineers. Activities: Operates employment clearinghouse and offers career guidance counseling. Conducts: studies and surveys; special programs for disadvantaged persons; legislation monitoring, analysis, and reporting; courses for graduate chemists and chemical engineers; radio and television programming. Administers the Petroleum Research Fund and other grants and fellowship programs; presents awards. Maintains library of 10,000 volumes.

American Forestry Association (AFA)

1516 P St. NW
Washington, DC 20005
Phone: (202)667-3300
Toll-free: 800-368-5748
Fax: (202)667-7751

Membership: A citizens' conservation organization. **Purpose:** Working to advance the intelligent management and use of forests, soil, water, wildlife, and all other natural resources. Promotes public appreciation of natural resources and the part they play in the social, recreational, and economic life of the U.S. Presents annual Distinguished Service Award, John Aston Warder Medal, William B. Greeley Award, biennial Fernow and Giono Awards. Sponsors Trees for People program which seeks to help meet national needs for forest products, enhance productivity of private nonindustrial forest resources, maximize benefits to private woodland owners, provide advice to forest owners, and make legislative recommendations at the federal level. Maintains 6000 volume library on forestry, conservation, and wildlife. **Publication(s):** *American Forests*, bimonthly. • *Resource Hotline*, biweekly. • Also publishes books, reprints, and the *National Registry of Champion Big Trees and Famous Historical Trees.*

American Geological Institute (AGI)

4220 King St.
Alexandria, VA 22302
Phone: (703)379-2480
Fax: (703)379-7563

Membership: Federation of national scientific and technical societies in the earth sciences. **Purpose:** Seeks to stimulate public understanding of geological sciences; improve teaching of the geological sciences in schools, colleges, and universities; maintain high standards of professional training and conduct; work for the general welfare of members. Provides career guidance program. **Publication(s):** *Directory of GeoScience Departments*, annual. • *Earthscience*, quarterly. • *Geotimes*, monthly. • Also publishes bibliographies, reports, dictionaries, guides, and technical books.

American Geophysical Union (AGU)

2000 Florida Ave., NW
Washington, DC 20009
Phone: (202)462-6900
Fax: (202)328-0566

Membership: Individuals professionally associated with the field of geophysics; associate membership is open to all others; supporting members are companies and other organizations whose work involves geophysics. Activities: Sponsors placement service at semiannual meeting. Promotes the study of problems concerned with the figure and physics of the earth; initiates and coordinates research that depends upon national and international cooperation and provides for scientific discussion of research results. Offers science and policy lecture series. Presents medals and awards.

American Horticultural Society

7931 E. Boulevard Dr.
Alexandria, VA 22308
Phone: (703)768-5700
Fax: (703)763-6032

The group's membership includes amateur and professional gardeners. It operates a free seed exchange, a discount book service, and a gardeners' information service for members. The society sponsors garden symposia and maintains a 4000-volume library. The American Horticultural Society publishes several bimonthly journals.

American Indian Science and Engineering Society (AISES)

1630 30th St., Ste. 301
Boulder, CO 80301
Phone: (303)492-8658
Fax: (303)492-3400

Membership: American Indian and non-Indian students and professionals in science, technology, and engineering fields; corporations representing energy, mining, aerospace, electronic, and computer fields. Activities: Operates placement service. Seeks to motivate and encourage students to pursue graduate studies in science, engineering, and technology. Sponsors science fairs in grade schools, teacher training workshops, and student chapters in colleges. Offers scholarships. Adult members serve as role models, advisers, and mentors for students. Bestows awards; maintains library.

Some personal improvement guides: *Marketing Yourself*, by Dorothy Leeds; *The Perfect Interview: How To Get the Job You Really Want*, by John D. Drake; and *The Management Skills Builder: Self-Directed Learning Strategies for Career Development*.

Source: *Library Journal*

American Industrial Health Council (AIHC)
1330 Connecticut Ave., NW, Ste. 300
Washington, DC 20036
Phone: (202)659-0060

The AIHC is a coalition of industrial and commercial firms and trade associations working to advocate and promote the implementation of scientific methods to identify potential industrial carcinogens and other health hazards. It seeks to develop a basis for the review, risk assessment, and regulation of substances which may pose significant chronic health risks. The group publishes an annual report and a quarterly newsletter.

American Institute of Biological Sciences (AIBS)
730 11th St., NW
Washington, DC 20001-4521
Phone: (202)628-1500
Fax: (202)628-1509

Membership: Professional biological associations and laboratories whose members have an interest in the life sciences. Activities: Operates placement service and maintains computerized job and meeting lists. Promotes unity and effectiveness of effort among persons engaged in biological research, education, and application of biological sciences, including agriculture, environment, and medicine. Conducts symposium series; provides names of prominent biologists who are willing to serve as speakers and curriculum consultants; provides advisory committees and other services to the Department of Energy, Environmental Protection Agency, National Science Foundation, Department of Defense, and National Aeronautics and Space Administration. Bestows Congressional Science Fellowships and Distinguished Service Award. Maintains educational consultant panel.

American Institute of Chemical Engineers (AIChE)
345 E. 47th St.
New York, NY 10017
Phone: (212)705-7338
Fax: (212)752-3294

Membership: Professional society of chemical engineers. Activities: Offers placement and employment services. Conducts Career Guidance Committee. Establishes standards for chemical engineering curricula. Sponsors petrochemical and refining, exposition, and continuing education programs. Sponsors competitions; bestows 16 awards. Maintains speakers' bureau; compiles statistics. Publishes quarterly student magazine, *Chapter One*, which includes advice on studying and future careers (free to members; $12.00/ year for nonmembers).

American Institute of Chemists (AIC)
7315 Wisconsin Ave., NW
Bethesda, MD 20814
Phone: (301)652-2447

Membership: Chemists and chemical engineers. Activities: Offers placement service. Presents Gold Medal, Chemical Pioneers, and Members and Fellows awards, and an Honorary Fellowship. Sponsors American Board of Clinical Chemistry; National Registry in Clinical Chemistry; Commission on Professionals in Science and Technology; National Certification Commission in Chemistry and Chemical Engineering; AIC Foundation; National Inventors Hall of Fame; Public Education Fund. Bestows awards.

American Meteorological Society (AMS)
45 Beacon St.
Boston, MA 02108
Phone: (617)227-2425
Fax: (617)742-8718

The Society is made up of 11,000 professional meteorologists, oceanographers, and hydrologists; interested students and nonprofessionals. It develops and disseminates information on the atmospheric and related oceanic and hydrospheric sciences; seeks to advance professional applications. The group's activities include a guidance service, scholarship programs, career information, certification of consulting meteorologists, and a seal of approval program to recognize competence in radio and television weathercasting. It issues monthly announcements of job openings for meteorologists and maintains a small, highly specialized historical meteorological library. The American Meteorological Society publishes a periodic newsletter and several monthly and bimonthly journals.

American Public Health Association (APHA)
1015 15th St., NW
Washington, DC 20005
Phone: (202)789-5600
Fax: (202)789-5681

Membership: Professional organization of physicians, nurses, educators, academicians, environmentalists, epidemiologists, new professionals, social workers, health administrators, optometrists, podiatrists, pharmacists, pharmacy assistants, dentists, dental assistants, nutritionists, health planners, health care workers, other community and mental health specialists, and interested consumers. Activities: Sponsors job placement service. Seeks to protect and promote personal, mental, and environmental health. Services include: promulgation of standards; establishment of uniform practices and procedures; development of the etiology of communicable diseases; research in public health; exploration of medical care programs and their relationships to public health. Presents Award for Excellence to individuals for outstanding contributions to the improvement of public health; also bestows the Drotman Award to a young health professional who demonstrates potential in the health field and Sedgwick Memorial Medal to those who have advanced public health knowledge and practices. Maintains Action Board and Program Development Board.

American Society for Biochemistry and Molecular Biology (ASBMB)
9650 Rockville Pike
Bethesda, MD 20814
Phone: (301)530-7145
Fax: (301)571-1824

Membership: Biochemists and molecular biologists who have conducted and published original investigations in biological chemistry and/or molecular biology. Activities: Operates placement service. Bestows semiannual Herbert Sober Award, annual William C. Rose Award, and annual ASBC-Merck Award.

These days, saving the environment most likely requires a degree in chemistry, for analyzing polluted groundwater samples; or engineering, for designing machinery to filter those pollutants; or communications, for creating educational programs to teach people how used motor oil tossed in an open field can contaminate their drinking water. Anyway you go about it, science—and math—are eventually required.

Source: *Garbage*

American Society for Cell Biology (ASCB)
9650 Rockville Pike
Bethesda, MD 20814
Phone: (301)530-7153
Fax: (301)530-7139

Membership: Scientists with educational or research experience in cell biology or an allied field. Activities: Offers placement service.

American Society for Healthcare Environmental Services of the American Hospital Association (ASHES)
c/o Paul J. Julius
840 N. Lake Shore Dr.
Chicago, IL 60611
Phone: (312)280-6245
Fax: (312)280-4152

Membership: Managers and directors of hospital environmental services, laundry and linen services, housekeeping departments, and long-term care units. Activities: Maintains placement services. Provides a forum for discussion among members of common problems including educational opportunities, professional development, and career advancement. Operates technical assistance center. Offers legal advocacy; maintains liaison between members and governmental and code-writing bodies. Bestows Phoenix and Actions for Professional Excellence awards annually.

American Society for Horticultural Science (ASHS)
113 S. West St., Ste. 400
Alexandria, VA 22314-2824
Phone: (703)836-4606
Fax: (703)836-2024

Membership: Educators and government workers engaged in research, teaching, or extension work in horticultural science; firms, associations, and others interested in horticulture. Activities: Offers placement service. Strives to promote and encourage interest in scientific research and education in horticulture. Presents ten annual awards for outstanding research papers, teaching, extension, and collegiate activities. Maintains committees and working groups.

American Society for Microbiology (ASM)
1325 Massachusetts Ave., NW
Washington, DC 20005
Phone: (202)737-3600

Membership: Scientific society of microbiologists. Activities: Offers placement service. Promotes the advancement of scientific knowledge in order to improve education in microbiology. Communicates microbiological scientific achievements to the public. Maintains numerous committees and 22 divisions; biographical archives; compiles statistics. Sponsors competitions; bestows awards. Affiliated With: International Union of Microbiological Societies.

American Society for Photogrammetry and Remote Sensing (ASPRS)
5410 Grosvenor Ln.
Ste. 210
Bethesda, MD 20814-2160
Phone: (301)493-0290
Fax: (301)493-0208

Membership: Firms, individuals, and government agencies engaged in photogrammetry, photointerpretation, and remote sensing and their application to such fields as archaeology, geographic information systems, military reconnaissance, urban planning, engineering, traffic surveys, meteorological observations, medicine, geology, forestry, agriculture, construction, and topographic mapping. Activities: Maintains placement service. Sponsors student scholarships and issues awards for outstanding achievement. Offers voluntary certification program open to persons associated with one or more functional area of photogrammetry and remote sensing. Maintains small library and speakers' bureau; holds symposia and congresses. Surveys the profession of private firms in photogrammetry and remote sensing.

American Society of Agronomy (ASA)
677 S. Segoe Rd.
Madison, WI 53711
Phone: (608)273-8080

Membership: Professional society of agronomists, plant breeders, physiologists, soil scientists, chemists, educators, technicians, and others concerned with crop production and soil management, and conditions affecting them. **Purpose:** Presents achievement awards and Agronomy Club awards; sponsors fellowship program and student essay and speech contests. Provides placement service. **Publication(s):** *Agronomy Abstracts*, annual. • *Agronomy Journal*, bimonthly. • *Agronomy News*, monthly. • *ARCPACS Consultant Directory*, periodic. • *International Directory*, periodic. • *Journal of Agronomic Education*, semiannual. • *Journal of Environmental Quality*, quarterly. • *Journal of Production Agriculture*, quarterly. • Also publishes agronomy monograph series and special publication series.

American Society of Consulting Arborists (ASCA)
3985 Upham St., No. 12
Wheatridge, CO 80033
Phone: (303)420-9554

An organization made up of persons experienced in arboriculture who are professionally concerned with developing, growing, and caring for shade trees and who act as consultants in this field. ASCA encourages exchange of information regarding shade and ornamental trees; establishes guidelines for procedures in evaluating such trees; and seeks to provide an improved consultation service on the use and care of these trees. Publishes an annual directory and a bimonthly journal.

American Society of Consulting Arborists Membership Directory

American Society of Consulting Arborists
3895 Upham St., No. 12
Wheatridge, CO 80033
Phone: (303)420-9554

An annual directory listing arborist consultants. The publication is organized by state.

American Society of Plant Physiologists (ASPP)

15501 Monona Dr.
Rockville, MD 20855
Phone: (301)251-0560
Fax: (301)279-2996

Membership: Professional society of plant physiologists, plant biochemists, and other plant scientists engaged in research and teaching. Activities: Offers placement service for members. Presents annual and biennial awards for outstanding research in plant physiology. Conducts educational programs.

American Water Works Association (AWWA)

6666 W. Quincy Ave.
Denver, CO 80235
Phone: (303)794-7711
Fax: (303)795-1440

Membership: Water utility managers, superintendents, engineers, chemists, bacteriologists, and other individuals interested in public water supply; municipal- and investor-owned water departments; boards of health; manufacturers of waterworks equipment; government officials and consultants interested in water supply. Activities: Offers placement service via member newsletter. Develops standards and supports research programs; conducts in-service training schools and prepares manuals for waterworks personnel. Maintains hall of fame and biographical archives. Compiles statistics; sponsors competitions; presents awards. Conducts training programs. Offers children's services. Maintains on-line database, WATERNET (file 245), and a technical library and information center.

Association for Practitioners in Infection Control (APIC)

505 E. Hawley St.
Mundelein, IL 60060
Phone: (708)949-6052
Fax: (312)566-7282

Membership: Physicians, microbiologists, nurses, epidemiologists, medical technicians, sanitarians, and pharmacists. **Purpose:** To improve patient care by improving the profession of infection control through the development of educational programs and standards. Promotes quality research and standardization of practices and procedures. Develops communications among members, and assesses and influences legislation related to the field. Conducts seminars at local level. **Publication(s):** *American Journal of Infection Control*, bimonthly. • *Newsletter*, quarterly.

Best Business Schools in Executive Education

1. Harvard University
2. Stanford University
3. Northwestern University
4. University of Michigan
5. University of Pennsylvania

Source: *US News & World Report*

Association of Applied Insect Ecologists (AAIE)

1008 10th St., Ste. 549
Sacramento, CA 95814
Phone: (916)392-5721

Membership: Professional agricultural pest management consultants, entomologists, and field personnel. Activities: Offers placement service. Promotes the implementation of integrated pest management in agricultural and urban environments. Provides a forum for the exchange of technical information on pest control. Conducts local seminars.

Association of Boards of Certification (ABC)

208 5th St.
Ames, IA 50010-6259
Phone: (515)232-3623
Fax: (515)232-3778

Membership: Governmental certification authorities for water utilities and pollution control operating personnel and laboratories, including those that deal with hazardous wastes. **Purpose:** Seeks to strengthen state certification laws, their administration and effectiveness, and to establish uniform certification requirements among members. Promotes certification as a means to more efficient operation of public utilities; assists newly-created boards in implementing certification programs. Conducts uniform program for reciprocity, wherein certified operators are recognized as such by member boards after passing a standardized test produced by the ABC. Maintains speakers' bureau and biographical archives; compiles statistics; bestows awards. **Publication(s):** *Certifier*, monthly. • Also publishes certification tests, test manuals, and books on water and waste treatment.

Association of Consulting Chemists and Chemical Engineers (ACC&CE)

295 Madison Ave., 27th Fl.
New York, NY 10017
Phone: (212)983-3160
Fax: (212)983-3161

Membership: Chemists and chemical engineers engaged in consulting practice as individuals, partners, or executives of organizations. **Purpose:** Operates Clearing House for Consultants, through which industry is introduced to qualified and experienced members in any given field. **Publication(s):** *Consulting Services*, biennial. • Also issues press releases.

Association of Energy Engineers

4025 Pleasantdale Rd.
Atlanta, GA 30340
Phone: (404)447-5083
Fax: (404)446-3969

Engineers, architects, and other professionals with an interest in energy management and cogeneration. The group promotes the advancement of the profession and contributes to the professional development of members. Publishes several journals and a newsletter.

Association of Federal Safety and Health Professionals (AFSHP)

7549 Wilhelm Dr.
Lanham, MD 20706-2104
Phone: (301)552-2104

Membership: Federal safety and health personnel. Activities: Sponsors job referral program. Promotes the advancement of accident prevention through cooperation with other professional organizations; seeks to ensure the establishment of comprehensive accident prevention programs by federal agencies. Provides professional development opportunities for health and safety personnel. Encourages the maintenance of competency standards. Monitors potential abuses of position classification, downgrades, and job postings. Maintains liaison with Congress. Sponsors conference programs in conjunction with federal seminars.

Association of Ground Water Scientists and Engineers (AGWSE)

6375 Riverside Dr.
Dublin, OH 43017
Phone: (614)761-1711
Fax: (614)761-3446

Membership: Hydrogeologists, geologists, hydrologists, civil and environmental engineers, geochemists, biologists, and scientists in related fields. Activities: Offers placement service. Conducts educational programs, seminars, short courses, symposia, and field research projects. Maintains speakers' bureau and museum; sponsors competitions; compiles statistics. Operates library of 15,000 volumes on groundwater science and water well technology. A technical division of the National Water Well Association.

Biophysical Society (BPS)

c/o Emily M. Gray
Biophysical Society Office
9650 Rockville Pike, Rm. 512
Bethesda, MD 20814
Phone: (301)530-7114
Fax: (301)530-7133

Membership: Biophysicists, physical biochemists, and physical and biological scientists interested in the application of physical laws and techniques to the analysis of biological or living phenomena. Activities: Maintains placement service. Publishes *Careers in Biophysics* brochure.

Botanical Society of America (BSA)
c/o Gregory J. Anderson
Ecology and Evolutionary Biology
75 N. Eagleville Rd.
U-43 Univ. of Connecticut
Storrs, CT 06269-0043
Phone: (203)486-4322

Membership: Professional society of botanists and others interested in plant science. **Purpose:** Conducts special research programs; bestows awards. **Publication(s):** *American Journal of Botany*, monthly. • *Botanical Society of America—Membership Directory*, biennial. • *Career Bulletin*, periodic. • *Plant Science Bulletin*, bimonthly.

Co-op America
2100 M St., NW, Ste. 310
Washington, DC 20036
Phone: (202)872-5307
Toll-free: 800-424-2667

A group of both individuals and organizations interested in developing and supporting an economy that is socially and environmentally responsible. It provides services to members, including socially responsible financial planning tools, a credit union, health and medical insurance programs, and a travel service. Co-op America publishes a catalog of environmentally conscious products, a quarterly magazine, and several annual guides.

Coalition for Environmentally Responsible Economies
711 Atlantic Ave.
Boston, MA 02111
Phone: (617)451-0927

A coalition of groups that created an environmental code of conduct for companies called the Valdez Principles.

Earth Island Institute (EII)
300 Broadway, Ste. 28
San Franscisco, CA 94133
Phone: (415)788-3666
Fax: (415)788-7324

The organization is made up of individuals working to coordinate environmental and wildlife protection projects. It seeks to prevent the destruction of the environment; promotes ecologically sound development in order to preserve the natural environment and diversity of wildlife. EII publishes a quarterly international environmental news magazine.

Earthwatch
680 Mt. Auburn St.
Box 403
Watertown, MA 02272
Phone: (617)926-8200

Research and educational organization that allows individuals who have an avocational interest in science and the humanities to become working members of research teams led by highly qualified scientists. Currently sponsors 110 research expeditions a year. Provides a career training scholarship program.

> Managers are turning to tried-and-true as well as innovative imperatives to boost staff performance. Among them: communicate, creatively and often, through electronic bulletin boards, multimedia presentations, videotapes, handwritten notes, and employee-generated mottoes; build role-playing into training efforts; bring problem-solving and decision-making down to as low an organizational level as possible, giving everyone the training, information, and tools they need to make the right choices; set up incentive programs that are linked to both team effort and individual performance.
>
> Source: *Working Woman*

Environmental Action Foundation (EAF)
6930 Carroll Ave., 6th Fl.
Takoma Park, MD 20912
Phone: (202)745-4870

EAF is an environmental research and educational organization that serves as a resource for concerned citizens and organizations in the areas of energy policy, toxic substances, and solid waste reduction. It advocates recycling, source reduction and control of hazardous waste, energy efficiency measures, and renewable energy sources. The group operates Energy Project, which acts as a resource and information clearinghouse. They also publish a bimonthly news journal, pamphlets, brochures, and fact packets.

Environmental Careers Organization
286 Congress St.
Boston, MA 02210
Phone: (617)426-4375

Upper-level undergraduate, graduate, and doctoral students, or recent graduates seeking professional experience relevant to environmental careers. Their purpose is to foster professional development and the resolution of priority environmental issues in the public and private sectors. Organizes regional activities, facilitates exchange of information on environmental issues, and provides career couseling. The group publishes career publications and places students and recent graduates in short-term professional positions.

By the year 2000, 41 percent of new jobs created will require average or above-average skills, compared with fewer than 24% in 1992.

Source: *The Futurist*

Environmental Defense Fund (EDF)
257 Park Ave., S.
New York, NY 10010
Fax: (212)505-2375

EDF is a public interest organization of lawyers, scientists, and economists dedicated to the protection and improvement of environmental quality and public health. It conducts environmental public service and education campaigns and promotes research, public education, and administrative and legislative action. The group publishes an annual report and a bimonthly newsletter on environmental protection activities.

Environmental Law Institute (ELI)
1616 P St., NW, Ste. 200
Washington, DC 20036
Phone: (202)328-5150

The group seeks to conduct and sponsor research on environmental law and policy; maintain a clearinghouse for information regarding environmental law; and engage in related educational activities. Has conducted environmental law courses with law schools, governmental agencies, and other nonprofit organizations. ELI conducts a summer and annual internship program for law students. They also publish journals, newsletters, brochures, and reports.

Environmental Mutagen Society (EMS)
1600 Wilson Blvd., Ste. 905
Arlington, VA 22201
Phone: (703)525-1191
Fax: (703)276-8196

Membership: Bioscientists in universities, governmental agencies, and industry. Activities: Offers placement service. Promotes basic and applied studies of mutagenesis (the area of genetics dealing with mutation) and the avoidance of environmental mutagens. Bestows annual award for outstanding service in the field. Affiliated With: International Association of Environmental Mutagen Societies.

Federation of American Societies for Experimental Biology (FASEB)
9650 Rockville Pike
Bethesda, MD 20814
Phone: (301)530-7000
Fax: (301)571-1855

Membership: Federation of scientific societies with a total of 30,000 members: American Association of Immunologists; American Association of Pathologists; American Institute of Nutrition; American Physiological Society; American Society for Biochemistry and Molecular Biology; American Society for Cell Biology; American Society for Pharmacology and Experimental Therapeutics. Activities: Maintains placement service.

Geological Society of America (GSA)
PO Box 9140
3300 Penrose Pl.
Boulder, CO 80301-9140
Phone: (303)447-2020
Fax: (303)447-1133

Membership: Professional society fo geologists. Activities: Maintains placement service. Promotes the science of geology. Annually awards small research grants to geologists and graduate students in geology.

Greenpeace U.S.A.
1436 U St., NW
Washington, DC 20009
Phone: (202)462-1177
Fax: (202)462-4507

A group of conservationists who believe that verbal protests against threats to environmental quality are not adequate. Greenpeace initiates active, nonviolent measures to aid endangered species around the world. It monitors conditions of environmental concern including the greenhouse effect, radioactive and toxic waste dumping, and nuclear weapons. The organization publishes a quarterly publication and fact sheets and reports.

Hazardous Materials Control Research Institute (HMCRI)
7237 Hanover Pkwy.
Greenbelt, MD 20770
Phone: (301)982-9500

Association of corporations, consultants, engineers, scientists, professors, administrators, students, and others concerned with the safe management of hazardous materials and waste prevention, control, and cleanup. Publishes a newsletter that lists positions available in environmental service fields.

Hazardous Waste Treatment Council (HWTC)
1440 New York Ave., NW, Ste. 310
Washington, DC 20005
Phone: (202)783-0870

Membership: Firms dedicated to the use of high technology treatment in the management of hazardous wastes and to the restricted use of land disposal facilities in the interests of protecting human health and the environment. Activities: Provides placement assistance to members. Advocates minimization of hazardous wastes and the use of alternative technologies in their treatment, including chemical and biological treatments, fixation, neutralization, reclamation, recycling, and thermal treatments such as incineration. Encourages land disposal prohibitions. Promotes reductions in the volume of hazardous waste generated annually and expansion of EPA hazardous waste list. Advocates use of treatment technology as a more cost-effective approach to Superfund site cleanups. Works with state, national, and international officials and firms to assist in the development of programs that utilize treatment and minimize land disposal. Sponsors special studies, technical seminars, and workshops; participates in federal legislation, litigation, and regulatory development. Maintains library of materials on new technologies; operates speakers' bureau; compiles statistics and mailing list.

> With big corporations no longer rewarding loyalty and performance with lifetime guarantees of employment, individuals are transforming themselves into itinerant professionals who sell their human capital on the open market. "Instead of climbing up the ladder, people now have to develop a portfolio of skills and products that they can sell directly to a series of customers," explains Charles Handy, visiting professor at the London Business School and author of *The Age of Unreason,* a book about the changing nature of work. "We are all becoming people with portfolio careers."
>
> Source: *Business Week*

Human Environment Center
1001 Connecticut Ave. NW, Ste. 827
Washington, DC 20036
Phone: (202)331-8387

Provides forum for discussion and debate and promotes joint activities and efforts among environmental and social equity groups. Encourages minority participation in environmental issues and professions. Maintains the Environment Consortium for Minority Outreach, which helps professionals of color find employment in environmental fields.

Inform
381 Park Ave., S.
New York, NY 10016
Phone: (212)689-4040

An environmental research and education organization, Inform's purpose is to report on practical actions for the protection and conservation of natural resources, clarify the extent of corporate social responsibility, and identify specific constructive options for change. The group publishes a quarterly newsletter updating research projects and outreach activities.

Instrument Society of America (ISA)

PO Box 12277
67 Alexander Dr.
Research Triangle Park, NC 27709
Phone: (919)549-8411
Fax: (919)549-8288

Activities: Sponsors placement service. Educational organization dedicated to advancing the knowledge and practice related to the theory, design, manufacture, and use of instruments and controls in science and industry. Operates training center for industry; conducts symposia; develops standards; recognizes individual achievement. Maintains library and speakers' bureau.

International Society of Arboriculture (ISA)

303 W. University Ave.
PO Box 908
Urbana, IL 61801
Phone: (217)328-2032

The organization is made up of those engaged in commercial, municipal, and utility arboriculture; city, state, and national government employees; municipal and commercial arborists; and others interested in shade tree welfare. ISA disseminates information on the care and preservation of shade and ornamental trees. It publishes a monthly journal and distributes videotapes.

Junior Engineering Technical Society (JETS)

1420 King St., Ste. 405
Alexandria, VA 22314
Phone: (703)548-JETS

High school students interested in mathematics, science, engineering, and technology. Chapters operate in high schools under the guidance of a teacher. Practicing engineers serve as volunteer technical advisors. National and state offices provide engineering career guidance activities, seminars, academic and engineering design competitions, and engineering aptitude tests. Publishes a newsletter on national exams, competitions, developments in the field, and JETS activities.

Korean Scientists and Engineers Association in America (KSEA)

6261 Executive Blvd.
Rockville, MD 20852
Phone: (301)984-7048
Fax: (301)984-1231

Membership: Scientists and engineers holding single or advanced degrees. Activities: Operates placement service. Sponsors symposium. Maintains speakers' bureau and biographical archives. Bestows awards; compiles statistics. Maintains 100 volume library of scientific handbooks and yearbooks in Korean.

National Action Council for Minorities in Engineering (NACME)

3 W. 35th St.
New York, NY 10001
Phone: (212)279-2626
Fax: (212)629-5178

Seeks to increase the number of African American, Hispanic, and Native American students enrolled in and graduating from engineering schools. Offers incentive grants to engineering schools to recruit and provide financial assistance to increasing numbers of minority students. Conducts educational and research programs, bestows awards, and compiles statistics. Publishes an annual report, a newsletter, and a financial aid guide.

National Association of Black Geologists and Geophysicists (NABGG)

PO Box 720157
Houston, TX 77272

Membership: Black geologists and geophysicists. Activities: Assists minority students in their pursuit of summer employment and members interested in obtaining employees for summer positions. Informs minority students of career opportunities in geology and geophysics. Helps minority geologists and geophysicists to establish professional and business relationships. Seeks to motivate minority students to utilize existing programs, grants, and loans. Provides scholarships and oversees the educational careers of scholarship recipients.

National Association of Environmental Professionals (NAEP)
PO Box 15210
Alexandria, VA 22309-0210
Phone: (703)660-2364

Persons whose occupations are either directly or indirectly related to environmental management and assesment. Goal is to improve interdisciplinary communications and to advance the state of the art of the environmental planning process.

National Association of Minority Engineering Program Administrators (NAMEPA)
c/o Yvonne Green
College of Engineering
Felger Hall, Rm. 221
Norman, OK 73109
Phone: (405)325-4161

Membership: Administrators of college minority engineering programs; community, corporate, and technical group representatives. Activities: Acts as liaison among students and industry to facilitate job placement and the development of internship programs. Places administrators as interns in the industry to gain insight into problems faced by students. Sponsors job fairs, internship and in-service training programs, and workshops. Examines the issue of enrollment constraint concerning overcrowding in schools of engineering and the practice of establishing higher enrollment requirements and restricting financial aid for minority students; cooperates in and sponsors studies regarding student retention. Provides assistance to pre-college programs and directors in properly matching potential students with member institutions; offers counseling and guidance services.

National Audubon Society
950 3rd Ave.
New York, NY 10022
Phone: (212)832-3200

The group is made up of persons interested in ecology, energy, and the conservation and restoration of natural resources. It conducts research programs to aid endangered species, supports a force of 35 wardens to patrol wildlife sanctuaries, produces educational materials for school children, and bestows awards. The National Audubon Society also publishes several bimonthly journals.

National Consortium for Black Professional Development (NCBPD)
PO Box 18303
Louisville, KY 40218-0308
Phone: (502)896-2838

Membership: Industrial corporations and business firms; universities, including schools of business, science, and math, and public school systems; affiliates. Activities: Maintains clearinghouse and placement bureau for black professionals seeking employment. Goal is to increase substantially, by the year 2000, the number of black professionals in business administration, communications, applied and natural sciences, engineering, and law. Sponsors a science and engineering competition for black students and Ph.D. programs in the agricultural sciences and business administration. Provides recruitment service for universities seeking qualified black faculty and students. Services several federal contracts.

> "Hazardous waste cleanups are a social problem, not a technical problem," says Ecova founder Bill St. John. "When insurance companies and industries squabble over who should pay for Superfund cleanups, costs for lawyers and studies can consume 88 cents of every cleanup dollar."
>
> Source: *E Magazine*

National Environmental Health Association (NEHA)
720 S. Colorado Blvd., Ste. 970, South Tower
Denver, CO 80222
Phone: (303)756-9090
Fax: (303)691-9490

Membership: Professional society of persons engaged in environmental health and protection for governmental agencies, public health and environmental protection agencies, industry, colleges, and universities. Activities: Offers placement service. Conducts national professional registration program and continuing education programs. Provides self-paced learning modules for field professionals. Bestows awards; compiles statistics. Maintains speakers' bureau, biographical archives, and 1000 volume library on environmental health and protection. Plans to offer an electronic bulletin board service.

National Environmental Training Association (NETA)

2930 E. Camelback Rd.
Phoenix, AZ 85016
Phone: (602)956-6099

Professional society for environmental training professionals organized to promote better operation of pollution control facilities by means of personnel development.

Best books for new bosses

1. *Servant Leadership*, Robert K. Greenleaf, 1977
2. *The Female Advantage*, Sally Helgesen, 1990
3. *The Grace of Great Things*, Robert Grudin, 1990
4. *301 Great Management Ideas from America's Most Innovative Small Companies*, from *Inc.* magazine, 1991

Source: Selected by Nancy K. Austin, co-author of *A Passion for Excellence*, *Working Woman*

National Geographic Society (NGS)

17th & M Sts., NW
Washington, DC 20036
Phone: (202)857-7000
Toll-free: 800-638-4077

A 10-million-member organization that aims to increase and diffuse geographic knowledge. National Geographic sponsors expeditions and research in geography, natural history, archeology, astronomy, ethnology, and oceanography. It disseminates information through its magazine, maps, books, monographs, television documentaries, films, filmstrips, and information services for press and radio. The society also operates a library and an educational program.

National Network of Minority Women in Science (MWIS)

c/o American Association for the Advancement of Science
Directorate for Education and Human Resource Programs
1333 H St., NW
Washington, DC 20005
Phone: (202)326-6670

Membership: Asian, Black, Mexican American, Native American, and Puerto Rican women involved in science-related professions; other interested persons. Activities: Serves as clearinghouse for identifying minority women scientists. Goals are to: promote the advancement of minority women in science fields; improve the science and mathematics education and career awareness of minorities; support public policies and programs in science and technology that benefit minorities. Compiles statistics. Offers writing and conference presentations, seminars, and workshops on minority women in science and local career conferences for students. Local chapters maintain speakers' bureaus and placement services, offer children's services, sponsor competitions, and bestow awards.

National Organization for the Professional Advancement of Black Chemists and Chemical Engineers (NOPABCCE)

525 College St., NW
Washington, DC 20059
Phone: (202)667-1699

Membership: Black professionals in science and chemistry. Activities: Maintains placement service. Provides volunteers to teach science courses in selected elementary schools; sponsors scientific field trips for students; maintains speakers' bureau for schools; provides summer school for students of the U.S. Naval Academy. Conducts technical seminars in Africa; operates exchange program of scientific and chemical professionals with the People's Republic of China. Sponsors competitions; presents awards for significant achievements to individuals in the field. Maintains library of materials pertaining to chemistry, science, and black history; keeps archive of organization's books and records. Compiles statistics. Affiliated With: American Association for the Advancement of Science.

National Recycling Coalition
1101 30th St., NW
Washington, DC 20007
Phone: (202)625-6406
Fax: (202)625-6409

The Coalition works to promote the recovery, reuse, and conservation of materials and energy, and to make the benefits of recycling more widely known. It acts as an information network for persons interested in recycling, and publishes an annual report and a quarterly newsletter.

National Society for Black Engineers (NSBE)
1454 Commerce St.
Alexandria, VA 22306
Phone: (703)549-2207
Fax: (703)683-5312

NSBE seeks to increase the number of minority graduates in engineering and technology. The group bestows awards, and sponsors seminars and workshops geared toward preparing students for careers in the industry. Publishes an annual report, a bimonthly newsletter, and a pamphlet.

National Society of Professional Engineers
1420 King St.
Alexandria, VA 22314
Phone: (703)684-2800
Fax: (703)836-4875

Qualified professional engineers, graduate engineers, student members, and registered land surveyors who are interested in social, ethical, and economic considerations of engineering as a profession. Encompasses programs in public relations, employment practices, education, and career guidance. Monitors legislative and regulatory actions of interest to the engineering profession. Publishes a directory, a quarterly newsletter, and a monthly magazine on engineering.

National Solid Wastes Management Association
1730 Rhode Island Ave., NW, Ste. 1000
Washington, DC 20036
Phone: (202)659-4613

The group maintains a speakers' bureau, compiles statistics, conducts research programs, sponsors competitions, and presents awards. Publishes a monthly magazine on the waste industry.

National Water Well Association (NWWA)
6375 Riverside Dr.
Dublin, OH 43017
Phone: (614)761-1711
Fax: (614)761-3446

Membership: Water well drilling contractors, water system contractors, manufacturers and suppliers of drilling equipment, groundwater scientists such as geologists, engineers, public health officials, and others interested in the problems of locating, developing, preserving, and using underground water supplies. Activities: Offers placement services. Conducts seminars and 125 continuing education programs per year. Encourages scientific education, research, and the development of standards. Compiles market statistics. Maintains speakers' bureau, museum, 70,000 volume library, and software clearinghouse. Offers charitable program. Bestows awrds.

National Wildlife Federation (NWF)
1400 16th St., NW
Washington, DC 20036-2266
Phone: (202)797-6800

A federation of state and territorial conservation organizations and associate members, NWF encourages the intelligent management of the earth's resources and promotes greater appreciation of these resources, their community relationship, and wise use. The group gives organizational and financial assistance to local conservation projects, annually awards fellowships for graduate study of conservation, and publishes conservation education teaching materials.

Natural Science for Youth Foundation (NSYF)
130 Azalea Dr.
Roswell, GA 30075
Phone: (404)594-9367
Fax: (404)594-7738

Activities: Maintains placement service. Sponsors natural science centers, junior nature museums, native animal parks, and trailside museums. Provides information service. Conducts training courses in museum and nature center management. Presents Henry Gund Award, Naumburg Award, Founders Award, and Hornaday Gold Medal.

The Nature Conservancy (TNC)
1815 N. Lynn St.
Arlington, VA 22209
Phone: (703)841-5300

Dedicated to the preservation of biological diversity through land and water protection of natural areas. Provides long-term stewardship for 1600 conservancy-owned preserves and makes conservancy lands available for nondestructive use on request by educational and scientific organizations.

Good negotiating skills are not just more important in times of social and economic change, they are also more difficult to master, according to Max H. Bazerman and Margaret A. Neale, authors of *Negotiating Rationally*. "Negotiation is used every day to resolve differences and allocate resources," they explain; negotiating rationally means making the best decisions to maximize your interests. It's especially important for the job seeker.

Source: *Library Journal*

Radiation Research Society (RRS)
1819 Preston White Dr.
Weston, VA 22901
Phone: (703)648-3780
Fax: (703)648-9176

Membership: Professional society of biologists, physicists, chemists, and physicians contributing to knowledge of radiation and its effects. Activities: Maintains placement service. Promotes original research in the natural sciences relating to radiation; facilitates integration of different disciplines in the study of radiation effects. Presents RRS Travel Award and RRS Research Award annually.

Sierra Club
730 Polk St.
San Francisco, CA 94109
Phone: (415)776-2211

The Sierra Club promotes protection and conservation of the natural resources of the world, educates others on the need to preserve and restore the quality of the environment and the integrity of those ecosystems. The group publishes a bimonthly magazine that reports on environmental politics, conservation movement, and outdoor adventure.

Society for Cryobiology (SC)
c/o Federation of American Societies for Experimental Biology
9650 Rockville Pike
Bethesda, MD 20814
Phone: (301)530-7120
Fax: (301)530-7001

Membership: Investigators in the field of low temperature biology and medicine. Activities: Offers placement service. Promotes interdisciplinary approach to freezing, freeze-drying, hypothermia, hibernation, physiological effects of low environmental temperature on animals and plants, medical applications of reduced temperatures, cryosurgery, hypothermic perfusion and cryopreservation of organs, cryoprotective agents and their pharmacological action, and pertinent methodologies. Maintains biographical archives and operates charitable program. Conducts symposium and workshops.

Society for Industrial Microbiology (SIM)
PO Box 12534
Arlington, VA 22209-8534
Phone: (703)941-5373
Fax: (703)941-8790

Membership: Mycologists, bacteriologists, biologists, chemists, engineers, zoologists, and others interested in biological processes as applied to industrial materials and processes concerning microorganisms. Activities: Maintains placement service. Serves as liaison between the specialized fields of microbiology. Conducts surveys and scientific workshops in industrial microbiology. Presents annual Charles Thom Award for contributions to research in microbiology; awards annual ONR Lectureship to a distinguished microbiologist.

Society for Range Management (SRM)
1839 York St.
Denver, CO 80206
Phone: (303)355-7070

Membership: Professional international society

of scientists, technicians, ranchers, administrators, teachers, and students interested in the study, use, and management of rangeland resources for livestock, wildlife, watershed, and recreation. Activities: Sponsors placement service and maintains Employment Affairs Committee. Maintains library of 5000 books and periodicals on range management and related subjects. Bestows awards.

Society of American Foresters (SAF)

5400 Grosvenor Ln.
Bethesda, MD 20814
Phone: (301)897-8720
Fax: (301)897-3690

Membership: Professional society of foresters and scientists working in related fields. **Purpose:** Serves as accrediting agency for professional forestry education. Provides professional training. Supports 28 subject-oriented working groups. Bestows awards. **Publication(s):** *Forest Science*, quarterly. • *Journal of Forestry*, monthly. • *Northern Journal of Applied Forestry*, quarterly. • *Southern Journal of Applied Forestry*, quarterly. • *Western Journal of Applied Forestry*, quarterly.

Society of Exploration Geo-physicists (SEG)

PO Box 702740
Tulsa, OK 74170
Phone: (918)493-3516
Fax: (918)493-2074

Membership: Individuals having eight years of education and experience in exploration geophysics or geology. **Purpose:** Promotes the science of geophysics, especially as it applies to the exploration for petroleum and other minerals. Encourages high professional standards among members; supports the common interests of members. Maintains SEG Foundation, which receives contributions from companies and individuals and distributes them in the form of scholarships to students of geophysics and related subjects. Offers short continuing education courses to geophysicists and geologists. Presents several awards. Maintains 37 committees including: Development and Production; Engineering and Groundwater Geophysics; Mining and Geothermal; Offshore Exploration and Oceanography. **Publication(s):** *Geophysics*, monthly. • *Geophysics: The Leading Edge of Exploration*, monthly. • *Roster*, annual. • Also publishes monographs.

Society of Hispanic Professional Engineers (SHPE)

5400 E. Olympic Blvd., Ste. 225
Los Angeles, CA 90022
Phone: (213)725-3970

Membership: Engineers, student engineers, and scientists seeking to increase the number of Hispanic engineers by providing motivation and support to students. Activities: Maintains placement service. Sponsors Society of Hispanic Professional Engineers Foundation. Bestows awards; operates speakers' bureau. Hosts annual career conference each February.

When training is unavailable free on the job, the next cheapest way to acquire new skills may be right in the back yard. The majority of Americans live within 30 miles of one of the nation's nearly 1,200 community and technical colleges, which are rapidly gaining importance as centers of retraining.

Source: *U.S. News & World Report*

Society of Petroleum Engineers

PO Box 833836
Richardson, TX 75083-3836
Phone: (214)669-3377
Fax: (214)669-0135

A professional society of engineers in the field of petroleum engineering. The group conducts videotape courses, continuing education courses, and lecturer programs. It sponsors contests, presents awards, and offers scholarships. SPE publishes a newsletter advertising jobs, educational programs, etc.

Society of Spanish Engineers, Planners and Architects (SSEPA)

384 149th St., Ste. 300
Bronx, NY 10455
Phone: (212)292-0970

Membership: Hispanic professionals in the areas of engineering, planning, and architecture. Activities: Maintains placement service and provides internship programs. Fosters cooperation among industry, government, and academic and professional communities to improve education and employment opportunities for Hispanics. Provides counseling and financial assistance to Hispanic students in the physical development fields; sponsors precollege workshops. Operates speakers' bureau. Sponsors competitions.

Society of Women Engineers (SWE)

345 E. 47th St., Rm. 305
New York, NY 10017
Phone: (212)705-7855
Fax: (212)319-0947

Membership: Educational service society of women engineers; membership is also open to men. Activities: Assists women engineers in preparing for return to active work following temporary retirement and offers career guidance. Publishes *Profile of the Woman Engineer* and career guidance pamphlets. Supplies information on the achievements of women engineers and the opportunities available to them. Serves as an informational center on women in engineering. Administers several certificate and scholarship programs. Presents awards; offers tours and professional workshops. Conducts surveys; compiles statistics; maintains archives.

Soil Science Society of America (SSSA)

677 S. Segoe Rd.
Madison, WI 53711
Phone: (608)273-8080
Fax: (608)273-2021

Membership: Professional soil scientists, including soil physicists, soil classifiers, land use and management specialists, chemists, microbiologists, soil fertility specialists, soil cartographers, conservationists, mineralogists, engineers, and others interested in fundamental and applied soil science. **Publication(s):** *Journal of Environmental Quality*, quarterly. • *Journal of Production Agriculture*, quarterly. • *110-Year Indices*, periodic. • *Soil Science Society of America—Journal*, bimonthly. • *Soil Survey Horizons*, quarterly.

Spill Control Association of America (SCAA)

400 Renaissance Center, Ste. 1900
Detroit, MI 48243
Phone: (313)567-0500
Fax: (313)259-8943

Membership: Third party contractors; manufacturers or suppliers of pollution control and containment equipment; individuals in private or governmental capacities involved with spill clean-up and containment operations; associate companies. Activities: Maintains placement service. Organized to provide information on the oil and hazardous material emergency response and remediation industry's practices, trends, and achievements; to establish liaison with local, state, and federal government agencies responsible for laws and regulations regarding pollution caused by oil and hazardous materials; to cooperate in the development of industry programs and efforts so that pollutants are properly controlled and removed from land and water. Provides certification for hazardous material technicians. Maintains Spill Control Institute, Technical Services Division; collects and disseminates educational and technical information; conducts seminars. Operates library and speakers' bureau; conducts research; bestows awards.

Student Conservation Association (SCA)

Box 550
Charlestown, NH 03603-4301
Phone: (603)826-4301
Fax: (603)826-7755

Membership: Individuals, garden clubs, foundations, corporations, and groups who support the Student Conservation Program. The program, conducted in cooperation with the National Park Service, the U.S. Forest Service, and other federal, state, local, and private agencies which manage public lands, enlists the voluntary services of high school and college age persons to aid in preserving the natural beauty and resources of the national parks, forests, and resource areas. High school work group participants repair structures, maintain trails, and rehabilitate over-used areas. Older students assist the rangers and naturalists in interpretive and management projects, such as giving nature talks, cataloging materials, and trail patrol. Activities: Operates placement service.

Conducts educational and vocational programs providing job skill training, work experience, and exposure to career options in natural resource fields. Publishes *Earth Work*, a monthly magazine including career information for those working in conservation ($29.95/year).

Teratology Society (TS)
c/o Alexandra Ventura
9650 Rockville Pike
Bethesda, MD 20814
Phone: (301)571-1841
Fax: (301)530-7133

Membership: Individuals from academia, government, private industry, and the professions. Activities: Maintains placement service. Objective is to stimulate scientific interest in, and promote the exchange of ideas and information about, problems of abnormal biological development and malformations at the fundamental or clinical level. Sponsors annual education course, lectures, presentations, and workshops; bestows student travel awards. Is establishing archives of society documents and history.

Tissue Culture Association (TCA)
8815 Center Park Dr., Ste. 210
Columbia, MD 21045
Phone: (301)992-0946

Membership: Professional society of individuals using mammalian, invertebrate, plant cell tissue, and organ cultures as research tools in chemistry, physics, radiation, medicine, physiology, nutrition, and cytogenetics. Activities: Operates placement service. Aims to disseminate information on the maintenance and experimental use of tissue cells in vitro, and to establish evaluation and development procedures. Bestows student awards.

United States Committee for the United Nations Environment Program (USUNEP)
2013 Q St., NW
Washington, DC 20009
Phone: (202)234-3600
Fax: (202)332-3221

This program is made up of individuals interested in raising public awareness of the importance of a global environment effort. It sponsors educational programs and children's services and publishes several newsletters.

U.S. Public Interest Research Group
215 Pennsylvania Ave., SE
Washington, DC 20003
Phone: (202)546-9707

The group conducts research, monitors corporate and government actions, and lobbies for reforms on consumer, environmental, energy, and governmental issues. It sponsors an internship program for college students, provides opportunities for students to receive academic credit for activities such as investigative journalism, legislative research, lobbying, and public education. The group publishes a quarterly newsletter.

> To economize on headhunters' fees and classified advertising, a growing number of companies are now filing the resumes that snow in each year where they might actually do job seekers some good: in an electronic database.
>
> Source: *U.S. News & World Report*

Water Environment Federation (WEF)
601 Wythe St.
Alexandria, VA 22314-1994
Phone: (703)684-2400
Toll-free: 800-666-0206
Fax: (703)684-2492

Membership: Technical societies representing municipal engineers, consulting engineers, public health engineers, water pollution control works superintendents, chemists, operators, educational and research personnel, industrial wastewater engineers, municipal officials, equipment manufacturers, and university professors and students dedicated to the ehancement and preservation of water quality and resources. **Purpose:** Seeks to advance fundamental and practical knowledge concerning the nature, collection, treatment, and disposal of domestic and industrial wastewaters, and the design, construction, operation, and management of facilities for these purposes. Disseminates technical information; promotes good public relations and regulations that improve water pollution control and the status of individuals working in this field. Maintains job bank for wastewater facility employees; conducts educational programs. Sponsors High School Science Fair National Award. Maintains library of 6000 volumes on water pollution and related topics. **Publication(s):** *The Bench Sheet*, bimonthly. • *Highlights*, monthly. • *Job Bank*, biweekly. • *Literature Review*, annual. • *Operations Forum*, monthly. • *Research Journal Water Environment Federation*, bimonthly. • *Safety and Health Bulletin*, quarterly. • *Washington Bulletin*, monthly. • *Water, Environment, and Technology*, monthly. • Also publishes training materials including *Manuals of Practice*, public education brochures, and a water quality curriculum for schoolchildren.

"It is clear from the destruction that has been the price of today's uneven and unsatisfactory development that the world cannot afford much more of the same," asserts Martin W. Holdgate of The World Conservation Union. "We need something different. To use today's catch-word, we need development that is sustainable—that is, it must not overcrop soil, pastures, forest, or fisheries or create products that spread from a beneficial activity, like industry, to blight other essential ones, like agriculture, the supply of drinking water, or the stability of the world's ecosystems."

Source: *Environment*

The Wilderness Society (TWS)

900 17th St. NW
Washington, DC 20006-2596
Phone: (202)833-2300
Fax: (202)429-3958

Purpose: Purposes are the establishment of the land ethic as a basic element of American culture and philosophy, and the education of a broader and more committed wilderness preservation and land protection constituency. Focuses on federal, legislative, and administrative actions affecting public lands including national forests, national parks, wildlife refuges, and Bureau of Land Management lands. Encourages Congress to designate appropriate public lands as wilderness areas. Programs include grass roots organizing, lobbying, research, and public education. Presents annual awards; compiles statistics. **Publication(s):** *Annual Report*. • *Wilderness*, quarterly. • Also publishes press releases, notices, and alerts on critical conservation issues.

The Wildlife Society (TWS)

5410 Grosvenor Ln.
Bethesda, MD 20814-2197
Phone: (301)897-9770
Fax: (301)530-2471

Scientific and educational society of wildlife biologists, research scientists, conservation law enforcement officers, resource managers, and others interested in resource conservation and wildlife management on a sound biological basis.

Women in Agribusiness (WIA)

PO Box 10241
Kansas City, MO 64111

Membership: Women in agribusiness. Activities: Offers placement, networking, and peer/mentor support services. Provides a forum for the discussion of ideas and information related to agribusiness. Bestows annual awards to outstanding women in agribusiness.

WorldWIDE Network

1331 H St., NW, Ste. 903
Washington, DC 20005
Phone: (202)347-1514
Fax: (202)347-1524

Promotes strengthening of role of women in the development and implementation of environmental and natural resource policies. The group educates and promotes communication among members concerning the consequences of decisions affecting the environment. WorldWIDE publishes an annual directory and a bimonthly bulletin.

Employment Agencies and Search Firms

Aaron Personnel and Aaron Engineering
151 West Passaic St., Ste. 7
Rochelle Park, NJ 07662
Phone: (201)845-6011

Employment agency.

ABC Employment Service
25 South Bemiston, Ste. 214
Clayton, MO 63105
Phone: (314)725-3140

Employment agency.

Accro Personnel Services
1355 Willow Way, Ste. 230
Concord, CA 94520
Phone: (415)682-6800

Employment agency.

The Adams Group
7840 Madison Ave.
Ste. 185
Fair Oaks, CA 95628
Phone: (916)966-5050
Fax: (916)966-7070

Executive search firm.

Agra Placements, Ltd.
4949 Pleasant St., Ste. 1
West 50th Place III
West Des Moines, IA 50265
Phone: (515)225-6562
Fax: (515)225-7733

Executive search firm. Branch offices in Peru, IN, and Lincoln, IL.

Agri-Associates
500 Nichols Rd.
Kansas City, MO 64112
Phone: (816)531-7980
Fax: (816)531-7982

Executive search firm.

Agri-Personnel
5120 Old Bill Cook Rd.
Atlanta, GA 30349
Phone: (404)768-5701

Executive search firm.

B-W and Associates, Inc.
4415 W. Harrison
Hillside, IL 60162
Phone: (708)449-5400

Employment agency.

If an ad requests salary information, provide it or you'll find your resume in the wrong pile. The reason firms want the information is to ensure they're interviewing candidates they can afford. Interviews take time and cost money.

Source: *Business Monday/Detroit Free Press*

Biomedical Search Consultants
330 Main St.
Danbury, CT 06810
Phone: (203)744-4027

Employment agency.

Central Tech-Search, Inc.
463 N. Seneca
Wichita, KS 67203
Phone: (316)267-0281

Employment agency.

Channel Personnel Services, Inc.
7007 Gulf Fwy., Ste. 214
Houston, TX 77087
Phone: (713)643-8001

Executive search firm.

Chemical Scientific Services
PO Box 7135
Columbus, OH 43227
Phone: (614)231-4401

Employment agency.

Claremont-Branan, Inc.
2150 Parklake Dr., Ste. 212
Atlanta, GA 30345
Phone: (404)491-1292

Employment agency. Executive search firm.

Colli Associates of Tampa
PO Box 2865
Tampa, FL 33601
Phone: (813)681-2145

Employment agency. Executive search firm.

One thousand unsolicited resumes typically arrive in the daily mail at Fortune 50 companies. Four out of five are tossed after a quick perusal.

Source: *U.S. News & World Report*

The Energists
10260 Westheimer, Ste. 300
Houston, TX 77042
Phone: (713)781-6881
Fax: (713)781-2998

Executive search firm.

Engineer One, Inc.
PO Box 23037
Knoxville, TN 37933
Phone: (615)690-2611

Employment agency.

Networking isn't talking about yourself. You can get information only if the other party is talking about himself or herself, his or her company and associates. If you find networking is your-sided, you'd better rethink your approach.

Source: *Business Monday/Detroit Free Press*

Environmental Professional Associates
9454 Wilshire Blvd., Ste. 650
Beverly Hills, CA 90212
Phone: (213)273-5320

Executive search firm. Focuses on environmental positions.

General Industrial Technology
108 S. Franklin Ave.
Valley Stream, NY 11580
Phone: (516)561-1300

Employment agency. Places staff in regular or temporary positions.

Hansen Employment and Counseling Service
110 N. Cleburn
Grand Island, NE 68801
Phone: (309)382-7300

Employment agency. Handles placements in a variety of fields on a regular or temporary basis.

Hayden and Associates
7825 Washington Ave. S., Ste. 120
Minneapolis, MN 55435
Phone: (612)941-6300
Fax: (612)941-9602

Employment agency. Executive search firm. Fills openings in a variety of fields.

Health and Science Center
PO Box 213
Lima, PA 19037
Phone: (215)891-0794

Employment agency. Executive search firm.

Industrial Recruiters Associates
630 Oakwood Ave., Ste. 318
West Hartford, CT 06110
Phone: (203)953-3643

Employment agency.

Intech Summit Group, Inc.
11772 Sorrento Valley Rd., Ste. 10
San Diego, CA 92121
Phone: (619)792-5711

Employment agency.

International Staffing Consultants
19762 MacArthur Blvd.
Irvine, CA 92715
Phone: (714)752-6228

Employment agency. Provides placement on regular or temporary basis. Affiliate office in London.

Jobs Company
E. 8900 Sprague Ave.
Spokane, WA 99212
Phone: (509)928-3151

Employment agency. Has division specializing in engineering and scientific openings.

JR Professional Search
7477 E. Broadway
Tucson, AZ 85710
Phone: (602)721-1855

Employment agency.

LOR Division, NIHRRI
418 Wall St.
Princeton, NJ 08540
Phone: (609)921-6580

Employment agency. Executive search firm.

Lybrook Associates, Inc.
PO Box 572
Newport, RI 02840
Phone: (401)847-2210
Fax: (401)683-9153

Executive search firm.

Mainline Personnel Service, Inc.
401 City Ave.
Bala Cynwyd, PA 19004
Phone: (215)667-1820

Employment agency.

Management Search, Inc.
2800 W. Country Club Dr.
Oklahoma City, OK 73116
Phone: (405)842-3173

Executive search firm.

Pattison's Agency
770 E. Shaw, No. 214
Fresno, CA 93710
Phone: (408)244-6060

Employment agency.

The Personnel Institute
1000 Connecticut Ave., NW, Ste. 702
Washington, DC 20036
Phone: (202)223-4911

Consulting firm.

Professional Placement Associates, Inc.
11 Rye Ridge Plaza
Port Chester, NY 10573
Phone: (914)939-1195
Fax: (914)939-1959

Employment agency.

A recent study by Northwestern National Life Insurance Company found that 46 percent of American workers worry about their jobs and feel more pressured to prove their value because of the recession. . . Unfortunately, the more you worry about whether you are doing a good enough job, the more likely you are to erode your efficiency, creativity and morale—and damage your health.

Source: *Business Monday/Detroit Free Press*

Search and Recruit International
4455 South Blvd.
Virginia Beach, VA 23452
Phone: (804)490-3151

Employment agency. Headquartered in Virginia Beach. Other offices in Bremerton, WA; Charleston, SC; Jacksonville, FL; Memphis, TN; Pensacola, FL; Sacramento, CA; San Bernardino, CA; San Diego, CA.

Search Consultants International, Inc.
4545 Post Oak Pl., Ste. 208
Houston, TX 77027
Phone: (713)622-9188

Executive search firm.

Sierra Technology Corporation
4150 Manzanita Ave., Ste. 100
Carmichael, CA 95608
Phone: (916)488-4960

Employment agency. Provides placement on a temporary basis.

Source Engineering
4545 Fuller Dr., Ste. 100
Irving, TX 75038
Phone: (214)717-5005
Fax: (214)717-0075

Executive search firm. Many affiliate offices located throughout the U.S.

Staff Inc.
2121 Cloverfield Blvd., Ste. 133
Santa Monica, CA 90404
Phone: (213)829-5447

Employment agency.

T.R. Employment Agency
409 Santa Monica Blvd., Ste. 210
Santa Monica, CA 90401
Phone: (213)393-4107

Employment agency.

Between 1986 and 1989, 600 turtles were injured or killed along the New Jersey coast. Some deaths resulted from run-ins with boats, but many others occurred after plastics had been ingested. Fast-food wrappers, plastic straws, and garbage and sandwich bags are responsible for slow and painful deaths suffered by whales, dolphins, and sea turtles.

Source: *Wildlife Conservation*

Tri-Serv Inc.
100 West Padonia Rd.
Timonium, MD 21030
Phone: (301)561-1740

Employment agency.

Career Guides

The 100 Best Companies to Work for in America
Signet/NAL Penguin
1633 Broadway
New York, NY 10019

Levering, Robert, Moskowitz, Milton, and Katz, Michael. 1985. $5.95. 477 pages. Describes the best companies to work for in America, based on such factors as salary, benefits, job security, and ambience. The authors base their 'top 100' rating on surveys and personal visits to hundreds of firms.

300 New Ways to Get a Better Job
Bob Adams, Inc.
260 Center St.
Holbrook, MA 02343
Phone: (617)767-8100

Advocates a job search approach designed to meet the changing nature of the job market.

850 Leading USA Companies
Jamenair Ltd.
PO Box 241957
Los Angeles, CA 90024
Phone: (213)470-6688

Studner, Peter K. $49.95. Compatible with IBM and IBM-compatibles.

The American Almanac of Jobs and Salaries
Avon Books
1350 Avenue of the Americas
New York, NY 10019
Phone: (212)261-6800
Toll-free: 800-238-0658

John Wright, editor. Revised and updated, 1990. A comprehensive guide to the wages of hundreds of occupations in a wide variety of industries and organizations.

Becoming an Environmental Professional
Environmental Careers Organization
68 Harrison Ave.
Boston, MA 02111
Phone: (617)426-4375

The Berkeley Guide to Employment for New College Graduates
Ten Speed Press
PO Box 7123
Berkeley, CA 94707
Phone: (415)845-8414

Briggs, James I. $7.95. 256 pages. Basic job-hunting advice for the college student.

The Best Companies for Women
Simon and Schuster
Simon and Schuster Bldg.
1230 Avenue of the Americas
New York, NY 10020
Phone: (212)698-7000

1989. $8.95.

Best of the National Business Employment Weekly
Consultants Bookstore
Templeton Rd.
Fitzwilliam, NJ 03447
Phone: (603)585-2200
Fax: (603)585-9555

$5.00/booklet. Booklets summarizing the best articles from the *National Business Employment Weekly* on a variety of job hunting topics.

Botanist
Careers, Inc.
PO Box 135
Largo, FL 34649-0135
Phone: (813)584-7333
Toll-free: 800-726-0441

1992. Eight-page brief offering the definition, history, duties, working conditions, personal qualifications, educational requirements, earnings, hours, employment outlook, advancement, and careers related to this position.

The Career Fitness Program: Exercising Your Options
Gorsuch Scarisbrick, Publishers
8233 Via Paseo del Norte, Ste. F-400
Scottsdale, AZ 85258

Sukiennik et al. 1989. $16.00. 227 pages. Textbook, with second ha'f devoted to the job search process.

The Career Guide—Dun's Employment Opportunities Directory
Dun's Marketing Services
Dun and Bradstreet Corp.
3 Sylvan Way
Parsippany, NJ 07054-3896
Phone: (201)605-6000

Annual, December. $450.00; $385.00 for public libraries (lease basis). Covers: More than 5,000 companies that have a thousand or more employees and that provide career opportunities in sales, marketing, management, engineering, life and physical sciences, computer science, mathematics, statistics planning, accounting and finance, liberal arts fields, and other technical and professional areas; based on data supplied on questionnaires and through personal interviews. Also covers personnel consultants; includes some public sector employers (governments, schools, etc.) usually not found in similar lists. Entries include: Company name, location of headquarters, and other offices of plants; entries may also include name, title, address, and phone of employment contact; disciplines or occupational groups hired; brief overview of company; discussion of types of positions that may be available; training and career development programs; benefits offered. Arrangement: Companies are alphabetical; consultants are geographical. Indexes: Geographical, Standard Industrial Classification code.

There are two types of ads: open (the company identified) and blind. Open ads are great for job-hunters. They give you the opportunity to do some investigation on the firm. Be sure to tailor your cover letter with your knowledge of the company. If you're lucky, you may uncover a contact.

Source: *Business Monday/Detroit Free Press*

Career Information Question and Answer Sheet
Society of American Foresters (SAF)
5400 Grosvenor Ln.
Bethesda, MD 20814-2198
Phone: (301)897-8720

P. Gregory Smith, editor. 1992. Describes the differences between foresters and forestry technicians, including job duties, educational preparation, and employment opportunities.

Career Information Systems (CIS)
National Career Information System
1787 Agate St.
Eugene, OR 97403
Phone: (503)686-3872

Includes information on job search techniques and self-employment options. Also provides extensive career planning information.

Career Opportunities
Quanta Press, Inc.
1313 5th St. SE, Ste. 223A
Minneapolis, MN 55414
Phone: (612)379-3956

CD-ROM (Compact Disc-Read Only Memory) database that provides job titles and job descriptions and information on education levels, chances for advancement, average salaries, and working conditions.

Career Opportunities With the Agricultural Research Service
United States Department of Agriculture
Agricultural Research Service
Personnel Division
Personnel Operations Branch
Beltsville, MD 20705

1985. Describes the federal hiring process, eligibility requirements, salaries and benefits, and training opportunities with the agricultural service.

People assume that they get better within their careers over time, that growth is a step-by-step improvement. Studies have shown that growth occurs in episodic movement, often triggered by a small event. People tend to remain at a uniform level until some change propels them toward a new level of performance.

Source: *The Canadian Nurse*

Career Placement Registry (CPR)
Career Placement Registry, Inc.
302 Swann Ave.
Alexandria, VA 22301
Phone: (703)683-1085
Fax: (703)683-0246

Contains brief resumes of job candidates currently seeking employment. Comprises two files, covering college and university seniors and recent graduates, and alumni, executives, and others who have already acquired substantial work experience. Entries typically include applicant name, address, telephone number, degree level, function, language skills, name of school, major field of study, minor field of study, occupational preference, date available, city/area preference, special skills, citizenship status, employer name, employer address, description of duties, position/title, level of education, civil service register, security clearance type/availability, willingness to relocate, willingness to travel, salary expectation, and overall work experience. Available online through DIALOG Information Services, Inc.

Career Profiles: Forestry Conservation, Ecology, and Environmental Management
U.S. Department of Agriculture
Forest Service
PO Box 96090
Washington, DC 20090-6090
Phone: (202)205-0957

1987. Describes the job of forester; lists places of employment, educational requirements, and other characteristics needed to be successful in the field of forestry.

Career Strategies—From Job Hunting to Moving Up
Association for Management Success
2360 Maryland Rd.
Willow Grove, PA 19090

Six video cassettes. Kennedy, Marilyn Moats. $36.95/each. $203.70/set. 30 minutes each. Covers the following topics: planning the job hunt, networking, resumes, interviewing, negotiating salaries and benefits, and moving up on the job.

Careering and Re-Careering for the 1990's
Consultants Bookstore
Templeton Rd.
Fitzwilliam, NH 03447
Phone: (603)585-6544
Fax: (603)585-9555

Krannich, Ronald. 1989. $13.95. 314 pages. Details trends in the marketplace, how to identify opportunities, how to retrain for them, and how to land jobs. Includes a chapter on starting a business. Contains index, bibliography, and illustrations.

Careers
National Textbook Co.
4255 W. Touhy Ave.
Lincolnwood, IL 60646
Phone: (312)679-5500
Toll-free: 800-323-4900

1990. Includes a bibliography and an index.

Careers and the College Grad
Bob Adams, Inc.
260 Center St.
Holbrook, MA 02343
Phone: (617)767-8100
Fax: (617)767-0994

Ranno, Gigi. 1992. $12.95. 64 pages. An annual resource guide addressing the career and job-hunting interests of undergraduates. Provides company profiles and leads.

Careers in Agribusiness and Industry
Interstate Printers & Publishers, Inc.
510 N. Vermillion St.
PO Box 50
Danville, IL 61834-0050
Phone: (217)446-0500

Mark Bultman, Marcella Smith, and Jean M. Underman. Fourth edition, 1991.

Careers in Botany
Botanical Society of America, Business Office
1735 Neil Ave.
Columbus, OH 43210-1293
Phone: (614)292-3519

1988. Describes botany, the connection between botany and society, specializations in the field of botany, current issues, salary, and educational preparation.

Careers in Engineering and Technology
Macmillan Publishing Co.
866 Third Ave.
New York, NY 10022
Phone: (212)702-2000
Toll-free: 800-257-5755

George C. Beakley, Donovan L. Evans, and Deloss H. Bowers. Fourth edition, 1987. Includes bibliographical references and an index.

Careers in Exploration Geophysics
Society of Exploration Geophysicists (SEG)
PO Box 702740
Tulsa, OK 74170-2740
Phone: (918)493-3516

Explores careers in geophysics, briefly describing the fields and education preparation.

Careers in Geology
American Association of Petroleum Geologists (AAPG)
PO Box 979
Tulsa, OK 74101-0979
Phone: (918)584-2555

1991. Describes what geologists do, where they work, job outlook, and earnings.

Whether you're looking for your next job or your first job, networking must be a key element of your search. More jobs are found by networking than through any other source.

Source: *Business Monday/Detroit Free Press*

Careers in Geophysics, Solid Earth, Hydrologic, Oceanic, Atmospheric, and Space Sciences
American Geophysical Union (AGU)
2000 Florida Ave., NW
Washington, DC 20009
Phone: (202)462-6900

1993. Describes the geophysical disciplines, personal qualification needed for a career in geophysics, educational preparation, and employment oppportunities and outlook.

Careers in Public Gardens
American Association of Botanical Gardens and Arboreta
786 Church Rd.
Wayne, PA 19087
Phone: (215)688-1120

Brochure that describes the function of public gardens, the types of jobs available in public gardens, and the training required for positions in botanical gardens.

Chronicle Career Index
Chronicle Guidance Publications
PO Box 1190
Moravia, NY 13118-1190
Phone: (315)497-0330

Annual. $14.25. Provides bibliographic listings of career and vocational guidance publications and other resources. Arrangement: Alphabetical by source. Indexes: Occupation; vocational and professional information.

What makes one job better than another? High pay? Prestige? Pleasant working conditions? Or, these days, might the clincher be job security? The answer is that there is no single deciding factor. Truly great jobs offer all of the above and more . . . . Jobs, after all, are a complicated mix of pluses and minuses.

Source: *Money*

College Majors and Careers: A Resource Guide to Effective Life Planning
Garrett Park Press
PO Box 190E
Garrett Park, MD 20896
Phone: (301)946-2553

Paul Pfifer. 1993. Includes chapters titled "Biology", "Botany", "Physiology", and "Zoology". Lists 61 college majors, with definitions; related occupations and leisure activities; skills, values, and personal attributes needed; suggested readings; and a list of associations.

The Complete Guide to Environmental Careers
Environmental Careers Organization
68 Harrison Ave.
Boston, MA 02111
Phone: (617)426-4375

Directory that provides information on job hunting in the environmental field, including the areas of planning and communication, environmental protection, and natural resource management.

The Complete Job Search Book

John Wiley and Sons
605 3rd Ave.
New York, NY 10158

Beatty, Richard H. 1988. $12.95. 256 pages.

The Complete Job-Search Handbook

Consultants Bookstore
Templeton Rd.
Fitzwilliam, NH 03447
Phone: (603)585-6544
Fax: (603)585-9555

Figler, Howard. 1988. $12.95. 366 pages. Contains information on how to look for career opportunities every day. Focuses on 20 life skills in self-assessment, detective work, communication skills, and selling oneself. Includes skill-building exercises.

The Corporate Directory of U.S. Public Companies

Gale Research Inc.
835 Penobscot Bldg.
Detroit, MI 48226
Phone: (313)961-2242
Fax: (313)961-6241

1991. $325.00. Provides information on more than 9,500 publicly-traded firms having at least $5,000,000 in assets. Entries include: General background, including name, address and phone, number of employees; stock date; description of areas of business; major subsidiaries; officers; directors; owners; and financial data. Indexes: Officers and directors, owners, subsidiary/parent, geographic, SIC, stock exchange, company rankings, and newly registered corporations.

CSI National Career Network

Computer Search International Corporation (CSI)
7926 Jones Branch Dr., Ste. 120
McLean, VA 22102
Phone: (302)749-1635

Contains job listings from potential employers and candidate resumes from executive recruiting firms. Covers more than 40 technical and managerial job categories.

Directory of Employment Opportunities in the Federal Government
Arco Publishing Company
Simon and Schuster, Inc.
15 Columbus Circle
Order Dept., 16th Fl.
New York, NY 10023
Phone: (212)373-8931
Fax: (212)767-5852

1985. $24.95. Covers: Federal agencies offering employment opportunities in the U.S. government. Entries include: Agency name and address, geographical area served, subsidiary and branch names and locations, eligibility requirements, application and testing procedures, and job descriptions. Arrangement: Alphabetical. Indexes: Department name, position title, subject (occupational categories).

Dun and Bradstreet Million Dollar Directory
Dun's Marketing Services
Dun and Bradstreet Corp.
3 Sylvan Way
Parsippany, NJ 07054-3896
Phone: (201)605-6000
Fax: (201)605-6911

An annual directory covering 160,000 businesses with a net worth of $500,00 or more, including industrial corporations, utilities, transportation companies, bank and trust companies, stock brokers, mutual and stock insurance companies, wholesalers, retailers, and domestic subsidiaries of foreign corporations.

Encyclopedia of Career Choices for the 1990s: A Guide to Entry Level Jobs
Walker and Co.
720 5th Ave.
New York, NY 10019
Phone: (212)265-3632
Toll-free: 800-289-2553

1991. Describes entry-level careers in a variety of industries. Presents qualifications required, working conditions, salary, internships, and professional associations.

The Encyclopedia of Careers and Vocational Guidance
J.G. Ferguson Publishing Co.
200 W. Monroe, Ste. 250
Chicago, IL 60606
Phone: (312)580-5480

William E. Hopke, editor-in-chief. Eighth edition, 1990. Four-volume set that profiles 900 occupations and describes job trends in 71 industries.

The Encyclopedia of Careers and Vocational Guidance
J. G. Ferguson Publishing Co.
200 W. Monroe, Ste. 250
Chicago, IL 60606
Phone: (312)580-5480

William E. Hopke, editor-in-chief. ninth edition, 1993. Four-volume set that profiles 900 occupations and describes job trends in 71 industries. Volume 2—*Professional Careers*—chapters on biological scientists include "Biochemists" (p. 60) and "Biologists" (p. 63). Includes career description, educational requirements, history of the job, methods of entry, advancement, employment outlook, earnings, conditions of work, social and psychological factors, and sources of further information.

> In his widely acclaimed history of the conservation movement *John Muir and His Legacy*, historian Stephen Fox states, "On a practical level conservation has been sustained by this interplay between professionals and radical amateurs. Professionals keep the movement organized. Amateurs keep it honest."
>
> Source: *Buzzworm: The Environmental Journal*

The Experienced Hand: A Student Manual for Making the Most of an Internship
Carroll Press
43 Squantum St.
Cranston, RI 02920
Phone: (401)942-1587

Stanton, Timothy, and Ali, Kamil. 1987. $6.95. 88 pages. Guidance for deriving the most satisfaction and future benefit from an internship.

Exploring Careers in Agronomy, Crops, and Soils
American Society of Agronomy (ASA)
677 S. Segoe Rd.
Madison, WI 53711
Phone: (608)273-8080

1991. Describes agronomic sciences and the various roles which agronomists, crop scientists, and soil scientists fulfill. Includes description of various job opportunities as well as salaries in the agronomic sciences. Includes a list of colleges and universities offering degrees in agronomic science.

The United States economy is projected to provide 24 million more jobs in 2005 than it did in 1990, an increase of 20 percent.

Source: *Occupational Outlook Quarterly*

Exploring Nontraditional Jobs for Women
Rosen Publishing Group, Inc.
29 E. 21st St.
New York, NY 10010
Phone: (212)777-3017
Toll-free: 800-237-9932
Fax: (212)777-0277

Rose Neufeld. Revised edition. 1989. $13.95 per volume; $139.50 per set. Part of a 10 volume set that describes occupations where few women are found. Covers job duties, training routes, where to apply for jobs, tools used, salary, and advantages and disadvantages of the job.

Financial World—500 Fastest Growing Companies
Financial World Partners
1328 Broadway
New York, NY 10001
Phone: (212)594-5030

An annual directory listing 500 U.S. firms showing greatest growth in net earnings for the year.

Financial World America's Top Growth Companies Directory Issue
Financial World Partners
1328 Broadway
New York, NY 10001
Phone: (212)594-5030

An annual listing of companies selected on the basis of earnings per share growth rate over a 10-year period ending with the current year.

Forbes Up-and-Comers 200: Best Small Companies in America
Forbes, Inc.
60 5th Ave.
New York, NY 10011
Phone: (212)620-2200
Fax: (212)620-1863

An annual directory that lists 200 small companies judged to be exceptionally fast-growing on the basis of 5-year return on equity and other qualititative measurements.

Fortune Directory
Time, Inc.
Time and Life Bldg.
Rockefeller Center
New York, NY 10020
Phone: (212)586-1212

An annual directory that covers 500 of the largest U.S. industrial corporations and 500 largest U.S. non-industrial corporations.

Future Employment Opportunities in the Geological Sciences
Geological Society of America (GSA)
3300 Penrose Pl.
PO Box 9140
Boulder, CO 80301
Phone: (303)447-2020
Toll-free: 800-472-1988

1991. Examines employment opportunities in the petroleum, mining, and consulting industries; in academia; and in federal, state, and local governments. Gives some tips on resume writing and interviewing.

Geologist
Careers, Inc.
PO Box 135
Largo, FL 34649-0135
Phone: (813)584-7333
Toll-free: 800-726-0441
Fax: (813)586-0454

1990. Two-page occupational summary card describing duties, working conditions, personal qualifications, training, earnings and hours, employment outlook, places of employment, related careers, and where to write for more information.

Geoscientific Employment and Hiring Surveys
American Geological Institute (AGI)
c/o AGI Publications Center
PO Box 205
Anapolis Junction, MO 20701
Phone: (301)953-1744

Annual. Gives current and projected employment statistics and approximate starting salaries for graduates by degree level.

Get a Better Job!
Peterson's
PO Box 2123
Princeton, NJ 08543-2123
Phone: (609)243-9111

Rushlow, Ed. 1990. $11.95. 255 pages. Counsels the reader on job search techniques. Discusses how to win the job by bypassing the Personnel Department and how to understand the employer's system for screening and selecting candidates. Written in an irreverent and humorous style.

Get That Job!
Consultants Bookstore
Templeton Rd.
Fitzwilliam, NH 03447
Phone: (603)585-6544
Fax: (603)585-9555

Camden, Thomas. 1981. $24.95. Two 30-minute cassettes supplemented by a 45-page booklet that include dramatizations of interviews, cover what questions to expect, and how to respond to them. Provides sample resumes and letters.

Getting a Job in the Computer Age
Peterson's Guides, Inc.
PO Box 2123
Princeton, NJ 08543-2123
Phone: (609)395-0676
Toll-free: 800-338-3282

Harold Goldstein and Bryna S. Fraser. 1986. Includes about 75 occupations, based on a study of all occupations in which computers are used. Contains chapters titled "Writers" (p. 80) and "Technical Writers" (p. 79-80). Describes the type of equipment used; discusses types of computer training (most computer skills needed are learned on the job).

> In all cases, the people with an edge will be those who know how to use a computer to do their jobs more efficiently, who can present ideas cogently and who work well in teams.
>
> Source: *U.S. News & World Report*

Guide to Federal Jobs
Resource Directories
3361 Executive Pkwy.
Toledo, OH 43606
Phone: (419)536-5353
Toll-free: 800-274-8515
Fax: (419)536-7056

Rod W. Durgin, editor. Third edition, 1992. Contains information on finding and applying for federal jobs. Describes more than 200 professional and technical jobs for college graduates. Includes chapters titled "Geologist" (p. 221), "Geophysicist" (p. 215), and "Hydrologist" (p. 211). Covers the nature of the work, salary, and geographic location. Lists college majors preferred for that occupation. Section one describes the function and work of government agencies that hire the most significant number of college graduates.

Have You Considered. . .Geology?
Catalyst
250 Park Ave., S.
New York, NY 10003
Phone: (212)777-8900

1985. Describes educational preparation, on-the-job training, job location, salary, career paths, and internships available for geologists.

The Hidden Job Market
Peterson's
PO Box 2123
Princeton, NJ 08543-2123
Phone: (609)243-9111

1991. $16.95. Subtitled *A Job Seeker's Guide to America's 2,000 Little-Known but Fastest-Growing High-Tech Companies.* Listing of high technology companies in such fields as environmental consulting, genetic engineering, home health care, telecommunications, alternative energy systems, and others.

How to Get a Good Job and Keep It
VGM Career Horizons
4255 W. Touhy Ave.
Lincolnwood, IL 60646-1975
Phone: (708)679-5500

Bloch, Deborah Perlmutter. 1993. $7.95. Aimed at the recent high school or college graduate, this guide provides advice on finding out about jobs, completing applications and resumes, and managing successful interviews.

One way to improve your chances in the job hunt is to define "you" as broadly as possible . . . . Defining yourself in terms of your skills rather than your job history is the key.

Source: *Business Monday/Detroit Free Press*

Inc.—The Inc. 100 Issue
The Goldhirsh Group
38 Commercial Wharf
Boston, MA 02110
Phone: (617)248-8000
Fax: (617)248-8090

An annual directory listing the 100 fastest-growing publicly held companies in manufacturing and service industries that had revenues greater than $100,000 but less than $25 million five years prior to compilation.

Inc.—The Inc. 500 Issue
The Goldhirsh Group
38 Commercial Wharf
Boston, MA 02110
Phone: (617)248-8000
Fax: (617)248-8090

An annual directory that lists 500 fastest-growing privately held companies in service, manufacturing, retail, distribution, and construction industries, based on percentage increase in sales over the five-year period prior to compilation.

Internship Directory 1994: Internships and Summer Jobs at Public Gardens
American Association of Botanical Gardens and Arboreta
86 Church Rd.
Wayne, PA 19087
Phone: (215)688-1120

1989. Lists more than 500 summer jobs and internships at 122 botanical gardens, arboreta, and other horticultural institutions.

Internships: On-the-Job Training Opportunities for All Types of Careers
Peterson's Guides, Inc.
20 Carnegie Center
PO Box 2123
Princeton, NJ 08543-2123
Phone: (609)243-9111
Fax: (609)243-9150

Annual, December. $27.95., plus $3.00 shipping. Covers: 850 corporations, social service organizations, government agencies, recreational facilities (including parts and forests), entertainment industries, and science and research facilities which offer about 50,000 apprenticeships and internships in 23 different career areas. Entries include: Organization name, address, name of contact; description of internship offered, including duties, stipend, length of service; eligibility requirements; deadline for application and application procedures. Arrangement: Classified by subject (arts, communications, business, etc.). Indexes: Subject/organization name, geographical.

The Job Bank Series
Bob Adams, Inc.
260 Center St.
Holbrook, MA 02343
Phone: (617)767-8100
Fax: (617)767-0994

$12.95/volume. There are 18 volumes in the Job Bank Series, each covering a different job market. Volumes exist for the following areas: Atlanta, Boston, Chicago, Dallas/Fort Worth, Denver, Detroit, Florida, Houston, Los Angeles, Minneapolis, New York, Ohio, Pennsylvania, Phoenix, San Francisco, Seattle, St. Louis, and Washington D.C. Each directory lists employers and provides name, address, telephone number, and contact information. Many entries include common positions, educational backgrounds sought, and fringe benefits provided. Cross-indexed by industry and alphabetically by company name. Profiles of professional associations, a section on the region's economic outlook, and listings of executive search and job placement agencies are included. Features sections on conducting a successful job search campaign and writing resumes and cover letters.

Job Opportunities for Engineering, Science, and Computer Grads
Peterson's Guides, Inc.
PO Box 2123
Princeton, NJ 08543-2123
Phone: (609)395-0676
Toll-free: 800-EDU-DATA

Annual. Fourteenth edition, 1993. Gives job hunting advice including information on resume writing, interviewing, and handling salary negotiations. Lists companies that hire college graduates in science and engineering at the bachelor and master's level. Companies are indexed by industry, starting location, and major. Company profiles include contact information and types of hires.

Jobs Rated Almanac: Ranks the Best and Worst Jobs by More Than a Dozen Vital Criteria
World Almanac
200 Park Ave.
New York, NY 10166
Phone: (212)692-3830

Les Krantz. 1988. Ranks 250 jobs by environment, salary, outlook, physical demands, stress, security, travel opportunities, and geographic location. Includes jobs the editor feels are the most common, most interesting, and the most rapidly growing.

Joyce Lain Kennedy's Career Book
VGM Career Horizons
4255 W. Touhy Ave.
Lincolnwood, IL 60646-1975
Phone: (708)679-5500

Kennedy, Joyce Lain. Co-authored by Dr. Darryl Laramore. 1992. $17.95 paperback. $29.95 hardcover. 448 pages. Guides the reader through the entire career planning and job hunting process.

> Four out of five companies say their employees can't write well. But only 21 percent of corporate training aims at writing skills.
>
> Source: *U.S. News & World Report*

Moody's Corporate Profiles
Moody's Investors Service, Inc.
Dun and Bradstreet Co.
99 Church St.
New York, NY 10007
Phone: (212)553-0300
Fax: (212)553-4700

Provides data on more than 5,000 publicly held companies listed on the New York Stock Exchange or the American Stock Exchange or NMS companies traded on the National Association of Securities Dealers Automated Quotations. Available through DIALOG Information Services, Inc.

National Directory of Internships
National Society for Internships and Experiential Education
3509 Haworth Dr., Ste. 207
Raleigh, NC 27609
Phone: (919)787-3263

Biennial. $22.00. Covers over 30,000 educational internship opportunities in 75 fields with over 2,650 organizations in the United States for youth and adults.

North American Survey of Geoscientists, U.S. Section: Summary: Survey Results and Forecast of Employment Trends
American Geological Institute (AGI)
4220 King St.
Alexandria, VA 22302
Phone: (703)379-2480

Nick Claudy, editor. 1987. Profiles geoscientists in the United States and Canada. Each Profile includes information on employment, years of experience, annual income, occupational levels and objectives, educational background, and training.

> Approximately 31 percent of high-grade papers (including office papers) were collected for recycling last year, according to the American Forest & Paper Association. . . The recovery level for old newspapers rose to 55 percent in 1992. . .
>
> Source: *Resource Recycling*

Occupational Outlook Handbook
Bureau of Labor Statistics
441 G St., NW
Washington, DC 20212
Phone: (202)523-1327

A biennial directory containing profiles of various occupations, including description of occupation, educational requirements, market demand, and expected earnings.It also lists over 100 state employment agencies.

On Becoming a Biologist
HarperCollins Inc.
10 E. 53rd St.
New York, NY 10022
Phone: (212)207-7000
Fax: 800-822-4090

John Janovy. First edition, 1986. Includes a bibliography.

Opportunities in Agriculture Careers
National Textbook Co.
NTC Publishing Group
4255 W. Touhy Ave.
Lincolnwood, IL 60646-1975
Phone: (708)679-5500
Toll-free: 800-323-4900

White, William C. 1988. Contains details on more than 200 careers available in agriculture-related fields as a result of the application of technology to agriculture. Describes careers in agriculture production industries, food processing, marketing, environmental protection and communications.

Opportunities in Biological Science
National Textbook Co.
NTC Publishing Group
4255 W. Touhy Ave.
Lincolnwood, IL 60646-1975
Phone: (708)679-5500
Toll-free: 800-323-4900

Winter, Charles A. 1990. Includes a bibliography.

Opportunities in Environmental Careers
National Textbook Co.
NTC Publishing Group
4255 W. Touhy Ave.
Lincolnwood, IL 60646-1975
Phone: (708)679-5500
Toll-free: 800-323-4900

Odom Fanning. 1991. Describes a broad range of opportunities in fields such as environmental health, recreation, physics, and hygiene. Chapters include "Forestry" (pp. 87-90), "Range Manager" (pp. 90-93), "Soil Conservation" (pp. 96-98), and "Wildlife Conservation" (pp. 99-103). Lists federal government agencies, colleges and universities, and citizen organizations that provide opportunities in environment-related careers. Entries include organization name and address.

Peterson's Job Opportunities for Business and Liberal Arts Graduates
Peterson's
PO Box 2123
Princeton, NJ 08543-2123
Phone: (609)243-9111

1993. $20.95. 300 pages. Lists hundreds of organizations that are hiring new business, humanities, and social science graduates in the areas of business and management.

Professional's Job Finder
Planning/Communications
7215 Oak Ave.
River Forest, IL 60305-1935
Phone: (708)366-5297

$15.95. Discusses how to use sources of private sector job vacancies in a number of specialties and state by state, including job-matching services, job hotlines, directories, and more.

A Scientific Career With the Agricultural Research Service
United States Department of Agriculture
Agricultural Research Service
Personnel Division-Personnel Operations Branch
6303 Ivy Lane
Greenbelt, MD 20770
Phone: (301)344-2152

1985. Brochure describing the work of the agricultural research service and jobs with the service.

So You Want to Be in Forestry
American Forestry Association (AFA)
1516 P St., NW
Washington, DC 20005
Phone: (202)667-3300

Brochure describing forestry, how to become a forester, and employment opportunities and related fields.

Soil Conservationist
Careers, Inc.
PO Box 135
Largo, FL 34649-0135
Phone: (813)584-7333
Toll-free: 800-726-0441

1992. Two-page occupational summary card describing duties, working conditions, personal qualifications, training, earnings and hours, employment outlook, places of employment, related careers, and where to write for more information.

Soil Conservationists
Chronicle Guidance Publications, Inc.
66 Aurora St.
PO Box 1190
Moravia, NY 13118-1190
Phone: (315)497-0330

1990. Career brief describing the nature of the job, working conditions, hours and earnings, education and training, licensure, certification, unions, personal qualifications, social and psychological factors, location, employment outlook, entry methods, advancement, and related occupations.

Soil Scientists
Chronicle Guidance Publications, Inc.
Aurora St. Extension
PO Box 1190
Moravia, NY 13118-1190
Phone: (315)497-0330

1991. Career brief describing the nature of the job, working conditions, hours and earnings, education and training, licensure, certification, unions, personal qualifications, social and psychological factors, location, employment outlook, entry methods, advancement, and related occupations.

A career path should not be restrictive—there should be forks in the path, allowing you to adapt as changes occur within professional and personal lifestyles. The best intentions can go astray, leading to discouragement and disillusionment if alternative paths have not been prepared.

Source: *The Canadian Nurse*

Standard and Poor's Register of Corporations, Directors, and Executives
Standard and Poor's Corp.
25 Broadway
New York, NY 10004
Phone: (212)208-8283

An annual directory that covers over 55,000 corporations in the United States, including names and titles of over 500,000 officials and 70,000 biographies of directors and executives.

Ten Greatest Achievements of Chemical Engineers
American Institute of Chemical Engineer (AIChE)
345 E. 47th St.
New York, NY 10017
Phone: (212)705-7657

Describes the work that chemical engineers

have done in different fields such as medicine, textiles, pharmaceuticals, and rubber manufacturing.

Think About It
National FFA Center
5632 Mount Vernon Memorial Hwy.
PO Box 15160
Alexandria, VA 22309-0160
Phone: (703)360-3600

Outlines career opportunities in agricultural production, processing, research, agribusiness, and resource management.

Growth in employment is only one source of job openings. In fact, most openings arise because of the need to replace workers who transfer to other occupations or leave the labor force.

Source: *Occupational Outlook Quarterly*

VGM's Careers Encyclopedia
National Textbook Co.
4255 W. Touhy Ave.
Lincolnwood, IL 60646-1975
Phone: (708)679-5500

Norback, Craig T., editor. Third edition, 1991. Profiles 180 occupations. Describes job duties, places of employment, working conditions, qualifications, education and training, advancement potential, and salary for each occupation. Chapters include "Geologist" (pp. 171-172), "Geophysicist" (pp. 173-175), and "Oceanographer" (pp. 280-282).

Ward's Business Directory of U.S. Private and Public Companies
Gale Research Inc.
835 Penobscot Bldg.
Detroit, MI 48226
Phone: (313)961-2242
Fax: (313)961-6241

1993. Four volumes. Contains information on over 85,000 U.S. businesses, over 90% of which are privately held. Entries include company name, address, and phone; sales; employees; description; names of officers; fiscal year end information; etc.

Water/Wastewater Operator
Vocational Biographies, Inc.
PO Box 31, Dept. VF
Sauk Centre, MN 56378
Phone: (612)352-6516
Toll-free: 800-255-0752
Fax: (612)352-5546

1989. This pamphlet profiles a person working in the job. Includes information about job duties, working conditions, places of employment, educational preparation, labor market outlook, and salaries.

What Color Is Your Parachute?
Ten Speed Press
PO Box 7123
Berkeley, CA 94707
Phone: (415)845-8414

Bolles, Richard N. 1993. $12.95 paperback; $18.95 hardcover. Provides detailed and strategic advice on all aspects of the job search.

Where the Jobs Are: A Comprehensive Directory of 1200 Journals Listing Career Opportunities
Garrett Park Press
PO BOx 190
Garrett Park, MD 20896
Phone: (301)946-2553

1989. $15.00. Contains list of approximately 1,200 journals that publish advertisements announcing job opportunities.

Where the Jobs Are: The Hottest Careers for the '90s
The Career Press
180 5th Ave.
PO Box 34
Hawthorne, NJ 07507

Satterfield, Mark. 1992. $9.95. Provides a look at current trends in the job market and the industries that offer the greatest opportunity for those entering the work force or making a career change.

Where to Start Career Planning
Peterson's
PO Box 2123
Princeton, NJ 08543-2123
Phone: (609)243-9111

Lindquist, Carolyn Lloyd and Miller, Diane June.

1991. $17.95 315 pages. Lists and describes the career planning publications used by Cornell University's Career Center, one of the largest career libraries in the country. It covers more than 2,000 books, periodicals, and audiovisual resources.

Wildlife/Fishery Biologists
Careers, Inc.
PO Box 135
Largo, FL 34649-0135
Phone: (813)584-7333
Toll-free: 800-726-0441

1992. Eight-page brief offering the definition, history, duties, working conditions, personal qualifications, educational requirements, earnings, hours, employment outlook, advancement, and careers related to this position.

Women Exploring the Earth
Society of Exploration Geophysicists (SEG)
PO Box 702740
Tulsa, OK 74170-2740
Phone: (918)493-3516

1987. Profiles five women who have productive careers in geophysics.

Working for Life: Careers in Biology
Plexus Publishing, Inc.
143 Old Marlton Pike
Medford, NJ 08055
Phone: (609)654-6500

Thomas A. Easton. Second edition, 1988. Includes a bibliography.

Professional and Trade Periodicals

AABGA Newsletter
American Association of Botancial Gardens and Arboreta
786 Church Rd.
Wayne, PA 19087
Phone: (215)688-1120

A monthly publication that provides job listings, funding sources, and garden news.

ACS Washington Alert
American Chemical Society (ACS)
1155 16th St., NW
Washington, DC 20036
Phone: 800-227-5558

Paul Graves, editor. Biweekly. Focuses on such chemical issues as hazardous waste, air and water quality, biotechnology, and toxic substances, and how they are affected by government regulatory and legislative activities.

Agriculture & Food: An Abstract Newsletter
National Technical Information Service (NTIS)
U.S. Department of Commerce
5285 Port Royal Rd.
Springfield, VA 22161
Phone: (703)487-4630

Weekly. Publishes abstracts of reports on agricultural chemistry, agricultural equipment, facilities, and operations. Also covers agronomy, horticulture, and plant pathology; fisheries and aquaculture; animal husbandry and veterinary medicine; and food technology.

According to forestry consultant Henry S. Kernan, publicity results in more preservation of limited areas but does not stop the kind of forest destruction that governments promote: "In every tropical country with which I am acquainted, laws encourage the clearing and planting of forest land with agricultural crops. They thereby assure a drastic change of the forest resource."

Source: *The Conservationist*

Agronomy Journal
American Society of Agronomy
677 S. Segoe Rd.
Madison, WI 53711
Phone: (608)273-8080
Fax: (608)273-2021

J.L. Hatfield, editor. Six issues/year. Agriculture science trade journal.

American Forests
American Forestry Association
PO Box 2000
Washington, DC 20013-2000
Phone: (202)667-3300
Fax: (202)667-7751

Bill Rooney, editor. Bimonthly. Forest conservation magazine.

American Journal of Botany
Botanical Society of America
Ohio State University
1735 Neil Ave.
Columbus, OH 43210-1293
Phone: (614)292-3519
Fax: (614)292-2180

Nels Lersten, editor. Monthly. Magazine containing botanical research papers.

Interview proactively. Make a list of questions you'd like answered. Target the company's current and future plans, the job and where it could lead. You'll have the chance to ask most of them if you tie them into the answers you give on similar topics.

Source: *Business Monday/Detroit Free Press*

American Laboratory
PO Box 870
Shelton, CT 06484
Phone: (203)926-9300

A monthly journal for research chemists and biologists.

American Rivers
American Rivers
801 Pennsylvania Ave., SE, Ste. 400
Washington, DC 20003
Phone: (202)547-6900
Fax: (202)543-6142

Mary Ellen Kirkbride, editor. Quarterly. Concerned with the preservation and protection of natural rivers. Covers local, state, and federal action on river issues.

The Amicus Journal
Natural Resources Defense Council
40 W. 20th St.
New York, NY 10011
Phone: (212)727-2700
Fax: (212)727-1773

Francesca Lyman, editor. Quarterly. Journal covering national and international environmental affairs.

ARI Newsletter
Agricultural Research Institute (ARI)
9650 Rockville Pike
Bethesda, MD 20814
Phone: (301)530-7122
Fax: (301)571-1858

Editor(s): Stan Cath. Quarterly. Designed to keep members up-to-date on current work study panels, committees, and special task forces of the Institute. Provides a vehicle for exchange of professional information on agricultural research and related national policies and issues.

The Bench Sheet (WEF)
Water Environment Federation (WEF)
601 Wythe St.
Alexandria, VA 22314-1994
Phone: (703)684-2400

Bimonthly. Newsletter.

Buzzworm: The Environmental Journal
Buzzworm, Inc.
2305 Canyon Blvd., No. 206
Boulder, CO 80302
Phone: (303)442-1969

6x/year. Environmental magazine.

Certifier (ABC)
Association of Boards of Certification (ABC)
208 5th St.
Ames, IA 50010-6259
Phone: (515)232-3623

Monthly. Association and industry newsletter for operators and laboratory analysts involved in certification programs for distribution and collection of water and waste water and industrial waste treatment.

Clean Water Report
Business Publishers, Inc.
951 Pershing Dr.
Silver Spring, MD 20910
Phone: (301)587-6300

Editor(s): Elaine Eiserer. Biweekly. Provides information on water pollution control, drinking water supply and safety, and water resources issues. Covers national policy, legislation, regulations, enforcement and litigation, and state and local news.

Coal
Maclean Hunter Publishing Co.
29 N. Wacker Dr.
Chicago, IL 60606
Phone: (312)726-2802
Fax: (312)726-2574

Art Sanda, editor. Monthly. Coal production magazine.

Concentrates
Mining Foundation of the Southwest
PO Box 27225
Tucson, AZ 85726
Phone: (602)622-6257

Monthly. Monitors developments in the mining industry. Provides information on the Club's educational and social events for professionals in the industry.

The Conservationist
New York State Department of Environmental Conservation
50 Wolf Rd.
Albany, NY 12233
Phone: (518)457-5547
Fax: (518)457-1088

Robert DeVilleneuve, acting editor. Six issues/year. Magazine covering conservation issues.

The Cruiser
Forest History Society
701 Vickers Ave.
Durham, NC 27701
Phone: (919)682-9319

3 issues/year. Covers forest and conservation history.

E: The Environment Magazine
Earth Action Network, Inc.
28 Knight St.
Norwalk, CT 06851
Phone: (203)825-0061

Bimonthly. Environmental magazine.

Earth Work
The Student Conservation Association, Inc.
PO Box 550
Charlestown, NH 03603-0550
Phone: (603)543-1700
Fax: (603)826-7755

Monthly. This magazine covers conservation/environmental career issues and includes a comprehensive job listing with emphasis on career news and "how to" articles.

Engineering Outlook
College of Engineering
University of Illinois at Urbana-Champaign
112 Engineering Hall
1308 W Green St.
Urbana, IL 61801
Phone: (217)333-1510
Fax: (217)244-7705

Editor(s): Maureen L. Tan. Quarterly. Covers, in non-technical language, research at the University of Illinois in the areas of aeronautical, ceramic, agricultural, chemical, civil, computer, electrical, mechanical, industrial, and materials science engineering; as well as computer science, physics, theoretical and applied mechanics, and bioengineering.

When we consciously choose to do the work that we enjoy, not only can we get things done, but we can get them done well and be intrinsically rewarded for our effort, according to organizational psychologist Marsha Sinetar.

Source: *The Detroit News*

Environment Today
Enterprise Communications, Inc.
1483 Chain Bridge Rd.
McLean, VA 22101
Phone: (703)448-0322
Fax: (703)827-8214

Paul Harris, editor. 9x/year. $36/year. Magazine for environmental professionals, including waste generators, municipal utilities managers, and governmental decisionmakers. Focuses on trend-spotting and problem-solving.

Environmental Science & Engineering
Environmental Science Engineering Publications
10 Petch Cr.
Aurora, ON, Canada L4G 5N7
Phone: (416)727-4666

Tom Davey, Publisher. 6x/yr. Magazine on water, sewage, and pollution control.

EPA Journal
U.S. Environmental Protection Agency
401 M. St. SW, A-107
Washington, DC 20460
Phone: (202)260-4359

Monthly. Journal on regulations and the environment.

Garbage
Old House Journal Corp.
2 Main St.
Gloucester, MA 01930
Phone: (508)283-3200

6x/year. Magazine exploring environmental issues.

Some companies use creative gimmicks to motivate workers. Each year, John Brady Design Consultants, Pittsburgh, gives a jar of 12 marbles to its 18 employees, a different color for each person. Over the year, employees give the marbles as rewards to co-workers who help them out or achieve great feats. At year's end, the firm can see who recognizes others and who doesn't.

Source: *The Wall Street Journal*

Geological Magazine
Cambridge University Press
40 W. 20th St.
New York, NY 10011
Phone: (914)937-9600

C.P. Hughes; I.N. McCave; R.S.J. Sparks; N.W. Woodcock, editors. Six issues/year. Earth sciences periodical covering the entire spectrum of geological topics.

The Geological Newsletter
Geological Society of the Oregon Country
PO Box 907
Portland, OR 97207
Phone: (503)284-4320

Monthly. Disseminates news concerning geology and the earth sciences. Recurring features include reports on activities of the Society and news of research.

Graduating Engineer
COG Publishing Group
Peterson's
16030 Ventura Blvd.
Encino, CA 91436
Phone: (818)785-6252

Charlotte Chandler-Williams, editor. 4x/year. Magazine focusing on employment, education, and career devlopment.

IEEE Spectrum
Institute of Electrical and Electronics Engineers, Inc.
345 E. 47th St.
New York, NY 10017
Phone: (212)705-7016
Fax: (212)705-7589

Donald Christiansen, editor and publisher. Monthly. $7.50/year, members; $109/year, nonmembers. Magazine for the scientific and engineering professional. Provides information on developments and trends in engineering, physics, mathematics, chemistry, medicine/biology, and the nuclear sciences.

In Business: The Magazine for Environmental Enterpreneuring
J.G. Press
419 Stale Ave.
Emmaus, PA 18049
Phone: (215)967-4135

6x/year. Small business management magazine.

Journal American Water Works Association
American Water Works Assn.
6666 W. Quincy Ave.
Denver, CO 80235
Phone: (303)794-7711
Fax: (303)794-7310

Monthly. Magazine dealing with water supply, treatment, quality, and distribution.

Journal of Air & Waste Management Association
Air & Waste Management Association
PO Box 2861
Pittsburgh, PA 15230
Phone: (412)232-3444
Fax: (412)232-3450

Harold M. Eglund, editor. Monthly. $200/year. A journal on environmental science engineering.

Journal of Arboriculture
International Society of Arboriculture
303 University Ave.
PO Box 908
Urbana, IL 61801
Phone: (217)328-2032

A monthly publication free to members of the International Society of Arboriculture. Contains job listings.

Journal of Environmental Education
Heldref Publications
1319 18th St. NW
Washington, DC 20036-1802
Phone: (202)296-6267

Quarterly.

NAEP Newsletter
National Association of Environmental Professionals
PO Box 15210
Alexandria, VA 22309-0210
Phone: (703)660-2364

Bimonthly.

Natural Resources & Earth Sciences: NTIS Alerts
National Technical Information Service (NTIS)
U.S. Department of Commerce
5285 Port Royal Rd.
Springfield, VA 22161
Phone: (703)487-4630

2/year. Carries abstracts and bibliographic citations in the fields of mineral industries, natural resources management and surveys, soil sciences, geology and geophysics, and hydrology and limnology. .

NewsCAST
Council for Agricultural Science and Technology (CAST)
137 Lynn Ave.
Ames, IA 50010-7197
Phone: (515)292-2125

Editor(s): Robert J. Ver Straeten. Quarterly. Serves a consortium of 28 food and agricultural science societies, which promotes understanding by providing a factual background in agricultural science and technology. Carries features of interest to food and agricultural scientists and news of the organization's activities and programs.

NRDC Newsline
Natural Resources Defenses Council (NRDC)
40 W. 20th St.
New York, NY 10011
Phone: (212)727-2700

Quarterly.

At the same time that whale-size firms are whacking away the blubber, a net of 1.9 million new jobs will be created this year 1992, estimates Dun & Bradstreet, and 80 percent of them will be at companies with fewer than 100 employees.

Source: *U.S. News & World Report*

NTIS Alerts: Ocean Technology and Engineering
National Technical Information Service (NTIS)
U.S. Department of Commerce
5285 Port Royal Rd.
Springfield, MO 22161
Phone: (703)487-4630
Fax: (703)321-8547

2/month. Carries abstracts from publications concerned with marine engineering, dynamic oceanography, physical and chemical oceanography, biological oceanography, marine geophysics and geology, hydrography, and underwater construction and habitats.

Research Journal of the Water Environment Federation
Water Environment Federation
601 Wythe St.
Alexandria, VA 22314
Phone: (703)684-2400
Toll-free: 800-666-0206
Fax: (703)684-2492

Pete R. Piecuch, Editor. 6x/yr. Technical journal covering municipal and industrial water pollution control, water quality, and hazardous wastes.

The Research Reporter
Worcester Foundation for Experimental Biology
222 Maple Ave.
Shrewsbury, MA 01545
Phone: (508)842-8921
Fax: (508)842-9632

Editor(s): Patricia Kelleher Martin. Three issues/year. Monitors current activities at the Foundation and relates ongoing research in the areas of neurobiology, cancer and cell biology, and endocrine-reproductive biology. Recurring features include items on grants and awards, personal profiles, meeting and conference reports, and a column titled Distillations.

In today's competitive marketplace, people who have not thought about their future may not have one, or at least not a very bright one. Job seekers must be able to match their skills to the jobs available. You'll stand a better chance of having the right skills if you know which ones will be in demand.

Source: *Occupational Outlook Quarterly*

Science Agenda
Science Directorate
American Psychological Association
750 1st St., NE
Washington, DC 20036
Phone: (202)336-5500

K. Lee Herring, editor. Quarterly. Disseminates information on scientific psychology, including news on activities of the Association and congressional and federal advocacy efforts of the Directorate.

Science of Food and Agriculture
Council of Agricultural Science and Technology
137 Lynn Ave.
Ames, IA 50010-7120
Phone: (515)292-2125

Editor(s): Mary K. Adams. Two issues/year. Tracks developments in the science of food and agriculture.

Soil Science Society of America Journal
Soil Science Society of America
677 S. Segoe Rd.
Madison, WI 53711-1086
Phone: (608)273-8080
Fax: (608)273-2021

Robert Luxmoore, editor. Six issues/year. Soil research journal.

The Timberline
New England Forestry Foundation, Inc.
85 Newbury St.
Boston, MA 02116
Phone: (617)864-4229

L.J.G. Kopp, editor. Quarterly. Contains forestry-related articles.

Water & Pollution Control
Zanny Publications
190 Main St.
Unionville, ON, Canada M3R 2C9
Phone: (416)477-2922
Fax: (416)479-4834

Kate Fleming, Editor. Six times/yr. Water, sewage and pollution control market trade magazine with municipal and industrial focus.

Water Conditioning & Purification
Publicom Inc.
4651 N. 1st Ave., Ste. 101
Tucson, AZ 85718
Phone: (602)293-5446
Fax: (602)887-2383

Darlene J. Scheel, Editor. Monthly. Domestic and commercial water conditioning and purification magazine.

Water Environment Federation Highlights (WEF)
Water Environment Federation
601 Wythe St.
Alexandria, VA 22314-1994
Phone: (703)684-2400
Toll-free: 800-666-0206
Fax: (703)684-2492

Monthly. Newsletter.

Water Environment Federation Job Bank (WEF)
Water Environment Federation
601 Wythe St.
Alexandria, VA 22314-1994
Phone: (703)684-2400
Toll-free: 800-666-0206
Fax: (703)684-2492

Biweekly.

Water Environment Federation Safety and Health Bulletin (WEF)
Water Environment Federation
601 Wythe St.
Alexandria, VA 22314-1994
Phone: (703)684-2400
Toll-free: 800-666-0206
Fax: (703)684-2492

Quarterly.

Water Environment Regulation Watch (WEF)
Water Environment Federation
601 Wythe St.
Alexandria, VA 22314-1994
Phone: (703)684-2400
Toll-free: 800-666-0206
Fax: (703)684-2492

Monthly.

Water Technology
National Trade Publications, Inc.
13 Century Hill Dr.
Latham, NY 12110
Phone: (518)783-1281
Fax: (518)783-1386

Gregory Norton, Editor. Monthly. Magazine focusing on water treatment.

The Wildlifer
The Wildlife Society
5410 Grosvenor Ln.
Bethesda, MD 20814-2197
Phone: (301)897-9770
Fax: (301)530-2471

Bimonthly. Lists approximately 20 positions in conservation, wildlife, and natural resources in each edition.

Basic Reference Guides

AEG Directory
Association of Engineering Geologists (AEG)
323 Boston Post Rd.
Ste. 20
Sudbury, MA 01776
Phone: (508)443-4639

Annual.

AFSHP Directory
Association of Federal Safety and Health Professionals (AFSHP)
7549 Wilhelm Dr.
Lanham, MD 20706-2104
Phone: (301)552-2104

Biennial.

Women are nearly as likely as men to have many types of postsecondary degrees, but men hold professional degrees and doctorates at more than double the rate of women.

Source: *The Wall Street Journal*

Agricultural and Veterinary Sciences International Who's Who
Gale Research Inc.
835 Penobscot Bldg.
Detroit, MI 48226
Phone: (313)961-2242
Fax: (313)961-6241

1987. Two volumes; $450.00/set. Provides biographical profiles of about 7,500 senior agricultural and veterinary scientists from approximately 100 countries.

Agricultural Research Centres
Gale Research Inc.
835 Penobscot Bldg.
Detroit, MI 48226
Phone: (313)961-2242
Fax: (313)961-6241

Ninth edition, 1988. Two volumes; $400.00/set. Covers 2,000 main organizations controlling over 7,500 departments engaged in research in agriculture, fisheries, food, forestry, horticulture, and the veterinary sciences.

Agricultural Research Institute Membership Directory
Agricultural Research Institute
9650 Rockville Pike
Bethesda, MD 20814
Phone: (301)530-7122
Fax: (301)571-1858

Annual, spring. $4.00, postpaid. Covers: 100 members; also lists study panels and committees interested in environmental legislation, pest control, agricultural meteorology, biotechnology, food irradiation, agricultural policy, and research and development. Entries include: Name, title, affiliation, address, phone. Arrangement: Alphabetical.

Selecting a boss who is a good match for your work style can be critical to your job success. The mismatched, or wrong boss, can make your work life miserable, as well as significantly damage your career.

Source: *The Detroit News*

AGWSE Membership Directory
Association of Ground Water Scientists and Engineers (AGWSE)
6375 Riverside Dr.
Dublin, OH 43017
Phone: (614)761-1711
Fax: (614)761-3446

Triennial.

AIBS Membership Directory
American Institute of Biological Sciences (AIBS)
730 11th St., NW
Washington, DC 20001-4521
Phone: (202)628-1500
Fax: (202)628-1509

Biennial.

AIC Professional Directory
American Institute of Chemists (AIC)
7315 Wisconsin Ave., NW
Bethesda, MD 20814
Phone: (301)652-2447

Annual. Free to members; $50.00/copy for nonmembers. Includes professional biographical information.

AIChE Directory
American Institute of Chemical Engineers (AIChE)
345 E. 47th St.
New York, NY 10017
Phone: (212)705-7338
Fax: (212)752-3294

Periodic. Available to members only.

AIPG Membership Directory
American Institute of Professional Geologists (AIPG)
7828 Vance Dr., Ste. 103
Arvada, CO 80003
Phone: (303)431-0831
Fax: (303)431-1332

Annual.

American Industrial Hygiene Association Directory
American Industrial Hygiene Association
PO Box 8390
345 White Pond Dr.
Akron, OH 44320
Phone: (216)873-2442

Annual, September. Available to members only. Covers: 8,900 members concerned with the study and control of environmental factors affecting people at work. Entries include: Name, address, phone, affiliation. Arrangement: Alphabetical. Indexes: Employer, geographical.

American Men and Women of Science
R. R. Bowker
121 Chanlon Rd.
New Providence, NJ 07974
Phone: (908)464-6800
Fax: (908)665-6688

Triennial, latest edition January 1992. Biographical volumes set, $750.00; index volume, $85.00. Covers: 125,000 United States and Canadian scientists active in the physical, biological, mathematical, computer science, and engineering fields. Entries include: Name, address, personal and career data, memberships, research interest. Arrangement: Alphabetical. Indexes: Discipline (in separate volume).

ASA International Directory
American Society of Agronomy (ASA)
677 S. Segoe Rd.
Madison, WI 53711
Phone: (608)273-8080
Fax: (608)273-2021

Periodic.

ASHES Member Directory
American Society for Healthcare Environmental Services of the American Hospital Association (ASHES)
c/o Paul J. Julius
840 N. Lake Shore Dr.
Chicago, IL 60611
Phone: (312)280-6245
Fax: (312)280-4152

Annual.

ASHS Membership Directory
American Society for Horticultural Science (ASHS)
113 S. West St., Ste. 400
Alexandria, VA 22314-2824
Phone: (703)836-4606
Fax: (703)836-2024

Annual.

ASM Directory of Members
American Society for Microbiology (ASM)
1325 Massachusetts Ave., NW
Washington, DC 20005
Phone: (202)737-3600

Every 2-3 years. Available to members only.

ASPP Bulletins
American Society of Plant Physiologists (ASPP)
15501 Monona Dr.
Rockville, MD 20855
Phone: (301)251-0560
Fax: (301)279-2996

Annual. Directory.

Association of Consulting Foresters Membership Specialization Directory
Association of Consulting Foresters
5410 Grosvenor Lane, Ste. 205
Bethesda, MD 20814
Phone: (301)530-6795

Annual, August. $15.00, postpaid. Covers: Nearly 450 member forestry consulting firms and professional foresters who earn the largest part of their income from consulting. Entries include: Name, address, phone, specialties, background, career data, staff (if a consulting firm), geographic area served, capabilities, including equipment available and foreign language proficiency. Arrangement: Alphabetical. Indexes: Name, office location, language, international capability.

AWG Membership Directory
Association for Women Geoscientists (AWG)
10200 W. 44th Ave., Ste. 304
Wheat Ridge, CO 80033
Phone: (303)422-8527

Annual.

According to the American Association of Fund-Raising Counsel, the environmental movement took in $2.29 billion in 1990. That's almost double 1987 revenues, when the counsel started monitoring environmental giving.

AWMA Directory and Resource Book
Air and Waste Management Association (AWMA)
PO Box 2861
Pittsburgh, PA 15230
Phone: (412)232-3444
Fax: (412)255-3450

Annual.

AWWA Membership Roster
American Water Works Association (AWWA)
6666 W. Quincy Ave.
Denver, CO 80235
Phone: (303)794-7711
Fax: (303)795-1440

Quadrennial.

Biophysical Society Directory
Biophysical Society (BPS)
c/o Emily M. Gray
Biophysical Society Office
9650 Rockville Pike, Rm. 512
Bethesda, MD 20814
Phone: (301)530-7114
Fax: (301)530-7133

Biennial. Available to members only. Includes geographic listing.

The Biotechnology Directory
Stockton Press
15 E. 26th St.
New York, NY 10010

1989. $190.00. Covers biotechnology firms.

BSA Membership Directory
Botanical Society of America (BSA)
c/o Christopher Haufler
Univ. of Kansas
Dept. of Botany
Haworth Hall
Lawrence, KS 66045-2106
Phone: (913)864-4301

Biennial. Free to members; $10.00/copy for nonmembers.

Average starting salary for an M.B.A. with a liberal arts bachelor's degree: $35,734. A technical bachelor's degree adds $5,579.

Source: *U.S. News & World Report*

Challinor's Dictionary of Geology
Oxford University Press, Inc.
200 Madison Ave.
New York, NY 10016
Phone: (212)679-7300
Toll-free: 800-445-9714

John Challinor. Sixth edition, 1986.

Chemical Engineering Catalog
Penton Publishing
1100 Superior Ave.
Cleveland, OH 44114-2543
Phone: (216)696-7000

Annual, November. $40.00, postpaid. Send orders to: Penton Publishing, 1100 Superior Ave., Cleveland, OH 44114. Publication includes: List of manufacturers of equipment and chemicals for the chemical processing industries. Entries include: Company name, address, district sales offices' addresses and phone numbers. Arrangement: Alphabetical within product categories. Indexes: Company name, product, trade name.

Chemical Engineering Faculties
American Institute of Chemical Engineers (AICHE)
345 E. 47th St.
New York, NY 10017
Phone: (212)705-7338
Fax: (212)752-3294

Annual. Directory of faculty members, department heads, and placement officers of approximately 151 U.S. and 281 foreign chemical engineering schools.

Chemical Engineers' Handbook
McGraw-Hill, Inc.
1221 Avenue of the Americas
New York, NY 10020
Phone: (212)512-2000
Toll-free: 800-722-4726

Robert H. Perry, Don W. Green, and James O. Maloney, editors. Sixth edition, 1984. Contains illustrations. Includes bibliographical references and an index.

Conservation Directory
National Wildlife Federation
1400 16th St., NW
Washington, DC 20036
Phone: (703)790-4402
Fax: (703)442-7332

Annual, January. $18.00, plus $3.50 shipping; payment must accompany orders from individuals. Covers: About 90 federal agencies, 515 national and international organizations, 1000 state government agencies and citizens groups, and 113 Canadian agencies and groups concerned with conservation of natural resources and preservation of the environment; colleges and universities with environmental education programs. Entries include: Agency name, address, branch or subsidiary office name and address, names and titles of personnel, interests, activities, publications. Arrangement: Classified by type of organization. Indexes: Personal name, subject, publication title.

The Dictionary of the Biological Sciences
R. E. Krieger Publishing Co., Inc.
PO Box 9542
Melbourne, FL 32902
Phone: (407)724-9542
Fax: (407)951-3671

Peter Gray. 1982. Includes a bibliography.

Directory of African American Design Firms
San Francisco Redevelopment Agency
770 Golden Gate Ave.
San Francisco, CA 94102
Phone: (415)749-2423

Annual, December. Free. Covers: Nearly 90 architectural, engineering, planning and landscape design firms. Entries include: Firm name, address, phone. Arrangement: Alphabetical.

Directory of Certified Petroleum Geologists
American Association of Petroleum Geologists
Box 979
Tulsa, OK 74101
Phone: (918)584-2555

Biennial, even years. $40.00, postpaid. Covers: About 3,600 members of the association. Entries include: Name, address, education and other career data; whether available for consulting. Arrangement: Alphabetical. Indexes: Geographical.

The Directory of Chemical Engineering Consultants
American Institute of Chemical Engineers
345 E. 47th St.
New York, NY 10017

1988. $8.00.

Directory of Chemical Producers U.S.A.
SRI International
333 Ravenswood Ave.
Menlo Park, CA 94025
Phone: (415)859-3627
Fax: (415)859-2182

Annual, June; semiannual supplement. $1,390.00 per year. Covers: Over 1,500 United States basic chemical producers manufacturing nearly 10,000 chemicals in commercial quantities at 4,500 plant locations. Entries include: For companies - Company name, division or subsidiary name, corporate address, phone, telex, location of each subsidiary, division and manufacturing plant, and the products made at each plant location. For products - Producers' names and plant locations, alternate product names (if any), and plant-by-plant capacities for over 250 major chemicals. Arrangement: Companies are alphabetical by parent company; products are alphabetical and by group (dyes, pesticides, etc.); manufacturing plants are geographical.

Directory of Commercial Hazardous Waste Treatment and Recycling Facilities
Office of Solid Waste
Environmental Protection Agency
401 M St., SW
Washington, DC 20460
Phone: (202)260-4610

Irregular; latest edition August 1987. $23.00, plus $3.00 shipping. Send orders to: (National Technical Information Service), Springfield, VA 22161 (703-487-4808). Covers: About 500 commercial facilities that accept hazardous waste for treatment and/or recycling. Entries include: Facility name, address, phone, contact, types of treatments or processes used, types of wastes accepted. Arrangement: Alphabetical. Indexes: Geographical (in table form, with type of materials handled and processes used).

Citicorp is changing the way it uses interns, as are other companies. Instead of providing opportunities for students to examine various career paths, employers are taking a closer look at them as potential full-time employees. This means giving interns more responsibility.

Source: *Fortune*

Directory of Contract Service Firms
C. E. Publications, Inc.
Box 97000
Kirkland, WA 98083
Phone: (206)823-2222
Fax: (206)821-0942

Annual, January. $10.00. Covers: Over 1,015 contract firms actively engaged in the employment of engineering and technical personnel for 'temporary' contract assignments throughout the world. Entries include: Company name, address, phone, name of contact, description of needs and work locations. Arrangement: Alphabetical. Indexes: Geographical by location of firm.

Directory of Engineering Societies and Related Organizations
American Association of Engineering Societies
415 2nd St., NE
Washington, DC 20002
1987. $105.00.

Directory of Engineers in Private Practice
National Society of Professional Engineers
1420 King St.
Alexandria, VA 22314
Phone: (703)684-2800
Fax: (703)836-4875

Biennial, even years. $75.00. Covers: 2,000 consulting engineering firms and 11,000 individuals who are members of the society's Professional Engineers in Private Practice division. Entries include: For companies - Name, address, phone, name of principal executive, list of services. For individuals - Name, address; most listings include phone. Arrangement: Firms are geographical, then by specialty; individuals are alphabetical.

Nothing can be more frustrating than getting typecast at work. You can get typecast in a certain job or image. Then, when you're ready to move up or into a different area of expertise, you can't get anyone to see you in a different way . . . . One technique to change your image is to dress in a more professional manner. You must also position yourself with people who can help you. One good way is to become active in a professional group, which also can provide you with good contacts and news of opportunities throughout your industry.

Source: *Business Monday/Detroit Free Press*

Directory of Environmental Information Sources
Government Institutes, Inc.
4 Research Pl., Ste. 200
Rockville, MD 20850-3226
Phone: (301)921-2300

Covers more than 1400 federal and state government agencies; profesional and scientific organization; trade associations; publishers; database producers; and other organizations that provide information on the environment.

Directory of Foreign Manufacturers in the United States
Business Publishing Division
Georgia State University
University Plaza
Atlanta, GA 30303
Phone: (404)651-4253

Biennial, summer of even years; new edition expected 1993. $195.00, postpaid; payment must accompany orders from individuals. Covers: Over 4,800 United States manufacturing, mining, and petroleum companies, and the over 2,300 firms abroad which own them. Entries include: Company name, address, products or services, parent company name and address. Arrangement: Alphabetical by U.S. company name. Indexes: U.S. subsidiary location, foreign company name, geographical (foreign company location), product.

Directory of Japanese Company Laboratories Willing to Receive American Researchers
National Technical Information Service
5285 Port Royal Rd.
Springfield, VA 22161
Phone: (703)487-4650

Latest edition, June 1988. $35.00. Covers: Approximately 125 companies involved in various Japanese industries that accept foreign science and engineering researchers in their laboratories for periods of one to three years.

Directory of Minority and Women-Owned Engineering and Architectural Firms
American Consulting Engineers Council
1015 15th St. NW, Ste. 802
Washington, DC 20005
Phone: (202)347-7474
Fax: (202)898-0068

Irregular; latest edition June 1990. $15.00. Covers: Approximately 525 minority and women-owned engineering and architectural firms. Entries include: Firm name, address, phone; owners' names including percentage of ownership, sex, and race of each; registered professionals, size of staff, description of activities, minority status, branches; local, state, and federal MBE/WBE certification, if applicable. Arrangement: Geographical. Indexes: Firm name, area of experience.

Directory of National Environmental Organizations

U.S. Environmental Directories
Box 65156
St. Paul, MN 55165

Irregular, latest edition 1991. $54.00, postpaid; payment must accompany order. Covers: Over 500 organizations outside of government concerned with the environment and conservation. Entries include: Organization name, address, phone, contact name, year established, number of members, short description of activities and aims. Arrangement: Alphabetical. Classified by subject.

Directory of Natural Science Centers

Natural Science for Youth Foundation (NSYF)
130 Azalea Dr.
Roswell, GA 30075
Phone: (404)594-9367
Fax: (404)594-7738

Periodic.

Directory of State Departments of Agriculture

Financial Management Division
Agricultural Marketing Service
Department of Agriculture
14 Independence Ave., SW, Rm. 3964
Washington, DC 20250
Phone: (202)720-6920

Biennial, late summer of odd years. Free. Covers: State departments of agriculture and their officials. Entries include: Department name, address, phone, names and titles of key personnel, department branches. Arrangement: Geographical.

Directory of State Environmental Agencies

Environmental Law Institute
1616 P St., NW, No. 200
Washington, DC 20036
Phone: (202)328-5150

Latest edition September 1985; suspended indefinitely. $22.50, plus $2.50 shipping. Covers: State and territorial government agencies responsible for environmental supervision, issues, and programs. Entries include: Agency name, address, phone, authorizing legislation, geographic and industrial coverage of responsibility, specific responsibilities. Arrangement: Geographical.

Directory of U.S. Ocean Scientists and Engineers

American Geophysical Union (AGU)
2000 Florida Ave., NW
Washington, DC 20009
Phone: (202)462-6900
Fax: (202)328-0566

Periodic.

Directory of World Chemical Producers

Chemical Information Services Ltd.
PO Box 8344
University Station
Dallas, TX 75205
Phone: (214)340-4345
Fax: (214)340-4346

Triennial; latest edition 1992. Price: $500.00, payment with order. Covers: Over 5,000 chemical producers in 61 countries; does not include producers of chemical and pharmaceutical specialties or formulated mixtures. Entries include: Company name, address, phone, telex, TWX numbers, cable address. Arrangement: Geographical. Indexes: Product.

EI Environmental Services Directory

Environmental Information Ltd.
4801 W. 81st St., Ste. 119
Bloomington, MN 55437
Phone: (612)831-2473

Annual, December. $290.00, postpaid; payment must accompany order. Five regional directories are also available; $75.00 each. Covers: Over 450 waste-handling facilities, 600 transportation firms, 375 spill response firms, 1,700 consultants, 470 laboratories, 390 soil boring/well drilling firms; also includes incineration services, polychlorinated biphenyl (PCB) detoxification and mobile solvent-recovery services, asbestos services and underground tank services, summaries of states' regulatory programs. Entries include: Company name, address, phone, service, regulatory status, on and off site processes used, type of waste handled. Arrangement: Geographical. Indexes: Service.

Employment Guide for Engineers and Scientists
Institute of Electrical and Electronics Engineers
345 E. 47th St.
New York, NY 10017
Phone: (212)705-7560

Published 1986. $8.95 for members, $11.95 for nonmembers. Send orders to: IEEE Service Center, 445 Hoes Lane, Piscataway, NJ 08854 (201-981-0060). Publication includes: List of the top 100 employers of institute members, 50 employment agencies, and 50 outplacement agencies specializing in engineering fields. Entries include: Company name, address, phone, name of contact.

EMS Membership Roster
Environmental Mutagen Society (EMS)
1600 Wilson Blvd., Ste. 905
Arlington, VA 82201
Phone: (703)525-1191
Fax: (703)276-8196

Triennial. Free to members; $150.00/issue for nonmembers.

Some people will find the training they need right at the office. American companies desperate to produce more with fewer, better-skilled workers now are pumping $30 billion annually into employee-training programs that run the gamut from basic computer courses to company-sponsored M.B.A. degrees.

Source: *U.S. News & World Report*

Encyclopedia of Chemical Processing and Design
Marcel Dekker, Inc.
270 Madison Ave., 4th Fl.
New York, NY 10016
Phone: (212)696-9000

John J. McKetta and William A. Cunnigham, editors. 1976. Includes bibliographical references.

The Encyclopedia of Field and General Geology
Van Nostrand Reinhold Co., Inc.
115 Fifth Ave.
New York, NY 10003
Phone: (212)254-3232
Toll-free: 800-842-3636

Charles W. Finkl, editor. 1988. Contains information for practicing field geologists.

Engineering and Mining Journal International Directory of Mining
Maclean Hunter Publishing Company
29 N. Wacker Dr.
Chicago, IL 60606
Phone: (312)726-2802
Fax: (312)726-2574

Annual, November. $120.00. Covers: 2,100 companies and 3,000 mines and plants producing metals and nonmetallic minerals, worldwide. Also includes a list of over 500 consultants, contractors, and other service firms, and a directory of mining associations, government mine bureaus and geological surveys. Entries include: For company headquarters - Company name, address, phone, names of executives, number of employees, sales and capital, general area explored, type of business, products, SIC numbers. For mines and plants -Company name, address, phone, primary function (consulting, contracting, etc.), specific activities and fields engaged in, number of employees, principals, branch offices. Arrangement: Companies and consultants are alphabetical; mines and plants are geographical. Indexes: Personnel, type of ore or mineral.

Engineering Research Centres
Gale Research Inc.
835 Penobscot Bldg.
Detroit, MI 48226
Phone: (313)961-2242
Fax: (313)961-6241

Second edition, 1988. $400.00. Contains over 8,000 entries describing research and technology laboratories in over 70 countries. Provides details on industrial research centers and educational establishments with research and development activity. Indexes: Subject and title of establishments.

ENR Directory of Design Firms
McGraw Hill, Inc.
1221 Avenue of the Americas
New York, NY 10020
Phone: (212)512-2000
Fax: (212)312-2007

Biennial, fall of even years. $34.50. Covers: About 145 architects, architectural engineers, consultants, and other design firms; limited to advertisers. Also includes lists of top 500 design firms in the United States, top 200 international design firms, top 50 United States design-construction firms, and top 50 international design-construction firms, based on total amount of billings. Entries include: For advertisers - Company name, address, branch locations, subsidiaries, list of key personnel, territory served, capabilities. In ranked lists - Company name, address, phone; international firms include telex. Arrangement: Alphabetical.

ENR Top 500 Design Firms Issue

McGraw Hill, Inc.
1221 Avenue of the Americas
New York, NY 10020
Phone: (212)512-2000
Fax: (212)312-2007

Annual, August. $10.00, payment with order. Publication includes: List of 500 leading architectural, engineering, and specialty design firms selected on basis of annual billings. Entries include: Company name, location, code for type of firm, current and prior year rank in billings, types of services, number of *Engineering News-Record* subscribers. Arrangement: Ranked by billings.

ENR Top International Design Firms Issue

McGraw Hill, Inc.
1221 Avenue of the Americas
New York, NY 10020
Phone: (212)512-2000
Fax: (212)312-2007

Annual, August. $10.00. Publication includes: List of 200 design firms (including United States firms) competing outside their own national borders who received largest dollar volume of foreign contracts in preceding calendar year. Entries include: Company name, headquarters location, total value of contracts received in preceding year, design specialties, rank and countries in which they are operating in current year. Arrangement: Geographical by country.

Environmental Engineering Selection Guide

American Academy of Environmental Engineers (AAEE)
130 Holiday Ct., No. 100
Annapolis, MD 21401
Phone: (301)266-3311

Annual. Free. Directory listing environmental engineers in consulting, education, and manufacturing certified by the academy; also lists accredited environmental engineering programs.

Environmental Industries Marketplace

Gale Research Inc.
835 Penobscot Bldg.
Detroit, MI 48226-4094
Phone: (313)961-2242
Fax: (313)961-6083

Annual; semiannual update. Federal, state, and local agencies, legislative committees, public and private organizations, and individuals concerned with environmental issues.

Environmental Services Directory

Environmental Information Ltd.
4801 W. 81st St., Ste. 119
Bloomington, MN 55437
Phone: (612)831-2473
Fax: (612)831-6550

Annual, December. Covers over 450 waste-handling facilities, 600 transportation firms, 425 spill response firms, 1,900 consultants, 425 laboratories, 390 soil boring/well drilling firms; also includes incineration services, PCS detoxification and mobile solvent-recovery services, asbestos services and underground tank services, and summaries of states' regulatory programs.

Essentials of Forestry Practice

John Wiley and Sons, Inc.
605 Third Ave.
New York, NY 10158
Phone: (212)850-6000
Toll-free: 800-526-5368

Charles H. Stoddard and Glenn M. Stoddard. Fourth edition, 1987. Includes history and future trends in forestry. Covers managing forests and administration of forestry programs.

The Facts on File Dictionary of Biology

Facts on File
460 Park Ave., S.
New York, NY 10016
Phone: (212)683-2244
Toll-free: 800-322-8755

Elizabeth Toothill, editor. Revised edition, 1988.

Defines terms for all areas of the biological sciences.

The Facts on File Dictionary of Geology and Geophysics
Facts on File, Inc.
460 Park Ave., S.
New York, NY 10016
Phone: (212)683-2244
Toll-free: 800-322-8755

Dorothy F. Lapidus. 1987. Illustrated.

FASEB Directory of Members
Federation of American Societies for Experimental Biology (FASEB)
9650 Rockville Pike
Bethesda, MD 20814
Phone: (301)530-7000
Fax: (301)571-1855

Annual. Free to members; $1.00/copy for nonmembers.

A computer can make it easier to customize your resume. If you store your resume on a computer disk, you can copy it and rearrange it by skills, job chronology oralmost any other method, customizing it for each job you apply for.

Source: *Business Monday/Detroit Free Press*

Federal Personnel Office Directory
Federal Reports, Inc.
1010 Vermont Ave., NW, Ste. 408
Washington, DC 20005
Phone: (202)393-3311
Fax: (202)393-1553

Biennial, March of even years. $27.00. Covers: Over 1,500 federal government personnel offices that hire people for federal jobs; limited international coverage. Entries include: Government agency name, address, phone, description of services, restrictions for employment eligibility, branch office names and locations. Includes information on federal recruitment programs for disabled persons, women and minorities, veterans, students, and summer employment. Arrangement: Geographical, classified by department or agency.

Federal Staff Directory
Staff Directories Ltd.
Box 62
Mount Vernon, VA 22121-0062
Phone: (703)739-0900
Fax: (703)765-1300

Semiannual, December and July. $59.00. Covers: 30,000 persons in federal government offices and independent agencies, with biographies of 2,500 key executives; includes officials at policy level in agencies of the Office of the President, Cabinet-level departments, independent and regulatory agencies, military commands, federal information centers, and libraries, and United States attorneys, marshalls, and ambassadors. Entries include: Name, title, location (indicating building, address, and room), phone. Arrangement: By department or agency. Indexes: Personal name, subject.

Forestry Handbook
John Wiley and Sons, Inc.
605 Third Ave.
New York, NY 10158
Phone: (212)850-6000
Toll-free: 800-526-5368
Fax: (212)850-6088

Karl F. Wenger, editor. Second edition, 1984. This handbook was written for the practicing forester and contains information on logging and silviculture.

Geophysical Directory
Geophysical Directory, Inc.
Box 130508
Houston, TX 77219
Phone: (713)529-8789
Fax: (713)529-3646

Annual, March. $45.00, postpaid. Covers: About 3,600 companies that provide geophysical services, equipment, or supplies and mining and petroleum companies that use geophysical techniques; international coverage. Entries include: Company name, address, phone, names of principal executives, operations, and sales personnel; similar information for branch locations. Arrangement: Classified by product or service. Indexes: Company name, personal name.

Glossary of Geology
American Geological Institute (AGI)
4220 King St.
Alexandria, VA 22302
Phone: (703)379-2480

Robert L. Bates and Julia A. Jackson, editors. Third edition, 1988. Defines 36,000 geoscience terms including more than 4,000 mineral names.

GSA Membership Directory
Geological Society of America (GSA)
PO Box 9140
3300 Penrose Pl.
Boulder, CO 80301-9140
Phone: (303)447-2020
Fax: (303)447-1133

Annual.

Guide to Products and Services of Small Chemical Businesses
Division of Small Chemical Businesses
American Chemical Society
Box 14373
Columbus, OH 43214
Phone: (614)248-2976

Irregular. $9.00; payment must accompany order. Covers: Approximately 400 small chemical businesses (with less than 500 employees) related to the Division through persons who are members or affiliates. Entries include: Company name, address, phone, name and title of key personnel, description of products and services. Arrangement: Alphabetical. Indexes: Product/service.

Hazardous Waste Consultant Directory of Commercial Hazardous Waste Management Facilities Issue
McCoy and Associates, Inc.
13701 W. Jewell Ave., No. 202
Lakewood, CO 80228
Phone: (303)987-0333

Annual, March/April. $90.00. Publication includes: List of nearly 130 licensed commercial facilities that process, store, and dispose of hazardous waste material. Entries include: Facility name, address, phone, contact name, facilities, type of waste handled, methods of on-site treatment or disposal, Environmental Protection Agency identification number, restrictions, description of other services. Arrangement: Geographical. Indexes: Organization name.

Hazardous Waste Services Directory
J. J. Keller & Associates, Inc.
3003 W. Breezewood Ln.
Neenah, WI 54957
Phone: (414)722-2848
Fax: (414)727-7516

Base edition supplied upon subscription; semiannual updates. $95.00. Covers: Over 1,000 firms which provide services related to the handling of dangerous materials, including haulers, processors, disposal sites, operators, laboratories, and consultants. Entries include: Company name, address, phone, name and title of contact, services. Arrangement: Geographical.

Healthy Harvest: A Directory of Sustainable Agriculture and Horticulture Organizations
603 4th St.
Davis, CA 95616
Phone: (916)756-7177

Annual. $24.95, plus $3.00 shipping. Covers: More than 1,000 agriculture and horticulture training institutions, research institutes, development programs, political organizations, appropriate technology institutes, and sustainable agriculture design groups worldwide. Entries include: Organization name, address, phone, contact name, geographical area served, description of activities. Arrangement: Alphabetical. Indexes: Subject, geographical.

ICWM Directory of Hazardous Waste Treatment and Disposal Facilities
Institute of Chemical Waste Management (ICWM)
National Solid Wastes Management Association (NSWMA)
1730 Rhode Island Ave., NW, Ste. 1000
Washington, DC 20036
Phone: (202)659-4613
Fax: (202)775-5917

Annual. $7.00. Covers: More than 20 commercial hazardous waste management firms in the United States and Canada. Entries include: Firm name, address, phone, types and locations of facilities, services offered. Arrangement: Geographical.

International Engineering Directory
American Consulting Engineers Council
1015 15th St., NW
Ste. 802
Washington, DC 20005
Phone: (202)347-7474
Fax: (202)898-0068

January 1989. $25.00; payment must accompany order. Covers: Member engineering consulting firms practicing abroad. Entries include: Firm name, address, location of branch offices, names and titles of key personnel, services offered, areas of expertise, selected typical projects. Arrangement: Alphabetical. Indexes: Specialty.

International Society of Arboriculture Membership Directory
International Society of Arboriculture
303 University Ave.
PO Box 908
Urbana, IL 61801
Phone: (217)328-2032

An annual yearbook of the members of the International Society of Arboriculture.

Journal of Air and Waste Management
Air and Waste Management Assn.
PO Box 2861
Pittsburgh, PA 15230
Phone: (412)232-3444
Fax: (412)232-3450

Monthly. Environmental science engineering journal.

KSEA Membership Directory
Korean Scientists and Engineers Association in America (KSEA)
6261 Executive Blvd.
Rockville, MD 20852
Phone: (301)984-7048
Fax: (301)984-1231

Triennial.

Life Sciences Organizations and Agencies Directory
Gale Research Inc.
835 Penobscot Bldg.
Detroit, MI 48226
Phone: (313)961-2242
Fax: (313)961-6241

First edition 1988. $155.00. Covers: About 7,500 associations, government agencies, research centers, educational institutions, libraries and information centers, museums, consultants, electronic information services, and other organizations and agencies active in agriculture, biology, ecology, forestry, marine science, nutrition, wildlife and animal sciences, and other natural and life sciences. Entries include: Organization or agency name, address, phone, name and title of contact, description. Arrangement: Classified by type of organization. Indexes: Organization/agency name and keyword.

Municipal/County Executive Directory
Carroll Publishing Company
1058 Thomas Jefferson St., NW
Washington, DC 20007
Phone: (202)333-8620
Fax: (202)337-7020

Annual, June. $127.00, plus $8.00 shipping; payment must accompany order. Covers: Officials of 1,400 county governments (with populations over 25,000) and 2,000 municipalities (with populations over 1,000); includes elected, appointed, and career office holders. Entries include: Name, title, agency, address, phone. Arrangement: County officials are geographical, then by agency; municipal officials are by city name. Indexes: Personal name.

Municipal Year Book
International City Management Association
777 N. Capitol St., NE, Ste. 500
Washington, DC 20002-4201
Phone: (202)962-3700
Fax: (202)962-3500

Annual, April. $77.50. Covers: Incorporated municipalities with populations of over 2,500; counties; state municipal leagues and state associations of counties; councils of governments; state agencies for community affairs; Canadian provincial and territorial agencies for local affairs, local government chief administrative officers, associations and unions; professional and educational organizations serving local governments. Entries include: For municipalities - Municipality name, form of government, population,; names of mayor, city manager, city clerk, finance officer, other officials; and municipal phone number. For counties - County name, names of key officials, phone. For organizations - Company name, address, phone, description of services, products/services provided. Arrangement: Geographical; alphabetical by organization.

NACD Directory
National Association of Conservation Districts (NACD)
509 Capitol Ct., NE
Washington, DC 20002
Phone: (202)547-6223
Fax: (202)547-6450

Annual.

National Directory of Internships
National Society for Internships and Experiential Education
3509 Haworth Dr., Ste. 207
Raleigh, NC 27609-7229
Phone: (919)787-3263

Covers more than 30,000 educational internship opportunities in 75 fields with over 650 organizations in the United States. Includes information on deadlines, application procedures, contact names, and elegibility requirements.

National Directory of Local and Regional Land Conservation Organizations
Land Trust Exchange
1017 Duke St.
Alexandria, VA 22314

$10.00. Includes directors' names.

National Environmental Health Association Membership Directory
National Environmental Health Association (NEHA)
720 S. Colorado Blvd., Ste. 970, South Tower
Denver, CO 80222
Phone: (303)756-9090
Fax: (303)691-9490

Annual.

National Parks: Index
National Park Service
Department of the Interior
Box 37127
Washington, DC 20013
Phone: (202)208-6985

Biennial, odd years. $3.00, payment must accompany orders. Send orders to: Superintendent of Documents, U.S. Government Printing Office, Washington, DC 20402 (202-783-3238). Covers: Over 350 areas administered by the National Park Service, including parks, shores, historic sites, 80 national trails, and wild and scenic rivers. Entries include: Name, location, address, acreage (federal, non-federal, and gross), federal facilities, brief description. Arrangement: Most areas are geographical; wild and scenic rivers and national trails are alphabetical. Indexes: Alphabetical by area name.

National Weather Service Offices and Stations
National Weather Service
National Oceanic and Atmospheric Administration
Department of Commerce
1325 East-West Hwy.
Silver Spring, MD 20910
Phone: (301)427-7698

Annual, September. Free. Covers: Offices and stations operated by or under the supervision of the National Weather Service in the United States, Mexico, Caribbean, Central and South America, and Oceania. Entries include: Station and airport name, type of station, call letters, International Index Number, latitude, longitude, elevation; and number, type, and frequency of weather observations. Arrangement: Geographical.

The Nature Directory: A Guide to Environmental Organizations
Walker & Co.
720 5th Ave.
New York, NY 10019
Phone: (212)265-2632

Covers more than 120 environmental organizations and related government agencies in the United States.

NWWA Membership Directory
National Water Well Association (NWWA)
6375 Riverside Dr.
Dublin, OH 43017
Phone: (614)761-1711
Fax: (614)761-3446

Triennial.

Oil & Gas Directory
Geophysical Directory, Inc.
Box 130508
Houston, TX 77219
Phone: (713)529-8789
Fax: (713)529-3646

Annual, November. $60.00, postpaid. Covers: About 5,200 companies worldwide involved in petroleum exploration, drilling, and production, and suppliers to the industry. Entries include: Company name, address, phone, telex, names of principal personnel; branch office addresses, phone numbers, and key personnel. Arrangement: Classified by activity. Indexes: Company name, personal name.

Jeffrey A. Sonnenfeld, an Emory University management professor, divides US corporations into 4 categories: the Baseball Team—advertising, entertainment, investment banking, software, biotech research, and other industries based on fad, fashion, new technologies, and novelty; the Club—utilities, government agencies, airlines, banks, and other organizations that tend to produce strong generalists; the Academy—manufacturers in electronics, pharmaceuticals, office products, autos, and consumer products; and the Fortress—companies in fields such as publishing, hotels, retailing, textiles, and natural resources.

Peterson's Job Opportunities for Engineering, Science, and Computer Graduates 1993
Peterson's
PO Box 2123
Princeton, NJ 08543-2123
Phone: (609)243-9111

Compiled by the Peterson's staff. 1993. $20.95 paperback. 550 pages. Lists over 1,000 manufacturing, research, consulting, and government organizations hiring technical graduates. Explores how to match academic backgrounds to specific job openings. Provides information about opportunities for experienced personnel as well. Includes data on starting locations by city and state, summer jobs, co-op jobs, internships, and international assignments.

Professional Workers in State Agricultural Experiment Stations and Other Cooperating State Institutions
Cooperative State Research Service
Department of Agriculture
901 D St., NW
Washington, DC 20250

Biennial, even years; supplement in odd years. $15.00. Send orders to: Superintendent of Documents, U.S. Government Printing Office, Washington, DC 20402 (202-783-3238). Covers: Academic and research personnel in all agricultural, forestry, aquacultural, home economics, and animal husbandry fields at experiment stations and academic institutions with agricultural programs. Entries include: Station or institution name, address, phone; names of personnel, their degrees and titles, and, in some cases, individual phones; classified by major scientific or administrative areas. Arrangement: Geographical. Indexes: Personal name.

Reference Directory to Hazardous, Toxic, and Superfund Services
Rimbach Publishing, Inc.
8650 Babcock Blvd.
Pittsburgh, PA 15237
Phone: (412)364-5366

Annual, September. $40.00. Publication includes: List of about 300 hazardous waste management contractors, consultants, and contract analytical laboratories. Entries include: Company name, address, phone, services and equipment available. Arrangement: Geographical. Indexes: Alphabetical.

Register of the National Certification Commission in Chemistry and Chemical Engineering
American Institute of Chemists
7315 Wisconsin Ave.
Bethesda, MD 20814
Phone: (301)652-2447

Annual, November. $5.00. Covers: About 1,000 chemists and chemical engineers certified by the National Certification Commission. Entries include: Name, address, certification title (Certified Chemical Engineer or Certified Professional Chemist), and date of expiration of the certification. Arrangement: Alphabetical. Indexes: Geographical.

Roster of Registered Architects, Engineers, Land Surveyors and Landscape Architects
Minnesota State Board of Architecture, Engineering, Land
Surveying, and Landscape Architecture
133 7th St. E., 3rd Fl.
St. Paul, MN 55101
Phone: (612)296-2388

Biennial, December of even years. $5.00. Covers: About 11,500 architects, engineers, land surveyors and landscape architects in Minnesota; over 120 licensing boards throughout the United States. Entries include: For individuals -Name, address, field, license number; engineers also have a code for particular branch of engineering. For boards - Name, address, phone, name and title of contact. Arrangement: Individuals are alphabetical; boards are separate geographical lists for each profession.

SC Membership Directory
Society for Cryobiology (SC)
c/o Federation of American Societies for
Experimental Biology
9650 Rockville Pike
Bethesda, MD 20814
Phone: (301)530-7120

Annual.

Scientific and Technical Organizations and Agencies Directory
Gale Research Inc.
835 Penobscot Bldg.
Detroit, MI 48226
Phone: (313)961-2242
Fax: (313)961-6241

Latest edition June 1987. $195.00. Covers: Over 15,000 national and international organizations and agencies concerned with the physical sciences, engineering, and technology, including associations, computer information services, consulting firms, educational institutions, federal government agencies, general grant and assistance programs, libraries and information centers, patent sources and services, research and development centers, science-technology centers, standards organizations, state academies of science, and state government agencies in the fields of aeronautics and space sciences, chemistry, computer science specialties, geography, geology, machinery, mathematics, metallurgy, meteorology, mineralogy, nuclear science, petroleum, and gas, physics, plastics, transportation, water resources, and other areas. Entries include: Organization name, address, phone, and name of contact; additional descriptive text for most entries. Arrangement: By type of organization. Indexes: Organization name/keyword.

SEG Roster
Society of Exploration Geophysicists (SEG)
PO Box 702740
Tulsa, OK 74170
Phone: (918)493-3516
Fax: (918)493-2074

Annual.

SIM Membership Directory
Society for Industrial Microbiology (SIM)
PO Box 12534
Arlington, VA 22209-8534
Phone: (703)941-5373
Fax: (703)941-8790

Biennial.

SRM Mini-Directory
Society for Range Management (SRM)
1839 York St.
Denver, CO 80206
Phone: (303)355-7070

Periodic.

TCA Membership Roster
Tissue Culture Association (TCA)
8815 Center Park Dr., Ste. 210
Columbia, MD 21045
Phone: (301)992-0946

Triennial. Free to members; $150.00 for nonmembers.

Who's Who in Engineering
American Association of Engineering
Societies (AAES)
1111 19th St., NW, Ste. 608
Washington, DC 20036
Phone: (202)296-2237

Biennial.

Who's Who in Environmental Engineering
American Academy of Environmental Engineers (AAEE)
130 Holiday Ct., No. 100
Annapolis, MD 21401
Phone: (301)266-3311

Annual. Free to members; $50.00/copy for nonmembers. Hardbound directory of environmental engineers who are certified by the academy; primary listing is alphabetical by name, with secondary geographic and specialty listings.

Who's Who in Technology
Gale Research Inc.
835 Penobscot Bldg.
Detroit, MI 48226-4094
Phone: (313)961-2242
Fax: (313)961-6241

1989. $380.00. Covers: 38,000 engineers, scientists, inventors, and researchers. Entries include: Name, title, affiliation, address; personal, education, and career data; publications, patents; technical field of activity; area of expertise. Arrangement: Alphabetical. Indexes: Geographical, employer, technical discipline, expertise.

World Directory of Environmental Organizations
California Institute of Public Affairs
PO Box 189040
Sacramento, CA 95818
Phone: (916)442-2472

Covers more than 2100 governmental and nongovernmental environmental protection organizations in 218 countries, 165 intergovernmental agencies, and 300 international intergovernmental groups.

World Environmental Directory
Business Publishers, Inc.
951 Pershing Dr.
Silver Springs, MD 20910
Phone: (301)587-6300

Covers agencies, organizations, manufacturers, and professionals in the United States and Canada that emphasize environmental interests.

Zoological Parks and Aquariums in the Americas
American Association of Zoological Parks and Aquariums
Oglebay Park
Wheeling, WV 26003

1988. $20.00 for members; $50.00 for nonmembers, prepaid.

Master Index

Master Index

The Master Index provides comprehensive access to all four sections of the Directory by citing all subjects, organizations, publications, and services listed throughout in a single alphabetic sequence. The index also includes inversions on significant words appearing in cited organization, publication, and service names. For example, "Ward's Business Directory of U.S. Private and Public Companies" could also be listed in the index under "Companies; Ward's Business Directory of U.S. Private and Public."